MRS GRUNDY

STUDIES IN ENGLISH PRUDERY

MRS GRUNDY

STUDIES IN ENGLISH PRUDERY

PETER FRYER

LONDON · DENNIS DOBSON

First published in Great Britain in 1963
by Dobson Books Ltd,
80 Kensington Church Street, London, W.8

Printed in Great Britain by
C. Tinling & Company Ltd,
Liverpool, London & Prescot.

To Norma with love

CONTENTS

7

PART IV

UNKINDLING A WANTONNESS

PART V

DON'T DANCE, LITTLE LADY

LIST OF ILLUSTRATIONS

TEXT FIGURES

PLATES

Between pages 96 and 97

27(a) 'Who Is to Draw the Line: the Magistrate or the Ballet-Master?'
From *The Day's Doings*, 1870
Trustees of the British Museum

27(b) 'Wiry Sal' (Sarah Wright), the most famous of the Alhambra
cancan dancers
The Raymond Mander and Joe Mitchenson Theatre Collection

28 The future Lady Hamilton posing as Hygeia, goddess of health, at
Dr James Graham's Temple of Æsculapius. A satirical drawing by
Thomas Rowlandson, *c.* 1800
Trustees of the British Museum

29(a) Women entertainers of the middle ages
Trustees of the British Museum

29(b) 'Paphian Revels' in a London brothel: strippers of the eighteen-
forties. From *The Swell's Night Guide through the Metropolis*
[1841]
Trustees of the British Museum

29(c) The Judge and Jury Society at the Coal Hole in the Strand, with
Renton Nicholson, 'Lord Chief Baron', presiding
The Raymond Mander and Joe Mitchenson Theatre Collection

30(a) Maud Allan as Salome, 1908
The Raymond Mander and Joe Mitchenson Theatre Collection

30(b) Stasia Napierkowska in her disrobing 'Dance of the Bee', 1911
The Raymond Mander and Joe Mitchenson Theatre Collection

31(a) Lady Constance Stewart-Richardson
The Raymond Mander and Joe Mitchenson Theatre Collection

31(b) Strip-tease in the nineteen-sixties
Basil's Photographic Studio

32 In 1916 the Lord Chamberlain was shocked by these *Bystander*
impressions of C. B. Cochran's *Half-past Eight*, since the artist
'seemed deliberately to have created the effect of feminine garments
being blown up'. He ordered the removal of a framed copy from
the outside of the Comedy theatre
London Electrotype Agency

LIST OF ABBREVIATIONS

AL   Mencken, *The American Language* (various editions)

ARLD   *Annual Report of the Society for Promoting the Due Observance of the Lord's-day* (1834–1925)

DS   Partridge, *Dictionary of Slang* (5th edn, 1961)

F & H   Farmer and Henley (comp. and ed.), *Slang and its Analogues* (1890–1904)

H & E   *Health & Efficiency* (1918–   )

OED   Murray and others (ed.), *Oxford English Dictionary* (1933)

SBR   *Sun Bathing Review* (1933–59)

SV   [Cary?], *The Slang of Venery* (1916)

INTRODUCTION

It is often said that Mrs Grundy is today far less of a busybody, and in any case far less influential, than she used to be; and certainly young people are willing to put up with much less from her than their predecessors seem to have done, so that to most of them her name now means little. Nevertheless she remains (though rising 170)[1] a pretty energetic and persistent old person, who very much wants to regain her influence over people's lives. Nor is there any guarantee that she will not succeed.

Of her activities in Britain and other countries there was ample evidence in the first few weeks of my investigation into her ideas and her methods. There was the case of the young woman undergraduate who was expelled from her university after being found in bed with a man; it was a characteristic stroke of grundyism that the man was able to purge his offence with merely a fortnight's suspension. There was the London bookseller who refused to display copies of a book whose jacket bore a drawing of a naked young man by William Blake. There was the London composer who sought to prosecute the B.B.C. for broadcasting—for the seventh time since 1954—the 'obscene' sixteenth-century play *Gammer Gurton's Needle*. In the Lebanon, one of the lands where women dancers who rotate their pelves have for decades been observed with interest by tourists and other students of folk culture, the authorities decreed the prohibition of a new American dance, the twist. Before long the London Dance Institute followed suit, on the ground that the dance was 'far too uninhibited, abandoned and frankly sexy to be performed in Britain'. The Institute's managing director added that the twist 'belongs to the African bush'.[2] About the same time a man was jailed for three years, and fined £3,000, for keeping a 'disorderly house' at a London strip-tease club, the show being described by the prosecuting solicitor as more suitable for a sewer than a theatre. Meanwhile in Saigon a kinswoman of Mrs Grundy was inspiring an austerity law prohibiting private or commercial dancing, cabarets and beauty contests; while in Los Angeles her American cousin was prompting members of a local school board to consider banning all Tarzan books from young people's libraries, because of a complaint that Tarzan and his mate Jane were unmarried when they lived in their tree-house. At a hospital in Chesterfield, nurses were ordered to lengthen the skirts of their uniforms so as not to show their knees; if their skirts were any higher, said the matron, 'patients would see the girls' stocking tops when they bent down to tuck in the sheets'.[3] Precisely how this would impair the patients' recovery she did not reveal. And at Kingsbridge in Devon the rural district council expressed concern at the increase in the number of naked bathers on south Devon beaches during the previous summer, and asked the county council to adopt by-laws enabling the police to prosecute nudists who used public beaches.[4]

I had not expected to find so many examples of present-day grundyism in a period of barely six weeks. But what caused me still more surprise was to discover the lady I was studying firmly entrenched inside what I had always regarded as a stronghold of liberality and enlightenment—the British Museum library. How many people know that a great number of books and periodical publications held by that library are regarded by the authorities there as so unsuitable for readers to consult freely that their titles and press-marks do not even appear in the General Catalogue or subject index? Yet this is indeed the case. The matter would not be quite so serious, perhaps, if these 'Private Case' books were all ephemeral items of pornography (though even this genre of literature cannot be dismissed as unworthy of the attention of the serious student of sexual behaviour). It is hard to estimate accurately; but something like half the Private Case titles are works of irrefragable scientific, literary, and historical interest and importance. They include *The Slang of Venery* (1916); a French-English glossary, *Vocabula Amatoria* (1896); Κρυπτάδια (1883–1911), a valuable collection of folk-lore; John Davenport's *Aphrodisiacs and Anti-aphrodisiacs* (1869 [*sc.* 1873]) and *Curiositates Eroticæ Physiologiæ* (1875); numerous works on phallic worship; Bloch's *Sexual Life of Our Time* (1908); and many other sexological works. Such books were relegated to the 'Private Case' in less enlightened days than ours—though when *The Slang of Venery* arrived at the Museum it was classified for a time with books on hunting. Even the *Registrum Librorum Eroticorum* (1936) of

'Rolf S. Reade' (Alfred Rose) is in the 'Private Case', presumably because it lists other 'P.C.' works and gives their press-marks; fortunately, a copy is accessible on the open shelves of the London Library. It is only recently that certain editions of the works of the Earl of Rochester have been taken out of this British Museum limbo and admitted to the paradise of the General Catalogue; and, even in the year of the legal publication of Henry Miller's *Tropic of Cancer* in London, readers are still protected from knowing about the existence in the library of several mildly bawdy books of the seventeenth and eighteenth centuries. The British Museum is also said to possess a number of books which no readers (and precious few members of the staff) are ever allowed to see, and of which no catalogue is known to exist. This 'Hell' beneath the 'Hell' is spoken of as the 'S.S.' collection, the initials presumably standing for 'Secret Shelf'.

It is clearly necessary to protect valuable and, in some cases, irreplaceable books from thieves, mutilators, and scribblers, all of whom find erotica peculiarly attractive. But the protection of 'Private Case' works need not entail their omission from the catalogue. Anyone who is working up a subject needs to know all the books that deal with it, whether or not he means to use, or even consult, them all; the British Museum General Catalogue, and the subject indexes that are based on it, are deficient and misleading if they are censored. There is no guarantee whatever that the secret catalogue of 'Private Case' works is consulted efficiently and intelligently on one's behalf when one sends for one of them; twice, while writing this book, I had the experience of applying for a 'Private Case' work only to be told categorically that the Museum did not possess it; I then supplied the press-mark from Reade's *Registrum* and was duly sent the work I needed.

This vexatious state of affairs has not changed in essentials since Havelock Ellis and Edward Carpenter complained about it in 1913.[5] It remains what it was half a century ago: a fetter on free inquiry and scholarship. The Museum bibliotaphs, though otherwise as helpful as they can be to serious inquirers, are adamant in defending and perpetuating a system whereby such inquirers are handicapped by being denied access to an up-to-date list of 'Private Case' works. This rule, writes the Principal Keeper of the Department of Printed Books,

is of long standing and is designed to put a check on what I might perhaps call indiscriminate browsing in the field of erotica. It is quite true that the publication of Reade's *Registrum* has greatly weakened the force of this regulation but there have been a good many accessions since the publication of that work and, subject to a new direction from higher authority, I propose to continue to enforce it. Moreover, it is precisely in order to prevent the publication of another work similar to that of Reade that we normally do not disclose the press-marks of Private Case books.

I hope that these regulations do not seem to you unduly onerous. We certainly do not wish to hinder serious research, still less to act as censors, but it is my view that we are under an obligation to limit the use of these works to serious researchers.[6]

It seems a strange interpretation of censorship which does not see as inherently censorial the maintenance of a secret catalogue, the arbitrary definition of what is 'indiscriminate browsing', and the determination to 'prevent the publication' of a serious bibliographical work.

Prudery is fear and hatred of pleasure, primarily of sexual pleasure; and Mrs Grundy is a prude who carries this fear and hatred to the stage of more or less organized interference with other people's pleasures. The private prude and the prude-at-large are both obsessed by an awareness of the vast amount of unregulated pleasure that is being enjoyed in the world; this they call sin. When they inveigh or organize against sin they are consciously or unconsciously buttressing their own inner barriers against the pleasure they long for but fear to obtain. Sometimes their extreme shockability and militancy are pharisaical; but it is only a minority of prudes who are hypocrites. The majority are unaware of their real motives. To a healthy person sex is a very important part, but only a part, of life; so long as he is sexually satisfied his sexual needs are only from time to time in the forefront of his consciousness. The sexual behaviour of others may be of interest to him but is not an obsession; he is neither unduly stimulated nor disgusted by evidence of other people's sexuality. He can contemplate without distress forms of pleasure and fulfilment that do not correspond to his own habits and tastes, provided those forms do not infringe the freedom of choice of mature persons or the inviolability of the immature. To the prude and to Mrs Grundy, however, the sexual activity of others is simultaneously inflammatory and disgusting, and of such obsessive interest that it is rarely far from their thoughts. It stimulates their imagination and inventive powers. 'The dreaded subject', says one of the most sensible writers on prudery, 'is detected in a thousand innuendoes, in inanimate as well as animate forms.'[7] It is a constant and fascinating reminder of their own frustration and unhappiness; it perpetually awakens feelings whose existence they spend their lives denying and trying to suppress; it impels them to punish both their tormentors and themselves.

Prudery's first line of defence is the regulation of speech. Feelings of shame and guilt about the organs of sex, about the articles of clothing and underclothing that cover them, about sexual activity, about menstruation, pregnancy and birth, and about excretion and the places where one excretes, tend to become closely associated with the words that are used for these things. These words become taboo, and other words come into use, free from the emotions that now suffuse the original terms. As often as not, the new words themselves are felt sooner or later to have become tainted and to need replacement. By its very nature euphemism tends to lose its protective magic at a fairly rapid rate. The results are often laughable. Or rather, the euphemisms of past generations, and some of those used by some Americans today, strike us as comical; our own simply show how polite we are, and how considerate of other people's feelings.

In discussing verbal taboos I have given examples from the U.S.A. as well as Britain, though at first sight they seem to illustrate American prudery rather than English. But Americanisms, not least in the sphere of sex, are often fairly rapidly adopted in this country; and some of the most vivid dysphemisms and most vapid euphemisms in our common language originated in the U.S.A. And so the comparison with American modes of speech is not, I think, altogether without value. It would have been entertaining to continue such a comparison throughout the rest of the book, but there was not the space to do so. This has prevented, for instance, any mention of such a joyful extravaganza as the Society *for* Indecency to Naked Animals (it should have been 'against', but the founder was stricken in years when he drew up his will), which, in 1963, has designed bikinis for stallions, petticoats for cows, knickers for bulldogs, and boxer shorts for small animals, so as to shield the eyes of Americans from the sight of these animals' sex organs.

The prude has traditionally operated with energy and persistence in two fields which at first glance are unconnected with sex: the way people behave on their rest days; and the use of alcoholic drinks. But there is more than a trace of hatred of sex in both sabbatarianism and teetotalism; and this view of teetotalism is supported in a recent excellent study of prohibition in the U.S.A.[8] The Sunday observance bigot wishes to regulate the way people spend their days of rest because he is alarmed (not necessarily consciously) by the opportunities for sexual indulgence that would be available if Sundays were spent freely and with free access to places of social intercourse. People who are not allowed to be idle are less likely to get into mischief. The total abstinence bigot seeks to prevent the use of alcoholic drinks because he is alarmed (again, not necessarily consciously) by the fact that such drinks, taken in moderation, not uncommonly heighten sexual responsiveness and induce people to engage in sexual activity more frequently.

Clothing, especially the clothing of women, easily captures the attention of prudes. It is a commonplace that the changes in women's fashions are basically determined by the need to maintain men's sexual interest, and therefore to transfer the primary zone of erotic display once a given part of the body has been saturated with attractive power to the point of satiation. The prude finds each new, revealing fashion a profoundly shocking and disturbing experience. He cannot tear his eyes away from the ankles, or knees, or breasts, or backs, or buttocks, with which the world around him is suddenly filled. Others are pleased and amused for a time by the fresh evidence that women have both shapes and wiles; but the prude, fleeing from his own erethism, defends his peace of mind by attacking the new fashion as indecent and immoral.

There are other aspects of the body taboo. The prude may not approve of his wife being examined by a male physician. He may even object to his baby being delivered by a male obstetrician. And he will go to some trouble to be shocked by nudists.

Then there is the form of prudery which concerns itself with dancing. The prude finds the public embracing of men and women and their bodily contact in the dance intolerably suggestive. The dance is in one sense a mimetic representation of copulation, and, as such, a form of courtship. It presents itself to the prude, not as innocent enjoyment, but as a kind of licensed *frottage*. Worse still are the more overt and organized forms of erotic display by women entertainers: vestigial forms of ancient fertility dances, exemplified today in such dances as the cancan and in strip-tease performances. Displays of this kind have been a source of anxiety to many generations of prudes.

Thus far the present volume. There are of course many other forms of prudery, and I intend to discuss them in a further book.

I hope to show how the prude in authority becomes a censor, whose function is to protect his fellow men against images which he considers indecent and immoral, depraving and corrupting—especially against descriptions of sexual activity which present it as something pleasurable. Those the censor protects are put in the position of children being guarded from harm. They may not read books that someone else considers unsuitable; nor see plays or motion pictures before someone else has seen them and dictated whatever cuts he deems necessary; nor (at times) see certain paintings or pieces of sculpture that might, in the opinion of someone else, arouse sexual desire. Nor may they have access to photographs of sexual activity, which are held to be harmful—though no scientific inquiry has yet brought to light any evidence that people are in fact harmed by seeing such photographs. The prude-in-office himself is supposed to be impervious to the harmful influence of the mass of erotic material it is his distasteful duty to examine. Moreover the existence of even the most stringent censorship has never prevented the writing, publication, and distribution of large numbers of erotic books, and the distribution of erotic pictures in great quantities. Eroticism in art and literature is as old as art and literature themselves; which seems to show that prudes, with or without law enforcement officers to help them, have little chance of ever making sex uninteresting. Their efforts do however mean that the traffic in erotic books and pictures can be tolerably profitable to those who are willing to accept the risks attending the trade of pornographer.

I hope to show, further, that the effects of prudery have been specially unfortunate in the upbringing and education of children. At times the punishing of children for enjoying themselves in ways disapproved of by their parents or educators has taken unmistakably pathological forms. This was especially so in the middle of the nineteenth century, when public discussion of methods of inflicting pain on children was eager and widespread. This hatred of the flesh reached its climax in the harsh punishments reserved for masturbation, a form of sexual activity which many would now regard as not merely harmless, but essential to a child's healthy sexual development. The record of strait jackets, catheters, beatings, and warnings about insanity and death, is a sombre one.

The biggest efforts that organized prudes make are designed to combat prostitution, and I plan to include an account of the origin, growth, and activities of the various sex-obsessed anti-'vice' leagues in Britain, beginning with the Societies for the Reformation of Manners, some of whose activities are discussed in the present volume.

Lastly, I hope to give in the second volume some account of the efforts that have been made in various periods to put a stop to private sexual activity between adults whose union has not been registered in some way. This will entail a discussion of changing attitudes to chastity, sex education, contraception, and abortion.

Marxists and freudians and others will observe that I have not tried to draw any but the most obvious general conclusions. For those who want them, two highly seductive theories of prudery already exist. V. F. Calverton, in *Sex Expression in Literature* (1926), and Alec Craig, in *Sex and Revolution* (1934), relate the growth and decline of English prudery to the changing economic conditions of the nineteenth and twentieth centuries. Gordon Rattray Taylor, in *Sex in History* (1953) and *The Angel-Makers* (1958), suggests that society is at various times dominated by persons who have modelled themselves on their fathers ('patrists') or by persons who have modelled themselves on their mothers ('matrists'), these types being respectively restrictive and permissive towards expressions of the sexual instinct and towards many other things. There is much to be said for both these theories. But it seems to me impossible to explain the development of the different forms of prudery in this country in terms of a single formula. People who are fairly permissive in some ways are often pretty intolerant in others. Periods that are generally permissive are sometimes surprisingly intolerant in certain fields. And vice versa.

Four not very original generalizations may nevertheless be made. First, wars and revolutions tend to relax the dominant code of sexual behaviour and at the same time cause the defenders of that code to seek to apply it more rigorously. Secondly, different classes tend to have different standards of sexual morality; it would be an arduous undertaking to study the changing class attitudes to sex in this country over the last four hundred years, but the results of such a study might surprise both marxists and freudians. Thirdly, there is nothing new about the present-day animadversions upon the alleged immorality of young people; such criticisms have almost always been made; and there is no evidence to suggest that young people behave very differently nowadays—or that older people are any more, or less, disturbed by their behaviour. And lastly, though we seem to ourselves to live in a period of relative enlightenment and tolerance, there is no reason to assume that Mrs Grundy is incapable of returning to a position of influence. Even today, it is as well not to be too boastful about our attitudes to other people's pleasures. It is easy to laugh at the prudery of former generations; it is far from easy to detect our own, which we are in the habit of calling 'good taste'.[9]

It is a pleasure to record my gratitude to the staffs of the British Museum and the London Library for their ungrudging help, without which my spare-time research would have been far more laborious and far less fertile. I have, I fear, given some trouble to the Principal Keeper of the British Museum's Department of Printed Books and to his staff; whatever objection there may be to certain regulations, it would be churlish not to acknowledge the helpfulness and courtesy of the entire staff, down to the youngest attendants. In particular, I am indebted to Dr Eric Dingwall, whose valuable advice and information have done much to smooth my path.

I should like to acknowledge with thanks the permission granted, by the individuals and bodies whose names appear in the list of illustrations, to reproduce the illustrations against which their names appear. In some cases they went to much trouble to secure for me, or lend me, the picture or other document that I desired to use. I am grateful to Mr Peter Chapman, Mr John Moore, and Mr George Stock for a variety of technical help with the illustrations.

My thanks are due to Mr Terence Deakin, Mr Bernard Francke, Dr John Daniels, Mr Michael Rubinstein, Professor E. A. Thompson, Mr T. B. Thompson, Mr Ronald Whiting, and Mr Cecil Woolf, all of whom have helped in one way or another, and some of whom will find some interesting discussions shadowed in these pages.

I owe a special debt of gratitude to Mr Trevenen Peters, whose advice and criticisms have saved me from many blunders, and whose almost daily encouragement has spurred me over many obstacles. I was fortunate enough to have his detailed comments on the first draft, chapter by chapter; his suggestions were always apt, never less than fruitful, and frequently invaluable. I hope that his distaste for acknowledgements of this kind will not prevent his accepting my warmest thanks for help which, at every stage, has hastened the completion of this book.

COBHAM, Surrey, *May 19, 1963.*   P. F.

PART I

PLAIN WORDS, PRUDE WORDS, AND RUDE WORDS

A CURE FOR GOOSEFLESH

The great Roman orator Cicero advised his friends not to say 'little pavements' by adding a diminutive to *pavimenta*, for the word so formed, *pavimentula*, would suggest *mentula*, which meant 'penis'.[1] Two thousand years later, the British Ministry of Transport discreetly bans the use of certain combinations of letters on the registration plates of motor vehicles. The Aberdeen three-letter series starts at BRS; Birmingham jumps from BOC to DOC and from BOK to DOK; Leeds from AUM to CUM; London from EUC to GUC; Wolverhampton from EUK to GUK.[2] How much harm would be done to our wives and daughters, not to mention our servants, if this precaution were not taken, and approximations to demotic words for buttocks, penis, and copulation hit them in the eye at every bend in the road, so to say? One cannot tell; but it would be fascinating to see the minute that circulated in the Ministry when three-letter index marks were first authorized, in 1932. If four-letter marks were ever introduced the staff responsible for finding, considering, and advising against unsuitable permutations would no doubt have to be increased; otherwise matters might get out of hand.

The English-speaking peoples have long had a specially strong fear of words for the organs of sex and excretion and their functioning, and a correspondingly strong taste—or talent—for euphemism. The opposite to euphemism, known technically as dysphemism, has also flourished.[3] The abundance of vigorous dysphemisms for the tabooed organs and activities has no doubt been a reaction to the debilitating effect that euphemism has on language.

In 1791, twenty-seven years before the appearance of Thomas Bowdler's somewhat unjustly notorious work, we find the *Gentleman's Magazine* referring ironically to the rewriting of Shakespeare:

The publick . . . is much indebted to the modern Editors of Shakspeare . . . who . . . have taken care to substitute pleasing and fashionable words, instead of the obsolete and gross terms which sometimes occur in that admirable author. . . . All our mothers and grand-mothers used in due course of time to become *with-child*, or, as Shakspeare has it, *round-wombed* . . . but it is very well known, that no female, above the degree of a chamber-maid or laundress, has been *with-child* these ten years past: every decent married woman now becomes *pregnant*; nor is she ever *brought-to-bed*, or *delivered*, but merely, at the end of nine months, has an *accouchement*; antecedent to which, she always informs her friends that at a certain time she shall be *confined*.[4]

From this time on, the use of euphemism in England and America gradually increased until, in 1833, Noah Webster, the famous lexicographer, got down to the task of bowdlerizing the Bible. He replaced *teat* with *breast*, *in the belly* with *in embryo*, *stink* with *smell*, *to give suck* with *to nurse* and *nourish*, *fornication* with *lewdness*, *whore* with *lewd woman* and *prostitute*, *to go a-whoring* with *to go astray*, and *whoredom* with *impurities*, *idolatries* and *carnal connection*. He even cut out whole verses 'as beyond the reach of effective bowdlerization'.[5] This was the high point of euphemism, but it was at least four decades before there was any significant loosening of the strict mid-Victorian taboos; and it took the first world war to bring about a partial return to plain speaking, and even, in the U.S.A., 'a certain defiant looseness of speech'.[6] Nevertheless prudish modes of speech clung on tenaciously, and there were those who resisted change and recommended still greater strictness—one writer proposing, in 1922, to substitute *habit-disease* for *vice*, and *behavior problems* for *prostitutes*.[7] In the thirties the Hollywood list of banned words, which might never be spoken in any motion picture, included *cocotte, courtesan, eunuch, harlot, madam* (for 'brothel-keeper'), *slut, tart, trollop, wench, whore, son-of-a-bitch, sex*, and *sexual*. The words *virtuous* and *bum* were to be avoided, and the expression *traveling salesman* might not be used 'where reference is made to a farmer's daughter'.[8] During and after the second world war there was a further marked retreat from euphemism on both sides of the Atlantic. In 1961 *The Connection* came on the screen in both America and Britain with the word *shit* openly pronounced, which would have been unthinkable ten years before; and in 1960 the *Guardian* and the *Observer*, in articles on the *Lady Chatterley's Lover* trial, printed the word *fuck* without recourse to the dash or asterisks that, as the American philologist Allen Walker Read had pointed out a quarter of a century before, render the mutilated word, unlike the plain verb, really obscene.[9]

And so public opinion came rather closer to answering in a liberal fashion two questions that Read had asked: 'When a subject is admissible at all, why should not the plain, outspoken terms be the best to use?' and 'Is it a wise policy to leave an area of our language in a diseased condition, without attempting to cleanse it?'[10] (Or, as another American philologist, Richard Bache, had declared over half a century before: 'It is a shame that excellent words . . . which served our ancestors for hundreds of years, should be driven out of familiar use by prurient imaginations.'[11]) One taboo, if not yet by any means destroyed, had been somewhat weakened, having been broken in the only way it was possible to break it—by the word's being used 'unemotionally in its simple literal sense'.[12]

Carnoy, in *La Science du mot* (1927), defined euphemism as 'discretion', used in order to minimize a painful impression on the hearer. Social and moral taboos were one of six causes of euphemism that he listed, the others being: a desire to adapt oneself to the general sentiment suitable to the time, place and other circumstances (as when addressing children); an attempt to enhance the value of what one possesses or gives (e.g., *saloon* for *bar*); respect for the person addressed, or a desire to impress or please him (e.g., *charlady* for *charwoman*); the need to soften tragic news (e.g., *pass away* for *die*); superstition and religious taboos.[13] Partridge points out that these six reasons might be reduced to three: fear, kindness, and delicacy.[14] Of these, though the other two play a part, it is chiefly fear that gives rise to and nourishes the taboos lying behind the class of euphemisms we are here discussing. The reaction to certain words connected with excrement or sex, says Read, is 'a titillating thrill of scandalized perturbation. . . . The speaker or hearer regards [them], owing to the interference of a taboo, with a sneaking, shame-faced, psychopathic attitude'.[15] The plain word, says Wyld, 'chills the blood and raises gooseflesh'.[16]

In short, when a person calls a word obscene, indecent or dirty, this is an indication of his state of mind; neither the words themselves nor the things they stand for can properly be described as obscene, indecent, or dirty. It is to reduce or eliminate this state of mind, to avoid speaker or hearer having gooseflesh, to keep their blood temperature normal, that a polysyllabic Latin word replaces a short English one; or an obscure word replaces the one that would naturally spring to mind; or a metaphor is chosen; or a part of the human body is called by the name properly given to the general area in which it is situated, or to the internal organ of which it is the outward covering; or the corresponding parts of animals, or of articles of furniture, are renamed; or a word that merely sounds like a tabooed word, though it may mean something entirely different, is replaced.

Of the making of euphemisms there is indeed—alas! for the delicately minded who need them—no end. Once a euphemism becomes accepted and its primary meaning changes to the shameful thing for which it has come to stand, the taboo, if it be strong enough, tends to be transferred. The gooseflesh reappears. And some fresh, innocent, victim-word has to be sacrificed on the altar of propriety. As Weekley put it, 'the euphemism is, by inevitable association, doomed from its very birth'.[17] There are in fact whole chains of euphemisms, like the one from *privy* to *toilet* and *loo*, and the one from *whore* to *model*. In the chapters which follow, we shall see how such chains are constructed.

2

THE NUDE TRUTH[1]

Nearly half a century ago the American critic H. L. Mencken hit on the ingenious idea of arranging the parts of the body in an 'interior hierarchy' of eight classes, beginning with the highly respectable ones and ending with what in 1915 were regarded as unmentionable. Class I consisted of the heart, brain, hair, eyes, and vermiform appendix, 'five aristocrats, of dignity even in their diseases'. Class II included the collar-bone, the stomach (in America) and liver (in England), the bronchial tubes, arms (excluding elbows), tonsils, ears, cheeks, and chin. Descending to Class III, one had the elbows, ankles, teeth (if natural), shoulders, lungs, neck, etc. In Class IV came the stomach (in England) and liver (in America), hips, calves, nose, feet (bare), etc. Teeth (if false), heels, toes, knees, legs (female), and scalp were grouped in Class V; thighs, paunch, oesophagus, spleen, pancreas, gall-bladder, and caecum in Class VI. Mencken omitted to name the constituents of his two other classes, VII and VIII, because these 'entered into anatomical details impossible of discussion in a book designed to be read aloud at the domestic hearth'.[2] It is with the plain words, prude words, and rude words for these two lowly but not uninteresting—and nowadays quite mentionable—classes that we are concerned in this Chapter. But first let us glance at some words for bodily nakedness itself.

In 1936 a woman lunatic took off her clothes in St Paul's Cathedral. The *Daily Express*, *Daily Mail*, and *Daily Telegraph*, in their reports of the incident, described her as *unclothed*. The *Daily Herald* called her *nude* in a headline, but elsewhere used *unclothed*. The *News Chronicle* had *unclothed* and *unclad*. Not one single daily newspaper 'was able to face the horror'[3] of the decent old English word *naked*.

First recorded in the ninth century, this word, along with *bare* (before 1000),[4] was almost ousted by *nude* (1873) in the nineteenth; though, strangely enough, the Latin word *nudus*, from which *nude* is directly derived, is a cousin-word of *naked*. Yet *naked* was felt to be too stark long before the nineteenth century, it seems. For in Wycherley's *The Country-Wife* (acted *c.* 1672), when Sir Jaspar Fidget says, 'Faith to tell you the naked truth', his wife reproves him: 'Fye, Sir *Jaspar*, do not use that word naked.'[5] Those who, like Lady Fidget, have found verbal nakedness an affront to their susceptibilities have had plenty of euphemisms at their disposal: *uncovered* (*c.* 1400), *unclad* (*c.* 1420), *unclothed* (1440), *unrigged* (late C. 16), *undressed* (1613), *in buff* (C. 17) and *stripped to the buff* (C. 19), *abram* (C. 17–18; from 'auburn'), *in birthday gear* (1731), *in one's birthday suit* (1771) and *in birthday attire* (1860), *disrobed* (1794), *peeled* (1820), *in the altogether* (1894), *starkers* (*c.* 1910; Oxford University slang) and *starko* (*c.* 1910), and *in a state of nature*. And those for whom the plain word was not strong enough, or not expressive enough, have salted their speech with *stark-ballock* (or *starbolic*) *naked* (*c.* 1870).[6]

One of the earliest victims of verbal prudery was *belly* (1340), very gradually replaced by *stomach* (*c.* 1375). The Greek στόμαχος, from which the latter is derived, meant 'mouth', 'opening', then 'throat', 'gullet', 'oesophagus'; but its earliest use in English was for the internal organ in which the chief part of the digestive process takes place; then it began to oust *belly*; and eventually it 'was transformed, by some unfathomable magic, into a euphemism denoting the whole region from the nipples to the pelvic arch'.[7] Respectable Englishwomen used to be shocked if a Continental physician asked them whether the pain they complained of was in the belly; one foreign physician practising in Britain was told in 1900 that his blunt use of that 'dreadful' word had affected one female patient most unpleasantly.[8] Alec Craig recalls an incident at a party he attended in his childhood, where the small guests were amusing themselves by adding *y* to their various names: Alfy, Jamesy, Dorisy, and so on. 'The fact that one of the little girls was called "Belle" brought dire punishment and disgrace on the unfortunate who added the suffix to her name.'[9] *Belly-ache* (before 1552; Standard English till *c.* 1800) became *stomach-ache* (1763) and even *gastrodynia* (1804) and *gastralgia* (1822) and, later, *a pain in one's pinny*. No one seems to have thought of saying 'stomach-laugh'; but 'The Stomach Dance' is the title of an illustration by Aubrey Beardsley for the first English edition of Wilde's *Salome* (1894).[10] Eventually the more modest speakers found even *stomach* too coarse for their stomachs

—Trollope let his publisher change *fat stomach* to *deep chest* in *Barchester Towers* (1857)[11]—and descended to *tum* (1868), *tummy* (1868), *tum-tum* (before 1904), and *Little Mary* (1903; from Barrie's play of that name). For the less pompous there were *craw* (C. 16), *puddinghouse* (late C. 16), *middle story* (c. 1670–1800), *bread-basket* (1753),[12] *corporation* (1785), *middle pie* (c. 1870–1910), and *periphery* (before 1923), while for the more pompous there were always *abdomen* and even *viscera*. In 1933 the Los Angeles *Times* printed *sow-bosom* in place of *sow-belly*;[13] and as late as 1962 the London *People* printed *waist dimple* in place of *navel* (c. 725).[14]

The word *leg* seems to have engendered still more distress than *belly*, especially in the United States, where even *feet* was banned at one time,[15] and where, as is well known, the legs of pianofortes were solemnly dressed in frilly trousers to keep the very thought of legs of any kind out of people's minds.[16] The American habit of referring to the organs of support and locomotion as *limbs* caused some confusion among visiting Englishmen.

> An Englishman, to whom an American woman should say, 'I have the rheumatism in one of my limbs', might inquire 'Which?' if he did not happen to know that many women in [the U.S.A.], in speaking of their sex's legs to persons of the other sex, call them distinctively *limbs,* and there drop the subject, although they might not drop their skirts a hair's breadth.[17]

Some Americans, wrote Marryat, always said limb of a table or limb of a pianoforte; his female informant was 'not so particular'.[18] Bache met a woman

> who was all ankle to the waist, and all waist to the shoulders. . . . She, wishing to express her belief that New England women, of whom she was one, had as delicately shaped limbs—by which the writer means arms as well as legs—as the women of other sections have, stammered out that they had very fine—ah-ah-ah—extremities.[19]

There is a story about a young American woman, injured in an accident, who told the surgeon one of her limbs was broken. He asked her which limb it was. 'I can't tell you, doctor,' she replied, 'but it's one of my limbs.' 'Which is it,' the doctor demanded, 'the limb you thread a needle with?' 'No, sir,' she answered with a sigh, 'it's the limb

I wear a garter on.' The surgeon told her never to say the word 'limb' to him again in hospital, for if she did she would be passed by; when a woman got as bad as that, the sooner she died the better.[20] Longfellow, in *Kavanagh* (1849), quotes from the prospectus of a fashionable American boarding school: 'Young ladies are not allowed to cross their *benders* in school.'[21] Colloquial euphemisms for *legs* in Britain were *understandings* (1828) and *underpinners* (late 1850s).[22] The leg of a chicken became *second wing* in Britain, *second joint*, or *trotter*, or *the dark meat* in the U.S.A.; but gastronomic motives may have been at work here.

Women's *breasts* had always been known as their *bosoms*; the two words were both first recorded about the year 1000. But in the early part of the nineteenth century the first became indelicate, and across the Atlantic even the breast of a turkey was referred to as its bosom, as Marryat notes in his novel *Peter Simple* (1834):

> It was my fate to sit opposite to a fine turkey, and I asked my partner if I should have the pleasure of helping her to a piece of the breast. She looked at me very indignantly, and said, 'Curse your impudence, sar, I wonder where you larn manners. Sar, I take a lilly turkey *bosom* if you please. Talk of *breast* to a lady, sar; really quite *horrid.*[23]

Even *breastpin*, in the U.S.A., became *bosom-pin* (1855).

The possibly onomatopoeic Standard English word *bubbies*, first used in the latter part of the seventeenth century, remained in polite diction only a hundred years but survived in Britain as a colloquialism, along with its less common abbreviation *bubs* (C. 19), in the U.S.A. as *boobies*, *boobs*, and *boovies*. Even earlier was the euphemistic *milky way* (c. 1620), which was poetical Standard English till about 1800; it was followed by a number of similar colloquial euphemisms: *milk-shop* or *-walk* (C. 19), *feeding-bottle* (C. 19), *baby's public house* (1884; working class), and *dairy arrangements* (before 1923). A woman's *charms* were first referred to in the eighteenth century; this expression was Standard English until about 1840; compare the nineteenth-century *bust* (1819) and *figure* (c. 1870), and the twentieth-century *contours* and *curves*, the last three connoting buttocks as well as breasts. Another series of colloquial terms refers to the shape of the breasts: *globes* (c. 1860), and *hemispheres* (C. 19) are euphemistic; *dumplings* (before 1709), *fore-buttocks* (c. 1727; coined by Pope), *apple-dumpling shop* (late C. 18–19), *dumpling shop* (C. 19), and (*Cupid's*) *kettledrums* (c. 1770–1850) seem dysphemistic, as do two words that allude to breathing, *heavers* (mid-C. 17–early 19) and *panters* (C. 19), as well as *blubber* (late C. 18) and *meat-market* (C. 19). Literary euphemisms are endless; Cleland, the author of the famous *Memoirs of a Woman of Pleasure* [*c.* 1747–48], used *hillocks, semi-globes,* and *twin orbs*; others include *mounts of lilies, nature's founts, orbs of snow,* and *ivory hills*.[24]

If the plain word *breast* was indelicate in the nineteenth century, how much more so was *nipple* (1530)—especially in America. Even the technical use of this word for the device by which the percussion cap of a muzzle-loading gun was fixed and exploded became taboo; Sir Richard Burton's 1863 edition of Marcy's *The Prairie Traveler* had a sarcastic footnote explaining: 'The American "cone" is the English "nipple". Beg pardon for the indelicacy!'[25] In southern England *paps* (*c.* 1200) fell out of general use in the eighteenth century; in the nineteenth the still older *teats* (*c.* 950) was not a polite word, nor were its colloquial variants *tits* (C. 17 or before) and the nursery terms *titties* (*c.* 1740) and *diddies* or *diddeys* (*c.* 1780). The other ancient word for this part of the body, *dugs* (1530), has been a vulgarism since about 1880, though, as Partridge points out, it is still permissible in Standard English 'if used as a strong pejorative'.[26] *Cherrilets* or *cherrylets* (C. 16–17) was almost Standard English; *buds of beauty, rosebuds, ruby jewels,* and *strawberries* are other euphemisms of the past.[27]

Until the second half of the seventeenth century the word *arse* was Standard English. The glossary of Abbot Ælfric, compiled in the tenth century, gives *earslyre* as the English for *nates*.[28] The Old English *ears* or *aers* compares with the Old Frisian *ers*, Old High German *ars* (in Modern German it is *Arsch*), Old Norse *ars*, Hittite *arraš*, and Greek ὄρρος.[29] *The Chronicles of England* (printed by Caxton in 1480) tell how the women of England 'lete hange fox tailes . . . forto hele [cover] and heyde hire ars'.[30] In the seventeenth century Butler told in *Hudibras* (1663) how his knight and squire were

> mounted both upon their Horses,
> But with their faces to the Arses.[31]

And in Swift's *Battle of the Books* (1704) the spider says to the bee: 'Do you think I have nothing else to do, in the devil's name, but to mend and repair after your arse [i.e., behind you]?'[32] Except for Captain

Francis Grose, in the article on *arse* (verb) in his *Classical Dictionary of the Vulgar Tongue* (1785),[33] Swift was apparently the last writer to give the word in full—until the year 1930, when Frederic Manning defied Mrs Grundy by giving it without mutilation in his war novel *Her Privates We*.[34]

The similarity or identity in pronunciation of *arse* and *ass* (as well as the common practice of spelling both words *ass*) caused trouble in America for the latter long-suffering animal, whose name was printed *A—* in an 1855 issue of *Putnam's Monthly*,[35] and which eventually became a *donkey* (1785), *jackass* (1727), or *jack* (1785); while *ass* in the sense of 'fool' was replaced by *pinhead* (1896), *bonehead* (C. 20), *boob* (before 1912), etc.[36] In England, however, the word *jackass* had at an earlier period so offended the susceptibilities of one lady that she called the beast *Johnny bum*, for reasons recorded by Grose in his definition of that term: 'A he or jack ass; so called by a lady that affected to be extremely polite and modest, who would not say jack, because it was vulgar, nor ass because it was indecent.'[37]

Her '*bum*' is, of course, one of three other old-established English words for this part of the body. *Buttocks* (before 1300) and *fundament* (1297) have held their own; but *bum*, which is still older, has fared almost as badly as *arse*. It is popularly but erroneously supposed to be a contraction of *bottom* (1794); but in fact it is 'probably onomatopoeic':[38] compare *bump*. Defined by Johnson as 'the part on which we sit'[39] (which led a commentator to ask him: 'Do you mean a chair Doctor?'[40]), this 'good English word', writes Partridge, 'began to lose caste' about 1790, and about 1840 became a vulgarism 'and has been eschewed'.[41] Thus when Al Jolson's film *Hallelujah, I'm a Bum* was shown in Britain in the thirties, the title was changed to *Hallelujah, I'm a Tramp*.[42] *Bum* was no doubt kicked aside by such words as *rump* (c. 1440), *backside* (c. 1500), *breech* (before 1533), *podex* (1598), *seat* (1607), *posterior(s)* (1619), *nates* (1706), *behind* (1786), and *promontories* (1792).[43] The nineteenth century brought *sit-me-down*, *sit-upon*, *botty* (mid-C. 19; originally and mainly nursery), and *b.t.m.* (late C. 19; domestic); the twentieth, *sit-me-down-upon* (1926) and *the fleshy part of the thigh*, which was used jocularly from 1899 to about 1912, after the news came from South Africa that Lord Methuen had been wounded in that region.[44] *Derrière* was once much used in women's magazines, especially in the U.S.A.; *the lower back* once 'served to indicate a region that has baffled the descriptive fashion writer ever since'.[45] Yet even this wealth of euphemisms did not always prevent embarrassment. Graves tells of a soldier, shot through the buttocks at Loos, who was asked by a visitor where he had been wounded, and could only reply: 'I'm so sorry, ma'am, I don't know: I never learned Latin.'[46]

Tail (C. 14) was Standard English until about 1750 but became impolite—perhaps because the identical word was used for the pudenda; the same thing happened to *prat* (C. 16), presumably for the same reason. Another old Standard English word, *tout* (C. 14), became obsolete in the fifteenth century but was later revived as literary slang. *Stern* (late C. 16) and *poop* (c. 1640) were of nautical provenance; their contemporaries were *catastrophe* and *crupper*, the first a jocular euphemism that did not survive the nineteenth century, the second meaning literally 'a horse's rump'. *Bum(p)kin* (C. 17) and *bum-fiddle* (late C. 17–early 19) were presumably diminutives of *bum*, and *fun* (late C. 17–early 19) an abbreviation of *fundament*. The seventeenth century yielded also *nockandro* (used by Urquhart, the translator of Rabelais), *toby* (c. 1675; from the proper name), *blind cheeks*, and *double jug(g)s*; the eighteenth, *scut* (before 1709) *dopey*, *jutland* (C. 18–mid-19), *blind Cupid* (mid-C. 18–early 19), *cheeks* (c. 1750; sometimes *two fat cheeks and ne'er a nose*), *ars musica* (late C. 18–19), and *seat of vengeance* (1749) and *seat of honour* (1792)—a series completed in 1821 with *seat of shame*; the nineteenth, *bows* or *boughs* (c. 1810–70; used in the expression 'wide in the bows'), *nancy* (c. 1810–1910), the jocular *fundamental features* (1818), *flankey* (c. 1840), *jacksy* (*pardo* or *pardy*) (c. 1850; *jacksy* alone, late C. 19, army and navy), *latter end* (mid-C. 19; jocular; originally a boxing term), *corybungus* or *corybungo* (c. 1850–1900; boxing), *mottob* (before 1859; back slang), *droddum* (c. 1860), *Sunday face* (c. 1860), *hinterland* (c. 1880–90), *ampersand* (c. 1885–1914; '&' used to come at the end of nursery-book alphabets), *hinders* (c. 1890; dialect from 1857), *dummock, hind boot, hinder end, hinder parts, hinder world*, and *keel* (Scots). *Bim* (C. 20) originated in Scottish public schools. Cleland coined the terms *flesh cushions, Turkish beauties* and *white cliffs*, Marvell the term *western end*. Two dysphemisms for the posteriors are *cracker* (mid-C. 17–early 19) and *dilberry-maker* (before 1811).[47]

As might be expected, there are no euphemisms for the *anus* (1658), not in itself normally a topic of polite conversation. *Hole* dates from the fourteenth century; other more or less plain terms have included *port-hole* (*c.* 1660), *bung*(*-hole*) (late C. 18), *arse-hole* (C. 19), *shit-hole* (C. 19), *brown* (*hole*) (mid-C. 19), *bottom-hole*, *privy hole*, *hinder entrance* (C. 19), and *back passage*. There are such archaic terms as *siege* (1561), *fugo* (C. 17–18), *roby douglas* (*c.* 1780–1850), and *feak* (early C. 19). *Holloway, Middlesex* (*c.* 1865-1910) was a dysphemistic double pun; other dysphemisms were *trill* (? late C. 17–mid-19), (*brother*) *round mouth* (*c.* 1810–70; especially in the phrase 'brother round mouth speaks'), *spice island* (*c.* 1810–50), *dilberry creek, stinkhole bay, wind-mill,* and *wrong door*.[48]

The commonest demotic words for the male sex organ, *prick* (from Old English *prica*, 'point' or 'dot'[49]) and *cock* (from Old English *cocc*[50]) date back in written sources to the sixteenth and seventeenth centuries respectively. The former has been a vulgarism since the eighteenth century, the latter since about 1830 (somewhat earlier in the U.S.A.). Both words were suggested punningly by Shakespeare. 'The bawdy hand of the dial is now upon the prick of noon', says Mercutio in *Romeo and Juliet* [*c.* 1595]; 'Pistol's cock is up,/And flashing fire will follow', says Pistol in *King Henry V* [*c.* 1599].[51] Florio, in his Italian-English dictionary, *A Worlde of Wordes* (1598), renders *coglíuto* as 'one that hath a good prick'.[52] 'The main Spring's weaken'd that holds up his cock', says a servant to Sulpitia, Mistress of the Male Stewes, about a Dane exhausted in her service, in Fletcher and Massinger's play *The Custom of the Country* (composed between 1619 and 1622).[53]

The word *cock* seems to have had a specially strong aura in America, where, as the polite term for a male domestic fowl, *rooster* (1772) became cock of the walk early in the nineteenth century; it has remained so to this day. Bache protested energetically, but unavailingly:

> Why . . . should we substitute *rooster* for *cock*? Does not the hen of the same species roost also? We say *woodcock, peacock, weathercock*,—although some persons object to these,—why, then, should we not use the distinctive name from which the compounds are derived? . . . Or shall we read, where Peter denies the Master— 'the *rooster* crew'? The word *rooster* is an Americanism, which, the sooner we forget, the better.[54]

De Vere quotes an anonymous Englishman who professed to have heard a *rooster and ox* (i.e., cock and bull) story in the United States.[55] But even *rooster* was considered somewhat advanced; one New York boarding-house keeper preferred *barn-door he-biddy*,[56] and *game-chicken* (1846) and *crower* (1891) were quite frequent.[57]

Roaches started to oust American *cockroaches* in the eighteen-twenties; *haystacks* began to replace *haycocks* in the same decade; by 1859 *cockchafers* were being called *chafers*; and a young woman tells Judge Haliburton's *Sam Slick* (1838) that her brother is a *rooster swain* in the navy![58] It is, on the whole, surprising that the U.S.A. was the home of a drink called a *cocktail* (one colloquial English meaning of which is 'whore'). But these changes were not all. What Bartlett in 1877 called the 'mock modesty of the Western States' required that a male turkey should be called—a *gentleman turkey*.[59]

In comparison with the plain words *prick* and *cock*, such expressions as *member* (c. 1290), *privy member* (1297), *genitals* (1390), *privy parts* (1556), *pudenda* (1634), *penis* (1693), *arbor vitae* (1732), *tree of life* (1732), *means of generation* (1791), *genitalia* (1876), *private parts* (1885), *(male) organ*, and *sex* sound distinctly emasculate. So do the more literary euphemisms—*catso* (C. 17–early 18; from the Italian *cazzo*), *gadso* (late C. 17–mid-19; cf. *catso*; used in Dickens as an interjection), *cyprian sceptre*, *mentule*, *priap*, and *thyrsus*—and also the colloquial (but still respectable) ones: *thing* (C. 17), *(matrimonial) peacemaker* (mid-C. 18), *private property* (C. 19), *affair* (C. 19), *it* (C. 19), *concern* (c. 1840), *Athenaeum* or *the A* (before 1903), *thingummy* (C. 20), *contrivance*, *privates*, and *privities*. Less so, perhaps, Rochester's *rector of the females*, or *champion of women's rights*, or *nakedness*, or *phallus*. But the feebleness, or archness, of most of these terms is more than compensated for by a wealth of popular synonyms—*The Slang of Venery* lists about 600—both euphemistic and dysphemistic, which reflect the unquenchable verbal inventiveness, sexual vigour and pride (and, to a certain extent, cynicism) of Englishmen over several centuries.[60]

These synonyms fall into five main groups. First, there are words—colloquialisms or slang terms—which refer to the bodily position, appearance, or shape of the relaxed or tumescent penis. The majority of words in this group seem euphemistic—though we must bear in mind that both euphemism and dysphemism are relative terms, depending on the context and on the degree of social acceptability, in a specific milieu, of the plain word which the chosen synonym is replacing. The position of the penis is indicated by such terms as *middle finger* (C. 19), *middle leg* (C. 19), *middle stump* (C. 20) and *middle*; *best leg of three* (C. 19); *down-leg*; and *foreman*. For the organ in detumescence there are *tail* (mid-C. 14; Standard English until C. 18) and such compounds as *tail-pipe* and *tail-tree*; *flip-flap* (*c.* 1650); *flap-doodle* (late C. 17); *lobcock* (mid-C. 18); *flapper* (C. 19); *dingle-dangle* (*c.* 1895); and a nursery term, *worm*. Two other nineteenth-century euphemisms of this kind are *dropping member* (especially if gonorrhœa'd) and *hanging Johnny* (especially if impotent or diseased). *Little finger* (C. 20) is a female euphemism. There is a series of expressions likening the penis to a tool or machine-part or domestic article of some kind: *tool* itself (mid-C. 16; Standard English until C. 18), *master-tool*, and *instrument*; *pen* and *pencil* (late C. 19); *pin* (C. 17; used by Burns), *tail-pin* and *needle* (Standard English in C. 18); *pump(-handle)* (C. 18); *horn* (C. 18); *key* (C. 18); *rod* (C. 18), *rod of love* and *Aaron's rod*; *copper-stick* (C. 19); *pendulum* (C. 19); *pole* (C. 19); *button* (C. 19; baby's); *spout* (C. 19); *pestle* (C. 19); *machine* (C. 19); *(k)nob* (late C. 19), *broom-handle*, *broomstick*, *busk*, *candle*, *clothes-prop*, *cork*, *golden rivet*, *peg*, *spigot*, *sponge*, and *spindle*. Other names come from the kitchen or the sweet shop: *poperine-pear* (late C. 16–mid-17; used by Shakespeare); *pudding* (C. 17) and *roly-poly* (C. 19); *sugar-stick* (late C. 18) and *lollipop* (C. 19); *bone* (mid-C. 19; Cockneys'); *gristle* (*c.* 1850) and *marrowbone* (C. 19); *banana, potato finger, radish*, and *(live) sausage*. Others again, from the animal kingdom: *nag* (*c.* 1670–1750), *cuckoo* (C. 19; schoolboys'), *mole* (C. 19), *mouse* (C. 19), *goose's neck* (*c.* 1872), *winkle* (late C. 19; nursery and schoolboys'), *bird, goat, live rabbit, lobster, pony, snake*, and *trouser-snake*. The penis is also euphemized into a *prickle* (*c.* 1550; Standard English), a *pilgrim's staff* (C. 18), a *star-gazer* (C. 18), a *flute* (C. 18), *living, one-holed*, and *silent flute* (the latter, late C. 18–mid-19) and a *whistle*, a *pointer*, a *root* (C. 19) and an *Irish root* (*c.* 1830–1914), a *fiddle-bow* (*c.* 1830), a *stick*, a *fiddle-stick* (C. 19), a *drumstick* and a *night stick*, a *sceptre* (*of authority*), a *tent-peg*, and a *yard*. Among sailors it becomes a *stern-post* (mid-C. 19) or a *rudder*; in the countryside a *handstaff* (*c.* 1850). A whole armoury is drawn on: *weapon* itself (late C. 19); *dirk* (C. 18; Scots); *pikestaff* (C. 18), *pike of pleasure*, and *tail-pike*; *bow* and *(love's) arrow*; *bayonet*, *cutlass*, *(mutton) dagger, dart, nature's scythe, sabre, spear*, and *spike*;

club (C. 19) and *bludgeon*; *pistol* (late C. 19), *fowling-piece*, *gun*, and *cutty-gun* (Scots). Of the few dysphemisms in this group, three empha-size the phenomenon of erection: *bit of hard* (C. 19), *hard-bit*, and *bit of stiff* (C. 19). The other is *hairy wheel* (*c.* 1870).

In the second group, euphemisms are heavily outnumbered; this group contains words which refer, sometimes with gusto or with crudity, to the sexual or reproductive or excretory functions of the male sex organ. The euphemisms are *lullaby* (mid-C. 19), *badge* (or *label*) *of manhood, Cupid's torch, bed-fellow, carnal part, guest, little lover, lodger, love flesh, mark of the man, master of the ceremonies, object of enjoyment, ploughshare, sex's pride, thorn in the flesh,* and *unruly member*; *cuckold-maker* (*c.* 1610); *baby-maker* (late C. 19), *child-getter, brat-getter,* and *life-preserver* (*c.* 1840); *pee-wee* (C. 19; nursery), *P-maker* (mid-C. 19), *waterworks* (mid-C. 19), *water-engine* (late C. 19), and *make-water*. Many of the dysphemisms introduce into the name of the male sex organ a more or less direct allusion to the female sex organ: *trap-stick* (*c.* 1670–1900); *plum-tree shaker* (C. 17–18); *tickle-tail* (C. 17); *tickle-toby* (? C. 17–19), *plug-tail* (mid-C. 18–mid-19), *tail-trimmer,* and *tenant-in-tail* (punning upon the legal meaning of *tail*); *quim-wedge* (C. 19), *wedge, quim-stake* (C. 19), *crack-h(a)unter* (C. 19), *hunter, cracks-man, cranny-h(a)unter, cunny-catcher, gap-stopper* (C. 19), *gully-raker, chink-stopper,* and *touch-trap*; *rump-splitter* (*c.* 1560–1800), *arse-opener, arse-wedge, bum-tickler,* and *claw-buttock*; *beard-splitter* (C. 18–19), *hair-splitter* (*c.* 1810), *hair-divider* (*c.* 1850), *splitter* (1876), *quiff-splitter, bush-beater,* and *bush-whacker*; *leather-stretcher* (C. 18) and *leather-dresser, sky-scraper* (*c.* 1840), *button-hole worker* (C. 19), *holy iron* (*c.* 1860; punning), *gardener* (C. 19) and *garden-engine,* (*bald-headed*) *hermit* (late C. 19), *bung-starter, dilator, distender,* and *vestryman*; *split-mutton* (? C. 17–19), *kidney-wiper* (C. 20; used in 'The Highland Tinker') and *kidney-scraper, gut-stick, liver-turner, meat-skewer, spike-faggot, trouble-guts,* and *womb-brush*. Others make a fairly direct allusion to the movement of the penis in the act of copulation: *knocker* (*c.* 1650) and *knock* (C. 18), *wriggling pole* (late C. 17 or early 18), *jigger* (C. 19) and *jiggling-bone* (Irish), *gaying instrument* (C. 19), *fornicating-engine, -member,* and *-tool* (C. 19), *grinding-tool* (C. 19), *pile-driver* (C. 19), *tickler* (C. 19), *poker* (*c.* 1810) and *holy poker* (*c.* 1860), *ram-rod* (mid-C. 19) and *rammer* (mid-C. 19), *gooser* (*c.* 1871); *piston(-rod)* (C. 20), *sexing-piece* (*c.* 1925), *connecting-*

rod, coupling-pin, plunger, and *shove-devil.* Elsewhere the allusion to copulation is metaphorical, but the reference is plain and the effect dysphemistic: *angler* and *fishing-rod, butcher* and *chopper,* and *floater.* The penis is named as a provider of semen—*cream-stick* (C. 18), *gravy-giver* (C. 19), *butter-knife,* and *Old Slimy*—and of urine: *pisser* (C. 19). Its temperature at certain times is alluded to: *red-hot poker* (C. 19; female), *bonfire, burning rod,* and *firebrand.* It is seen as a source of sexual pleasure: *ladies' lollipop* (C. 19), *sweetmeat* (mid-C. 19), *merry-maker* (mid-C. 19) and *merry man, joy-stick* (late C. 19), *joy-prong* and *love-prong, giggle-stick* (C. 20), *shaft of delight, delight of women, plaything, toy,* and *yum-yum.* And there are names that appear to reflect the popular belief that the tumescent organ is not unduly troubled by pangs of conscience: *(belly-)ruffian* (? C. 17–19), *ranger* (C. 18; from *range,* 'to be inconstant'), *girl-catcher* (*c.* 1870), and *girlometer* (*c.* 1870).

The third group of synonyms, of great interest, consists of personifications of the penis; almost all are euphemistic. The Bible makes a large contribution: *Nimrod* (C. 19; 'a mighty hunter'), *the old Adam* (C. 19), *Jacob* (C. 19), *Nebuchadnezzar* (*c.* 1860–1915), *Abraham* (late C. 19), *Father Abraham, Jezebel,* and *Saint Peter* (who holds the keys of heaven). Greek myth supplies *Polyphemus* (C. 19); history, *Julius Caesar* (*c.* 1840) and *Old Rowley* (i.e., Charles II); literature, *Dr Johnson* (*c.* 1790–1880; 'perhaps', suggests Partridge, 'because there was no one that Dr Johnson was not prepared to stand up to'[61]); fable, *Bluebeard* and *Master Reynard.* The personal names that have been recorded start with *Roger* (*c.* 1650) and *Jock* (before 1790; compare *jock-strap*) and include *Jack, Jack-in-the-box* (C. 19; also, since *c.* 1870, as rhyming slang for *pox,* signifies syphilis) and *Jack Robinson,* the lately celebrated *John Thomas* (*c.* 1840; cf. *J.T.,* before 1923), *Thomas* (C. 19), *man Thomas, John Henry, Peter* (mid-C. 19), *Dick* (*c.* 1860; military), *Dick(e)y* (*c.* 1870; schoolboys'), *Little Davy* (Scots), *Billy-my-nag, Bob-my-nag,* and two nursery terms: *Timothy(-tool)* and the hypocoristic *Willie,* in use before 1847 and before 1905 respectively. *She,* a twentieth-century Londoners' term, is 'partly euphemistic, partly proleptic'.[62] *His Majesty in Purple Cap,* a *one-eyed man,* an *old man* (C. 19), a *bishop* (late C. 19), *the boy* (late C. 19), and two anonymous kinsmen, a *little brother* (mid-C. 19) and an *uncle,* complete the roll.[63]

The fourth group is made up of literary synonyms coined or used by English writers; a few have passed into the spoken language for a time. George Gascoigne gave us *Robin*; Shakespeare, *bauble*; Sir Thomas Urquhart, *aspersing-tool*, *bracmard*, *coral-branch*, *Don Cypriano*, *Don Orsino*, *gentle-tittler*, *Master John Goodfellow*, *Master John Thursday*, *nilnisistando*, and *nudinuddo*; Denham, *wand* and *ware*; Dorset, *tarse*; Rochester, *angle*; Cleland, *animated ivory*, *beloved guest*, *blind favourite*, *centre of sense*, *dear morsel*, *engine of love*, *(piece of) furniture*, *grand movement*, *handle*, *instrument of pleasure*, *man machine*, *master-member*, *mutinous rogue*, *nipple of love*, *picklock*, *playfellow*, *pleasure pivot*, *plenipotentiary instrument*, *sceptre member*, *sensitive plant*, *shaft*, and *standard of distinction*; Sterne, *sausage*; Burns, *dearest member*; Ann Radcliffe, *pego* (from the Greek πηγή, 'spring', 'fountain'). Whitman has *man-root*, *pond-snipe*, and *thumb of love*. All these may be classed as euphemisms; but up to the death of Smollett English writers were also in the habit of coining or using names intended to draw attention to the sexual function of the penis. Shakespeare has *pike*; Ebsworth, *Captain Standish*; Urquhart, *cunny-burrow ferret*, *crimson chitterling*, *generating-* (or *generation-*) *tool*, *intercrural pudding*, *jolly-member*, *live sausage*, *nervous cane*, *nine-inch knocker*, *placket-racket*, *shove-straight*, *Sir Martin Wagstaff*, *split-rump*, *touch-her-home*, and *trouble-giblets*; Rochester, *quickening-peg* and *whore-pipe*; D'Urfey, *what Harry gave Doll*; Cleland, *battering-piece* and *-ram*, *conduit pipe*, *gristle*, and *sensitive truncheon*; Burns, *plug*.

Lastly, there is a group of synonyms for the penis and testicles together. There was a plain word, *gear*, first used in the sixteenth century and Standard English until the nineteenth. Euphemisms include *the Netherlands* (C. 18), *place* (C. 18), *rule of three* (C. 18), *barber's sign* (late C. 18–19), *kit* (C. 19) and *kit of tools*, *bag of tricks* (mid-C. 19), *fancy work* (C. 20; a female euphemism for the male genitals, including the pubic hair), *pencil and tassel* (C. 20; nursery), *twig and berries* (C. 20; nursery) *wedding kit* (c. 1918; mostly army and air force), *Adam's arsenal*, *ladyware*, *luggage*, *other parts*, *parts*, *parts below*, *parts more dear*, *parts of shame*, and *watch and seals*. Dysphemisms include *meat* (C. 16), *raw meat*, (mid-C. 18) and *meat and two veg.* (C. 20), *beef* (C. 19), *marrowbone and cleaver* (C. 19), *oil can*, and *tail tackle*.[64]

Of plain English words for the human *testicles* (c. 1425) the oldest (slightly older even than *balls*) appears to be *beallucas*, which an Old English vocabulary of the tenth or eleventh century gives as the translation of the Latin *testiculi*.[65] Wycliffe, in his 1382 translation of the Bible, spelt it *ballokes*;[66] we are more familiar with it today as *ballocks*. Almost as venerable is *stones*, first recorded in the twelfth century and Standard English until the middle of the nineteenth, when—except for the testicles of a horse—it became a vulgarism.[67] An early word for *scrotum* (1597) was *cod* (1398)—i.e., 'bag'—which in the plural (1527), together with the diminutive *codlings*, signified 'testicles'; compare *codpiece* (c. 1460). By the nineteenth century *cod(s)* had fallen out of use; and about 1840 *ballocks* and *balls* became impolite.[68] Other ancient words were *callibisters*, *culls*, *cullions*, and *male mules*, all in use in the sixteenth and seventeenth centuries. *Pounders* (late C. 17–18) was used by Dryden. There were *tarriwags* (C. 17) and *talliwags* (late C. 18), *whirlygigs* (late C. 17–early 19), and *twiddle-diddles* (c. 1786), *jelly-bag* (C. 17), *nutmegs* (C. 17) and *nuts* (C. 18), *baubels* or *bawbels* (late C. 18–early 19), and *bobbles* (C. 19). A series of colloquial euphemisms—some of them still current—includes *gingam-bobs* and *gingumbobs* (C. 18), *thingumbobs* and *thingambobs* (1785), *thingummies* (C. 19), *thingumaries* (c. 1820), and *thingumajigs* (c. 1880). Nineteenth-century adaptations and coinages were *apples* and *goose-berries* (c. 1850), *knackers*, *nags*, *pebbles*, *seals*, *goolies* (late C. 19), and *pills* (late C. 19); twentieth-century ones, *booboos* (U.S.), *dusters* (army), and *charleys*. Cleland, fertile in this as in other directions, has *ladies' jewels*, *reservoirs*, *storehouse of nature's sweets*, and *treasure bag*. The only dysphemistic words for this part of the body appear to be *cannon-balls* (c. 1885), *swingers* (C. 19), and *spunkholders*.[69]

The American slang term *nerts* is derived from *nuts*; according to Mencken it originated in Hollywood in the early twenties, when there arose

> a fashion for using openly the ancient four-letter words that had maintained an underground life since the Restoration. It was piquant, for a while, to hear them from the lovely lips of movie beauties, but presently the grand dames of Hollywood society prohibited them as a shade too raw, and they were succeeded by euphemistic forms, made by changing the vowel of each to *e* and inserting *r* after it. *Nuts* was not one of these venerable words, but it had connotations that made it seem somewhat raw too, so it was changed to *nerts*, and in that form swept the country.[70]

America also provides the euphemisms *glands, interstitial* [*sic*] *glands,* and *sex glands.* In Kansas in the early twenties *bag* was banned, for 'when they hear . . . it they always think of *scrotum*'.[73]

This seems the appropriate point to refer to some euphemisms for the original *geld* (before 1300): *castrate* (1613), *emasculate* (1623), *neuter* (1903), and *doctor*; and, in the U.S.A., *alter* (1852), *change,* and *arrange*—'even on the farm', remarks Mencken[72]—or, in the Middle West, *cut*; in Georgia, *make a Baptist minister of.*[73]

The most venerable English word for the female sex organ, *cunt*, was once thought to derive from the Latin *cunnus*; but philologists find it hard to explain how the *t* got into Old and Middle English *cunte* (occasionally *counte*), Old Frisian *kunte*, Old Norse *kunta*, Middle Low German and Low German *kunte*, and Dutch *kunte*. The Old English word, says Partridge, was 'certainly cognate with' the Old English *cwithe*, 'the womb';[74] the root of the word is thought to be *cu* (in Old English, *cwe*), which apparently signified 'quintessential physical femineity'.[75] The word may be 'of common Medit[erranean] stock'; the Egyptian *ka-t* (Fig. 1) meant 'vagina', 'vulva', 'mother', 'women collectively'.[76]

Fig. 1

The mother knew how to produce life. This was the greatest wisdom, and so arose the symbol of the Great Mother. The root *cu* appears in count-less words from *cowrie, Cypris,* down to *cow*; and the root *cun* has two lines of descent, the one emphasizing the mother and the other knowledge: *Cynthia* and the underworld term for the external female organ, *cunt*, on the one hand, and *cunning*, on the other.[77]

But *cunt* is not an 'underworld term': as Partridge makes clear, 'it is not slang, nor is it cant: it definitely is a "language" word . . . belonging to the class of vulgarisms'.[78] ('Vulgarisms' is used here in the technical sense.) *Cunt* has long served to connote, not merely the female sex organ, but also 'the sexual pleasure produced by a woman in a man, and indeed all that a woman-as-sex signifies to a man, both physically and spiritually'.[79] Owing to this 'powerful sexuality'— it is what Edward Charles called a 'sexually energizing' word[80]—it has been avoided in written and polite spoken English since the fifteenth century, and between c. 1700 and 1960 it was, 'except in the reprinting of old classics . . . held to be obscene, i.e., a legal offence, to print it in full'.[81]

Alone among the so-called 'four-letter words', this one has the distinction of appearing as part of a once widespread English street-name. In 1279 there was a lane in the City of London called Gropeconte-lane; Magpie Lane (now Grove Street) in Oxford was Gropecuntelane in about 1230; Grape Lane in York was Grapecuntlane in 1376; Northampton had a Groppecuntelane in 1274, Wells in Somerset a Gropecuntelane in 1285–91, and Stebbing in Essex a Gropecountelane in about 1325.[82] This was in fact 'a common medieval name . . . for a dark and disreputable passage'.[83]

The word was used by Chaucer, who spelt it *queynte* or *queinte*; in *The Miller's Tale* Nicholas wooed Alison

And prively he caughte hire by the queynte.[84]

Shakespeare, in *Twelfth Night* [c. 1600–01], suggested it, when he made Malvolio say: 'By my life, this is my lady's hand! these be her very *C*'s, her *U*'s, and her *T*'s; and thus makes she her great *P*'s', Sir Andrew Aguecheek commenting, 'Her *C*'s, her *U*'s, and her *T*'s; why that?'[85] ('And' would no doubt be pronounced 'en'.) Fletcher, in *The Spanish Curate* (1622), suggested it more plainly: 'They write *sunt* with a *C*, which is abominable.'[86] Rochester is one of the few later writers who prints the word in full. Most lexicographers fought shy of it. Palsgrave, in his *Lesclarcissement de la langue Francoyse* (1530), had 'Count a womans shappe—*con*'.[87] At the beginning of the seventeenth century Cotgrave defined the French *con* as 'A womans &c.',[88] and Minsheu had 'a Cu&c.', with the definition, 'a womans &c. a Quaint, as Chaucer termes it'.[89] Grose, having omitted the word from the first edition of his dictionary (1785), gave it as 'C**T' in the second (1788), and defined it, perhaps not altogether seriously, as 'The κόννος of the Greek, and the *cunnus* of the Latin dictionaries; a nasty name for a nasty thing'.[90] In the third edition (1796), under 'Thingstable'—i.e., constable—he called that curious euphemism 'a ludicrous affectation of delicacy in avoiding the pronunciation of the first syllable of the title of that officer'.[91] Succeeding lexicographers omitted the word *cunt* entirely; Partridge points out that the legal situation would have been different if the editors of the great *OED* had had the courage to include the word and spell it in full.[92] But the relevant volume appeared in the nineteenth century, when it was impossible even to suggest the word in print, except in pornographic literature circulating clandestinely. Even *The Swell's Night Guide* [1841], a kind of *Ladies' Directory*, has: 'The dance was followed up by an out-and-out song by Mike Hunt, whose name was called out in a way that must not be mentioned to ears polite.'[93] Illicit literature apart, two of the few known nineteenth-century written uses of the word occur in one of Keats's letters and in the important collection of folk-lore known as Κρυπτάδια. Keats wrote to his brothers in 1818:

> There was an enquiry about the derivation of the Word C—t when while two parsons and Grammarians were sitting together and settling the matter Wᵐ Squibs interrupting them said a very good thing—Gentlemen says he I have always understood it to be a Root and not a Derivitive![94]

Under the heading 'An English Popular Story', Κρυπτάδια gives the following example of English humour:

> A young lady was out riding, accompanied by her groom. She fell off her horse and in so doing displayed some of her charms; but jumped up very quickly and said to the groom: 'Did you see my agility, John?' 'Yes, miss,' said he, 'but I never heard it called by that name before!'—Another version has it: 'Yes, miss, but we calls it cunt in the kitchen!'[95]

In the twentieth century, even before the 1960 edition of *Lady Chatterley's Lover*, there were books which printed the word in full without running foul of the law; D. H. Lawrence's *Collected Poems* (1932) is a case in point. In the dialect poem 'Whether or Not', a man observes:

> What bit o' cunt I had wi' 'er
> 's all I got out of it.
> An' 's not good enough, it isn't
> For a permanent fit.[96]

It was strange, therefore, that the blurb on the jacket of John Barth's *The Sot-Weed Factor* (1961) should be so delicate as to say: 'In *The*

Sot-Weed Factor there is no *Angst*; a spade is called a spade, a whore a whore, a c . . . a c . . . It is a man's world of strong action and bawdy talk.'[97]

Several other words for the female sex organ may claim the status of plain words: *tail* (mid-C. 14; Standard English until C. 18), *hole* (C. 16 or earlier), *gear* (late C. 16; Standard English until C. 19), *twat* (1656), and *quim* (C. 17). *Twat* (in C. 18, occasionally *twait*; a variant spelling—and the usual pronunciation—is *twot*) is admitted by the *OED*, which says it is 'of obscure origin'.[98] It occurs in a passage in the royalist rhymes *Vanity of Vanities* [1659]:

> They talk't of his having a Cardinalls Hat,
> They'd send him as soon an Old Nuns Twat.[99]

When Browning read this he took *twat* to mean some part of a nun's attire; and he liked the word so much that he used it in *Pippa Passes* (1841), in what is probably the worst howler in English literature:

> Then, owls and bats,
> Cowls and twats,
> Monks and nuns, in a cloister's moods,
> Adjourn to the oak-stump pantry.[100]

Quim, rejected by the *OED*, may be from the Celtic *cwm*, 'cleft', 'valley'.[101]

The list of cultured euphemisms for the organ whose components are known technically as the *vulva* (1548) and *vagina* (1682) begins with *flesh* (C. 16; cf. the later *fleshly part* and *love flesh*). *Commodity* was very widely used from the late sixteenth century to the nineteenth. The eighteenth century brought *masterpiece, novelty, place, mark (of the beast)* (c. 1715; cf. the later *mother mark*), *mother of all saints* (1785), *mother of all souls* (c. 1791), *monosyllable* (before 1788–before 1915), and *venerable monosyllable*. 'Addison, the best instructor of the small morals who ever lived, yet thought nothing, in papers designed for the breakfast-table and the ladies, as he says himself, to tell us, that a monosyllable was his delight.'[102] Nineteenth-century terms include *affair, private property*, and *it*, the latter being the title of the following lines attributed to a famous humorist and widely circulated orally inside and outside the medical profession:

The portions of a woman that appeal to man's depravity
   Are constructed with considerable care,
And what at first appears to be a simple little cavity
   Is in fact a most elaborate affair.

Physicians of distinction have examined these phenomena
   In numerous experimental dames;
They have tabulated carefully the feminine abdomina,
   And given them some fascinating names.

There's the vulva, the vagina, and the jolly perineum,
   And the hymen, in the case of many brides,
And lots of other little things you'd like, if you could see 'em,
   The clitoris, and other things besides.

So isn't it a pity, when we common people chatter
   Of these mysteries to which I have referred,
That we use for such a delicate and complicated matter
   Such a very short and ordinary word! [103]

Another euphemism with which verse is associated is *feminine gender* (before 1835); this was schoolboys' slang, and probably comes from the 'old schoolboys' rhyme' quoted in *The Slang of Venery*:

Amo, amas,
I loved a lass,
And she was tall and slender;
Amas, amat,
I laid her flat,
And tickled her feminine gender.[104]

Other nineteenth-century cultured euphemisms include *mother of masons* (c. 1810–70), *mother of St Patrick* (1811; Anglo-Irish), *concern* (c. 1840), *(leading) article* (mid-C. 19), and *almanach* (late C. 19). A twentieth-century example is *geography* (c. 1920).[105]

In many ways similar is a group of literary euphemisms coined by English and Scottish writers over six centuries. Chaucer has *belle chose* and *nether eye*; William Dunbar, *towdie*; Lindsay, *claff*; Shakespeare, *circle, dearest bodily part, peculiar river,* and *secret parts*; Donne, *centrique part, best-worst part,* and *exchequer*; Jonson, *socket*; Robert

49

Burton, *coynte*; Herrick, (*portal to the*) *bower of bliss*, *living fountain*, and *postern gate to the Elysian fields*; Carew, *cyprian strait* and *Grove of Eglantine*; Urquhart, *aphrodisiacal tennis court*, *carnal trap*, *contra-punctum*, *cunny burrow*, *hypogastric cranny*, *intercrural trench*, *skin coat*, *solution of continuity*, *trap*, *tufted honours*, and *water gap*; Richard Brome, *cellar*; Etherege, *toy*; Dorset, *best* and *towsie-mowsie*; John Crowne, *garrison*; Rochester (to whom the plain word came more naturally), *best in Christendom*, *bull's eye*, *crown of sense*, *et cetera* and *sport of Cupid's archery*; D'Urfey, *conjuring book*, *copy hold*, *placket box*, *sack*, *toll dish*, *Venus's honey pot*, *Venus's mark*, and *weather gig*; Motteux, *sweet-scented hole*; Allan Ramsay, *caldron*; Pope, *parts of shame*; John Boyle, *star over the garter*. To Cleland goes the credit for having coined almost as many synonyms as all these other writers put together, among them *charm of attraction*, *cleft of flesh*, *controlling part*, *cloven inlet*, *cloven stamp of female distinction*, (*delicate*) *glutton*, *delicious deep*, *devilish thing*, (*flesh* and *open*) *wound*, *furnace mouth*, *mysterious mark*, *mouth of nature*, *pleasure-girth*, *region of delight*, *quean seat*, *secret of nature*, *sensible part*, *small part*, *tender opening*, *tender part*, *treasury of love*, and *Venus's sphere*.[106] G. A. Stevens called it the *eye that weeps most when best pleased*, *life's dainty*, and *lock of all locks*; Sterne, *covered way*; and Burns, *canister*, *spleuchan*, and *wame*.

Turning now to more popular terms, we have a lengthy series referring to the physical structure or appearance of the organ: *crack* (C. 16); *hole of holes* (C. 16), *hole of content* (C. 16–19) and *queen of holes*; *ring* (C. 16, but rare after C. 18), *ring of flesh*, *Cupid's ring*, and (*Hans*) *Carvel's ring* (mid-C. 18–early 19), Hans Carvel being a jealous old doctor who, in bed with his wife, 'dreamed that the devil gave him a ring, which, so long as he had it on his finger, would prevent his being made a cuckold'; 'waking he found he had got his finger the Lord knows where';[107] *mouth thankless* (mid-C. 16–early 17; Scots), *mouth that cannot bite* (C. 18–mid-19), *mouth that says no words about it* (C. 18–mid-19), *lips* (*between the thighs*), and *nether mouth*; *nock* (i.e., 'notch'; late C. 16), *nick* (C. 18), *notch* (C. 18), and *nick-in-the-notch*; *cleft* (C. 17); *half moon* (C. 17); *pit* (C. 17), *pit-hole*, *pit-mouth* and *pit of darkness*; *port-hole* (c. 1660); *placket* (C. 17–18) and *purse* (C. 17), the latter very common, occurring, for example, in the broadside song *The Turnep Ground* [c. 1720]:

I ow'd my Hostess thirty Pound
And how d'ye think I pay'd her,
I Mett her in my Turnep Ground,
And gently down I lay'd her,

She Op't a Purse as black as Coal,
To hold my Coin when counted,
I Satisfied in the hole
And Just by Tayl She found it.[108]

The list continues with *pocket* and *pouch*; *road* (C. 17?), *love lane* (C. 19), *main avenue* (C. 19), *smock alley*, *(Cupid's) alley*, *Cupid's highway*, *Venus's highway*, and *turnpike*; *slit* (C. 17) and *chink* (C. 18); *horseshoe* (C. 18); *nest (in the bush)* (C. 18), *bird's nest*, *magpie's nest* (C. 18), *cuckoo's nest* (C. 19), *goldfinch's nest* (before 1827), *dove's nest*, *phoenix nest*, and *Cupid's nest*; *gap* (C. 18) and *gash* (C. 18), *cranny* (C. 19) and *crevice* (C. 19); *hoop* (C. 19), *pipe* (C. 19) and *shell* (C. 19); *button hole* (mid-C. 19); and *lucky bag* (mid-C. 19).[109] A similar group of terms relates to the organ's bodily position: *the Low Countries* (C. 18–mid-19), *the Netherlands* (C. 18), *the lowlands* (late C. 18–mid-19), *Antipodes* (C. 19), *forecastle* (C. 19), *front door* (C. 19), *Midlands* (c. 1830), and *Lapland* (c. 1840) are typical.[110]

Next comes a group likening the female sex organ to food of various kinds. It is seen as *meat* (late C. 16) or a *bit of meat*, as *cat's meat* or *man's meat*; or as *mutton* (c. 1670), or a *bit of mutton*, or a *bit of pork*, or *bacon*, or *tripe*. It is an *orange* (C. 17), *(a bit of) jam* (C. 19), a *pancake* (C. 19), a *cookie*, a *(bit of) fish* (c. 1850), an *oyster* (C. 19), a *bit of skate*, *ling*[111] or *trout*. Or it is simply a *tit-bit* (C. 17) or a *yum-yum*. Then there are words that liken it to a room or enclosed place of some kind: *Little Merlin's Cave* (1737), or *the thatched house under the hill* (c. 1770–1850) or the *cave of Cupid* (1792), for instance; or one's *(front) attic* (C. 19) or *(front) room* (C. 19). *(Cupid's) Hotel* seems equivocally euphemistic.[112] Similarly, it is seen as a *case* (C. 17) or *box*, or a vessel of some kind: a *pitcher* (C. 17) or *miraculous pitcher* (as in the mid-C. 18–mid-19 catchphrase *the miraculous pitcher that holds water mouth downwards*); or a *pipkin* (late C. 17–early 19), a *kettle* (C. 18), a *sugar-basin* (mid-C. 19), a *receptacle* (1876), a *bucket, can, chalice, pot, scuttle*, or *Venus's font*.[113]

The vegetable and animal kingdoms are laid under contribution. We have *garden* (C. 16), *hortus* (C. 18), *front garden* (C. 19)—and *Garden of Eden—orchard* (C. 19), *green meadow* (*c.* 1850),[114] and *vineyard*, as well as many of the things that grow in them: *flower* (C. 19; cf. *flower of chivalry* (C. 19), *flower pot* (C. 19) and *lady flower*), *rose* (C. 18; also a euphemism for 'hymen'), *moss rose, daisy, evergreen, fruitful vine* (C. 19),[115] *plum-tree* (used by Shakespeare), *medlar* (C. 17–mid-19), *fig* (C. 19) and *split fig, split apricot, gooseberry bush, pumpkin, parsley bed* (*c.* 1600), *cauliflower* (C. 18),[116] *cabbage* (and *cabbage-field, -garden,* and *-patch*) (C. 19), *mushroom* (C. 19), *nettle bed*—and *green grocery* (*c.* 1850). In 1741 'Philogynes Clitorides' wrote *The Natural History of the Frutex Vulvaria or Flowering Shrub* (terms that can be traced back to 1732); and a two-volume disquisition on woman-as-sex appeared in 1765 under the title of *The Fruit-shop*. The cat family provides a great many euphemisms, the most common ones still current being *puss* (C. 17) and *pussy* (C. 19)—though one philologist confesses that he has 'long been tantalized by the possibility that *puss* in its venereal sense may have developed from *purse*'.[117] The popularity of *cunny* or *cunnie* (C. 17; an obsolete form of *cony*, 'rabbit') may have been due to its suggesting the word *cunt*. *Titmouse* (C. 17), *tit* (C. 18), and *coyote* (C. 19) are also recorded.[118]

Like the male organ, the female organ is frequently personified. It was called the *toby* (*c.* 1678) and *Betty-land* (1684) in the seventeenth century, *Miss Brown* (late C. 18), *Madge* (*Howlet*) (*c.* 1780), and (*brown*) *jock* (before 1790) in the eighteenth and nineteenth. It is a *housewife* (C. 19), or one's *little sister* (C. 19), an *old lady* (C. 19), an *old woman* (C. 19), or one's *grandmother* (C. 20),[119] or *granny*. It may be called *Rufus* (C. 19), or *Mary Jane* (*c.* 1840), or *Lady Jane* (*c.* 1850), or—commonest of all—*Fanny* (*c.* 1860), *Fanny artful*, or *Fanny fair*, names we perhaps owe to Fanny Hill, the heroine of Cleland's *Memoirs of a Woman of Pleasure*. A woman might also refer to her *Aunt Maria* (before 1903) or her *chum*. It would hardly be employing euphemism, though, to call it *Miss Horner* (C. 19).

There are several kinds of mildly humorous name: a group of Latin names, [120] an eighteenth-century group using antiphony (i.e., a syllable or syllables are reduplicated with phonetic variation),[121] and a group of jocular phrases: *rest and be thankful* (C. 19), *rob-the-ruffian* (C. 19), *rough and ready* (C. 19), *Lord knows what, what-do-you-call-it* (sometimes spelt *washical*), *what's-her-name, what's-its-name,* and *you-know-what*.[122] Other jocular euphemisms are *Buckinger's boot* (*c.* 1740–

95; 'Matthew Buckinger was born without hands and legs; . . . he was married to a tall, handsome woman, and traversed the country, shewing himself for money'[123]), *(old) hat* (1754; 'because frequently felt';[124] used by Fielding), *Fumbler's Hall* (late C. 18–19; a *fumbler* is an impotent man or inadequate husband), *holy of holies* (C. 19), *agility* (c. 1870–1914),[125] and *book-binder's wife* ('manufacturing in sheets'[126]).

Lastly, there are innumerable expressions with a more directly erotic significance. Many view the female organ as a source of pleasure: *Merryland* (1740, in *A New Description of Merryland*, by 'Roger Pheuquewell'), *centre of bliss* (c. 1790), *(gentleman's) pleasure garden*, *agreeable ruts of life* (before 1903), *cup of pleasure*, *heaven* (cf. the C. 18 *hell*!), *love's paradise*, *love's playground*, *(privy) paradise*, *place of ease*, *plaything*, and *saint's delight.*[127] *Gate of horn, itcher,* and *itching Jenny* are nineteenth-century dysphemisms referring specifically to sexual excitement. Just as there are many popular names for the penis which allude to the female organ, so the latter is very often named with direct or indirect reference to the penis: *Pillicock Hall, mole-catcher* (C. 17–mid-18), *pin case* (C. 17), *(Cupid's) pincushion* (C. 17), *(velvet) mouse-trap* (shorter form, 1794), *needle-book* (C. 19), *needle-case* (C. 19), *bite* (late C. 17–early 19; probably cant), *hone* (C. 18–19), *magnet* (C. 18), *ladder* (C. 19), *mortar* (C. 19), *pintle-case* (C. 19), *rooster* (mid-C. 19), *gymnasium* (c. 1860), *mangle* (c. 1860), *(happy) hunting ground* (c. 1870), *old man's supper* (late C. 19; to 'warm the old man's supper' is to sit before the fire with skirts raised), *snatch* (late C. 19), *snatch-blatch* (c. 1890–1915), *snatch box* (before 1916), *candlestick, keyhole, little spot where Uncle's doodle goes, pistol pocket, scabbard, target,* and *way in.*[128] Or reference is made to semen, as in *honey pot* (C. 18–19), *seed-plot* (C. 19) and *seed-land, seminary* (mid-C. 19), and *spender.*[129] Apart from *saddle* (C. 17; rare since C. 18), *receipt of custom,* and *basket maker,* all the names which allude specifically to copulation seem to be dysphemistic: *man-trap* (c. 1775) and *manhole* (c. 1870), *rattle-ballocks* (late C. 18), *fuck-hole* (C. 19), *poke-hole* (C. 19), *poking-hole* (C. 19), *rasp* (C. 19), *shake-bag* (C. 19), *fool-trap* (c. 1840), *grindstone* (mid-C. 19), *bob-and-hit, coupler, salt cellar, salt horse,* and *salt meat* (*salt* meaning 'copulate'). Other dysphemisms allude to the temperature of the vagina in coition: *oven* (C. 18), *mustard-pot* (C. 19), *hot meat* (C. 19), *hot mutton* (C. 19), *hot lips, hot passage,* and *forge*; or to its humidity: *moist passage, wet passage,* and *slimy pit of sin.*

Urination,[130] menstruation,[131] reproduction,[132] and prostitution[133] are other functions reflected in popular terminology.[134]

It is significant that while *The Slang of Venery* lists over one thousand popular and literary English synonyms for the female pudenda as a whole, it lists only nine for the rudimentary organ analogous to the penis, the *clitoris* (1615). And these nine are, properly speaking, only seven, since four are pairs of duplicates; and of these seven, only three are genuinely popular synonyms: *button* (C. 19), (*little*) *boy in the* (or *a*) *boat* (late C. 19), and (*little*) *man in the boat* (late C. 19). Of the remainder, *fleshy excrescence*, *peeping sentinel*, and *sensitive spot* are literary, *penis muliebris* a technical term.[135]

The alleged virginal membrane has been known as the *maiden-head* since the thirteenth century, but is nowadays generally called the *hymen* (1615), which is derived from the Greek ὑμήν, meaning 'membrane'. Two eighteenth-century euphemisms were *rose* and *run goods* (*c.* 1786–1840), the latter a pun on the nautical sense of 'contraband'. The usual word in American popular speech is *cherry*. Other terms are *barrier*, *keep*, *ring of flesh*, *tail fence*, *virgin flower*, *virgin head*, *virgin knot*, *virgin membrane*, and *virginity*. Cleland, whose subject-matter necessitated frequent references to this part of the body, called it *bauble*, *darling treasure*, *flower*, *perishable commodity*, *trinket*, *unbroken passage*, and *virgin slit*.[136]

Perhaps the commonest present-day demotic term for the pubic hair is *bush*, which started off, according to Partridge, as a literary euphemism, becoming a low term in the middle of the nineteenth century.[137] It gave rise to the facetious *Bushy Park* (*c.* 1860; of women). Some other euphemisms are: *scut* (late C. 16), *furbelow* (C. 17–early 19; of women), (*silent*) *beard* (longer form late C. 17–early 19; of women), *muff* (late C. 17; of women), *fur* (C. 18; generally of women), *fleece* (? C. 18; of women), *parsley* (C. 18), *stubble* (C. 18; of women), *toupee* (mid-C. 18; of women), *fud* (late C. 18), *fluff* (C. 19; of women), *furze*(-*bush*) (C. 19; generally of women), *grass* (C. 19), *mattress* (C. 19), *shrubbery* (late C. 19; generally of women), *sporran* (late C. 19), *banner*, *brush*, *clover field*, *down*, *Downshire*, *feathers*, *fig leaf*, *forest*, *golden hedge*, *gooseberry bush*, *hedge* (*on the dike*), *kitten's ear*, *mole skin*, *moss*, *ringlets*, *silken floss*, *thatch*, *thicket*, *tuft*, *velvet*, and *wig*. Cleland has (*downy*) *cloth*, *mossy mounts*, and *silky hair*. The status of the main components of *cunt curtain*, *quim bush* (C. 19), *quim whiskers* (C. 19), *quim wig* (C. 19), and *twat rug* (before 1903) suggests that these should be classified as plain terms; but in fact all five are probably usually dysphemistic; and *front-door mat* (C. 19), *shaving-brush* (after 1838), *dilberry bush* (mid-C. 19), and *scrubbing-brush* (mid-C. 19) are certainly so.[138]

3

THEY SHOCKED Mrs BEETON

At the close of the eighteenth century the garments that lay next to legs, belly, buttocks and breast began to share the taboo that was more and more coming to surround these parts of the body. This was first noted immediately after the outbreak of the French revolution, whose challenge to property and propriety may have helped to inculcate new language habits among persons of refinement in England. The extension of the taboo to clothes was recorded by the satirist John Wolcot ('Peter Pindar') in 1790, in his *Ode to Affectation*:

> I've heard, that breeches, petticoats and smock;
> Give to thy modest mind a grievous shock;
> And that thy brain (so lucky its device)
> Christ'neth them *inexpressibles*, so nice![1]

The original English terms for the garments covering the lower half of a man's body were *breeches* (before 1000) and *trousers* (1681). The former, which were also called *knee-breeches* (1833) and *knickerbockers* (1859), came to just below the knee; *small-clothes* (1791) were breeches with a short extension on to the calf. Trousers were full-length and, if tight-fitting, were also known as *pantaloons* (1798), *panteys* (c. 1848–60; mainly U.S.), and *pants* (1842; extended to other trousers before 1874). *Inexpressibles*, as a delicate word for both types of garment, was closely followed by *irrepressibles* (1790), *indescribables* (1794), *ditto(e)s* (C. 19), *unexpressibles* (1810), *unspeakables* (1810), *don't mentions* (1818), *ineffables* (1823), *unmentionables* (1836; a word brought back from America by Dickens), *inexplicables* (1836; also given currency by Dickens), *nether-garments* (1836), *unwhisperables* (1837), *continuations* (c. 1840), *innominables* (c. 1840), *sit-down-upons* (1840), *sit-upons* (1841), *indispensables* (1841), *unutterables* (1843), *mustn't-mention-'ems* (c. 1850–1910), and *unhintables* (before 1904). Another word used in the

U.S.A. was *conveniences* (1842).[2] *Nether integuments* is recorded by C. Willett and Phillis Cunnington, and *femoral habilments* by John Davenport.[3]

Indispensable these garments undoubtedly were to the mid-nine-teenth-century gentleman; but if we had only Mrs Beeton as a guide to his dress we should have to conclude that he did not wear them. For that lady, describing—in 1861—the duties of a good valet, tells how he presents the various articles of the toilet as they are wanted, and then 'the body-linen, neck-tie . . . waistcoat, coat, and boots, in suitable order, and carefully brushed and polished. Having thus seen his master dressed. . . .'[4] The trousers were literally 'unmentionable'. One Ameri-can writer, perhaps not altogether seriously, used the term *limb-shrouders*;[5] another wrote satirically: 'His nether continuations were spotted here and there with diminutive banners of broadcloth secession [i.e., small holes].'[6] In the early part of the nineteenth century, to utter aloud in the presence of an American woman the word *shirt* was 'an open insult'[7] and 'a symptom of absolute depravity';[8] the acceptable euphemism was *linen*.

No one would today dare the old-fashioned plainness of speech which described a woman's *under-garments* (1530) from the waist down as her *clouts* (C. 19). At times the very mention of *underclothing* (1835) has been taboo. In nineteenth-century polite society 'one might mention only such feminine undergarments as were in part exposed to view. It was permissible, therefore, to use the word "petticoats", and, with circumspection, "stockings"; the rest was silence.'[9] In the 1860s the *Washington Union* dared not advertise shirts and men's drawers under any bolder heading than '*Gentlemen's Belongings*'.[10] In 1898 the Philadelphia *Ladies' Home Journal* announced that it would in future avoid all reference to women's *underwear* (1872), since 'the treatment of the subject in print calls for minutiae of detail which is [*sic*] extremely and pardonably offensive to refined and sensitive women'.[11] About this time one's *underclothes* (1884) were generally known as one's (*under-*) *linen* (longer form, 1862); or, if made of flannel, as one's *flannel* (1722) or *under-flannel* (1859), if of wool, as *woollens* (1800) or *woollies* (late C. 19); or, if so ornamented, as *frillies* (c. 1870) or *frillery* (c. 1888). *Smalls* and *under-things* are twentieth-century euphemisms for the underclothing of either sex; *intimate garments* for that of women. Women's magazines and shops have popularized *lingerie* (1835, but not in common use till the turn of the century) and *undies* (1918)—but not *neathie-set* (1933), which soon died a natural death. *Undikins* has been recorded in the U.S.A. Such playful nicknames, the Cunningtons point out, are given 'with an air of coy audacity which betrays . . . an erotic prudery still lurking about them'.[12]

'I'm resolv'd', says Miss Prue in Congreve's *Love for Love* (1695), 'I won't let Nurse put any more Lavender among my Smocks—ha, Cousin?' 'Fie, Miss;' replies Mrs Frail, 'amongst your Linnen, you must say—You must never say Smock.' And Miss Prue asks her if *smock* (before 1000) is a bawdy word.[13] A common euphemism for it was *shift* (1598)—i.e., a change of clothes. Yet in 1907, when a play by Synge was produced in Dublin, this harmless word caused offence; 'the audience broke up in disorder at the word *shift*'.[14] By then, the polite circumlocution was *chemise*, vulgarly called *shimm(e)y* (1837; shorter form, 1856). Leigh Hunt complained of these substitutions in his *Autobiography* (1850). His translation of the French fabliau *Les Trois Chevaliers et la chemise* had been published under the title *The Gentle Armour*, which was 'a puzzle for guessers'.

> The late Mr. Way . . . had no hesitation, some years ago, in rendering the French title of the poem by its (then) corresponding English words, *The Three Knights and the Smock*; but so rapid are the changes that take place in people's notions of what is decorous, that not only has the word 'smock' (of which it was impossible to see the indelicacy, till people were determined to find it) been displaced since that time by the word 'shift'; but even that harmless expression for the act of changing one garment for another, has been set aside in favour of the French word 'chemise'; and at length not even this word, it seems, is to be mentioned, nor the garment itself alluded to, by any decent writer![15]

At the same period it was 'considered extremely indelicate' in the western states of the U.S.A. to refer to *stockings* (1583), but *long socks* was 'pardonable'.[16] *Hose* (*c.* 1100) is today the usual commercial form, though hose were originally garments covering the abdomen as well as the legs. The mid-Victorian taboo extended, of course, to any mention of the stiffened inner *bodice* (1618; originally, *pair of bodies*) that is today variously known as *stays* (1608) or *corset* (1795).[17] Mrs Trollope told how in America 'a young German gentleman of perfectly good manners . . . offended one of the principal families . . . by having pronounced the word *corset* before the ladies of it'.[18] *Roll-ons* and *step-ins* were popular names for the *belt*, a later substitute for the corset. What was once known as the *bust bodice* (1889; cf. *B.B.*, *c.* 1920), or *underbodice* (1895), or *bust girdle* (1904), became a *brassière* (1912), a word frequently shortened to *bras* (*c.* 1910), pronounced and since *c.* 1940 usually spelled *bra* (*c.* 1934). The American *cup-forms* never caught on in Britain, perhaps because the term sounded indelicate. A combination of corset and brassière, the *corselette* (1921), was also known as the *foundation garment*. *Nightdress* (1712) and *nightgown* (1814) were given a euphemistic diminutive in *nightie* (or *nighty*) in the early 1890s.

The plain word for a two-legged garment suspended from the waist is *drawers* (1611). But this word came to be thought somewhat suggestive in the second half of the nineteenth century (when no lady could refer to a *chest of drawers* without blushing); after all, the garment in question may be drawn off as well as on.[19] Hence men's *(under)pants* (1874)[20] and women's *knickers* (1881; short for *knickerbockers*).[21] The great number of later synonyms, some for drawers of a particular design, some embarrassingly coy, demonstrates both the interest that these garments tend to arouse and the tendency of women (first and foremost, perhaps, women journalists) to give them 'fresh erotic values'[22]—by coining affectionate diminutives for them: *knicks* (C. 20), *(red) flannel(s)* (C. 20; derisive), *panties* (or *panteys*) (1905; Standard English by 1933), *divided skirt* (1906), *skirt knickers* (1908), *chemi(se)-knickers* or *cami-knickers* (1915), *cami-knicks* (*c.* 1917), *step-ins* (*c.* 1918; Standard English by 1940), *cami-comb(ination)s* (1919; short form, 1928), *as-is* (*c.* 1920), *draughters* (*c.* 1920), *pull-ons* (1923 or 1924; virtually Standard English by 1935), *cami-bockers* (1927), *scanties* (*c.* 1930), *trunks* (1930), *pullies* (*c.* 1932), *briefs* (1932 or 1933), *tighties* (*c.* 1933), *fullies* (1933), *pantie briefs* (*c.* 1938), *pantie trunks* (1939), and *knicker-briefs* (1939). During the second world war members of the Women's Auxiliary Air Force referred to the Service drawers they were issued with as *passion-killers* (1940); the winter-weight variety was also known as *black-outs* (1940; also used in the navy from *c.* 1918), the summer-weight as *twilights* (1940).

4

JUST BROWSING

Most of the non-sexual substances secreted by the bodies of animals, the acts by which some of them are excreted, and the places set apart by human beings for excretion, are referred to in English by euphemisms which are nowadays perhaps a shade more furtive, and more tenacious, than those employed for sexual activity. The taboo against any reference to the voiding of wind from the bowels, for instance, is currently rather stronger than many sexual taboos. And the plain English word for this act, the thirteenth-century *fart*, is today rarely heard in circles where it is regarded as smart to use the other 'four-letter words'. This taboo leads to a curious mistranslation in *The Albatross Book of Living Verse* (1933), whose readers are told that the line 'Bulluc sterteth, bucke verteth' in the well-known *Cuckoo-Song* [*c.* 1250] means: 'The bull rouses, the buck browses.'[1] But, despite Meredith's presumably innocent use of it in *The Ordeal of Richard Feverel* (1859)—first in a parody of *The Cuckoo-Song*, then in the sentence: 'Hippias . . . flew about in the very skies, *verting* like any blithe creature of the season'[2]—*verteth* does not mean 'browses'. The line is properly, and politely, translated as: 'The bullock leaps, the stag *breaks wind.*' We have used here a euphemism dating from 1552; two colloquial variants are *make a noise* (C. 19; in the nursery, often *make a rude noise*) and *cut one's finger* (C. 20); others, no longer in polite use, are *poop* (C. 18), *trump* (C. 18; as noun, mid-C. 19), *blow (off)*, and *let off (a fart).*[3]

The plain word *snot* (C. 15) was Standard English until the nineteenth century, when it became a vulgarism (though *snotty-nosed* (1610) remains Standard English).[4] *Mucus* (1661) is now generally used for this secretion. *Bog(e)y* is the usual nursery term (connoting desiccation), though *nose dirt* sometimes falls from the lips of especially fastidious persons when they are addressing children; compare *nose spasm* for *sneeze*.[5] And 'we have the absurd name *pocket handkerchief* [1530], i.e., pocket hand-cover-head, for a comparatively modern convenience, the earlier names of which have none of the directness of the Artful Dodger's "wipe". Ben Jonson calls it a *muckinder* [C. 15, as *mokedore*]'.[6]

Halitosis for *bad breath* is quite recent as anything but a technicality; but *perspire* for *sweat* dates from the end of the eighteenth century, when a writer complained ironically:

> It is well known that, for some time past, neither man, woman, nor child, in Great Britain or Ireland, of any rank or fashion, has been subject to that gross kind of exsudation which was formerly known by the name of *sweat*; and that now every mortal, except carters, coal-heavers, and Irish chairmen (animals all *sui generis*, and therefore not included within the general description of other British subjects,) merely *perspires*. Now, as the word *sweat* has for these twenty years past been gradually becoming more and more odious, and has indeed almost died out of our language, it is absolutely *certain* that Shakspeare could never have used that obsolete and disgustful term, which, doubtless, was as disagreeable in his days as it is now. . . . It is demonstrably clear, that the true reading of the line in *Hamlet* is, 'To *groan, perspire,* under a weary life'.[7]

The smell of moisture exuded from the skin is euphemistically known as *body odour* or *B.O.* (c. 1940); properly speaking this should refer to the smell of stale sweat,[8] but the manufacturers of deodorants seem to have gone a long way towards extending it to the smell of fresh sweat too. A condition in which the armpits are so coated with alcohol and hexachlorophane as to have 'no more smell than a piece of glass'[9] is referred to as *underarm daintiness*.

Webster, in his 1833 Bible, substituted *vomit* (1387) for *spew* (c. 897); the later *sick* (1614) has in this sense yielded among fastidious people to *ill*.[10] *Regurgitate, throw up,* and even *unswallow* have been recorded in the U.S.A.[11] *Eructate* (1638), *repeat* (1879) and, in America first, then to some extent in Britain, *burp* (1939)[12] have replaced *belch* (before 1000), now regarded as rather impolite. *Expectorate* (1827) for *spit* (c. 975) is largely an Americanism.[13]

The acts of defecation and urination, and the places where these acts are carried out, have long been referred to by a large number of euphemisms.

The plain word for *defecate* (1864) and *faeces* (1639), *shit* (or *shite*) is common to the Germanic languages (cf. also the French *chier*) and has existed in English as a verb since at least the fourteenth century, as a noun since the sixteenth.[14] The plain word for *urinate* (1599), *piss*, is derived from the Old French *pisser* and is found in Middle English. It too is a Standard English word, but has been considered a vulgarism since about 1760. Synonyms for *excrete* (1668) include popular expressions, women's words and nursery words. Among the first kind are *perform the work of nature* (1607), *ease nature* (1701), *obey the call(s) of nature* (1747), *do a job (for oneself)* (late C. 19; cf. the nursery terms *big job* and *little job*; *job* is also used by children as a verb, meaning 'defecate'), *pay a call*, *pay a visit*, *relieve nature* (or *one-self*), *see a man about a dog*, and *wash one's hands*. Women's words include *pluck a rose* (C. 18) and *pick a daisy* (c. 1860), which mostly refer to excreting in the open air, *(go to) see one's aunt(ie)* (c. 1850), and *powder one's nose*. *Number one(s)* and *number two(s)* are nursery terms, dating from the late nineteenth century, for urination and defecation respectively. Euphemisms for *shit* as a verb include *go to siege* (c. 1400), *stool* (1545), *evacuate (the bowels)* (1607), *pass one's stools* (1799), *bury a Quaker* (c. 1800; originally and mainly Anglo-Irish), *go to (the) bog* (1811), *pass a motion* (1822), *bog* (c. 1870) and *have a bog*, *go to* (or *visit*) *Sir Harry* (C. 19; now dialect), *rear* (c. 1890; originally university; general slang c. 1905; said to be the accepted word in the boy scout movement), *go and post a letter* (C. 20), *go and sing 'Sweet Violets'*, and *do one's business* (of animals and children).[15] The sound of *piss* was so offensive to the ears of American country-people in the middle of the last century that some of them taught their children to call what had hitherto been known as *pismires*, not 'ants', but 'ant-mires'.[16] Euphemisms for *piss* (and the C. 19 variants, *do a piss* and *have a piss*) include the catechristic *micturate* (1842) and a series of popular expressions: *make water* (1375), *leak* (c. 1590) and *do* (or *have*) *a leak* (mid-C. 19), *do* (or *plant*) *a sweet-pea* (mid-C. 19; mainly women's), *water one's* (or *the*) *nag* (or *dragon*) (mid-C. 19), *pass water* (1860; usually with reference to obstruction or the absence of it), *shake hands with an old friend* (c. 1880),[17] *shoot a lion* (c. 1880), *spend a penny* (c. 1880), *strain one's taters* (1873), *rack off* (late C. 19; from wine-making), *draw off* (C. 20), *have a run-out* (C. 20), *have a slash* (C. 20), *wring one's sock out* (C. 20; Partridge calls this 'jocular rather than euphemistic'[18]), and *have a run off* (*c.* 1930). As might be expected, there is a host of nursery euphemisms: *pee* (1788), *do* (or *have*) *a pee* (C. 19), *pee-wee* (C. 19), *do pee-pee* (late C. 19), *do* (or *have*) *a wee-wee* (late C. 19), *wee-wee* (C. 20), *widdle* (C. 20; on *piddle*), *tinkle*, and *do a puddle*.[19]

One of the longest chains of euphemisms, most of them sooner or later unseated by successors, relates to the room set aside for the act of excretion. The original English name for this room seems to have been *privy* (1375), though Chaucer, in *The Parson's Tale*, has *gong* (obsolete by 1800, as was *gong-house*). Fifteenth-century terms were *siege* (*c.* 1400), *siege-house*, (1440) and *siege-hole* (1477); sixteenth-century ones, *stool* (1542), *jakes* or *jacques* (1530s; 'Jack's place'?; Standard English till mid-C. 18),[20] and the Standard English term *boggard* (1552), from which were derived the slang terms *bog-house* (*c.* 1670), *bog-shop* (*c.* 1840–1910), and *bog(s)* (*c.* 1840; originally either printers' or public schoolboys' slang). Seventeenth-century names were *draught(-chapel)*, *house of office*, *necessary-vault* (1609), *necessary-house* (1611), *latrine* (1642)—used especially for a privy in a camp, barracks or hospital—*closet of ease* (1662), and *necessary-place* (1697). *Water-closet* dates from 1755; the use of *closet* alone in this sense (1869) led to the avoidance of the word in any sense.[21] Other eighteenth-century words were *necessary* (1756) and the slang term *coffee-house* (or *-shop*) (late C. 18). The nineteenth century brought *convenience, little house, petty(-house) place, Sir John*, and *W.C.*; *cloaca* (1840); *lavatory* (1845; literally, a vessel or place for washing); *House of Commons* (mid-C. 19); *dike* (mid-C. 19); *jerry-come-tumble* (before 1860), *the West Central* (before 1860; London); *chapel (of ease)* (*c.* 1860); *Mrs Jones* (*c.* 1860); *where the Queen goes on foot* (*c.* 1860–1915); *where the Queen sends nobody* (*c.* 1860–1915); *(my) aunt Jones* (*c.* 1870–1905); and *the W.* (late C. 19; working class). Barbara Charlton (1815–98), in her memoirs, recalled two relatives of hers who refused to use what she called the 'place of *general interest*' lately built inside the house.[22] The twentieth century brought *cloakroom, geography of the house, the John*,[23] *lav., smallest* (or *littlest*) *room (in the house)*,[24] *throneroom, toilet* (a name of American provenance that is nowadays probably the commonest working-class euphemism in Britain; the commonest middle-class euphemism seems to be *loo*, derived from either *l'eau* or *lieu*), and *the place where you cough* (*c.* 1920), together with a number of

American names that do not seem to have crossed the Atlantic: *boudoir*, *can*, *dressing-room* and *Fred*.[25]

So far we have been discussing the names given to this room when it is in or adjacent to a private house; other euphemisms describe the places set apart in theatres, inns, etc., or installed in the streets, for the purpose of excretion: *urinary* (1828), *urinal* (1851), *(public) convenience* (in America, 1883), and *place of convenience*—a place once known in Edinburgh as a *forty-twa* (c. 1820–90), from the number of seats it contained, in London as a *fountain palace* (or *temple*) (1890s), in the U.S.A. as a *public comfort station* (1904). A punning dysphemism is *where the (k)nobs hang out*. The commonest present-day euphemisms in Britain are *the gents'*, *(the) gents' toilet*, and *the ladies' (room* or *toilet*), from the more polite of the identifying notices at the entrances. 'Gentlemen' and 'Ladies' are usually found in the West End and its equivalent in provincial cities, 'Men' and 'Women' in the East End and similar districts, though they may coexist. Odette Keun claimed to have seen in a London street 'two little edifices, each of which had two doors. One little edifice was marked: "Gentlemen, One Penny"; "Men, Free"—the other little edifice was marked: "Ladies, One Penny"; "Women, Free".'[26] When the straightforward words 'Men' and 'Women' on a 'new public convenience' were discussed recently at Llantrisant and Llantwit Fardre rural council, Mr Albert Martin said: 'I suppose they used those words because there is so much discussion on sex these days.'[27] Lyall tells of 'a certain big London cinema, in whose lobby there are two doors. The one on the left is labelled "Gentlemen's Smoking Room" and the one on the right is labelled "Ladies' Retiring Room".'[28] Variants of the latter are *(ladies') wash-room*, *powder-room*,[29] and *rest-room*. *The little boys'* (and *little girls') room*, dating from 1944, were imported from the U.S.A. Worse have followed them: *gunroom*, *his and hers*, *Adam and Eve*, *cocks and hens*, *lads and lassies*, *gulls and buoys*. . . .

Lastly, the names for the vessel into which a person may empty his bladder without quitting his bedroom. From the middle of the fifteenth to the middle of the eighteenth century this was known in Standard English as a *piss-pot*, though *urinal* was also used from 1475, *chamber-pot* ('in the crockery-trade, often euphemized as *chamber*'[30]) from 1570, and *pot* from 1705. In the nineteenth century one referred to it as a *po*; or a *jeroboam* (c. 1820–80) or *jerry* (c. 1825); or simply as *it*.[31]

Close-stool was used from 1410 for a utensil enclosed in a box or seat, *stool of ease* from 1501, *stool* alone from 1516, *necessary-stool* from 1761, and (*chamber*) *commode* from 1851.

There is one other discharge from the human body for which numerous euphemisms have been employed, that of the *menses* (1597), an early and now obsolete Standard English term for which was (*monthly*) *flowers* (C. 15–*c.* 1840; from the Latin *fluere*, 'to flow', through French).[32] *Monthly courses* is also obsolete; *monthlies* (1872), obsolescent. A little-used technical term is *catamenia* (1754). In practice, a woman at one time would have said that *the captain is at home* (or *come*) (late C. 18–early 19); or that *my* (*little*) *friend has come* (C. 19); or would have spoken of *domestic afflictions* (*c.* 1850); or would have said that she was *so* (mid-C. 19), or *feeling poorly*, or having her *poorly time* (before 1887), or *having the painters in* (C. 20); or would ask another, '*Have you seen anything?*' (mid-C. 19). Nowadays she would be most likely to say that she had *got the curse* (late C. 19), or was *unwell*,[33] or had started, or was having, her *period*;[34] but there are many women who use the plain word *menstruate* (1382) without *mauvaise honte*.[35]

5

THE 'BLOODY' TABOO

It has been suggested that the swear-word *bloody* (C. 17) was especially abhorrent (for almost two centuries) because it evoked the idea of the menstrual discharge; but most philologists would tend to agree with Partridge that this 'ingenious' explanation is 'much too restricted to be valid'.[1] The popular derivation from *by'r Lady* has many times been exploded. The word was not tabooed before about 1750; Swift could write to Stella that it was 'bloody hot walking today'.[2] It first appears in print as an oath in Dana's *Two Years Before the Mast* (1840);[3] forty years later Ruskin was writing of the 'corruption' in 'the use of the word "bloody" in modern low English, not altering the form of the word, but defiling the thought in it'.[4] The taboo made necessary two groups of substitute-words: one for *bloody* in its original meaning (for it was 'with bated breath that the editor of a London newspaper wrote about the prospects of "a b——y war" '!),[5] the other consisting of expletives less shocking than *bloody* had come to be. Thus *Beeton's Manners of Polite Society* [1876] warns that 'all meats served in mass should be carved in thin slices . . . carefully avoiding . . . offending the delicacy of ladies . . . by too-ensanguined pieces'.[6] Other substitute-words were *severe*, *cruel*, and *sanguinary*. Besides the written *b——* and spoken *b* (once used by policemen giving evidence), mild, semi-euphemistic deputies for *bloody* as an intensive were *blasted* (mid-C. 18), *bleeding* (c. 1857; this soon became as forceful as *bloody*, or even more so), *blooming* (1882), *bally* (1884), *blinking* (c. 1890), *flaming* (early 1890s), *blistering* (C. 20), *blood-stained* (C. 20), *ruddy* (c. 1905),[7] *sanguinary* (1909), *blurry* (not later than 1910), *Pygmalion* (1912),[8] *burning* (before 1923), *roseate* (before 1923), and *rose-coloured* (before 1923). By 1893 it had become 'impossible for a cockney to read with proper sympathy Jeffrey's appeal to Carlyle, after a visit to Craigenputtock, to bring his "blooming Eve out of her blasted paradise" '. [9]

In 1911 John Masefield used *bloody* in *The Everlasting Mercy*,[10] and in the following year the taboo was broken on the London stage in Shaw's *Pygmalion*, the interest in the first English performance of which 'centered in the heroine's utterance of this banned word. It was waited for with trembling, heard shudderingly, and presumably, when the shock subsided, interest dwindled.'[11] Soon after Mrs Patrick Campbell's line had caused this shock the censor refused to allow a London revue to be called *Not B—— Likely*.[12] And it was not till 1935 that the word was heard again on the stage, in a play by Noel Coward.[13] In the following year the newspapers, discussing an order issued by Lord Beatty to Captain Sir Ernle Chatfield at the battle of Jutland ('There must be something wrong with our bloody ships, Chatfield. Turn two points to port') all substituted a dash. In September 1936 the Bath magistrates fined a fascist open-air speaker for using the word in a speech. Mr Justice Humphreys, however, 'laid it down that the word "bloody" is neither indecent nor obscene'.[14] Just after the second world war started, a Labour M.P., Mr William Dobbie, referring in the House of Commons to the failure to pay allowances to the wives of serving soldiers, said this was 'a bloody disgrace to the whole government'. Next day he apologized.[15] The virtual end of the taboo—or so it seemed at the time—was signalled by D. B. Wyndham Lewis in the spring of 1941:

> Clashing her wiry old ringlets in a kind of palsied glee at her own audacity, Auntie *Times* has printed a little poem containing the line, 'I really loathe the *bloody* Hun', and all Fleet Street stands aghast.... 'Bloody' ('————', or 'the Shavian adjective') is one of the hardest-worked words in current speech and in constant use by duchesses and dustmen alike, but to find Auntie *Times* spelling it in full is a shock.[16]

By the autumn of 1942 a local newspaper in Lancashire was happily printing *bloody* in full in a report of a speech by a clergyman before the Rochdale Rotary Club—a speech opposing bowdlerization.[17]

And yet, as late as May 1962, 'shocked' Post Office officials refused permission to the Crime Club to advertise on its envelopes a book called *Bloody Instructions*. 'The words . . . may offend quite a number of people', they explained.[18]

It only remains to recall the ancient story of the working-man who, unable to understand the election slogan, 'One man, one vote', was told by his friend that it meant 'One bloody man, one bloody vote', and replied: 'Then why don't it say so?'[19]

6

SEX, PREGNANCY, AND PROSTITUTION

The sexual differentiation of animals and human beings is a powerful source of verbal taboos, the act of sex an even more powerful one. The avoidance of the very word *woman* (*c.* 893) in America in the last century, and its replacement by *female* (in Britain a term of contempt) seems largely to have been a sexual taboo—unlike the social taboo which has turned the words *woman* and *man* (*c.* 1000) into terms of opprobrium for a Llantrisant councillor and for millions of Englishmen, so that everyone is a *lady* (C. 18) or a *gentleman* (C. 19). In turn, *female* came to be thought indelicate or degrading in America. When the Vassar Female College was founded in 1861, Mrs Sarah Josepha Hale, editor of *Godey's Lady's Book*, spent six years in securing the removal of the offending adjective from the college sign. This was done by taking away the single long stone on which it had been carved and inserting another with a plain surface, so that the two remaining words were separated by a space many feet long. That long, black stone, symbol of 'the honor of womanhood', became 'the pride of Vassar's heart'.[1] Under the pressure of the same kind of taboo a man's *wife* (*c.* 888) became his *lady* or, a usage now regarded as vulgar, his *good lady* (1796). Still more suggestive was the word *virgin* (before 1310); Mencken tells how, when his play *The Artist* was presented in Philadelphia in 1916, a local newspaper that reprinted some of the dialogue altered the name of one of the characters from *A Virgin* to *A Young Girl*.[2]

To rural Americans the names of male animals are so unbearably suggestive of sexual activity as to be virtually unmentionable; *bull*, above all, is held to be indecent.[3] When Longfellow's 'Wreck of the Hesperus' (1841) was recited, one verse had to be edited for modesty's sake, so that it read:

She struck where the white and fleecy waves
Looked soft as carded wool;
But the cruel rocks they gored her side,
Like the horns of a *gentleman cow*.[4]

This and no fewer than forty-one other substitutes for *bull* were current in New England thirty years ago, and many of them no doubt still are. They included *male, sire, animal, critter, gentleman, beast, male animal, male cow, he cow, seed ox, the he, old man, gentleman heifer, master, brute,* and *cow man*.[5] There is indeed 'a certain amount of verbal genius among a people who can invent forty-two circumlocutions in order to avoid uttering one undesired syllable'.[6] In the Ozarks such words as *boar, buck, ram, jack,* and *stallion* were 'absolutely taboo', and two women in Arkansas raised a great clamour for the arrest of a man who had used the word *bull-calf* in their presence. The words *bull-frog, bull-fiddle,* and *bull-snake* had to be used 'with considerable caution'; one Missouri preacher told his flock that Pharaoh's daughter found the infant Moses in the *flags:* 'he didn't like to say bull-rushes!'[7] In 1917 the word *male-cow* was to be found in an American scientific journal;[8] and some years later the following advertisement appeared in a Florida newspaper: 'Found—Young male cow. Owner may have same by calling 2020 North Hayne.'[9]

Frequently tabooed, too, are the names of female animals. *Mare* used to be a prohibited word in the U.S.A.[10] And some English people will still refer to a *bitch* (*c.* 1000) as a *lady dog*. 'How we pet lovers secretly resent our beloved female dogs being referred to as "bitches" ', declared a recent letter in a women's magazine. 'Have any readers suggestions for alternative names which would be both appropriate and acceptable to the various dog Societies?'[11] No doubt *bitch* continues to smack of indelicacy to some people because, since before 1400, it has also signified a lewd woman. By the late eighteenth century it had become 'the most offensive apellation that can be given to an English woman', and Billingsgate and St Giles's whores, if the word was applied to them, would reply with the catch-phrase: 'I may be a whore, but can't be a bitch.'[12] Coleridge's poem *Christabel* (1816) contains the lines:

Sir Leoline, the Baron rich,
Hath a toothless mastiff bitch;[13]

According to Thomas Allsop, Charles Lamb advised the poet to alter these lines to:

> Sir Leoline, the Baron round,
> Had a toothless mastiff hound.

But Coleridge, who had 'no alacrity in altering',[14] changed them to:

> Sir Leoline, the Baron rich
> Hath a toothless mastiff, which

in the copy he presented to David Hinves in 1816, and embodied the change when he reprinted *Christabel* in 1828.[15] The present-day non-canine meaning of *bitch* is 'a spiteful, treacherous woman'; it was not till the end of 1934 that the word became acceptable in this sense on the West End stage, a dramatic critic reporting that he had heard it twice in one week and so presumed it might be taken as naturalized.[16]

The plain English word for the act of sex, *fuck* (verb and noun), is no longer supposed by philologists to be derived from the related Greek φυτεύω, Latin *futuere* or French *foutre*. A closer relative is the German *ficken* ('to strike', hence, 'to copulate with'), and both this word and its English cousin might be derived from a presumed archaic word *fücken*. Partridge, who puts forward this hypothesis, and who suggests a Celtic origin, points out that the ultimate source is nevertheless probably earlier than both Latin and Celtic, and draws attention to 'a strikingly ancient etymon': the Egyptian *petcha* ('to copulate with', of the male), 'the hieroglyph [Fig. 2] being an ideogram of un-

Fig. 2

mistakably assertive virility'.[17] A somewhat far-fetched supposition was that of the late James Barke, who took the English word to be 'an onomatopoeic word equivalent of the sound made by the penis in the vagina'.[18]

In its present spelling or a near approximation, the word appears several times in sixteenth-century Scottish poems. Its first known use was in the poem 'Ane Brash of Wowing' ('A Bout of Wooing') [*c.*

1503] by the Franciscan friar, or pretended friar, William Dunbar, a poet sometimes compared to François Villon:

> In secreit place this hyndir nycht
> I hard ane beyrne say till ane bricht,
> 'My huny, my hart, my hoip, my heill,
> I have bene lang your luifar leill,
> And can of yow get comfort nane;
> How lang will ye with danger deill?
> Ye brek my hart, my bony ane!'
>
> His bony beird was kemmit and croppit
> Bot all with cale it was bedroppit,
> And he wes townysche, peirt, and gukit,
> He clappit fast, he kist, and chukkit,
> As with the glaikis he wer ouirgane;
> Yit be his feirris he wald have fukkit;
> Ye brek my hart, my bony ane![19] *

Three decades or so later, reproving King James V of Scotland for his licentious mode of life, his usher Sir David Lindsay of the Mount wrote 'The Answer quhilk Schir Dauid Lindesay maid to the Kingis Flyting' [c. 1535], which contained the lines:

> For, lyke ane boisteous Bull, ʒe rin and ryde
> Royatouslie lyke ane rude Rubeatour,
> Ay fukkand lyke ane furious Fornicatour.[20] †

Alexander Scott (c. 1530–c. 1584), in 'Ane Ballat maid to the Derisioun and Scorne of wantoun Wemen', wrote:

> Fairweill with chestetie
> Fra wenchis fall to chucking,
> Thair followis thingis thre
> To gar thame ga in gucking
> Brasing, graping, and plucking;
> Thir foure the suth to sane
> Enforsis thame to fucking.[21] ‡

* *this hyndir nycht*, last night *beyrne*, man *bricht*, maiden *hoip*, hope *heill*, health *leill*, loyal *deill*, deal *cale*, broth *townysche*, lively *gukit*, foolish *glaikis*, feeling *ouirgane*, overcome *feirris*, manner

† *rin*, run *Rubeatour*, libertine *ay*, ever

‡ *fra*, when, as soon as *chucking*, fondling *gar*, cause, make *gucking*, fooling *brasing*, embracing *graping*, feeling *plucking*, pulling about *thir*, these *suth*, truth *sane*, say

One anonymous poet of this period, in some touching verses called 'In Somer quhen Flouris will smell', quoted the words of a young woman who would not 'ly still':

> Allace! said scho, my awin sweit thing,
> Your courtly fukking garis me fling,
>   Ye wirk so weill;
> I sall yow cuver quhen that ye clyng,
>   So haif I seill.[22] *

And another, in 'A Lewd Ballet' (1571), poked fun at the priest:

> for quha wald not lauche q[u] his hart grew soir
> To se forett þe holy frere his fukking so deploire?[23]

Apart from the works of Rochester, who uses the word often, this was virtually its last appearance till the twentieth century in literature written for general circulation; though in *The Merry Wives of Windsor* [*c.* 1600–01] Sir Hugh Evans asks William Page what is the 'focative' case, and there is a sequence of bawdy puns.[24] Robertson of Struan has *f—k*, and the word occurs in numerous old Scottish folk songs collected, and in some cases published in polite versions, by Burns.[25]

Two instances are known however of the word's appearing in print (in other than clandestine literature[26]) in the middle of the Victorian era—and in *The Times* at that. One winter morning in 1882 the readers of that newspaper must have rubbed their eyes when they came to the following passage in the report of a speech by the Attorney-General, Sir William Harcourt:

> I saw in a Tory journal the other day a note of alarm, in which they said, 'Why, if a tenant-farmer is elected for the North Riding of Yorkshire the farmers will be a political power who will have to be reckoned with.' The speaker then said he felt inclined for a bit of fucking. I think that is very likely. (Laughter.)

This was baiting Mrs Grundy with a vengeance. So profound was the shock in Printing House Square that it was four days before the paper printed an apology, which went like this:

garis me fling, makes me toss about   *seill*, happiness

No pains have been spared by the management of this journal to discover the author of a gross outrage committed by the interpolation of a line in the speech by Sir William Harcourt reported in our issue of Monday last. This malicious fabrication was surreptitiously introduced before the paper went to press. The matter is now under legal investigation, and it is hoped that the perpetrator of the outrage will be brought to punishment.[27]

That was an unlucky year for *The Times*. In June the unknown joker—or an emulator—struck again, this time in an advertisement which must have convulsed the book trade as much as it scandalized parents:

Every-day Life in Our Public Schools. Sketched by Head Scholars. With a Glossary of Some Words used by Henry Irving in his disquisition upon fucking, which is in Common Use in those Schools. . . . Church Times.—'A capital book for boys.' Record.—'The book will make an acceptable present.'[28]

It was in *The Times*, too, that an *r* found its way into the name Figgins. But it was in another daily paper that, on the occasion of the birth of a royal child, 'the substitution of an F for a B in the name of the palace where the Queen was confined gave the heading of the notice a suspiciously suggestive appearance'.[29]

In 1898, when the great *New English Dictionary on Historical Principles* was in progress, its editors had an opportunity, as an American scholar has put it, 'to offset the remissness' of many of their predecessors.[30] To be sure, the word *fucke* had appeared in Florio's Italian-English dictionary (1598), as one of five English equivalents of *fottore*.[31] The first English dictionary to give the word an entry in its correct alphabetical order was Stephen Skinner's *Etymologicon Linguæ Anglicanæ* (1671);[32] no doubt it was this work that Elisha Coles had in mind when he complained in his own dictionary, which came out five years later, that some of his predecessors had been 'too plain (stufft with obscenity not to be named)'.[33] Eighteenth-century lexicographers were divided between those who agreed with Coles and banned the word from their pages (e.g., Samuel Johnson, and Marchant, who took 'especial Care to exclude all those Terms that carry any Indecency in their Meaning, or have the least Tendency to corrupt the Minds of Youth'[34]) and those whose linguistic sense was stronger than their prejudices. Thus Nathaniel Bailey, a Seventh Day Baptist who kept a boarding-school at Stepney, gave the word an entry in the 1721 edition of his dictionary, defining it as *'subagitare fœminam'* ('to lie with a woman'); nine years later he added 'a term used of a goat'.[35] John Ash, in 1775, called it a 'low, vulgar word', giving as one definition 'to have to do with a woman'.[36] Francis Grose included it (as *f—k*) in his *Classical Dictionary of the Vulgar Tongue* (1785), giving also the combinative with *duck*, which he defined as 'the man who has the care of the poultry on board a ship of war'.[37] But Dr Edward Harwood deleted the word from the twenty-fourth edition of Bailey, which appeared in 1782, and his example was followed by dictionary-makers throughout the nineteenth century. And so, though the *OED* was 'conceived in a scientific spirit', one looks in vain for this word in its pages; and it is 'to the lasting shame' of its editors Murray and Bradley that they failed to 'dissociate themselves from the warped outlook of their age'.[38]

Following the *Lady Chatterley's Lover* trial and the subsequent printing of the word *fuck* in full in two national newspapers, authors, editors, printers and publishers felt free to follow suit: and the *Quarterly Review*, the editor and publishers of a new edition, with English translations, of the poems of Rimbaud, and the publishers of a new dictionary of American slang and of a history of erotica, all did so. So did three women novelists.[39] It is hard to suppose that future lexicographers will not do the same.[40]

Over 1,200 English synonyms for this word have been recorded;[41] their 'vivid expressiveness' and 'vigorous ingenuity', says Partridge, 'bear witness to the fertility of English and to the enthusiastic English participation in the universal fascination of the creative act'.[42]

There are many archaic terms that probably rank as plain words. The oldest is *sard* (*c.* 950), which occurred in the old Nottingham saying: 'Go teach your Grandam to sard.'[43] Perhaps the sucking of eggs in the more familiar version is euphemistic. Others are *swive* (*c.* 1386; hence 'the Queen of Swiveland' for Venus), *line* (1398; used by Shakespeare), *jape* (before 1450), *flesh* (*it*) (C. 16; cf. *flesh one's sword*), *job* (C. 16; cf. *do a woman's job for her, c.* 1850), *occupy* (C. 16–early 19; regarded as obscene in C. 17 and 18)[44], *leap* (1530; cf. *do a leap,* C. 19), *tick-tack* (noun; mid-C. 16), *niggle* (*c.* 1565–1820),[45] *foin* (late C. 16–17), *jumble* (late C. 16–18), and *salt* (?C. 17–early 18).

The list of formal and technical synonyms begins with *to know* (before 1200; cf. *have knowledge of*, before 1425, and *have carnal knowledge of*, 1686). *To do* (or *work*) *one's kind* (before 1230) was commoner later as *do the deed* (or *act*) *of kind. Ride* is recorded before 1250 (remaining Standard English till *c.* 1780) as a verb, but not till the nineteenth century as a noun, in such expressions as *get* (or *have*) *a ride*, of which Partridge remarks that they are generally used by women, adding: 'cf. the scabrous smoke-room story of the little boy that wanted "a ride on the average".'[46] *Love-work* dates from *c.* 1250, *fornication* and *lie with* from before 1300, *meddle* (*with*) from 1340, *familiarity* (as in *have* (or *be on terms of*) *familiarity with*) from 1387, *couple* (*with*) from C. 15, *be* (*too* or *over-*) *familiar with* from before 1450, *copulation* from 1483, and *enjoy* from 1598.[47] Another sixteenth-century word, still a widely used vulgarism, was *have*. The seventeenth century brought *Venerean mirth* (1611), *Venus escuage* (1611), *coition* (1615),[48] *commerce* (1624), *the last favour* (1676),[49] *intimacy* (1676), and *priapize* (before 1693); the eighteenth, *have connexion* (*with*) (1791) and (*sexual*) *intercourse* (shorter form, 1798);[50] the nineteenth, *be* (*improperly*) *intimate* (*with*) (1889). Other euphemisms of this kind include *go in unto* (Biblical), *go to bed with, go with, have* (*conjugal* or *sexual*) *relations* (*with*), *have sex with, interfere with* (which also means 'feel'),[51] *make love* (*to*) (cf. the U.S. *love*), *oblige* (of women), *possess* (*carnally*), *sleep with* (or *together*), *spend the night with*, and *take* (a favourite of C. P. Snow's).[52] Akin to these are euphemisms employing synecdoche —(*close*) *hug* (C. 18-early 19), *caress, cuddle, embrace, fondle, kiss*, and *stroke*—and literary terms coined, or mainly used by, writers: *mell* (Lydgate), *come aloft* (Spenser), *do the act of darkness, go groping for trout in a peculiar river, make the beast with two backs, plough, pluck*, and *trim* (Shakespeare), *jog* (Middleton), *go bed-pressing* and *go vaulting* (Marston), *bob* and *ferret* (Fletcher), *play at cherry-pit* (Herrick), *do* (or *perform*) *the act of androgynation, do the culbatizing exercise, foraminate, jumm* (and *go jumming*), *play at belly-to-belly, play at grapple-my-belly, play the close-buttock game, play the loose-coat game*, and *rub bacons* (Urquhart), *ride a post* (Cotton), *get what Harry gave Doll, have a bedward bit, join faces*, and *play cuddle-my-cuddle* (D'Urfey), *taste* and *towsel* (Fielding), *do a lassie's by-job* and *get hilt and hair* (Burns), *do the divine work of fatherhood* (Whitman), and *futter* (Sir Richard Burton; from the French *foutre*).[53]

Passing to popular synonyms, we have first a group of euphemisms referring to the male sex organs: *pizzle*, *plug*, *play prick-the-garter*, and *thumb* (all C. 18); *have a brush* (*with the cue*) (shorter form mid-C. 18); (*have a*) *ro(d)ger* (1750); *pestle*, *play at stable-my-naggie*, *rake* (*out*), and *stick* (all C. 19), *peg* (*c.* 1850), *bury one's wick* (*c.* 1860); *take Nebuchadnezzar out to grass* (*c.* 1860–1915); *get outside* (*it*) (*c.* 1870; of women); *get a bit of the goose's neck* (after *c.* 1872; of women); *dip one's wick* (*c.* 1880); *strop one's beak* (late C. 19); *introduce Charley* (or *Charlie*) (C. 20); and *shaft*.[54] The female sex organ (or pubic hair) is referred to in another group: *nock* (late C. 16), *take a turn in the parsley-bed* (C. 17), *get shot in the tail* (C. 17?; of women), *wag* (or *turn up*) *one's tail* (C. 17?; of women; hence *tail-wagging*), *get one's kettle mended* (C. 18; of women), *have a bit of cauliflower* (C. 18–19), *nick* (C. 18), *arrive at the end of the Sentimental Journey* (C. 19), *be among the cabbages* (C. 19), *do a bit of front-door work* (C. 19), *feed the dummy* (C. 19), *labour* (or *stretch*) *leather* (C. 19), *take a turn in Bushy Park* (or *Girl Street*, or *Love Lane*) (C. 19; cf. *an ejectment in Love Lane*); *get* (or *be*) *there* (*c.* 1860; cf. *be all there but the most of you*), *be up her way* (late C. 19), *take a turn on Shooter's Hill* (late C. 19), *take a turn on Mount Pleasant* (*c.* 1880), and *be on the nest* (C. 20).[55] Other euphemisms contrive to include a reference to the pudenda of both sexes: *the one with t'other* (C. 17–18), *get Jack in the orchard* (C. 19), *impale* (C. 19), and *make ends meet* (C. 19).[56]

Terms which allude to the buttocks,[57] or to other parts of the body, or the disposition of the body,[58] seem all dysphemistic. There are euphemisms introducing the idea of entry: *invade* (C. 17), *do* (or *have*) *a put(-in)* (C. 19), *put it in*,[59] *get in(to)* (C. 18), and *have it in* (late C. 19); the idea of falling: *tumble* (1602), *have* (or *do*) *a tumble-in* (C. 19), and *do a tumble* (*c.* 1840; of women);[60] and the idea of ascent: (*mount* (late C. 16), *jump* (C. 17), *scale* (C. 17), *do a leap in the dark* (or *up the ladder*) (C. 18), *get up* (as transitive verb, C. 17; intransitive, C. 17 and 'prob[ably] S[tandard] E[nglish]'[61]), *be up* (mid- or late C. 19), *to up* (mid-C. 19), *do a mount* (*c.* 1860), and *run up* (before 1910).[62] Except perhaps for *shake* (verb, C. 16?; noun, *c.* 1860), those expressions which refer, often in mechanical terms, to the thrust of the penis, seem to be all dysphemisms;[63] so, from the nature of the case, are those which allude to semen.[64] The position adopted in sexual intercourse gives rise to several euphemisms: *lift one's leg* (or *get one's leg lifted*)

(C. 18; of women), *pray with knees upwards* (1785; of women), *lie feet uppermost* (C. 19), *go star-gazing* (or *studying astronomy*) *on one's back* (mid-C. 19; of women), *see stars lying on one's back* (of women), and *get on* (*c.* 1870).[65] The names of animals are used in others;[66] still others —notably *get a green gown* (C. 17–early 19; of women; also signifies 'to be deflowered')—mention garments.[67] The idea that sexual activity is pleasurable is embodied in such expressions as *have a good time* (C. 17; originally Standard English; reintroduced from the U.S.A., *c.* 1870; virtually Standard English again by 1930), *have a bit of fun* (*c.* 1850), *have a four-legged frolic* (*c.* 1850), *relish* (noun; C. 19), *fun and games*, and *pleasure* (noun). In slang, the association between sex and food is a close one, and men speak of having *pudding* (C. 17), *a bit of jam* (C. 19), *a nibble* (C. 19), one's *crumpet* (*c.* 1880; also signifies woman-as-sex), *a beanfeast* (*in bed*) (C. 20), and one's *oats* (before 1923).[68] Games are well represented: *play at put-pin* (mid-C. 16–mid-C. 18), *in-and-in* (C. 17–early 19), *in-and-out* (C. 17), *push-pin* (C. 17–18), *uptails-all* (*c.* 1640–1750; from the name of a song), *pickle-me-tickle-me* (mid-C. 17–18), and many more.[69] So is dancing, with *jig-(a)-jig* (as *Jiggajoggies*, 1603-04), *Moll Peatley's* (or *Pratley's*) *gig* (C. 18–early 19), *the goat's gig*(*g*) (or *jig*) (mid-C. 18–early 19), *the blanket hornpipe* (*c.* 1810), and *jiggle* (*c.* 1845).[70] But music, with only *strum* (*c.* 1780), and the U.S. *jazz*, hardly comes into it.[71]

Of considerable interest from both the philological and psychological points of view is a group that might be labelled 'sadistic', comprising terms which view coition as essentially or wholly aggressive: *thrum* (C. 17–early 19), *wap* (C. 17–early 19; cant; from an expression signifying 'throw (down) violently'), *(have a) knock* (shorter form, 1604),[72] *swinge* (*c.* 1620–1750),[73] *switch* (1772), *be done over* (C. 18; of women), *snabble* (late C. 18–early 19), *get stabbed in the thigh* (C. 19; of women; cf. *get stabbed with a mutton dagger*, or *pork sword*), *jolt* (C. 19), *(have a) ram* (C. 19), *rummage* (C. 19), *flimp* (*c.* 1850; cant), and *(have a) bang* (C. 20). A very common twentieth-century word is *do*, which in 1934 led to the banning of this verb in any sense in songs broadcast on the U.S. radio, whose syndics felt it was 'a bit too suggestive'; Mr Rudy Vallee was thus deprived of the use of one of his 'greatest stage and radio vehicles', *Let's Do It*, as well as *Do It Again* and *You Do Something to Me*.[74] Other aggressive terms are *batter* (C. 20), *prang* (1940; R.A.F.), *have a bout* (apparently a favourite of Mr Griffith-Jones,

senior Treasury Counsel in the *Lady Chatterley's Lover* trial), *to club,
have a double fight, pound,* and *trounce.*

Lastly, there are some euphemisms used of, and often by, women,
which have not been classified elsewhere: *stand the push* (C. 18–19),
get hulled between wind and water (C. 19), *do a spread* (*c.* 1840; cf.
spread to), *do the naughty* (mid-C. 19), *give way* (before 1870), *give the
old man his supper* (late C. 19), suffer *a fate worse than death* (jocular),
do it (which signifies 'be in the habit of copulating, or generally ready
to'), *go all the way* (=copulate, as opposed to petting), and *grant the
favour,* of which Partridge says:

> Euphemistic not unconventional. . . . 90 per cent of the world's obscene
> terms and locutions are the result of euphemism: neither the frank nor the
> mealy-mouthed realize that to call, e.g., the genitals by the one name and
> to eschew all others would soon lead to a lack of both obscene and euphe-
> mistic words and perhaps even minimize both euphemism and obscenity.[75]

A number of miscellaneous terms,[76] as well as Scots words,[77] cant
words,[78] and synonyms—mostly popular euphemisms—for coition
of specific kinds, or in specific positions or circumstances,[79] will be
found in the notes.

Euphemisms for the manifest sign of sexual excitement in the male
are comparatively few: one may speak of an *erection* (1594), or *priapism*
(1598), or *tumescence* (1859), if it is desired to avoid the plain word
horn (mid-C. 18; in C. 19 often used of women; *have the horn* dates
from late C. 18).[80] The present-day plain word for *ejaculate* (1578),
or experience an *orgasm* (1802), is *come* (*off*) (C. 19; of either sex),
itself originally a euphemism for *spend. Fetch* (late C. 19) and *go* (*off*)
(longer form, C. 20) are euphemistic, *shoot* (mid-C. 19), *get the dirty
water off one's chest* (C. 20; usually in reference to masturbation), and
spew, dysphemistic. In general, Mrs Grundy draws her skirts deter-
minedly aside from such phenomena, and there is consequently a
dearth of polite circumlocutions for them, as for *semen* (1398), known
in plain English three centuries ago as *mettle, jelly, pudding,* or *milk*
(*c.* 1660), today as *spunk* (C. 19), or *cream* (C. 19) or, in the U.S.A.,
gism (or *jism;* from *orgasm*?).[81] There is no such lack when one has
occasion to speak of the *contraceptive* (1897) whose invention is generally attributed to Dr (or Colonel) *Cundum* (*c.* 1665; nowadays usually
spelt *condom*).[82] Though normally described in print as *rubber goods*

or *specialities*, this *sheath* has long been known to every Englishman as a *French* (or sometimes *American, Italian,* or *Spanish*) *letter* (*c.* 1870), to Frenchmen as a *capote anglaise*: Mencken records an apparently unsuccessful attempt, after the *entente cordiale*, to change the French name to *capote allemande.*[83] 'Letter from France' or 'Letter from Paris' is often seen as a headline in English newspapers; 'French Letter', never. *Froggy* (or *froggie*) (*c.* 1910) is a schoolboys' and naval term; other naval expressions, from *c.* 1920, are *free issue* and *froth bugle*. *French safe* and *safe* are U.S. terms, dating from *c.* 1916; another American name, *rubber*, leads to comical misunderstandings, it is said, in offices where both English and American staff are employed, and the former ask for the loan of what the latter call an 'eraser'.

Among the superabundance of euphemisms for other aspects of sexual life and behaviour may be mentioned *betrayed* and *deceived* for *seduced* (*c.* 1560), specified in a sheet of 'Don'ts for Reporters and Sub-Editors' of the *Daily Express*;[84] *criminal* (or *improper*) *assault, felonious attack*, and *statutory offence*, which are newspaperisms for *ravish* (1436), *rape* (1481), *violate* (*c.* 1440), and *outrage* (1590); *dinner without grace* for sex without (or before) marriage; *friend* and *housekeeper* for *concubine* (1297) and *mistress* (1430) (though, somewhat surprisingly, *friend* in this sense dates back to 1490); and the seemingly endless thesaurus of expressions such as *a certain suggestion, an improper suggestion, unnatural relations, take advantage of, indecent behaviour*, and *misconduct*.

In September 1933 the Iowa Farmers' Union passed a resolution condemning 'the scheme to raise livestock prices by slaughtering pigs and *enceinte* sows'.[85] This word (1599, as *insented*) was one of the earliest attempts to draw a genteel veil over the state of being *pregnant* (1545), which itself, as we have seen,[86] was a substitute for plain terms that by *c.* 1745 apparently struck even Smollett as coarse; hence his use of *in an interesting condition*, a phrase echoed by Dickens (*in a delicate state of health,* 1850) and the *News of the World* (*in a certain condition*); another variant is *in a delicate condition* (late C. 19). The use of *confined* (1772) and *confinement* (1774) for *in childbed* (*c.* 1200) and *labour* (1595) led to many misunderstandings in Victorian times. There was the lady who was reading to some friends a letter she had received: 'We are in great trouble. Poor Mary has been confined—'. That was the last word on the sheet; the next sheet had fallen to the floor; and poor Mary, unmarried, was in an extremely interesting condition until the missing sheet was found and the sentence could be completed: '—to her room for three days with what, we fear, is suppressed scarlet fever.'[87] And there was the young woman 'of delicate appearance' who applied for some medicine at a dispensary and was told: 'You look very pale.' She replied: 'I have only come from my confinement three weeks.' At length it turned out that she had recently been confined—in prison.[88] Popular euphemisms for pregnancy include *to be in the pudding* (or *pudden*) *club* (C. 19; *to join*, etc., is C. 20), *to have been playing tricks* (C. 19), *bow-windowed* (1840s), *expecting* (*c.* 1870), *in the familiar way* (before 1891; a jocular variant of *in the family way*), *in trouble* (1891; of unmarried pregnancy), *awkward* (late C. 19), *obvious* (1897–*c.* 1914; Society slang), *to have been doing naughty things* (C. 20), *up the pole* (*c.* 1908; especially Cockneys'), *Irish toothache* (or *I.T.A.*) (before 1909), *up the stick* (*c.* 1920; especially Cockneys' and north of England), and *living in seduced circumstances* (*c.* 1920; of unmarried pregnancy).[89]

An *abortion* (1547) is still referred to in some mass-circulation newspapers as a *criminal operation* or a *certain result*, performing one as *producing a certain state*.

The word *bastard* (1297), elbowed out by *illegitimate* (1673), has descended to the level of a colourless swear-word. But not a meaningless one: in the first world war a special Army Order had to be issued to the British troops on the Piave front, 'explaining the meaning of the common Italian expression *basta* in order to lessen the number of fights to which a very natural misunderstanding gave rise'.[90] Not even *illegitimate* was veiled enough for the lawmakers of New York, who in 1925 laid it down that

in any local law, ordinance or resolution, or in any public or judicial proceeding, or in any process, notice, order, decree, judgment, record or other public document or paper, the term *bastard* or *illegitimate child* shall not be used, but the term *child born out of wedlock* shall be used in substitution therefor, and with the same force and effect.[91]

Popular euphemisms have included *bantling* (late C. 16), *by-blow* (late C. 16), *by-scape* (mid-C. 17), *bachelor's son* (*c.* 1670), *squeaker* (*c.* 1670) *stall whimper* (before 1676; cant), *by-slip* (late C. 17), *quae(-)gemes* (C. 18–early 19), *bachelor's baby* (mid-C. 19), *fly-blow* (before 1875), *illegit.* (C. 20; schoolboys'), *war baby* (late 1916), *get*, and *love child*.[92]

In 1934 a play called *Within the Gates* was presented in New York. One of the characters appeared simply as 'The Young Whore'. The New York *Sun* changed this to 'The Young Prostitute', the *World-Telegram* to 'The Young Harlot' and the *American* to 'A Young Girl Who Has Gone Astray'. A fourth paper solved the problem by omitting the cast altogether.[93] But the word *whore* (before 1100), cognate with the Latin *carus* ('dear'), must itself have been at one time 'a polite substitute for some word now lost'.[94] Later euphemisms were *strumpet* (1327), *harlot* (1423), *Winchester geese* (C. 16)—many of the Southwark stews were under the jurisdiction of the Bishop of Winchester—*trull* (1519), *aunt* (mid-C. 16–*c.* 1830), *baggage* (1596), *brothel-drab* (1598), *brothel-stale* (1598), *Paphian* (1599), *brothel-trull* (1599), *prostitution* (1603), *money-creature* (1603–04), *prostitute* (1613), *Bankside ladies* (C. 17), *quail* (C. 17–early 18), *nocturnal* (late C. 17), *natural* (c. 1685), *one of my cousins* (late C. 17–early 19), *quædam* (late C. 17–18), *incognita* (C. 18), *girl about* (or *of the*) *town* (1711), *girl* (c. 1770), (*lady of*) *easy virtue* (shorter form, c. 1780), *one of them* (C. 19), *moonlighter* (c. 1850), *nymph of the pavé* (before 1859–1890), *anonyma* (c. 1860–79), *bawdy-house belle* (1870), *nocturne* (c. 1875–1915), *perfect lady* (c. 1880), *tart* (before 1920), *trollop* (c. 1923), and *call girl* (c. 1945). But this list merely skims the surface. In newspaper English, a whore used to be a *fallen woman*, an *unfortunate*, or a *woman of a certain class*. Nowadays she is a *vice girl*, a *good-time girl*, or a *business girl*. To a certain old-fashioned type of man, she is a *pretty lady*, a *fille de joie*, a *soiled dove*, or a member of *the frail sisterhood*. To writers of official reports she is a *streetwalker*; in 1931 the Chattanooga police, 'on arresting a man for picking up a streetwalker on the street, announced that he was charged with "walking the streets accompanied by a woman", and it was so reported in the local papers'.[95] To herself, since c. 1921, she has been a *business girl*, but she advertises nowadays as a *French teacher*, an *ex-showgirl*, or a *model* (providing *personal service*, *private strip-tease*, or *repairs to gentlemen's clothing*). The appellation *model* has recently induced legitimate models to insist on being called *mannequins*. Other terms are still sometimes employed. Graves tells of a worried old country clergyman who, directed by a fellow priest, went to the old Empire Lounge, a resort of whores, in search of a son who had run away from home with money from the parish organ fund.

A woman swooped down on him at once: 'Are you looking for a naughty little girl?' The old clergyman beamed gratefully at her. 'No, Madam, I thank you kindly all the same: I am looking for a naughty little boy.' The woman threw up her hands. 'I don't know what's to become of us poor women these days.'[96]

Prostitution itself is variously described as being *on the game* (C. 17), *on the loose* (c. 1860), *on the bash* (C. 20), *on the streets*, or—in the *News of the World*—engaged in a *mode of living*.[97] There are various appellations for the *bawd* (1362), *pander* (1450), or *procurer* (1632). In the U.S.A. 'even prostitutes shrink from the forthright *pimp* [1607], and employ a characteristic American abbreviation, *P.I.*—a curious brother to *S.O.B.* [*son of a bitch*]';[98] three English equivalents are *bully* (1706), *rich friend* (c. 1805–70), and *souteneur* (1906). To the *News of the World*, pandering was at one time *having, for purposes of gain, exercised influence over the movements of*.[99] The *stew* (1362), having become successively a *bawdy house* (1552), *brothel* (1593), *leaping-house* (1596), and *bagnio* (1624), was further euphemized into a *place of sixpenny sinfulness* (C. 17), a *house of ill repute* (before 1726), a *house of ill fame* (1756–57), a *naughty house* (C. 19), a *house of evil fame* (1821), and a *disorderly house* (1877). *Sporting house* (1894) is an American equivalent. Other euphemisms include three jocular ones: *nunnery* (late C. 17), *(finishing) academy* (shorter form, late C. 17–18), and *ladies' college*. Dysphemisms range from *pushing-school* (late C. 17) to *knocking-joint* (C. 20).[100] The London district of St John's Wood was at one time known as *Apostle's Grove* and the *Grove of the Evangelist*, presumably because its reputation was such that its real name came to engender gooseflesh.[101]

'On my fidelitie', says one character to another in John Jones's *Adrasta* (1635), 'you are the foule mouth'dst gallant that ever wore Cloves in's Gummes: you say an Italian Count has the pox. . . . In a Nobleman 'tis abusive; no; in him the *Sarpigo*; in a Knight the *Grincomes*; in a Gentleman the *Neapolitan* scabb; and in a Servingman or Artificer the plaine Pox.'[102] Pox (1503, as *French pox*) was the Standard English word till the middle of the eighteenth century, but a desire to soften the plain word is shown towards the end of the sixteenth, when there begins a long series of what Mencken calls 'sportive synonyms':[103] *French marbles* (1592; from an old French word *morbilles*, 'pox'), *French disease* (1598), the adjective *French-sick* (1598–c. 1700), *French mole* (1607), *French measles* (1612), *French cannibal* (1614) and *French goods* (1678), as well as *French crown* (C. 17–19), *French gout* (C. 17–19), *Frenchman* (C. 19), *French aches*, *French fever*, and Shakespeare's *malady of France*. The French were not however the only nation after whom this malady was named; *Italian, German, Spanish* (C. 17–early 19), and *Indian pox* were spoken of, besides *Spanish gout* (late C. 17–early 19), the *Spanish needle* (early C. 19), and *American* (1611). Other euphemisms were: *bone ache* (late C. 16–17), *the pip* (late C. 16–17; not, apparently, the origin of the phrase 'You give me the pip'), *crinkums* (C. 17–early 19), *goodyear* (C. 17), *court scab* (1603), *Barnwell ague* (c. 1670–1850), *Covent Garden ague* (late C. 17–early 19; cf. *Common Garden gout*, late C. 17–18, and *Garden gout*, C. 19), *coals* (C. 19; nautical; in the phrase 'take in one's [winter] coals'), a *dose* (c. 1860), *bad disease, bad disorder, ladies' fever*, and *Venus's curse*. The word *syphilis* dates from 1718. The plain word for *gonorrhœa* (1598), *clap* (1587), was Standard English till about 1840.[104] *Venereal disease* (often abbreviated to *V.D.*) dates from 1658; the word *disease* itself, as McKnight points out, is a product of euphemism, meaning literally 'discomfort'.[105]

Neither the word *syphilis* nor the word *gonorrhœa* was permissible in the U.S.A. till the mid-thirties, and efforts to diminish these diseases were hampered in both the U.S.A. and Britain by prudery, especially the prudery of newspapers, which insisted on referring—when they could be induced to make any reference at all—to *blood-poison, specific blood-poison, secret diseases, vice diseases, preventable disease, communicable diseases, certain dangerous diseases*, and (the *News of the World*, this one) *a certain illness*. Even newspapers that approved of anti-V.D. campaigns went to fantastic lengths to avoid printing the word *venereal*. Nor was this prudery confined to newspapers. Many American physicians, in private letters to colleagues, would write that a patient had a *specific stomach* or a *specific ulcer* when they meant he had syphilis; and the *Journal* of the American Medical Association received a paper discussing the question, 'Can a positive woman have a negative baby?' —i.e., could a woman with a positive Wassermann, indicating syphilis, have a baby free from that disease?[106] Shortly before the second world war the British Ministry of Health prepared some outspoken anti-V.D. advertisements designed to reach the simplest people. But the Copy Committee of the Newspaper Proprietors' Association objected to the way they were written, and certain changes had to be made. The words *pox* and *clap* were deleted; so was the sentence, 'Professional prostitutes are not the only source of infection'; so, twice, was the term *sex organs*. Despite these changes, the *Daily Express* and the *Evening Standard* refused to print the advertisements at all.[107] Similar advertisements prepared by the U.S. War Advertising Council were objected to by the national commander of Catholic War Veterans Inc., who said they would 'weaken the sense of decency in the American people, . . . increase immorality by promising to make promiscuity safe' and 'ignore a fundamental fact in human conduct, that shame and embarrassment are among the strongest deterrents to the sins that spread V.D.'[108]

Quite 'harmless' words may come to be avoided because they merely sound like a tabooed word, though their meaning may be totally different. Thus, some Americans avoid saying *bellicose, chamber-maid, circumscribe, elicit, excavate* (associated with 'evacuate'), *excrescence* (associated with 'excrement'), *masticate, mensuration, privet, rapier, rumpus, sects, titter, vile* (associated with 'bile'), and *vowels*.[109] And some English people avoid using *frustrated, inhibited, intercourse, intimacy, promiscuous,* and *venereal* in the primary senses of these words; there are many who do not even realize that the primary meanings of the first five are non-sexual. Another example is the word *improper*. This has long meant 'indecent', too. When Dr Johnson published his great dictionary, a woman of his acquaintance expressed her satisfaction that he had not included in it any 'improper' words. He is traditionally supposed to have replied: 'No, Madam. I hope I have not daubed my fingers. I find, however, that you have been looking for them.'[110] It is to be hoped that no words to which the epithet 'improper' could justly be applied will have been found in this Part. On the other hand, an American philologist very sensibly advised 'those who think euphemism a disease which passes with time' to consider 'the many veiled and polite terms utilized by linguists in discussing euphemisms';[111] the reader of the present discussion will no doubt have made allowance for this.

PART II

THE GRUNDY SUNDAY

7

MERRY ENGLAND'S REVELLING DAY

A poor Norfolk woman was washing her linen one Saturday afternoon, after three o'clock—the hour the sabbath was deemed to begin—when a divine messenger appeared to her and warned her to desist. She refused, saying she would be in danger of starving if she did not do her usual work. There then appeared a coal-black beast like a sucking-pig, that fastened itself to her left breast and sucked her blood till she died.

This was how supernatural forces, long before the rise of puritanism, were doing their best to make the people of England abstain from work on the first day of the week.

The story dates from the beginning of the thirteenth century, when Eustache, Abbot of St-Germer-de-Flai, was sent to this country by Pope Innocent III to obtain recruits for a crusade. He brought with him a copy of a letter that had fallen from heaven on to the altar of a Jerusalem church—an event which had caused the people of that area to lie on the ground for three days and nights, together with their spiritual advisers, imploring the mercy of God. This heaven-sent document, which the abbot took from town to town on a preaching tour against Sunday trade, warned that violations of the fourth commandment would be punished by a rain of stones, wood and scalding water at night; in addition, the fruit trees would wither, the fountains would dry up, the pagan nations would come and slay the transgressors, and, as if all this were not enough, fearful animals would devour their women's breasts. Moved by these threats, and by the French abbot's exertions, the people vowed not to let anything be sold on the Lord's day, except meat and drink to travellers; not to work on that day; and to give money to the Church. King John however, 'instigated by the devil', had those who overturned the stalls of Sunday venders arrested.

But it was not so easy in those days to suppress manifestations of the divine will. At Beverley a carpenter and a weaver who went on working after three o'clock one Saturday were struck with the palsy. At a village in Lincolnshire dough put in a hot oven after that hour stayed unbaked till the Monday; elsewhere a man who had baked a cake on a Saturday evening found that it bled when he bit into it next day; while a miller trying to work his mill on a Sunday discovered, no doubt to his horror, that blood gushing from between the stones was preventing them from turning.[1]

Some not very successful attempts were made by the secular authorities to stop people from amusing themselves on the first day of the week. Sunday football and tennis were banned in the reign of Richard II— but this prohibition was intended to encourage archery practice rather than the performance of religious duties. Sunday fairs and markets were forbidden by Henry VI. Despite such laws the average pre-Reformation Englishman, having made a formal appearance at church, used to spend the rest of his Sunday drinking in the tavern or dancing and otherwise making merry on the village green.[2] 'In the Sunday', wrote a moralist of Chaucer's time, 'reigneth more lechery, gluttony . . . and other sins . . . than reigned all the week before.'[3]

Under Henry VIII it was laid down, in a document sometimes known as *The King's Book* (1543), that Sunday should be spent in holy works; but those who passed the time in idleness, gluttony, riot, or other vain or idle pastimes would be better occupied labouring in the fields. As for women, they 'should better bestow their time in spinning of wool, than upon the sabbath day to lose their time in leaping and dancing, and other idle wantonness'.[4] This was a somewhat more liberal view of Sunday labour than most of the puritans were to take.

Henry VIII's instructions seem to have had little effect. In 1547 Thomas Cranmer, Archbishop of Canterbury and chief architect of the *Book of Common Prayer*, who nine years later was to be burnt at Oxford for his theological opinions, was complaining of 'drunkenness, quarrelling, and brawling' on the holy day.[5] His chaplain, Prebendary Thomas Becon, was more specific. To sanctify the sabbath day was

> not to pass over that day idly in lewd pastimes, in banqueting, in dicing and carding, in dancing and bear-baiting, in bowling and shooting, in laughing and whoring, and in such like beastly and filthy pleasures of the flesh; nor yet in bargaining, buying and selling . . . but . . . to apply our whole mind and body unto godly and spiritual exercises.[6]

Canterbury has the distinction of being the first place in England where sabbath-breaking was made a penal offence.[7] This was in 1554–55, under the Catholic Queen Mary—a curious anticipation of her Protestant successor's Act of Uniformity (1558), which rendered all who did not attend their parish church on Sunday liable to a fine of twelve pence (approximately a carpenter's daily wage) for each offence. But this was directed more against recusants than against sabbath-breakers. Elizabeth I was by no means a sabbatarian; her attitude was 'in the nature of a compromise between the extreme Protestant view and the Roman Catholic view'.[8] She herself did not kick so high on a Sunday—but she did dance. And when she visited the Earl of Leicester at Kenilworth Castle she was entertained one Sunday evening 'with a grand display of fire-works',[9] a week later with a bride-ale (i.e., a wedding feast), a morris dance, some sports, a play, and 'an Ambrosiall Banket'.[10] She is said to have used her influence against a Bill for postponing Sunday fairs and markets to the next working day;[11] she vetoed a Bill for the 'better and more reverent observing of the Sabbath';[12] and she gave a licence to a poor man 'having foure small children and fallen into decaye' to play various games on nine Sundays 'for his better releif'.[13]

This permissiveness was contrary both to the attitude of the State Church and to that of the puritan preachers, whose agitation was becoming increasingly clamant. The former regarded Sunday work as on the whole preferable to Sunday pleasure:[14] the latter, generally speaking, lumped every form of Sunday activity neither specifically religious nor essential to maintain life under the general heading of 'sabbath-breaking'. Both regarded Sunday games, Sunday performances in the theatre, and Sunday drinking as the dishonouring of God.

The official Anglican view was sharply expressed in *An Homily of the Place and Time of Prayer* (1574), which attacked as the worse sort of sabbath-breakers those who, while not travelling or working on the first day of the week, would nevertheless not rest in holiness but 'in ungodliness and filthiness, prancing in their pride, pranking and pricking, pointing and painting themselves, to be gorgeous and gay; they rest in excess and superfluity, in gluttony and drunkenness, like rats and swine; . . . they rest in wantonness, in toyish talking, in filthy fleshliness'. In short, the devil was better served on Sunday than on all the other days of the week.[15]

Non-puritan and puritan sabbatarians alike had the spirit of Merry England to contend with; and it was not easy to quench that spirit. The common people enjoyed playing, going to the theatre, dancing, drinking, and making love on their day off (just as their betters did on theirs). They called it their 'reuelying day'. Employers found it impossible to stop their servants from staying out on Sunday night, engaging in 'drunkennes, and whoredome'.[16] Young people in particular made the most of the one day of the week they did not have to devote to toil. Complaints against their conduct on holy days have a distinctly modern ring: 'Hel breakes loase [when] wee permit our youth to haue their swinge. . . . I feare me, their harts are more alienated in two houres from virtue, than againe maie wel be amended in a whole yeare.'[17]

The puritans concentrated their main fire against Sunday games. Their most famous spokesman on this subject was the acid-penned Phillip Stubbes, whose first work was a broadside ballad characteristically entitled *A fearfull and terrible example of Gods iuste iudgement executed vpon a lewde Fellow, who vsually accustomed to sweare by Gods Blood* [c. 1581]. Before long Stubbes subjected all the other lewd fellows in the kingdom to a furious onslaught in his *Anatomie of the Abuses in England* (1583), a highly readable, colourful, and instructive compendium of the pleasures enjoyed by the majority of Elizabethans. On Sundays they annoyed Stubbes by frequenting bawdy stage-plays, maintaining lords of misrule, May games, church-ales (i.e., festive gatherings held in connexion with a church), feasts, and wakes; piping, dancing, playing dice, cards, bowls, tennis, and football, 'and such other deuilish pastimes'; bear-baiting, cock-fighting, hawking, and hunting; holding fairs and markets; reading lascivious and wanton books; 'and an infinit number of such like practises and prophane exercises . . . whereby the Lord God is dishonoured . . . and his People meruelously corrupted'.[18] Stubbes seems to have been particularly incensed against football, which he called 'a bloody and murthering practise'.[19] Like later puritans, he was not slow to seize on accidents that befell Sunday pleasure-seekers, as illustrations of divine anger at their wickedness. One Sunday in the January before his book was published, seven or eight people had been killed and many injured when the scaffolding collapsed at a Southwark bear-house; Stubbes hailed this as 'A Fearfull Example of God His Iudgement vpon the prophaners of his Sabaoth'.[20] Similarly, a severe earthquake shock in

1580 was attributed, in a special admonition read from the pulpits, to the fact that Sunday was spent 'full heathenishly in taverning, tippling, gaming, playing, and beholding of bear-baiting and stage-plays'.[21] Yet not everyone was prepared to believe that disasters and earthquakes were the voice of God. At Beverley, while many people were at a bear-baiting, the church fell down during evensong and buried part of the congregation; Sir Thomas More quotes a wag who commented: 'Now maie you see what it is to be at euensong whan ye should be at the bere baytynge.'[22]

The objections raised to Sunday performances of plays had little effect. The Court was tolerant towards them; and people insisted on flocking to them, no matter what the preachers might say. 'Wyll not a fylthye playe, wyth the blast of a Trumpette, sooner call thyther a thousande, than an houres tolling of a Bell, bring to the sermon a hundred?' asked the Master of Tonbridge Grammar School. In some places, he complained, the players came and danced around the church while the service was on, and there were 'men naked dauncing in nettes, which is most filthie'.[23] In 1580 the City of London magistrates succeeded in getting from the Queen a decree banning Sunday plays in the city, and the Privy Council made a similar order next year, and extended it to the rest of the country two years later; but these bans do not seem to have been strictly observed for long.[24]

Many writers and preachers objected to people spending the first day of the week 'in Tauerns & Alehouses, tossing of Pots';[25] the less fanatical among them held that it was better to work on that day than 'to passe the time, in dronknes . . . w^t a nomber of other abhominable vices'.[26] These other vices were the trouble, of course; drinking on the sabbath led to worse things, and 'all kinde of loosenesse' was sold in the alehouses on Sundays, as well as victuals.[27] Out in the provinces men who got drunk on the sabbath might be compelled to stand in the aisle of their parish church and confess their sin 'with lowde voyces' and say they were 'verie hartilie sorrie', as two Ely men did in 1595;[28] London was far less strict. Thomas White, forestalling by almost four centuries the views of a London magistrate about the laxity of the metropolis, fulminated at St Paul's Cross:

> The wealthyest Citizens haue houses for the nonce: they that haue none, make shift with Alehouses, Tauernes, and Innes, some rowyng on the water, some rouing in the field, some idle at home. . . . Is this the Lordes

daye or no? if it be, howe intollerable, nay howe accursed & moste con-
demnable are these outragious *Bachanalia*, *Lupanaria*, I can not tell what
to call them, such as Heathē menne were euer ashamed of (I am sure,) and
therefore practised better maters, although prophane exercises: but ours
sauors so of *Venus* Court and *Bacchus* kitchin, that it may rightly be
entituled an abhominable and filthy Citie.[29]

8

NO MORE CAKES AND ALE?

One Sunday, 'coming from dancing', Nicholas Ruddock and Katherine Canker made love. Their association was fruitful, their sin severely punished. The court ordered that both of them should be whipped through the high street of Glaston till their bodies were bloody; and while they were being whipped two fiddles should be played in front of them 'in regard to make known their lewdness in begetting the said base child upon the Sabbath day'.[1]

Such harshness towards human frailty was to be more characteristic of Cromwell's time than of the reign of James I; but, as we have just seen, the provinces were stricter than London, and the combination of fornication and sabbath-breaking was one peculiarly apt to make the puritan conscience tingle self-righteously.

When the seventeenth century opened, the first day of the week was a popular holiday once church was over. By the time Queen Anne came to the throne, just over a hundred years later, the holiday had become a holy day; despite the partial reaction against puritanism that the Restoration brought about, the first day of the week had acquired the main features of the 'English Sunday'. Not that the partisans of a gloomy Sunday won without a battle. For practically the entire century, it rained books and pamphlets on the sabbath question. One such publication appeared, on the average, every ten months. Sunday, in the vivid phrase of one of the controversialists, became 'as a Ball, betwixt two Rackets, bandied this way and that way, by mutuall contradiction'.[2] Nor were there merely two sides in these polemics: those who wanted stricter observance of Sunday and those who disagreed. There were also those who supported the Norfolk minister Theophilus Brabourne when, in a treatise somewhat daringly dedicated to Charles I, he demonstrated that Sunday was an ordinary working day and that it was Saturday which should be hallowed as the sabbath, as rigidly as the

Jews hallowed it.[3] After eighteen months in the insanitary Newgate jail, however, Brabourne found that his arguments were untenable.

The sabbatarians took the offensive with great energy. In various parts of the country they preached that to do any work on a Sunday was as great a sin as murder or adultery; that to throw a bowl on that day was as great a sin as murder; that to hold a feast or wedding dinner on the sabbath 'is as great a sinne, as for a Father to take a knife and cutte his childes throate'. Even to ring more than one bell to call people to church was accounted as great a sin as murder.[4] Sometimes cited as a good example for christians was the story of the Jew of Tewkesbury who fell into a large privy one Saturday and, for reverence of his sabbath, would not be pulled out, 'chosing rather to dye in that filthie stincking place'.[5] Many preachers preferred however to make their congregations' flesh creep with awful examples of what happened to sabbath-breakers. A curious book, copies of which circulated secretly (its authorship is not certain, but the two men who might each have written it were both jailed under Charles I, and one of them was fined £5,000 and had his ears cut off for allegedly libelling that monarch) gives fifty-five examples of divine judgment against sabbath-breakers. In Dorset a Sunday bowler is killed by a blow from a bowl; at Enfield a young woman dies after dancing on Sunday; a Sussex bell-ringer is struck down with a sickness, from which he afterwards dies, before he can carry out his promise to ring the bells next Sunday; fourteen young men playing football on the frozen river Trent are drowned when, on their 'comming alltogether in a scuffle', the ice suddenly breaks.[6] Such writings could hardly be said to represent the intellectual cream of seventeenth-century sabbatarianism; but even the more intelligent pamphleteers on the subject left extraordinary loopholes for opponents' ridicule. Thus the Suffolk minister Nicolas Bownd, the most influential of them, said that 'Noblemen and great personages . . . because they represent in some measure the Maiestie of God on the earth'—together with 'Knights, Esquires, and Gentlemen . . . in whom also is some image of the Lord to bee seene'—might be permitted to indulge in feasts on the sabbath.[7] 'Hee hoped to finde good welcome for this dispensation', observed Peter Heylyn, an anti-puritan writer, a trifle unkindly.[8] But Bownd's inconsistency did not prevent his view of the fourth commandment—that it was morally binding in its literal sense—soon becoming what Heylyn called 'the most bewitching

THE
LAMENTABLE
COMPLAINTS
OF
NICK FROTH the Tapster, and
RULEROST the Cooke.

*Concerning the reftraint lately fet forth,
againft drinking, potting, and piping on the Sabbath day, and againft felling meate.*

Printed in the yeare, 1 6 4 1.

A protest against puritan dictatorship, 1641

I

10 of May the Boocke of Sportes upon the Lords day was burnt by the Hangman in the place where the Croſſe ſtoode, & at Exchange

The burning of the *Book of Sports*, 1644

Severall Young men playing at foote-ball on the Ice upon the LORDS-DAY *are all Drownd*

One of several *Divine Examples of God's Severe Judgment upon Sabbath-Breakers.* From a broadsheet of 1672

4

Above: 'Reformation—or, the Wonderful Effects of a Proclamation! ! !' A satirical print by Thomas Rowlandson, 1787

Below: 'PROTECTING THE SABBATH! ! ! Or, Coercion for England.' An early nineteenth-century cartoon against sabbatarianism

5

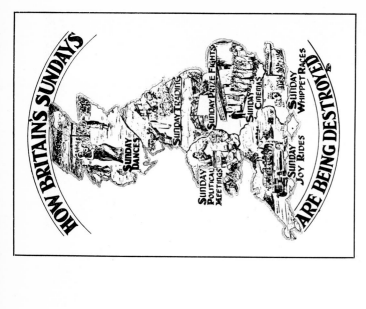

The above composite picture helps to illustrate the many encroachments which are being made on the Christian Sunday up and down the land. With such a challenge ringing in our ears, let us count it a joy and an honour to stand for the *LORD'S* Day, to witness for Him Whose Day it is.

John Bull : **Woodman, spare that Tree!**
Touch not a single bough ;
In youth it sheltered me,
And I'll protect it NOW.

Sabbatarianism between the wars. Two cartoons of the Lord's Day Observance Society.

Sabbatarianism today. Two recent productions of the Lord's Day Observance Society

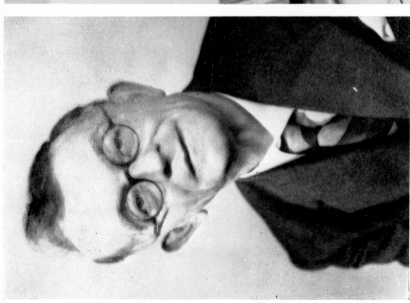

(a) H. M. ('Misery') Martin (1882–1954), secretary of the Lord's Day Observance Society, 1925–51

(b) Harold Legerton, secretary of the Lord's Day Observance Society

Errour, the most popular Deceit, that had ever beene set on foot in the Church of *England*'.[9] Another historian was soon to echo this estimation. Of Bownd's almost total opposition to Sunday work and recreation, the author of a history of the British Church from the birth of Christ wrote:

> It is almost incredible how taking this *Doctrine* was ... so that the *Lords Day* ... began to be precisely kept. ... On this *day* the *stoutest fencer* laid down the *buckler*, the most skillful Archer *unbent his bow*, counting all *shooting* besides the Marke; *May-games* and *Morrish-dances* grew out of request, and good reason that *Bells* should be silenced from gingling about mens leggs if their very *Ringing* in *Steeples* were adjudged unlawfull: some of them were ashamed of their former pleasures, like *children* which grown bigger, *blushing* themselves out of their *rattles,* and whistles. Others forbear them for fear of their Superiors; and many left them out of a Politick Compliance, least otherwise they should be accounted licentious.[10]

Now James I, in a proclamation in the year of his accession, had banned Sunday bear-baiting, bull-baiting, and plays.[11] But fourteen years later, on his way through Lancashire, it was put to him that puritan magistrates and 'precise people' there had been punishing those who indulged in 'honest exercises' after the afternoon service. His rebuke to these killjoys led to his famous *Book of Sports* (1618), which permitted 'lawfull Recreation' after the end of divine service. Bear- and bull-baiting, interludes, and ('in the meaner sort of people') bowling were still forbidden; but the people were not to be discouraged from such 'harmlesse' amusements as dancing, archery, leaping, vaulting, and the erection of maypoles. The king recognized that to prohibit such recreation gave rise to 'a number of idle and discontented speeches' in the alehouses.[12] And he asked: 'When shall the common people have leave to exercise, if not upon the Sundayes and holy daies, seeing they must apply their labour and win their living in all working daies?'[13]

The *Book of Sports*, in Heylyn's words, 'occasioned much noyse and clamour', being the first blow which had been given in James I's time to 'the new *Lords-Day-Sabbath*, then so much applauded'.[14] There were various puritan counter-attacks, both inside Parliament (Sunday observance Bills of 1621 and 1624, which James vetoed) and outside (the Lord Mayor stopped the royal carriages passing through the City of London at the time of divine service because they made such a noise). The *Book of Sports* was reissued under Charles I, in 1633, and again many ministers would not read it in their churches. One, at Shaftesbury, preached against it 'in a most high kind of "terrification", as if it were a most dreadful thing, and near damnable, if not absolutely damnation, to use any recreations on the Sabbath'.[15] Whatever the king might say, the provincial guardians of public morality knew better: like the Oxfordshire churchwardens who kept their eyes peeled for people working, dancing, drinking, having their hair cut, and playing cards at sermon time—as well as people fornicating, 'sicking in the Church', and making water in the church.[16]

One of the first acts of the Long Parliament was to read a Bill forbidding bargemen to load or unload goods on Sundays; and one of this Parliament's first victims, on the eve of the civil war, was a chaplain of Charles I, Dr John Pocklington, whose sermon *Sunday no Sabbath*, brought out as a pamphlet in 1636 and much read by students, led to his being charged with propagating 'Jewish, Popish, Superstitious and Antichristian Doctrines'. He was deprived of his benefices and his pamphlet was burnt by the common executioner—a fate it was soon to share with the *Book of Sports*. Pocklington had to make a recantation; he began it by saying: 'If *Canto* be to Sing, *Recanto* is to Sing again', and continued with a defence of his sermon.[17] But he died soon afterwards—of a broken heart, it was said.

The civil war and the Commonwealth witnessed a series of ever stricter and ever less enforceable laws to regulate people's Sunday behaviour. A régime that could abolish Christmas, Easter, and Whitsuntide was not going to let a small matter like sabbath-breaking offend the Lord. An ordinance of February 1643 called on the nation to repent for sins that included 'wicked prophanations of the Lords Day, by Sports and Gamings, formerly encouraged even by Authoritie';[18] next year Sunday trade, Sunday travel without reasonable cause (penalty ten shillings), Sunday work (penalty five shillings), and all Sunday games, sports, and pastimes (penalty five shillings) were prohibited. Existing maypoles ('a Heathenish vanity, generally abused to superstition and wickedness') had to be taken down, and no new ones put up. Publications against the fourth commandment were to be burnt. And whoever could not pay the fines laid down was to spend three hours in the stocks.[19]

A law passed in 1650 obliged travellers to return to their inn or lodging before midnight on Saturday and forbade them to leave again before one a.m. on Monday. No boats, horses, coaches or sedan-chairs might be used on Sunday, 'except it be to or from some place for the service of God, or upon other extraordinary occasion'. The penalty was ten shillings (five for a boatman or coachman) and six hours, this time, in the stocks for failure to pay.[20] Seven years later constables, churchwardens and overseers of the poor were given the right to 'Demand Entrance into any Dwelling-House' to see if anyone inside was profaning the Lord's day.[21] There was some controversy in Parliament, however, before this measure was passed. One Member, Colonel Holland, complained:

> These laws are always turned upon the most godly. . . . The last Bill for the Lord's Day, I remember, was passed on a Saturday, and carried on with great zeal. Then I told them they had tied men from coming to church by water or coach. Next day I, coming to Somerset House to sermon, had my boat and waterman laid hold on for the penalty.[22]

A clause in the original draft, prohibiting 'idle sitting, openly, at gates or doors, or elsewhere' and 'walking in church-yards' on Sundays, was dropped from the Bill by a margin of only two votes.[23]

How were people supposed to spend their Sundays? One bishop said the day should be spent in singing or reading psalms, recounting the great works of God, attending church 'early and cheerfully', staying patiently throughout the service, 'and gladly also hearing the Sermon'.[24] And it was officially laid down that the time between, or after, acts of public worship, should be spent 'in Reading, Meditation, Repetition of Sermons (especially, by calling their families to an account of what they have heard) and catechizing of them, holy conferences, prayer . . . singing of Psalms . . . and such like duties . . . accounting the Sabbath a delight'.[25]

How far in fact did people live up to such stringent rules? Some tried very hard. The Parliamentarian general Sir William Waller set himself a Sunday programme of two public services, four sessions of family prayers or psalm singing, four sessions of private prayer, and one of prayer with his wife, together with meditation and repetition of the sermons.[26] The ordinary people seem to have flouted the Sunday laws when they thought they could get away with it; on occasion they did their best to bring these laws into contempt. For instance, a visitor to the Gloucestershire village of Barnsley, where children were allowed neither to play nor to walk on Sunday, reported that

> two Women who had beene at Church both before and after Noone, did but walke into the fields for their recreation, and they were put to their choice, either to pay sixpence apiece (for prophane walking,) or to be laid one houre in the stocks; and the pievish willfull women (though they were able enough to pay) to save their money and jest out the matter, lay both by the heeles merrily one houre.[27]

Many people were convicted for such Sunday wickedness as baking, heating an oven, travelling, getting drunk, and trimming a man's hair or beard;[28] the Mayor of Coventry put three Quakers in the cage for travelling on Sunday;[29] alehouses were suppressed in Wiltshire because they tended to the profanation of the sabbath;[30] and one Sunday in 1652 three hundred people armed with muskets, bandoleers and swords, 'with a drummer and fidler . . . went in a riotous and warlike manner to Pewsey, and there very disorderly danced the Morris dance, drinking and tippling till many of them were drunk'.[31] The Merry English did not lightly surrender their Sunday pleasures.

But the English Sunday never really recovered from the interlude of triumphant puritanism. Charles II took a middle course. His former tutor, the Earl of Newcastle, advised him to revive Sunday sports after evening prayers, and painted a charming picture of 'the Countereye People with their fresher Lasses to tripp in the Toune Greene aboute the May pole, to the Louder Bagg-Pipe ther to be refreshte with their Ale and Cakes', adding sagely: 'The devertismentes will amuse the peoples thaughts, & keepe them In harmles action which will free your Matie from faction & Rebellion.'[32] Nevertheless Charles did not republish the *Book of Sports*, for the very good reason that 'there was still a mass of puritan or semi-puritan feeling which it would be unwise to outrage'.[33] The strength of this feeling seems to have varied from place to place. We find a minister himself going out and rebuking the young people who were playing on the village green, and a few years later complaining that 'this day, a day of holy rest, is now the sport and pleasure day of the generall rout of people';[34] elsewhere men were brought before the court for playing football during Sunday service.[35]

Once more barbers and tailors worked on a Sunday, and people went to pleasure resorts for Sunday recreation. Once more Sunday was a regular day for Privy Council or Cabinet meetings; in 1667 Pepys (who in the year of the Restoration had for the first time travelled by water on the sabbath[36]) was amazed to see the Queen and other notables playing cards on a Sunday.[37] Pepys himself one Sunday, after drinking 'mighty good store of wine', settled down to read *L'Escholle des filles*— 'a lewd book, but what do no wrong once to read for information sake'.[38]

The puritan reaction against this partial relaxation in people's Sunday manners took two forms, one legislative, the other exhortatory. A Bill for the better observance of the Lord's day passed both Houses of Parliament in 1663, but when it was ready for the King's consent it mysteriously disappeared from the table of the House of Lords.[39] The sabbatarians were luckier in 1667, when there was passed an Act prohibiting Sunday vending and Sunday work—works of necessity and charity excepted. Drovers, waggoners, and butchers were forbidden to travel on a Sunday; boating on that day was made a misdemeanour. In 1690 Queen Mary—herself rebuked twelve years earlier by her chaplain for sabbath card-playing—banned the use of hackney carriages on Sundays, and is said to have occasioned universal laughter by stationing constables at street corners to intercept puddings and pies on their way to the bakers' ovens.[40] Next year she sent a special letter to the Middlesex justices of the peace recommending that laws against the profanation of the Lord's day and all other lewd practices should be put into force.[41]

In default of the kind of legislation they would have liked to see on the statute-book, the sabbatarians intensified their propaganda, reciting still more awful examples of the Lord's displeasure. An immense book called *The Practical Sabbatarian* (1668), which has been described as 'the most tedious of all the Puritan productions about the Sabbath',[42] listed example after example: a drover is struck dead while driving cattle on the sabbath; a sabbath drunkard is drowned; a husbandman who tries to plough on the sabbath finds the iron stuck fast to his hand, and has to carry it about with him for two years; a vintner, drinking on a Sunday, is swept away by a whirlwind and never seen or heard of again; a 'great man' who hunts in sermon time has a child by his wife 'with a head like a dog, and it cryed like a hound'; Tiverton and

Stratford-on-Avon are each twice on fire because their citizens have profaned the Lord's day. . . .[43] *A Dreadful Warning to Lewd Livers* [*c.* 1682] is the title of a broadsheet, sometimes attributed to the industrious divine Richard Baxter, which collected a number of tales guaranteed 'to make the ears to tingle, and their hearts to ake that Read and consider them'. Eight drunkards are refused wine by a tavern-keeper, who advises them to go to church and hear the word of God. The devil in the likeness of a young man appears to them with a flagon of wine in his hand, and says: 'Sirs, be merry, you shall have Wine enough, you seem Good fellows, and I hope you will pay me well.' They answer, with horrible oaths, that they will either pay him or give him their bodies and souls. They go on swilling 'till they could hardly see each other', when their host appears 'in a most frightful shape', tells them they must pay in hell for evermore, 'and thereupon brake all their necks upon the place'. Lewd livers who remained unmoved by this warning no doubt resolved to reform forthwith when they read the following story:

> Some Children at *Lambeth-Marsh*, being on the Lords day in the after-noon at play in a Gentlemans house, and having got some drink, a Girl about eleven years old would needs drink a health to the Devil, using these words; *Here's a Health to the Devil, and if he do not come and pledge me, he is a Son of a Whore*; but before their Devilish Health was gone round, something, as they did affirm, did appear to them like a black Bear, which frighted them so, that one of them was not able to speak a word till the next day, and the rest all fear'd almost out of their wits.[44]

9

INFORMERS AND REFORMERS

The first society for suppressing other people's pleasures was formed in England in the last quarter of the seventeenth century by five or six young men of the Anglican persuasion, some of whom (we are told) had formerly been guilty of great lewdness.[1] They were soon joined by 'several Persons of considerable Rank and Fortunes',[2] and in forty-four years the 'Societies for the Reformation of Manners' were responsible for prosecuting no fewer than 101,683 persons in the London area alone, mostly for sabbath-breaking, swearing, drunkenness, lewdness, brothel-keeping, and sodomy.[3]

The undesirability of pleasure, especially on Sundays, greatly exercised eighteenth-century clerics, many of whom supported the Societies for the Reformation of Manners with appropriate sermons. 'There is in the young', wrote the Dean of Carlisle in a letter on Sunday card-playing, 'a Turn to Pleasure, that wants the most powerful Correctives.'[4] 'The *less* Pleasure Men take on Sundays, the better', declared the Vicar of Ware, Hertfordshire.[5] 'Let us ... give ourselves', coaxed the Bishop of Chester, 'a little respite [on Sundays] ... from the *fatigue* of pleasure.'[6] And the above-quoted dean, who believed that most executed persons blamed Sunday pleasure as a first step to their downfall, gave a graphic description of how taking long walks on Sundays led to thirst, and thirst led to drinking, and drinking led to lewd desires, and 'when the whore may be had, where the Bottle has raised the inclination to her, and at the very Moment she becomes agreeable; it can hardly be questioned, but that as little Regard will soon be paid to Chastity, as to Sobriety'.[7] That was where Sunday travelling led one.

The members of the Societies for the Reformation of Manners believed in combating 'publick Enormities'[8] by laying information before magistrates and so compelling them to implement the laws. Some magistrates, it appears, were not too well disposed towards informers; but those who were would be greatly encouraged by the Societies' activities,[9] just as the Societies themselves were greatly encouraged by the 'Proclamation for the Encouragement of Piety and Virtue, and for the Preventing and Punishing of Vice, Prophaneness and Immorality' issued by Queen Anne at her accession.[10] The informer was no more popular a figure in those days than he is today; not altogether surprisingly, the members of the Societies at first concealed their names from public knowledge and took special care not to let strangers be present at their meetings.[11] But a Nottingham vicar called John Disney, in a kind of vade-mecum for snoopers, insisted that 'there is nothing we need to blush at in turning Informers against Vice; 'tis an honourable undertaking, and the Cause of GOD; and whosoever is ashamed of it deserves neither the Work nor the Reward'.[12] Disney went on to lay down certain guiding rules for members of the Societies. They must never allow blasphemy, sodomy, or bestiality to escape conviction. Lewd-houses, those 'scandalous *Nurseries* of Vice', should be destroyed root and branch. While public offences should be informed against, secret sins should first be reproved. Informers should set aside considerations of party, friendship, or family; they should not proceed too zealously at first, nor provoke men into sin; they should keep a strict guard on their own morals; they must be sure of the facts before they laid information. They should inform against any persons they saw trading on Sundays—against bakers with their baskets, barbers with their basins, and other tradespeople. And they should be deferential and respectful to the magistrates.[13]

By 1698 the Societies had succeeded in having several Sunday markets suppressed;[14] glimpses of their later efforts may be obtained from the annual accounts of their progress, which generally showed the number of persons prosecuted by them for exercising their trades or ordinary callings on the Lord's day. In the years for which we have records, the Societies bagged a weekly average of about a dozen sabbath-breakers.[15]

The reaction of the eighteenth-century man in the street, and man in the alehouse, to these activities, is reflected in an anonymous satiric poem called *The Heaven-Drivers*, which appeared in 1701. It told how

> some Tygers of the Peace,
> Hungry as Hawks, and wise as Geese,
> Began to purge this sinful Nation,
> By *In* which they Call *Reformation*,*
> A goodly Word, which, well apply'd,
> Will all clandestin Int'rest hide.

The poem described how the self-appointed guardians of other men's virtue used to enter taverns and even coffee-houses on Sundays, in some cases coming to blows with the indignant customers.

> To *Drink,* tho dry as Dust, or worse,
> Or *Eat,* if Hungry as a Horse,
> In *Publick Houses* tho' at Noon,
> Or *Night* when ev'ry Church was done,
> Was, on the *Sabbath,* as they say,
> A Profanation of the Day:
> These Vanities, with many more,
> Were signs the *Babylonian* Whore,
> Had Conquer'd *England* with her Charms,
> And hug'd the Nation in her Arms.
>
> * * *
>
> O sinful sad Abomination,
> A Scandal to a Christian Nation,
> That on a *Sunday* sober Men
> Should be so wickedly profane,
> To Coffee drink, since all Men know,
> They might to stronger Liquor go.[16]

Almost the last we hear of a Society for the Reformation of Manners is a denial, in 1760, of what had evidently been a persistent rumour—that it had tried to convict people for cooking their Sunday dinners. With this went the boast that through its efforts 'a considerable check hath been put to the horrid prophanation of the Lord's Day'.[17] A somewhat similar organization, the Society for Preventing the Profanation of the Sabbath, was formed in 1775; its members used to go out at eight a.m. each Sunday, 'or sooner, if necessary', to report any sabbath-breaking they could find going on.[18] And there were parsons and mayors whose sabbatarian zeal tended also to compensate for the defi-

* i.e., by *in*formation, which they call *re*formation.

ciencies of the law—men like William Grimshaw, minister of Haworth in the West Riding, and Thomas Powell, Mayor of Deal. The former would leave church just before he was due to preach the sermon, and drive into church any who were 'idling their time in the church-yard, the street, or the ale-houses'; on at least one such occasion men jumped out of the lower windows of a public house because 'they were more afraid of their parson than of a justice of the peace'. Grimshaw also went out into the countryside in an effort to suppress 'the generally prevailing custom in country places, during the summer, of walking in the fields on a Lord's day, between the services or in the evening'.[19] Powell similarly patrolled the town in search of sabbath-breakers, and seems to have terrorized local publicans and shopkeepers into shutting their doors on Sundays ('if any company is within, 'tis very privately done') and coach-drivers into abandoning Sunday services from Deal.[20] In Manchester, in 1785, the streets were patrolled every Sunday by constables, who took stragglers into custody.[21]

Thanks to activities of this kind, people took their Sunday pleasure by stealth. The hallmark of the English Sunday was hypocrisy. Many who would not walk in the fields for pleasure, where their wickedness would be seen and commented on, did not scruple to drink all day in private alehouses.[22] If one were rich enough, one could be more open about Sunday recreation—go in for coach racing, perhaps, for very heavy wagers,[23] or play cards in West End houses, a practice observed by several foreign visitors. The sabbath, wrote a German, was kept in London with more outward decency than he had seen in many countries; around London the public houses were very full indeed, but there was no music, dancing, or card-playing—except for the concerts and card tables at the houses of persons of quality.[24] And Voltaire noted that there were

> no operas, no plays, no musical entertainments in London on Sundays; even cards are so expressly forbidden that it is only persons of quality and what are called gentlefolk that play on that day; the rest of the nation goes to church, to the tavern, and to the houses of women of pleasure.[25]

An attempt in 1780 to open a Sunday promenade at Carlisle House (admission three shillings) was frustrated by the Bishop of Chester, to whom the purpose was clearly 'to draw together dissolute people of both sexes, and to make the Promenade a place of assignation; and, in fact, it was a collection of the lowest and most profligate characters that could possibly be assembled together from every part of London. . . . Even foreigners were shocked and scandalized. . . .'[26] An even worse threat to the English Sunday than the scandalous promenade was a proposal to hold Sunday debates on theological questions—an idea fraught with 'infinite mischief'. The Bishop therefore carried through Parliament in 1781, against the opposition of Wilkes and other libertarians, an 'Act for preventing certain Abuses and Profanations on the Lord's Day, commonly called Sunday', thus putting a stop simultaneously to two evils which 'together threatened the worst consequences to public morals'.[27]

In the first half of the eighteenth century there was very little Sunday travelling; even the highwaymen rested, not wishing to waste their time. Some towns were very vigilant in stopping coaches from passing through at service time; Lord Chancellor Harcourt was thus stopped, with 'an humble apology', by the Abingdon constables.[28] By 1767 the roads were less deserted; in that year a clergyman proposed anonymously that the turnpike rate for coaches be quadrupled on Sundays.[29]

Work on the first day of the week was frowned on almost as much as pleasure. Dr Johnson, on his death-bed, is said to have asked Sir Joshua Reynolds to promise him not to work on the sabbath.[30] The number of barbers fined for working on the first day of the week was 'enormous';[31] the Vicar of Ware held that farmers must not harvest corn or hay on that day even when the weather was bad and the crop in danger of being spoiled.[32] But in 1794, when information was laid against the Middlesex magistrates for refusing to convict a man who baked meat puddings and pies on a Sunday, the judge felt it reasonable that bakers should bake for the poor.[33] Although the reformers pressed the prosecution of those who shaved people or cooked food on a Sunday, and although in 1757, in the midst of war with France, there was a successful nonconformist protest when Parliament proposed to allow Sunday drilling by the militia,[34] a blind eye was turned on glass-works and collieries, where men worked to keep the fires going over the weekend.[35]

Judging by the number of tracts that were thought necessary in the eighteenth century telling people how to spend the Lord's day, public reverence for it was scarcely more than skin-deep. One authority said the day should be employed in attending church twice; reading the

Bible and 'good Books'; instructing one's family; seriously reflecting on one's duties, on the temptations to which one might be exposed, and on what was likely to be one's doom and state throughout eternity; and in earnest prayer. He added: 'To spend the sacred Time in Amusement, and Idleness, or in frequenting Coffee-houses, Taverns, or Alehouses . . . is an high Affront to the Authority of God . . . an unspeakable injury to Yourself, to your Family, and to the Nation.'[36] Another taught that while you got dressed on Sunday morning you should 'think on sin, that was the cause of your soul's nakedness', and while combing your hair, too, you might reflect that however numerous your hairs might be, your sins were more numerous still.[37] To at least one clergyman, even Saturday night was 'a very improper time to spend the evening out anywhere'.[38] Among people too timid to defy these teachings, but lacking the requisite degree of pious enthusiasm, Sunday became, as William Wilberforce put it, 'a *heavy* day', the larger part of which 'dully draws on in comfortless vacuity or without improvement is trifled away in vain and unprofitable discourse'.[39] Nothing was more dreary and tedious, wrote a French police official in 1784, than an English Sunday, whether in London or in the country. 'It is the finest sight in the world', he added ironically, 'to see men, women, and children looking at each other gloomily and yawning as they trudge along, or sitting with folded arms close by their windows—which are always shut—counting the passers-by.'[40]

10

DAY OF GLOOM

Wilberforce is famous for freeing the Negro slaves; his efforts to make his own countrymen slaves to his conception of virtue are less well known. It was through his persuasion that the Privy Council issued in 1787 a proclamation which prohibited playing at dice, cards, or any other game on Sunday, either in public or private houses, and which urged the energetic enforcement of the laws against 'excessive Drinking, Blasphemy, profane Swearing and Cursing, Lewdness, Profanation of the Lord's Day, or other dissolute, immoral or disorderly Practices . . . loose and licentious Prints, Books and Publications', and the selling of refreshments during the time of divine service.[1] Two years later there came into existence, with Wilberforce as vice-president, an organization generally known as the Proclamation Society. This body of philanthropists gave serious attention to sabbath-breaking, and, since the penalties for that crime were 'of almost ridiculous smallness', tried to start an association 'among persons of weight and influence' for the better observance of the Lord's day; public response was disappointingly tepid.[2] Nothing daunted, the Society was instrumental in having places of entertainment closed on Sunday evenings; one such place, shut down through its efforts, had been a 'resort of the licentious and abandoned of both sexes' and had 'exhibited a scene of the most horrid profaneness and the most shocking indecency'.[3]

Rather than the activities of Wilberforce and his friends, however, it was the French revolution which frightened the English upper classes into a rather higher standard of Sunday observance. 'The churches were well attended, and sometimes even crowded. It was a wonder to the lower orders, throughout all parts of England, to see the avenues to the churches filled with carriages. This novel appearance prompted the simple country-people to inquire what was the matter?'[4]

In 1798 we find the Proclamation Society annoying the Speaker of

the House of Commons by trying to get him to stop his Sunday entertaining, a suggestion he took as a personal insult.[5] In 1802 a much more
energetic organization came into being: the Society for the Suppression
of Vice and the Encouragement of Religion and Virtue throughout the
United Kingdom. In one year alone this Society's subcommittee for
dealing with people's behaviour on Sundays successfully prosecuted
280 publicans and 340 shopkeepers for Sunday trading, and warned
between two and three thousand others. No longer were there 'scenes of
the most dissolute riot' in the public houses on Sundays.[6] A Society for
Promoting the Observance of the Christian Sabbath is heard of briefly
in 1809; it modestly disclaimed any intention of 'setting up . . . a
competition of vices, merely to shew that [sabbath-breaking] is the
worst of them, or the ringleader of all the others'.[7]

No such modesty informed the work of the Society for Promoting
the Due Observance of the Lord's-day, which was set up in 1831 and
has been with us ever since. Its founders were mainly Church of
England clergymen and laymen, the most prominent of them the Reverend Daniel Wilson, later Bishop of Calcutta; its aim was summarized,
jestingly, as 'the bitter observance of the sabbath'.[8] The Society's
inaugural meeting expressed alarm at attempts to release men's con-
sciences from the paramount claims of a 'primeval ordinance', and
dismay at such violations of the Lord's day as 'the multiplication of
tea-gardens and other places of public resort for amusement and
dissipation'. Profanation of the Lord's day was threatening a general
dissoluteness of manners, and loosening those bonds of civil order
and religious obedience by which the tranquillity of nations was maintained.[9] The Society's members, who by 1837 numbered something
over two hundred,[10] paid a subscription of half a guinea a year, or five
guineas for life.

At the Society's first annual meeting, in 1832, its committee declared
themselves 'deeply convinced of the necessity of some alteration in the
existing laws relative to the Sabbath'.[11] The man they chose to lead the
agitation in Parliament was the Irish landowner Sir Andrew Agnew, on
whose Edinburgh tombstone appears the motto of his life, 'Remember
the Sabbath-day', and of whom a fellow M.P. once said that he

> hanged his wicked cat on Monday,
> Because she killed a mouse on Sunday.[12]

A man of the most rigid principles, he once ordered a mutton chop in an inn a few minutes after the midnight dividing Sunday from Saturday, and an M.P. who heard him do so was unsporting enough to mention this lapse in the House of Commons. This was a lesson to Agnew. Taunted on another occasion with eating hot potatoes with his cold Sunday dinner, he 'never again ate a hot potatoe on Sunday, but substituted bread and butter'.[13]

Agnew lost no time in moving the appointment of a select committee to inquire into Sunday observance; it was in the debate on this motion that Lord Sandon uttered the notorious remark that 'the recreations of the rich affect themselves only, whilst the recreations of the poor affect society in general'.[14] The committee heard, from magistrates and others, evidence about Sunday drinking and trading of which Agnew's biographer wrote:

> A more appalling spectacle of human depravity, on a large and systematic scale, has seldom been brought to light. It was as if a curtain had been lifted up, revealing to the eyes of the Christian public, as to those of the ancient prophet, the scenes of abomination done in the midst of Israel.[15]

The committee recommended increased penalties for Sunday marketing and for the improper use of houses of public entertainment. Agnew's next move was to introduce a Bill making illegal all Sunday work except works of necessity and mercy, and laying down penalties ranging from five shillings to £5; *The Times* called this Bill a 'monstrous piece of absurdity' and proposed that the printed copies of it be 'converted into fools'-caps'.[16] After three successive defeats the second reading of the Bill was carried in 1837, but the dissolution of Parliament prevented its reaching committee stage.

That was the year of the accession of Queen Victoria, one of whose first actions as monarch was to issue yet another 'Proclamation for the Encouragement of Piety and Virtue, and for the Preventing and Punishing of Vice, Profaneness, and Immorality'. Her Majesty's loving subjects were prohibited once more from playing at dice, cards, or any other game on the Lord's day, either in public or in private; they were again commanded to attend church, and again forbidden to sell alcoholic beverages at the time of church services.[17] Though Agnew's efforts in Parliament had been widely ridiculed, this proclamation signalling the start of the Victorian era gave the green light to the sabbatarians, who worked untiringly to make Sunday, as far as they could, a day of unrelieved gloom. From now to the end of the century the current was more or less in their favour. And they made the most of it.

There were some things they were powerless to prevent: Sunday travel, at the height of the Railway Age, was one of them. Opposition was strongest in Scotland, where tram-cars did not run on Sundays till the turn of the century; when a railway engineer M.P. introduced a Bill for regulating Sunday travelling on the railways, one Scots opponent called it 'repugnant to our historical associations,—to our laws,—to our convictions, feelings, and habits'.[18] Advocates of Sunday trains were quick to pounce on anomalies in their opponents' own behaviour. A mineowner who was against Sunday trains was asked if his pit was worked on a Sunday. 'Oh, no,' he replied, 'only the water is pumped out.' A whisky distiller of similar views made whisky on Sundays; when neighbours objected, he simply shut the distillery windows and went on distilling.[19] Clergymen were sometimes tempted to avail themselves of new-fangled travelling facilities that were as convenient as they were irreligious. One who went by train from Glasgow to Edinburgh to see his dying wife was reproached by the Presbytery, and confessed that 'it would not be for edification' if he acted in the same way again.[20] A Derbyshire conference, in 1860, discussed ways of putting a stop to Sunday railway travel, which it regarded as on a level with riding and driving in the parks, pleasure boats, the opening of tea- and public gardens, 'desecrations by persons of high rank, and by foreigners'—and cheese-making.[21] Zealots prevented the sailing of a Sunday steamboat at Ipswich in the 1850s.[22] But this was a lost battle from the beginning, and by the last quarter of the century there was little point in anything but a rather forlorn rearguard action against 'the evil of Cheap Excursions on the Lord's-day'.[23]

Somewhat less of a forlorn hope—though the Lord's-day Society was ultimately defeated on this issue too—was the struggle to prevent the Sunday opening of the British Museum and the National Gallery. To those who held that working people, on the one day in seven they did not work, should have an opportunity to see the nation's historical and artistic treasures, the sabbatarians replied that the opening of these institutions on the first day of the week would involve the labour of a great many attendants and transport workers. 'In this happy result the hand of God is discernible', said the Society in 1855, when the corn merchant Sir Joshua Walmsley's Commons motion for the opening of the British Museum and the National Gallery after Sunday morning service was defeated by a heavy majority.[24] When a similar motion was defeated in the following year, Greville, Clerk to the Council, took a different view. 'Cant and Puritanism', he wrote in his journal, 'are in the ascendant, and ... it will be very well if we escape ... stringent measures against Sunday occupations and amusements. . . . It is stated that the Sabbatarians are so united and numerous . . . that . . . they would be able to influence and probably carry any election.'[25] The Society had collected 106,179 signatures to its petitions; the newly formed National Sunday League, an 'evil confederacy'[26] whose adherents included the 'infidel' Bradlaugh, apostrophized some of the remoter petitioners in a pamphlet entitled: *London and the Londoners. A Letter Addressed to the Inhabitants of Llanfairmathafarneithaf, Llanfihangel-nant-brane, Cambusnethan, Longformacus, Llangristiolus, Tintwistle, Brynguran, Polperro, Egloskerry, Kizziemuir, Twitchen, Mawcop, Chokey, Troon, Crook, Wix, Gad, &c., All Which Places, (together with Many Others Equally Remote and Little Known), Have Petitioned Parliament against the Opening of the British Museum and National Gallery on Sunday* (1856).[27] Later petitions were said to include the signatures of Sunday school children, as well as many names all in the same handwriting.[28]

Though the House of Lords voted in favour of the principle in 1886, it was another decade before the Sunday opening of national museums and art galleries became a reality, the Lord's-day Society having 'used every available means to induce Members of Parliament to come to a wiser decision'.[29] Even by 1896, of 208 towns possessing museums, art galleries, and libraries, only 46 had opened them on Sundays—and 14 had closed them again.[30] The trouble with art galleries, it was felt, was that the contemplation of paintings led to immorality. 'That modern city', observed one writer sternly, 'which has been distinguished above all others for the studious cultivation of the arts—Munich—is also distinguished for this terrible fact,—that one out of every two births is illegitimate.'[31] The Reverend John Gritton, secretary of the Lord's-day Society, was still more outspoken: collections of statuary and paintings were 'quite as likely to inflame the passions as to purge the life'. Gritton's evidence for this judgment was a letter from an English clergyman who had visited the Bordeaux picture gallery but had very soon come away, 'as I could hardly look in any direction without being distressed and disgusted by seeing on the walls paintings of females in a state of perfect nudity'.[32]

Similar efforts were made to prevent the opening of parks and public gardens. The Sunday opening of Kew Gardens in 1852 was 'an arrangement greatly to be regretted'.[33] A lecturer told a Rochdale audience that a young man who went for a pull on the river or visited Kew got home 'jaded and tired' after 'a day of riotous pleasure'.[34] For people to spend their Sundays walking or sitting in parks—or, worse still, listening to music there—came dangerously close to the sabbatarians' favourite bugaboo: the dreaded Continental Sunday, of which the Parisian Sunday was the most glitteringly wicked variety. One of the Lord's-day Society's earliest publications was its *Hints to Travellers on the Continent*;[35] the Society reported with approval a protest in the Common Council of the City of London against the Lord Mayor's having gone to a Sunday fête while on an official visit to Paris.[36] Protesting against two-hour Sunday concerts by military bands in Kensington Gardens, one writer warned: 'If our rulers should go on in this course, we shall soon see our English Sabbath made like that of Paris or Vienna.'[37] Another gave the following description of a Sunday in Paris:

> Aware of the scenes presented on this holy day in the French capital, he did not leave his hotel but for Divine Worship. Early in the evening, an English fellow-traveller came in and enquired, 'Have you been in the *Champs Elysées* this evening?' To which the writer replied, No. Then he remarked, 'O you should go and see it, for it *wants nothing but the flame to make it hell*!'—He afterwards stated that there were Bands, Theatres, Saloons, Mountebanks, Jugglers, Dancers, &c., &c., all surrounded with crowds who appeared to be highly gratified. Such is the kind of Sabbath to which the spirit of Sunday Bands would eventually conduct this land!

This writer's emotions at such a prospect were apparently so strong that he could not adequately express them in prose. He went on:

> Thou land of fiddling, gay Voltaire,
> Say, can we find Heaven's blessing there?
> No,—Heaven's blessing takes its flight,
> Where States deny the Sabbath right.[38]

When the Archbishop of Canterbury requested that Sunday concerts in the parks be stopped, Prime Minister Palmerston withdrew the military bands. Concerts were then provided by private subscription in several cities, despite the continuing protests of the sabbatarians, to whom they were 'a very great evil' because they attracted 'numbers of young persons . . . to congregate in the parks'.[39] Even the programmes were objected to, as 'more than usually profane—quite the theatre and ball-room style'.[40] Those who wanted indoor Sunday concerts contrived to find loopholes in the law—like registering the Alhambra music-hall as a nonconformist chapel for the purpose of holding Sunday concerts there under licence from the London County Council.[41]

Much was done to limit and even suppress Sunday wakes, revels, and feasts in the countryside. An association was formed in Herefordshire in 1838 for this purpose, the wakes being condemned as 'the occasion of tumultuous and disorderly assemblages both of men and women, and of a debauching and a revolting profligacy, baffling all description'.[42] The towns had little or no tradition of Sunday wakes; but here there was Sunday drinking to be suppressed, if possible. According to Taine, drinking went on in the taverns behind closed doors while the sermon was being preached.[43] The Lord's-day Society greeted 'with joy' the Act that closed Welsh public houses on the first day of the week.[44] One of the Society's supporters, describing a Sunday visit to thirty-four London public houses, told of seeing 'nine bad women' in one, while in another he had great difficulty in getting away from a group of women who surrounded him. Elsewhere 'many rejected my tracts with cursing and bitterness'; but a group of shoemakers displayed uncommon patience with this gentleman who asked them how often they washed themselves! One replied, no doubt with perfect gravity, that he had not washed for a fortnight; his practice each morning, he added, was merely to 'rub my hands over my face to equalize the dirt'.[45]

There was a lengthy battle over the Sunday opening of the Crystal Palace. To frustrate the Act of 1781 forbidding the taking of money for admission to Sunday entertainment, it was thrown open without charge on the Trinity Sunday of 1861, and 40,000 people crowded through the gates. 'Organized gigantic wickedness' was how the Lord's-day Society described the games that were played; one feels rather let down on discovering that these games were pole-climbing, leap-frog, and jumping over handkerchiefs.[46] The 1781 Act, which 'operated as a wholesome check on the selfishness and greed of Sunday pleasure-seekers and Sunday money-makers',[47] was challenged more directly in the 1870s by the proprietors of the Brighton Aquarium. One outcome of some exceedingly complex litigation was an Act making it impossible to oppose Sunday amusements in the courts without the Attorney-General's fiat. When a young woman undertook to walk 1,250 miles in 1,000 hours—including the sabbath hours—in the grounds of a Hastings hotel, the Society tried to stop this 'foolish and demoralizing' exhibition; but 'legal evidence sufficient to secure a conviction was difficult to procure'.[48] Another highly undesirable amusement was the Sunday funeral, an 'occasion of evil' and an excuse for 'unseemly conviviality'.[49]

As far as Sunday work and trading were concerned, the sabbatarians found themselves compelled by the growth of industrialization to retreat, very gradually; though at times they were able to pose, not without success, as protectors of the working man. A pamphleteer who believed that the consequence of Sunday work was, in many cases, insanity or premature death suggested that where Sunday work or travel was necessary the police ('after having had proved to them the necessity of the case') should be authorized to issue a licence. On Sundays the police would be empowered to demand the production of this licence by anyone they found working or travelling, 'and should such licence not be produced, the person so found should be dealt with as the law might direct'.[50] As early as 1797 Bishop Porteus had complained of the printing and sale of Sunday newspapers.[51] The Lord's-day Society, at its inaugural meeting, condemned 'the enormous evil of the Sunday Newspapers, which are published and vended with pernicious diligence, openly trampling upon the first duties of Christianity'.[52] The Society's opposition was later whetted by an item in *The Times* in 1899, revealing that the New York Sunday papers carried pictures of 'coloured petticoats, stockings, and other matters of female apparel . . . coloured and uncoloured pictures of women and men in every condition of *décolletage*, and . . . dishabille . . . effigies of celebrated beauties . . . [and] scandalous stories'.[53] It was hard to make out a plausible case for banning necessary work: but how did one define 'necessary'?[54] Apparently the work of the post offices was not necessary, and the Society successfully opposed the Sunday opening of the London Post Office; nor was the Sunday harvesting of crops in the wet autumn of

1881 necessary, and the Society opposed it;[55] in Scotland it was not necessary to draw drinking-water on the sabbath, and by order of the authorities a public well in Thurso was locked up from Saturday night to Monday morning.[56] Education on the sabbath was in Scotland considered not merely unnecessary, but positively sinful; so that in the 1850s, though 6,000 of the children attending Scottish Sunday schools were unable to read, the teachers were forbidden by the clergy to teach them.[57]

The sabbatarians took a low view, on the whole, of the morals and likely fate of sabbath-breakers. The editor of the *Leeds Mercury*, a Sunday school teacher for thirty-eight years, believed that one of the worst habits a child could be given was that of 'rambling in quest of amusement' on the Lord's day. 'When we see this habit once formed . . . we tremble for our girls as exposed to the greatest dangers.'[58] Multitudes of criminals had acknowledged that the violation of the sabbath 'was their first step in the downward road'.[59] And the Vicar of St Bride's, Fleet Street, declared: 'The great mass of Sabbath-breakers are ripe for all wickedness.'[60]

To check their sabbath-breaking tendencies, children were subjected to improving stories about what happened to this category of sinner. Typical was the tale of little Lewis, who went swimming in the mill-stream one Sunday and was crushed by the great mill-wheel: 'Scarcely had his last cry reached the ear of the miller, before his mangled corpse came out from under the wheel.' And the author drew the following moral for his young readers:

> Every Sabbath should be pass'd
> As if we knew it were our last;
> For what would dying people give
> To have one Sabbath more to live?[61]

No wonder that children tended to be shocked when informed that heaven resembled an everlasting sabbath day.[62] Nevertheless members of the Lord's-day Society were given to insisting, not without heat, that they looked 'just as joyous and pleasant'[63] as the infidels advocating a weekly holiday in place of a Sunday that most people found 'weary, dull, stale, and unprofitable'.[64]

11

'MISERY' MARTIN

versus

THE TWENTIETH CENTURY

This Hill Is Dangerous was the title of a leaflet with which the Lord's-day Society greeted the twentieth century. It was addressed to Sunday cyclists, whose weekly excursions into the countryside with light hearts and still lighter clothing were a dangerous sign of the times. The combination of a new century and a new monarch, whose standard of Sunday observance was not as high as the sabbatarians would have wished—who, indeed, seemed to prefer the 'Continental Sunday', and with whose Sunday habits the Society soon lost patience[1]—was scarcely calculated to promote the cause of Sunday gloom. The new generation was bent on emancipating itself from scriptural guidance, and there was open rejoicing at the 'silent revolution in the observance of the first day of the week'.[2] The Continental Sunday, it was alleged, was already spoiling the quietness of English streets and the character of English people.[3]

From now on the Society, unlike little Lewis, was swimming against the stream—and much of what it did had to be done behind the scenes. Members were told in 1912 that 'the public would probably be astonished to find that much which they hear of in connexion with the Lord's Day has emanated from the Lord's Day Observance Society', but that 'it would not be in the interests of the work to publish details'.[4] This was evidently a reference to the pressure the Society and its local 'auxiliaries' put on municipal councillors who had to decide, for example, whether or not to permit 'improper and mischievous'[5] Sunday cinema shows. The Society's annual reports were filled with items about the prosecution of sponsors of such shows; the banning of

Sunday trams in Edinburgh, Llandudno, and Doncaster; the Sunday closing of libraries at Bermondsey and Sheffield, and of Cheltenham art gallery; the banning of Sunday concerts in Newcastle, Worthing, Bath, Brighton, Bournemouth, and Harrogate, Sunday tennis at Clifton, Sunday boating at Rhyl, and Sunday golf at Cromer, Portrush, and Burton; the closing of Ilford skating rink; and the stopping of cheap Sunday trains into the Vale of Glamorgan and of Sunday excursion steamers to the Isle of Man. On the eve of the first world war the Society was protesting to the War Office about a Sunday march 'which resulted in the death of a sergeant', and to the National Rifle Association about the 'very regrettable decision' to open the Bisley rifle ranges for Sunday practice.[6]

The war itself presented the sabbatarians with still greater problems, now that military exigencies, the well-being of the troops, and civilian morale might be held to necessitate goods traffic, entertainments, and labour on the first day of the week. There was little to be done however but express the view that 'the Country is doing foolishly' and the hope 'that, before it is too late, there may be a return to right paths'.[7] Especially to be regretted was the Archbishop of Canterbury's approval of Sunday farm work, for 'the Word of God is . . . most explicit in special reference to the food supply and the Sabbath'.[8]

If one result of the war was 'a greatly desecrated Lord's Day', the first few post-war years were 'especially disappointing'.[9] The banning of Sunday games in certain London parks did the sabbatarians' hearts good (until the London County Council committed the 'mistake and wrong' of lifting the ban[10]); the Sunday closing of the Poultry Exhibition and the British Empire Exhibition were pleasing victories; and it was gratifying to be able to report that they had prevented the Sunday evening opening of 597 theatres and music-halls. But the Society was clearly in the doldrums; not even the incorporation of the Working Men's Lord's Day Rest Association and the League against Sunday Travelling could revitalize it;[11] an infusion of new energy was needed.

Salvation came in the shape of Herbert Henry Martin, who in 1925, 'after much prayerful consideration',[12] was chosen from 132 candidates as secretary of the Society. Few Englishmen in the present century have done as much as 'Misery' Martin, as the popular Press christened him, to stop people enjoying themselves in ways he disapproved of. Ascetic and self-denying ('in everything except his food',[13] for he relished a good steak), he was an anti-sin campaigner of the old school, who believed he could tell a young man's character by the way he got out of bed in the morning,[14] and who always remembered, as one of the sorriest sights of his life, an exhibition of 'the latest jazz dances' one Sunday evening in 1919. The scene was Brighton.

> The windows were open and I saw it all—the jazz costumes—the painted-faced ladies—the half-drunken demeanour of the male dancers—whilst the 'Jazz music' (!) and the whirl of the jazzers were about as frivolous and as sensual as they possibly could be. But the saddest fact of all has yet to be told. On that Lord's Day evening I saw little girls of about nine or ten years of age being taught all the movements of the Jazz and the Fox-trot in the fetid, hellish atmosphere of that saloon.[15]

What 'Misery' Martin saw that evening through a Brighton window led him to the view, held by so many of his predecessors, that 'neglect of God's Day is nearly always the first step in a downward career. *Everyday experience proves this.*'[16] Again like so many of his predecessors, 'Misery' Martin punched home his argument with verse:

> Hold fast by your Sundays! Of pleasure take heed
> Which seek [sic] from God's Temple your footsteps to lead;
> The flower of such pleasure is surely a weed,
> It stings as you pluck it, and bears deadly seed.[17]

'Misery' Martin gingered up the work of the Society, secured new offices bang opposite those of the National Sunday League, persuaded the Solicitor-General, Sir Thomas Inskip, to accept the presidency and a rising barrister-M.P., Mr W. S. Morrison (later Speaker of the House of Commons), to act as counsel, gave its annual report and quarterly magazine a thorough face-lift, introducing newsy headlines and crude but vigorous cartoons—and boosted the Society's income from an annual £1,600 to ten times that amount in five years.[18] At the end of his first year of office he had to his credit a long list of battles against 'attempts on the quiet and sanctity of God's Day': among these attempts were Sunday jazz band performances in London parks,[19] the debasing spectacle of women's boxing contests, the reintroduction of cock-fighting, and the innovation of girls' races with betting.[20]

'Misery' Martin was never content to sit behind a desk; he went out into the field to see, and to judge, for himself. So he was able to give his no doubt horrified readers a first-hand description of 'The Devil's Counter-Attraction to the Sunday School': a fair at Southend which 'out-Wembled the Wembley Amusements Park at its height', with 'Tip the Ladies out of Bed' (two young women dressed in pyjamas tumbling out of bed with loud shrieks amid the spectators' nasty observations) and 'Moulin Rouge de Paris' (admission twopence: 'can be better imagined than described'), 'Gay Life on the Continent' and 'Life in Gay Paris' (titles 'full of suggestion').[21] He could give them an eyewitness account of a Sunday morning market at Walworth, where men were selling 'disgusting French picture cards' (twopence each: 'Gay Girls of Paris' and 'What Billy Saw in Paris' were titles 'amplified by salacious comments calculated to appeal to lustful minds'; 'Sweet Mabel; Life in St John's Wood' also 'commanded a ready sale') and, from a neighbouring stall, 'filthy birth control contraceptives' ('I saw a number of customers pay him 2d. each, and walk away shamefacedly with the contraceptives supplied').[22] That visit led to prosecutions. And when Martin and his first wife Gertrude, accompanied by two plain-clothes policemen, visited a Sunday dance club in Ealing, the club closed down soon afterwards.[23] 'Misery' Martin knew his statute-book, as the sponsors of Sunday dog-racing at Southend, motor-cycle racing at Aylesbury, and concerts at Colchester all found to their sorrow. Where he could not use the law he used his pen—as in a protest against the inclusion of stained glass figures of Sunday golfers 'among the saints' in a window of a Wallasey church.[24]

The Southend and Walworth versions of gay Paris, shocking though they were, did not completely satisfy all the members of the Lord's Day Observance Society. Some wanted to see for themselves the 'abounding gaiety and pleasure-seeking and reeking sin' of a Sunday in Paris.[25] Accordingly there was set up a 'Continental Sunday Commission', which in the summer of 1928 spent seventeen days in Belgium, Holland, France, Switzerland and Italy—with Sundays in Ostend, Montreux and Paris—at a cost of nineteen guineas per head. From their report it is not clear that the thirty-one Commissioners, among whom were 'Misery' Martin and his wife, ever set collective foot in a Paris night club, whatever some of them may have done as individuals; but they expressed dutiful horror at the pavement cafés and the crowded streets, the theatres and cabarets in full swing, the wines, songs, and revelries till past midnight, and summed up their impressions, fairly predictably, as follows:

> The frivolity—hilarity—betting—gambling—excitement—and revelries . . . made the Commissioners more than ever resolved [to oppose] the establishment of the 'Continental Sunday' in our beloved land. . . . The Continental Sunday, with its immoderate Pleasure-seeking, encourages a . . . Pagan idea of life. . . . The Continental Sunday, with its Gambling, Drinking, and other Revelries, is a cause of moral feebleness and laxity. . . . Our . . . Sunday . . . in Paris . . . was a Day of Desecration we shall never forget. . . .[26]

When 'Misery' Martin visited Paris again twenty-one years later he found that things had, if anything, got worse. Gaiety, gambling, and godlessness were supreme, with 'Daring Shows', 'Pin-up Girls', and 'French Can Can' among the attractions. But Martin was not a man to be lured into the 'doubtful Dancing Halls' and 'Night Club Cabarets' that street touts tried to persuade him to enter; 'their seductive, low appeals', he wrote, 'were in vain'.[27]

Despite its having secured, in the 1929 general election, pledges from 259 M.P.s that they would resist the passing of a Sunday Theatres Bill, the Society soon had to endure a hurtful defeat. Sunday cinema performances in London and certain provincial towns were authorized in 1932, in spite of the 550,000 postcards the sabbatarians had caused to be sent to M.P.s, and in spite of the 1,457,683 signatures they had collected to a national petition ten miles in length. The Sunday Entertainments Act opened 'the floodgates of Sabbath Desecration':[28] a four-page 'Solemn and Respectful Protest' went to all M.P.s. But there were some victories, too, in the thirties. A chain store withdrew with alacrity a 'suggestive' gramophone record of a song called 'Sunday School Stories' consisting of 'vulgar caricatures of Bible characters'.[29] Sunday games were prevented in the parks of Liverpool, Manchester, and Glasgow, along with air pageants in the Isle of Wight, fairs at Morecambe, Cardiff, and Great Yarmouth, motor-cycle races at Pevensey and Rossendale, ice-hockey matches at Earls Court, rodeos at White City (after legal action), a gala and carnival ball at Belle Vue, Manchester, and the Sunday opening of the Chinese Art Exhibition. Local guerrilla operations against Sunday cinema shows 'made the Cinema Exhibitors squirm' and 'afraid to ask for what was granted them by law'.[30] A strong protest was registered against a Sunday evening wireless debate in 1935 between Bernard Shaw and Madeleine Carroll on the subject of sex appeal in films. An even stronger—and successful—protest was made in 1938 against a Sunday evening mud-wrestling match between women. 'Can there be imagined', asked the Society's annual report, 'a more revolting defiance of God's Sabbath commands than such happenings during the hallowed hours of a Sabbath evening?'[31] It would certainly have made Bishop Daniel Wilson sit up; revolting or not, however, a drawing of the match appeared on the opposite page for the edification of readers of the report.[32]

When the second world war broke out the Society had its hands full campaigning against Sunday cinemas, theatres, dances, variety shows, games, harvesting—and the B.B.C. Forces Programme, about whose Sunday items it commented in 1941: 'It seems pathetic that men face to face with the realities of eternity should be regaled with Dance Music, Variety, Cabaret, Sporting Items and other inanities during the hallowed hours of each Lord's Day.'[33] But then, sabbath profanation was by now one of Britain's national sins, along with the drink curse, the gambling mania, moral laxity among all classes, and inordinate pleasure-seeking.[34] It was in 1941 that 'Misery' Martin scored the biggest victory of his life when, sitting in the Strangers' Gallery of the House of Commons, he watched a majority of M.P.s defeat a government order permitting the Sunday opening of theatres and music-halls. Even forcing the Reverend R. W. Sorenson M.P. and the Dean of Ely to apologize to the Society—the former had stated that it had stopped Sunday entertainments for the troops, the latter that its members acted as common informers[35]—was not such sweet success as this blow for Sunday gloom struck at the height of the war.

The ending of the war made many people thankful. 'Misery' Martin had victories of another kind to celebrate. A headline 'On to Victory' in the January 1945 issue of the *Lord's Day Magazine* referred, not to the victory that most other people were hoping for, but to the locking up of children's swings on Sundays: 'We . . . thankfully report that two Councils . . . have decided in the interests of the moral and spiritual welfare of the children to refuse to allow the games apparatus to be open for use on Sundays.'[36]

Before his retirement in 1951 (he died three years later, aged seventy-two and worth £2,780) 'Misery' Martin put a stop to a Sunday hypnotism display at Hastings, and—a crowning triumph—was largely responsible for the House of Commons decision not to open the Festival of Britain pleasure gardens on Sundays.[37]

His successor Harold Legerton, a 200-words-a-minute confounder of television interviewers, soon showed his mettle when the Society collected over half a million signatures in six weeks to a petition against a Bill which would have ended most prohibitions on Sunday entertainments, including professional football and cricket matches. The Bill was defeated by a heavy majority. Its sponsor complained that he had received many abusive letters from people who wanted him to be drowned with a millstone round his neck; others told him they would like his eyes put out—and to be there to see it happening.[38] The Society quickly dissociated itself from these extreme examples of sabbatarian zeal.

In recent years the Lord's Day Observance Society has attracted most attention for its criticisms of the Duke of Edinburgh's Sunday polo. 'The term "Duke baiting" ', it declared, '. . . does not describe our attitude to His Royal Highness . . . but we shall not cease to rebuke him for his regrettable example of Sunday Sport.'[39] When the Headmaster of Eton decided to allow Sunday afternoon games on the well-known playing-fields the Society asked sadly: 'What can we expect when the first gentleman of the land sets so bad an example by persistently playing polo on the Lord's Day?'[40] And when the Queen (after watching the Duke playing polo) received two Russian statesmen one Sunday, 'Britain disgraced herself'.[41]

No one could accuse the Lord's Day Observance Society of not being impartial. It puts a stop to Sunday music and ballet in the ruins of the old Coventry cathedral with the same self-righteous loathing with which it puts a stop to the 'foul sin' of Sunday strip-tease shows[42] or opposes the dancing of the twist on Sunday in a church youth club (quoting Ginger Rogers's view that the twist is 'THE MOST OBSCENE DANCE I'VE EVER SEEN').[43] It censures Sunday bingo in the same breath as it condemns Sunday work by undertakers.[44] An embarrassment to clergy who have sought to move with the times, the Society flourishes on the present irrational mishmash of archaic Sunday laws. It holds that no change in these laws is needed, but rather a more complete knowledge of the laws on the part of the police and local authorities, together with a greater determination to enforce them and strict vigilance to prevent their being broken.[45] In other words, 'a return to the spirit of the Puritans', which would mean 'a return to Britain's glory and true joy'.[46] Is it in fact too late for the clock to be put back in this way? It would be rash to be quite certain that it is.

PART III

THE TEETOTALITARIANS

12

OUR DIZZY ISLAND

Though the licensing of inns dates back to 1552, temperance societies were unknown in England till the nineteenth century; had there been any in Elizabethan times, they would most likely have been as moderate and permissive as the sixteenth-century Order of St Christopher in Germany, whose members were pledged not to drink more than seven goblets of wine at one meal 'except in cases where this measure was not sufficient to quench their thirst'.[1] In those days Englishmen used to drink a great deal of strong beer; though there were plenty of moralists who opposed drunkenness, it occurred to very few of them to extend their opposition to drinking. Even so thorough-going a puritan as Stubbes complained, not of drinking as such, but of excesses: the practice, for instance, of tippling all night long, or a whole week together, so long as any money was left, some staggering, some spewing, some 'pissing vnder the boord as they sit'.[2] The lawful use of strong drink was not to be rejected, wrote John Downame in 'A Disswasion from the Sin of Drunkennes', one of four treatises against four 'hainous' sins (the others being swearing, whoredom, and bribery); but it was high time the magistrates and ministers suppressed the vice of drunkenness, which had grown to impudent boldness, and which caused ribaldry and obscene filthiness that made chaste ears glow as much with heat as a drunkard's face with wine.[3] To other pamphleteers drunkenness was 'England's bane';[4] and the royalist preacher Thomas Reeve called England 'the Dizzy iland', whose inhabitants 'drink, as if . . . we were nothing but *spunges to draw up moisture*, or we had *tunnels in our mouthes*'.[5]

To be sure, William Prynne, the great enemy of the theatre, proved that it was sinful and utterly unlawful for christians to drink to the health of their friends;[6] Thomas Hall, a minister five times imprisoned in the civil war, regarded the drinking of healths by young women on their knees during maypole festivities as abominable;[7] and the anonymous author of *A Warning-piece to all Drunkards and Health-Drinkers* (1682) believed that the drinking of healths was 'an Engine invented by the Devil to carry on the Sin of Drunkenness with the greater ease and Infallibility'.[8]

But these were, upon the whole, extreme views. Though the poet Richard Brathwait complained that healths were sometimes drunk out of old hats 'well peopled with footed vermin', 'old shooes which some base Pesant hath worne to the bottom' and 'Chamber-pots with the very lees or excrements of the Urine it self', he found the amorous exploits of young men in their cups far less unhygienic, poking fun at 'Weake Oratory to fence the besieged fort of Maids virginity'—'Pray Sir, let me be gone; your hand from under the table Sir; faire play above boord; Forbeare sir to seeke what you cannot finde'—and discussing with mock solemnity 'whether he who . . . forcibly puts his hand into a maids bosome, may be sued for a trespasse'.[9] It was the drunkard, not the drinker, whom the dramatist Thomas Heywood 'opened, dissected, and anatomized' in his *Philocothonista* (1635); it was the drunkard, not the drinker, who was so inflamed with lust—according to an 863-page analysis of *The Drunkard's Character* (1638) generally attributed to Richard Younge—that 'were his power equall to his desire . . . he would not leave a Virgin in the world';[10] it was immoderate drinking, wrote George Freman, that 'disposeth vehemently to the pleasures of sense, and to a gigling impertinent mirth . . . precipitateth to the acts of uncleanness, and exciteth all the Passions'.[11] It was drunkenness, not mere drinking, whose effects a Suffolk parson described so luridly in what might be called a seventeenth-century example of sick humour:

> I'th' next mans face Another spues,
> Who doth, with nimble Repartee, retort
>   His own, and his Assailants juice,
>   And so returns him double for't.
>   One with a Horizontal mouth,
>   Discharges up again into the Air,
> Which falls again in Perpendicular;
>   *   *   *
> Nor was this all. The surly Element
>   With Orall Channels not content,
> Reverberates; and downward finds a Vent
>   Which my Nice Muse to tell forbears,
> And begs, for what is past, the pardon of your Ears.[12]

And John Wesley felt tobacco and tea to be more objectionable than wine; it was spirits the early methodists had to avoid buying or selling.[13]

Even the formidable Thomas Trotter, the grossly underpaid physician to his Majesty's fleet, a pioneer of anti-scurvy treatment and author of a book of poems entitled *Sea Weeds* (1829), who was personally responsible for the shutting down of two hundred gin shops at Plymouth, and who attributed to drunkenness a list of ailments including apoplexy, palsy, epilepsy, hysterics, convulsions, bad dreams, brain fever, rheumatism, pleurisy, gastritis, enteritis, ophthalmia, carbuncles, jaundice, indigestion, dropsy, emaciation, palpitation, fainting fits, diabetes, lockjaw, ulcers, madness, melancholy, impotency, and abolition of the sexual appetite ('the sot', *pace* the author of *The Drunkard's Character*, 'loses all feelings of love'[14])—even Trotter admitted that a healthy man might need wine when he arrived at the age of forty.[15] A generation later a movement arose which regarded any such admission as totally impermissible, and one single noggin of the lightest of light ales as a fatal step to 'vice, crime, poverty, suffering, disease, and mortality'.[16]

13

INTEMPERATE TEMPERANCE

The first known total abstinence pledge was taken in 1637 by the Reverend Robert Bolton, a Northamptonshire vicar. From that day forward to the end of his life, he wrote on the blank leaf of an old Bible, he would never drink a health, nor drink a carouse, in a glass, cup, bowl, or other drinking instrument whatever, 'except the necessity of nature do require it'. Neither king nor friend, neither all the gold in the world nor an angel from heaven ('who I know will never attempt it'), would ever persuade him to do so.[1] In 1809 the Reverend William Cowherd, a convert from the Church of England to the mystical doctrines of Swedenborg, made total abstinence from all intoxicating liquors a condition of membership of his Bible Christian Church in Salford, in which non-alcoholic wine alone was used at the Lord's supper. After compiling a gigantic book consisting of 6,144 numbered articles illustrating Bible truths,[2] Cowherd died at fifty-four of a disease induced by too close application to study and want of exercise.[3] One of his supporters, the cotton magnate Joseph Brotherton, later M.P. for Salford, was the author of the first total abstinence tract, in which he declared drinking to be the root of almost every evil in society.[4]

Despite these efforts, and despite the formation of an Abstinence Society in Skibbereen, County Cork, in 1817, the real history of the British temperance movement does not begin until 1829. In the summer of that year a Belfast professor of theology named John Edgar launched an anti-spirits campaign by opening his parlour window and emptying into the gutter his stock of fine old malt whiskey. Then he sat down and wrote a letter to the local Press; but the editor of the Belfast *Guardian* refused to print it, on the ground that the professor was clearly demented. A few months later, twelve enthusiasts in Greenock were signing a pledge to abstain from drinking for two years.[5] By the end of 1830 there were about a hundred temperance societies in Scotland, with about 15,000 members; within six months thirty such societies had been formed in England, people rushing into them 'without thought',[6] but with great enthusiasm.

The movement that was springing up so quickly was still almost exclusively a movement for moderation, not for total abstinence. The emphasis was on not drinking spirits; most of the initial reformers had no objection to the moderate use of beer or wine. Indeed, a brewery was built in Belfast as part of the early temperance campaign there. Far from being bigoted, the temperance reformers were trying to reduce the harm caused by excessive drinking of cheap and often adulterated spirits by men, women, and children. Between 1818 and 1830 the consumption of spirits had doubled; and in ninety-eight trades there were three hundred different drinking usages, virtually compulsory, which encouraged hard drinking among workmen.[7] But the great demerit of the temperance movement was that it largely ignored the social causes of drunkenness. A young German, resident in Manchester in the early eighteen-forties, wrote:

> The working-man comes from his work tired, exhausted, finds his home comfortless, damp, dirty, repulsive; he has urgent need of recreation, he *must* have something to make work worth his trouble, to make the prospect of the next day endurable. . . . His enfeebled frame, weakened by bad air and bad food, violently demands some external stimulus; his social need can be gratified only in the public-house, he has absolutely no other place where he can meet his friends. How can he be expected to resist the temptation? It is morally and physically inevitable that, under such circumstances, a very large number of working-men should fall into intemperance. . . . Drunkenness has here ceased to be a vice, for which the vicious can be held responsible; . . . They who have degraded the working-man to a mere object have the responsibility to bear.[8]

None of the multitude of tracts, pamphlets, and books that the temperance reformers were producing at the same time shows anything approaching this insight.

The total abstinence trend which by 1838, after severe conflict, had substantially captured the English temperance movement, is generally supposed to have begun in Preston. It was there that the kind-hearted cheesemonger[9] Joseph Livesey drew up the pledge—'We agree to *abstain* from all liquors of an *intoxicating quality*, whether ale, porter, wine or ardent spirits, except as medicine'[10]—said to have been signed by the celebrated Seven Men of Preston in 1832. Yet, according to a historian concerned to prove that the first English total abstinence society was formed, not in Preston in 1832, but in Warrington in 1830, most of the traditional story is pure romance: the seven never signed any pledge drawn up together, and two of them later admitted that before long they had gone back on the bottle.[11] And in fact none of them, except Livesey and perhaps one other, was of any note, nor did they form a Society, or even a Committee, for the Promotion of Total Abstinence.[12] The real origins of the total abstinence trend are also clouded by the later desire on the part of some of its founders each to put himself forward as the most prominent pioneer of all, and by their not altogether unusual conviction that they had been selected as the special agents of divine providence.[13] Livesey himself was known to his admirers as 'the father of the Reform'. And he was unquestionably the most dynamic personality among these pioneers. For some years he wrote and published, practically single-handed, a monthly paper with the resounding title: *The Moral Reformer, and Protestor against the Vices, Abuses, and Corruptions of the Age* (1831–33). He opened, in 1833, the first temperance hotel, and next year founded the first total abstinence magazine, *The Preston Temperance Advocate* (1834–37). When giving his famous lecture on malt liquor, which made a great many converts, it was his custom to set fire to about four ounces of proof spirit that he had extracted from a quart of the best ale; the blaze was quite impressive. Prostrated with rheumatic fever, and told by his doctor that his only hope of recovery was to drink brandy, he answered: 'I WILL NOT DRINK THE STUFF. . . . If I am to die, *I will die now*.'[14] He lived, however, without the aid of brandy, to the age of ninety.

If the origins of teetotalism are confused, the origin of the word 'teetotal' is no less so. One authority attributes it to the secretary of an American temperance society, who is supposed to have put a 'T' after the names of those taking the total abstinence pledge.[15] Others, including the *OED*, prefer Livesey's explanation—that a working-man named Dicky Turner told a meeting in 1833: 'I'll have nowt to do with this moderation botheration pledge; I'll be reet down out-and-out tee-tee-total for ever and ever.'[16] Turner, whose great gift was summoning open-air meetings with a rattle, had a markedly individual touch with language. One of his long-remembered utterances was: 'We will go with our axes on our shoulders, and plough up the great deep, and the ship of Temperance shall sail gallantly over the land.'[17]

The total abstinence movement sailed still more rapidly over the land than the original temperance movement had done. In 1834 Lancashire and Yorkshire were—to add one further metaphor—on fire with teetotalism. In the Preston area alone there were seventy-seven regular public speakers; missionaries were sent to other places; at what were later known as 'experience meetings', reformed drunkards held forth in the Preston Cock-pit for five successive nights; and a door-to-door canvass of the intemperate was undertaken, the town being divided into twenty-eight districts, each under a 'captain'. The good people of Preston became ashamed to be seen fetching ale; women would carry their jugs under their aprons.[18]

Though their president was an earl, the pioneers of teetotalism were mostly manual workers,[19] many of whom appeared to the moderates as men of coarse minds and little character, not above using abusive language about their opponents within the movement, making violent personal charges against brewers and publicans, and retailing obscene anecdotes about the effects of drunkenness.[20] The moderates alleged that teetotallers substituted opium and laudanum for alcohol, and that their soirées pandered to the lowest tastes.[21] When Livesey visited London in 1834 to lecture, the aged porter employed by the British and Foreign Temperance Society was threatened with dismissal if he gave any help to this Preston heretic.[22]

It was not long before divisions arose within the ranks of the tee-totallers themselves over the nature of the total abstinence pledge. There was a 'short' pledge and a 'long' one: the former entailed total personal abstinence; the latter added an obligation to refrain from selling, giving, or offering intoxicants to others.[23] (Still more extreme was the Independent Order of Horebites, whose members pledged themselves to drink only water.) It would be a tedious task to list the various societies that arose, split, and were amalgamated, and still more tedious to enumerate their many newspapers and other periodicals. By the end of the nineteenth century there were thirteen general societies, eight women's organizations, five juvenile associations, seventeen religious societies, four philanthropic institutions, ten legislative bodies, seven trade and sectional societies, and nine orders and friendly societies, all dedicated to the proposition that alcohol was poison.

From the first, the activities of most of these bodies were marked by a combination of aggressiveness and intolerance that struck many besides brewers, publicans, and topers as disagreeable. They forbade the sale of intoxicating drinks on the steam packets they hired for aquatic excursions, and those buying tickets were asked not to bring any; on at least one occasion a bottle was snatched from the hand of a defiant excursionist and flung overboard.[24] The Church of England Temperance Society (formed in 1862), though viewed with some contempt by its more militant rivals, did 'aggressive work' on race-courses, at agricultural shows (where 'stokos', an oatmeal drink flavoured with lemon, was given away to any who would accept it), and among hoppickers (in whose midst there was much 'intemperance and sin', and to whom the Society's missioners gave illustrated addresses with magic lanterns).[25] No less edifying was the employment of informers by the C.E.T.S., which advised its agents to find out the antecedents of applicants for new public-house licences, and to keep observation on the use of public houses by 'disorderly persons' (i.e., whores), so as to discover 'whether they . . . leave with a person of the opposite sex and where they go on leaving. . . . In cases of this description there is generally a good chance of enlisting the help of some one or more residents in the neighbourhood.'[26] Total abstainers never hesitated to prevent the sale of drink when they could do so. Thus when a Miss Ryland gave Cannon Hill Park to the citizens of Birmingham, the deed of grant stipulated that no intoxicating liquors should be sold within its limits. On the estate of the Hon. George Howard, M.P., heir to the earldom of Carlisle, there was a brewhouse that furnished beer for all visitors, including tenants visiting the castle. But the Hon. Mrs Howard signed the pledge; and when her husband succeeded to the title in 1889 he not only shut down the brewhouse, but the public houses on his Yorkshire and Cumberland estates as well, as fast as the leases expired.[27] There were teetotallers who campaigned for the ending of the beer allowance to paupers in workhouses.[28] And at a meeting in North Meols, Lancashire, the spirit distilled from a quart of ale was given to two dogs, one of which died on the spot, the other within thirty-six hours; the experiment was considered worth while, since 'several drunkards signed in consequence'.[29]

The movement attracted its due share of eccentrics. A rich merchant named Edward Thomas used to give free tickets to Bristol fishwives, offering a free feed if they would come and hear him speak. They made so much noise that he would shout from the platform: 'Silence there, you women!'; but they paid little attention. Thomas had only one joke and one recitation. His reply to the question 'What's to become of the barley if the people drink no malt liquor?' was to serve up a large amount of barley pudding. His entertainments were very popular.[30] Another notable orator was the ex-alcoholic John Bartholomew Gough. He used to say, contesting the idea that alcoholic drinks gave one strength, 'If you sit down on a wasps' nest, it will be stimulating but not strengthening.'[31] And there was Thomas Swindlehurst, who styled himself 'King of the Reformed Drunkards', called his wife 'the Queen' and signed his letters 'Thomas Rex'. Many of these ex-alcoholics broke the pledge, and it was 'a matter of deep lamentation' that there were so many backsliders.[32]

Numerous prominent men, alive and dead, were claimed as total abstainers, or, at least, enemies of drinking: John the Baptist and Benjamin Franklin, John Locke and John Milton, Newton and Dr Johnson, Shakespeare and Burns, the Duke of Wellington and Sir Henry Havelock (the hero of Lucknow), David Livingstone (who nevertheless was admitted to take brandy occasionally as medicine), Samuel Plimsoll, Garibaldi, and Blondin. It was Thomas Cook who, in 1840, started the *Children's Temperance Magazine*. The teetotallers were not gratified by the royal family's refusal to join this illustrious company. A 'painful impression' was created in 1848 when the young Queen drank some whisky during a royal visit to a distillery;[33] two hundred memorials were addressed to the Prince of Wales in 1877 when he agreed to preside at the jubilee dinner of the Licensed Victuallers' Asylum; on ascending the throne, he refused to declare publicly that his health could be as loyally drunk in water as in wine.[34]

The propagandists of teetotalism painted alcohol in one shade only: black. There was nothing good to be said for it. It was a subtle poison curling through the veins,[35] a poisoning conqueror[36] which *must* do harm, since water was the only fluid suitable for drinking.[37] Intoxicating liquors sapped sobriety, diminished industry, consumed wealth, ruined health, weakened intelligence, corrupted morality, and prevented the means of religion from doing their appointed work.[38] In a word, they let the devil into the soul;[39] and the physician who wrote this no doubt believed it to be literally true, for he was the author of *A Scientific Justification of Miracles and Demoniacal Possession* (1908).

Half the diseases were caused by alcohol;[40] at least a third of the nation's lunatics owed their sad condition to drink;[41] probably all who drank alcohol at all died earlier than they otherwise would.[42] It was frequently alleged that 60,000 persons died annually in the United Kingdom through the effects of drinking, but the basis of this calculation was never made clear. Drink was held to be one of the main causes of crime.[43] Under the effects of drink, men's worst passions were inflamed, and they committed crimes so dreadful that they could never be told; but for drink, nine-tenths of the prisons might be closed.[44] Public houses were 'the starting chair for the gallows';[45] their atmosphere consisted of 'stale tobacco smoke, spirit, lemon, and saw-dust fumes, blasphemy, lies, obscenity, music, singing, jabbering, the wild laugh of despair, and other ingredients'.[46] One reverend gentleman, who entered a public house in the Whitechapel Road to see for himself what went on in such places, objected, not only to 'the language uttered' and 'the atmosphere breathed', but also to the 'hilarity indulged in'.[47] There were even attacks on inn signs. The Red Lion? 'Strong drink is a Lion [which] has killed millions.' The Angel? 'If you must have an Angel, let him be a fallen one.' Suggested substitutes were: 'The Ruined Daughter', 'The Handcuff, the Jail and the Transport Ship', 'The Murderer and Gallows Tree', and 'The Dying Drunkard'.[48]

But the teetotallers reserved their fiercest strictures for the practice and practitioners of moderate drinking. A Wigan minister wrote that moderate drinking was the chief cause of intoxication, adding: 'Our most immoral authors have penned their worst passages when they were "warm with wine" '.[49] And a Manchester pamphleteer argued that it was as absurd to speak of the 'temperate' or 'moderate' use of alcoholic drinks as it would be for a man to plead he was a temperate liar or a moderate thief. Since alcohol was a virulent brain poison, total abstinence from the dietetic use of alcoholic drinks in every shape, form, and quality was the only logical temperance and moderation in regard to them.[50]

Efforts made to prevent the use of alcohol in the treatment of disease included the formation of a British Medical Temperance Association in 1876; suggested medical substitutes for alcohol included nitroglycerine.[51] For the healthy, many less explosive non-alcoholic drinks were suggested: a drink made of boiling water and oatmeal; one made of boiling water, rhubarb, and ginger; buttermilk and water; fig and apple water; toast water; and cold tea.[52] There was a recipe for making bread without yeast.[53] Some temperance drinks contained such substances as liquid ammonia, ether, chloroform, phosphoric acid, and acids made by treating calcined bones with sulphuric acid. Others, including certain 'non-alcoholic' wines and cordials, as well as stone ginger beer, were found to have a pretty high alcoholic content.[54]

Special attention was paid to two sections of the population: women and children. Unmarried female teetotallers used to promise that they would not accept the addresses of any man who would not sign the total abstinence pledge, married ones that they would use 'affectionate' means to influence their husbands to sign it.[55] There was opposition to the employment of women as barmaids: if a girl retained her purity behind the bar of a public house it must be in spite of the frightful temptations with which she was surrounded.[56] For juvenile abstainers a Band of Hope was first formed in Leeds in 1847, when twelve-year-old George Mitchell, his nine-year-old brother and 198 other children signed a pledge 'to abstain from all Intoxicating Liquors, and from Tobacco in all its forms'.[57] The Band of Hope Union (formed in 1855) employed lecturers to visit schools and give 'scientific temperance lectures',[58] demonstrating to the pupils the poisonous nature and effects of alcoholic drinks by means of painted anatomical diagrams and chemical experiments. A course of instruction for Band of Hope children under sixteen, published in 1900, gave this 'blackboard summary' of 'The History of Drinking in England':

BRITONS⎫
ROMANS ⎬ OCCASIONALLY INTEMPERATE

SAXONS ⎫
DANES ⎬ GREAT DRINKERS

NORMANS: COPIED ENGLISH INTEMPERANCE
PLANTAGENETS: LIVED LUXURIOUSLY
TUDORS: INTEMPERANCE INCREASED
STUARTS: WILD EXCESSES
HANOVERIANS: DRUNKENNESS BECAME A NATIONAL VICE[59]

The work of the Bands of Hope produced children who, in a later age, might have been thought priggish. A small girl who had signed the pledge was sent with sixpence for a quart of ale. Reminded that according to her pledge she was neither to touch, taste, nor handle, she took back to her mother a quart of treacle beer and fivepence in copper.[60] A boy of six told his grandmother, who drank porter with her meals, 'Grandmamma, I cannot eat my dinner with that abominable stuff upon the table.'[61] To at least one opponent of teetotalism there was something objectionable in pledging children as to what they should do in any matter when they came of age; it was quite enough, he thought, for parents or guardians to teach a child, without interfering with its future liberty as a man.[62]

An extraordinary mass upsurge of the total abstinence movement came in the early eighties when the Gospel Temperance, or Blue Ribbon, movement spread from the U.S.A. to Britain. Its leading spokesman here was the thirty-six-year-old American, Richard Booth, who, from his arrival in England in August 1880 till his health collapsed in November 1882, visited fifty towns and was responsible for over 600,000 people signing the pledge. The revivalist atmosphere that Booth brought with him is well caught in this contemporary description of a typical Gospel Temperance meeting:

> Young America . . . throws off his coat . . . and . . . walks excitedly up and down the platform, beating time with his hands, perhaps slapping a rheumatic old clergyman upon the back, as he exclaims 'What do you think of it now, brother?' . . . The clapping of hands is succeeded by the stamping of feet, and shouts of joy seem to be crowning the demonstration, when Mr Booth's keen eye descries a young woman waving a white handkerchief, far away towards the back of the hall. He fumbles in his coat pocket for his own, and can't find it. Anybody else's will answer as well, so he helps himself—perhaps takes the Chairman's, and waving it high above his head, signals for the whole congregation to do likewise. Then the wave of enthusiasm rolls higher and higher and the sea of heads becomes capped as though with white-crested breakers. Tears are brought to the Chairman's eyes. . . . The audience laugh and cry. . . . No one is allowed to speak after Mr Booth . . . has 'got through'. Without a break, he calls for 'the kingly men and queenly women'. 'Won't you come tonight, men?' he pleadingly says, and instantly a dozen working men are seen elbowing their way through the crowd. Hundreds follow, whilst ladies and gentlemen go out in search of wavering ones. All this time Mr Booth is pacing to and

fro the platform, and the choir is singing half-way through the hymn-book. . . . Still the ladies are pinning the Blue Ribbon to the coats of con-verts. Now and then a cheer breaks forth as an old 'tippler' presses forward to register his promise.

Thirty policemen were needed to clear a way for Booth to his coach. After tasting 'a morsel' of food he retired, 'sometimes to toss nervously upon his bed, at others, to address great Temperance meetings in dreamland'.[63]

Gladstone is said to have remarked that the Blue Ribbon movement was the only temperance movement that commanded his implicit confidence.[64]

It was not hard to poke fun at the teetotallers. They were called 'ghostly', 'white', and 'thin', or 'milk-and-water men', or, more learnedly, Manicheans. Opponents mocked their processions, their bands that played wretchedly out of tune,[65] their questionable hymns,[66] their 'hunted and overdone' appearance, their revelling in fat, oil and sweets for the want of a little alcohol at mealtimes, their well-known intemperance in the use of tea and coffee.[67] Some anti-teetotallers vigorously counter-attacked the 'deleterious narcotic' tea, which contained a poison so deadly that one could distil from it an essential oil five drops of which would kill a full-grown dog in a few minutes.[68] Others argued that unnatural abstinence was the parent of unnatural excess: that the unnatural restriction of one appetite would prove the strongest incentive to the unnatural gratification of others.[69] A piquant comparison was made by a polemic who pointed to a sin more secret and more soul-destroying even than excess of drinking; 'and because it exists, are we all to be warned from childhood to strive after a condition of life which it is not given for everyone to undertake?'[70] (i.e., presu-mably, chastity). Another early argument was the danger of the teetotallers' organizations being utilized by the chartists[71]—though in fact some socialists had been turned out of a teetotal gala in 1840, and their tracts had been torn up.[72]

The main argument heard against teetotalism, however, was that it was unchristian; this view was largely based on the miraculous trans-formation of water into wine by Christ and the use of wine in the Lord's supper. A baptist minister called teetotalism 'a libel on the character of God';[73] another critic asserted that total abstainers dishonoured the

Lord's cup, stirred up pernicious controversies in the Church, and branded drinkers of communion wine as wine-bibbers;[74] while to a third, some teetotal arguments were little, if anything, short of blasphemy, and tantamount to denying the divinity of Christ.[75] Thomas Smeeton, for twelve years a total abstainer, went over to the moderate wing because, as he explained in his *Confessions of a Convert from Teetotalism to Temperance* (1849), teetotalism 'reflects upon the personal character and conduct of the Lord Jesus Christ ... [who] both made wine for others and used it temperately himself'.[76] A year later Smeeton was convicted of embezzlement.

The teetotallers' answer was twofold. First, they denied—usually at some length and with a great show of learning—that wine, when it was referred to approvingly in the Bible, was anything other than the unfermented, and hence non-alcoholic, juice of the grape. When it was referred to disapprovingly, then a fermented and intoxicating liquor was meant, of course! 'Avarice and appetite' had united to per-suade people that Christ made, drank, and gave others to drink, intoxicating liquids; this was the result of the arch-fiend's audacity.[77] The text 'Drink no longer water, but use a little wine for thy stomach's sake, and thine often infirmities' was explained by one teetotal exegete as meaning that the wine was to be rubbed on externally, as a liniment![78] This view that God did not wish men to drink fermented grape-juice (any more than he wished them to eat rotten meat[79]) had to be sustained at all costs, for there were teetotallers who declared that if they thought God had made either malt or grapes for the purpose of yielding an intoxicating liquor, they would never worship him again.[80]

In the second place, the teetotallers advocated the use of unfermented wine at the sacramental table—and the Reverend Francis Beardsall of Manchester actually manufactured and sold a thousand bottles of it annually. The Dean of Rochester viewed this as a presumptuous and profane innovation: 'I verily believe that they ... would have us read that the Good Samaritan poured in oil and water and took the poor wounded Jew to a temperance hotel.'[81] An earlier critic had warned that anyone who drank the unfermented juice of the grape as a beverage should be provided with the medicine proper in the case of an attack of diarrhoea, since the must it contained was a powerful laxative.[82]

The enemies of total abstinence did not confine themselves to verbal opposition. The proprietors of a Shropshire colliery dismissed eighty teetotal miners in 1838; in 1842 the Medical Officer of the Luton Poor Law Union was not re-elected to office because, as a teetotaller, he seldom prescribed intoxicating liquors for his patients. And there was much physical violence, often—or so the total abstainers alleged—fomented by publicans or brewers. In Salisbury in the early eighteen-forties an abstainer was chased through the streets by an angry crowd shouting: 'There goes a teetotaller!' Beer and less intoxicating substances used to be thrown over the speakers; in brewing districts men would bring ale into the meetings and drink it in concert; at Hoddesdon, sparrows were let into a meeting and the speaker was stoned. In Northamptonshire speakers were pelted with dust, rotten eggs, and tin kettles, and their cart was thrown in a village pond. In the west country brickbats and the dead carcasses of animals were thrown, and fights resulted in broken shins and bruised heads. Thomas Whittaker was drummed out of Scarborough, and his effigy was burned on the sands; some years later, however, he became mayor of the town. At Kirkby Lonsdale a brass band was sent to drown the speaker; when the players grew tired the windows of an hotel were thrown open and the hotel-keeper's two daughters played the piano 'with all the vigour they were capable of'.[83]

The total abstainers hit back. In 1842 copies of an anti-teetotal pamphlet were publicly burned in Newlyn, a resolution having been passed 'that the town crier, in the absence of the hangman, should burn the production of [the author's] brainless skull'.[84] At Lewes a publican blew tobacco smoke into a speaker's open mouth, until the speaker, with a swing of his billycock, broke the publican's pipe. Mockers met their match in William Gregson. Given a glass of grog or beer by a jeering opponent, Gregson, his hat and coat front sometimes dripping with rotten eggs, would accept it ('Is this mine?' 'Yes.' 'All of it?' 'Yes.'), say a few words about the liquid, pour it deliberately on the ground, and finally pocket the glass. This last gesture usually enraged the crowds. Successfully defying publicans and even chief constables, Gregson gradually built up a 'museum' of glasses and jugs acquired in this way.[85]

14

FOR SOTS AND TOTS

A catalogue published in 1887 by the National Temperance Publication Depot recorded 64 'standard temperance works', six historical works, 13 statistical works, 27 works on temperance legislation, six school books, three catechisms for juveniles, six 'anecdotal', 28 biographies and autobiographies, eight 'social', 397 story-books (at prices ranging from a penny to six shillings, and including *A Dog's Protest against Intemperance*), 47 'orations, lectures, essays, &c.', 31 series of 'tracts in packets', four series of illustrated tracts, 190 other tracts, 18 leaflets and small tracts, 17 books of poetry, 44 'reciters, readers, &c.', 66 'dialogues, entertainments, &c.', 43 books of 'temperance music, songs, hymns, &c.', nine pledge books, 36 pledge cards, five temperance societies' books, 19 Band of Hope requisites, 26 pieces of Good Templar literature, 27 publications of the Blue Ribbon movement (as well as blue ribbon itself, at 2s. 9d. per piece of 36 yards), 12 publications of the coffee tavern movement, four 'birthday books', six series of illuminated texts, 38 wall papers and placards, 11 health manuals, two annuals, and no fewer than 39 periodicals.[1]

The literary quality of this vast heap of publications was uneven. One of the most readable, most sensational, and most widely circulated of the novels inspired by teetotalism is *Danesbury House* (1860) by Mrs Henry Wood, 4,000 copies of which were sold each year for two decades after its publication. It opens with a drink-fuddled nurse giving poison by mistake to her nine-months-old charge, whose mother, returning home in haste, is soon killed in an accident caused by a gatekeeper's drunkenness. Subsequent events continue this pattern. Though the author was not herself an abstainer, the fate of all her characters seems to depend on the amount they drink. We are left in no doubt that to drink one single glass puts us in great peril, and that only massive exertions can then save us from imps in the bed or some other fairly disagreeable form of destruction. Almost as dramatic is a tale which appeared in the same year, Mrs Clara Lucas Balfour's *The Victim*. The victim is Lucy, who is persuaded by a woman friend to visit the Vulture tavern, where she finds 'young men in troops, almost all engaged in drinking, and its filthy accompaniment, smoking'; they are 'lounging and gazing at the females present, with an expression that no modest woman could endure, without humiliation'. Lucy is soon separated from her friends, whereupon a gentleman wearing a pair of green spectacles over-persuades her to drink a glass of negus. He and his female relative escort her into a conveyance, where she falls asleep. By now an experienced reader of such tales has almost guessed that the person in green spectacles, far from being a gentleman, is a 'hoary libertine'. Lucy's insensible form is taken into a 'guilty abode' tenanted by 'harpies who look on youth and beauty as their prey'. At the crucial moment there is a row of asterisks across the page. Lucy soon dies of brain fever, while the faithless friend who lured her to an 'evening's amusement' goes mad through intemperance and ends up in a private madhouse, beyond hope of recovery.

Most temperance novels were still more thinly disguised tracts, in which chunks of moralizing were put into the mouths of one or more of the characters. Thus in William Gourlay's *Oinosville* (1902) a physician not altogether surprisingly casts a deep silence over a dinner-party that includes half a dozen 'lively girls' when he states very gravely that he would rather see the devil any day than a beautiful woman raising a glass of wine to her lips. Someone has to break the deep silence; at length the doctor himself does so, remarking:

> Alcohol in any shape or form begins at once to undermine the . . . moral character . . . of womanhood. The girl in her late teens . . . who feels on better terms with herself and those around her after her first sip or two of champagne, has already placed her dainty foot on the topmost rung of the ladder that leads to the bottomless pit of the lowest social life.[2]

A little later, fascinating Lizzie Jenkins, the late barmaid at the Royal Hotel, is narrating, with tears in her eyes, the folly she has been guilty of in selling kisses at a shilling apiece in aid of the Indian Famine Fund, a device suggested by the squire's eldest son. Her confidante feels very thankful that Lizzie has been removed from a life that must have ended in her ruin.[3]

Nowadays most temperance stories appear to be written for children. An example is *Shawn in Peril* [*c.* 1948] by Robert Tayler, the present general secretary of the United Kingdom Band of Hope Union. A young woman who is being made to drink 'moonshine' at gun-point throws the contents of a pepper-pot in her captor's face; at the end of the story the villain dies of alcoholic poisoning.

Short plays have always been popular in teetotal circles; they sometimes take the form of a trial of brewers and publicans. But at *The Trial of John & Jane Temperance* [1882] the prosecutors were Sergeant Muddle and Robin Quicktipple, and the prosecution witnesses included Caleb Catchem, a publican, John Soaker, a carpenter, Mrs Slysup, a housewife, and Grab Muchprofit, Esq., a brewer. The defence advocates were Sir Joseph Straightpath and Silas Quickenham, and their witnesses included persons named Freeman, Goodheart, Steadyman, and Everstraight. Fortunately the judge's name was Farsight, and his summing-up left little, if any, doubt that the jury must find the prisoners not guilty of slandering publicans. Allegory was less common, but *An Account of the Drunken Sea* [1877] by A Physician shows that Bunyan did not write in vain. Nothing could exceed the beauty of the Drunken Sea from the beach of Soberland—as far as Point Just-Enough, that is. But beyond the latter lay Tipsy Island (discovered by Noah), the Port of Paphos, the Temple devoted to the Worship of Venus, three sunken rocks called the Horrors, the Liver Sands, Fatuous Fog, and the Mountains of No-Hope. Another curiosity of teetotal prose, standing out even in a genre where eccentricity of presentation is never unexpected, is *Tippling and Temperance* (1890) by Charles Bateman. Every one of its 1,289 words begins with the letter *t*, and 'this terse treatise . . . trenchantly traverses tattling, time-serving table-talkers' temerarious tolerance to the trivial, trifling, truckling toss-pot'.[4]

There was something about teetotalism that turned an uncommonly high proportion of its pledge-takers into versifiers. The most graceful lines on the evils of alcohol appeared in *Punch* in 1843 ('Gin! Gin! a Drop of Gin!/What magnified Monsters circle therein!'[5]) and might, just possibly, have been intended satirically. The movement's own poets preferred the bludgeon to the rapier. They delighted in adapting —not to say parodying—well-known hymns, transforming them into spirited denunciations of spirituous liquors. With a little effort, one can

hear the abstainers' voices raised at the conclusion of their evening
meetings, to the tune of *Babylon is Fallen*:

> Shout aloud, Teetotal choir,
>   Higher still your voices raise;
> See, old Alcohol all on fire,
>   Clap your hands, and fan the blaze.
> Burn the mash-tubs; stave the barrels;
>   Throw the coolers out of doors:
> Drunkenness is falling, to rise no more.
>
> Kidley-winks* must fall for ever
>   At Teetotaler's powerful stand
> Public Houses too must quiver,
>   Landlords' signboards shall come down.
> We shall conquer, we shall conquer,
>   Onward! cry from shore to shore—
> Drunkenness is falling, to rise no more.[6]

Another version has the lines:

> See the poison venders quaking,
> Calling us *tee-total fools*.
> See their splendid hell-holes shaking,
> Since we've found superior schools.[7]

The Great McGonagall of the teetotal movement was unquestionably
the Reverend James Dawson Burns; none other achieved quite the
same combination of daring, banality, and bathos:

> If strong drink I touch not, no stain is on my soul
> From bloodshed or foul crime caused by the toxic bowl;
> This root of thousand plagues I do nothing to nurse,
> But try my best to rid the world from this great curse.[8]

In Dawson Burns's 'The Repentant Father', a daughter goes to a
temperance meeting, and is greeted thus by her father when she advises
him not to touch strong drink:

* Beershops.

147

'Silence, girl!' the father stormed,
　'Will you dare to lecture me?
'What your prating words deserve,
　'You shall very quickly see.'

And again he beat his child—
　Beat her blue and beat her black,—
After which he flung her down
　On her lacerated back.

Repentance follows, however, and

Soon he signed the Temperance pledge,
　And a noble man he grew,
And no happier home than his
　Can be seen the country through.[9]

The results of drinking were frequently described in such terms as these:

Little drops of porter,
　Frequent sips of stout,
Make the breathing shorter,
　Cultivate the gout.[10]

And the alternative?

Oh, water for me! bright water for me!
And wine for the tremulous debauchee!
It cooleth the brow, it cooleth the brain;
It maketh the faint one strong again.

* * *

My hand is steady, my eye is true,
For I, like the flowers, drink nought but dew.[11]

A large number of teetotal poems were written about children, or addressed to children, or designed for recitation by children to predominantly adult audiences. As Dawson Burns put it:

Each little child a hero may be,
　And strike with the Temperance spear;
And when the Drink-dragon is wounded to death,
　All good men will raise a grand cheer.[12]

'What Can Little Children Do?' asked Hettie M. Hawkins:

> What can little children do
>> For the Temperance Band?
> Mother says we can all work
>> Voice, and feet and hand.
>
> I can tell the other ones
>> Not to touch the drink;
> I can sing you pretty songs
>> With my voice, I think.[13]

T. H. Evans's 'I'm Nothing But a Tiny Tot' was written for recitation by a very small girl:

> Although I'm but a tiny tot,
>> (I hope you all can hear,)
> An 'ittle pedge tard I have dot,
>> I drink no wine nor beer.
>
> Before my head was high enough
>> To reach the window ledge,
> My mother took my hand in hers,
>> And helped me sign the pedge.
>
> But though I'm such an 'ittle mite—
>> You'll hardly think it true—
> I've dot six lovely darling dolls,
>> And they're teetot'lers too.
>
>   *   *   *
>
> If there are any here to-night,
>> Who're fond of beer and wine,
> Pray do what I should *make* you do,
>> Were you a doll of mine.[14]

It was not uncommon for the tracts that printed verses of this kind to carry also advertisements for cocoa.

Each generation of Band of Hope members gets the verse its mentors think it deserves. But the basic treatment changes little, the basic idea not at all:

Dump him in the varnish;
Pop him in the dye;
Who wants alcohol in drinks?
Not I ! Not I ! Not I ![15]

Of a rather different character from most of the literature we have been glancing at, and from most of the drawings in the teetotalist magazines, were the temperance pictures of the caricaturist George Cruickshank. His *Worship of Bacchus* is a vast canvas on which a thousand figures demonstrate the drinking habits of all classes, showing how drinking leads to the workhouse, to prison, to the madhouse, and to the gallows. Queen Victoria had the picture taken to Windsor Castle, where the artist himself explained it to her. A public appeal raised £1,260, and *The Worship of Bacchus* was presented to the nation.

15

THE BRITISH PROHIBITIONISTS

Some of the British teetotallers were greatly impressed by the thorough-going law, enacted in 1851 by the American state of Maine, prohibiting the sale of alcoholic drinks. So in 1853 they formed the United Kingdom Alliance, with the aim of procuring 'the Total and Immediate Legislative Suppression of the Traffic in all Intoxicating Liquors as Beverages'.[1] In other words, a Maine Law for Britain.

The United Kingdom Alliance owed its establishment above all to the initiative of the Manchester cotton manufacturer and quaker, Nathaniel Card. Its first president was the naturalist and landowner Sir Walter Trevelyan, who was noted both for his herd of short-horned cattle and for his temerity in denouncing, at a banquet in honour of a former Home Secretary, the custom of drinking toasts. Its first secretary was Samuel ('Jumbo') Pope, a barrister who afterwards became first Recorder of Bolton. And its parliamentary spokesman (and president from 1879 to 1906) was Sir Wilfrid Lawson, 'the apostle of temperance', who, referring to a popular description of alcohol as 'the devil in solution', once said that the object of temperance reformers was to bring the devil into dissolution;[2] this kind of thing earned him his other sobriquet, 'the witty baronet'. His youth had been spent in hunting, shooting, fishing, and mixed reading; it was presumably the latter occupation that led him to the view that alcohol ought to be restricted to the chemist's shelf along with opium and other poisons.[3] Nevertheless he once attacked a sorbet with vigorous appreciation, despite its being so heavily charged with kirsch that it gave those who ate it a headache; he had been told that the flavour was syrup.[4]

The first meeting of the new organization, having listened to papers on 'The Delusion of the Drinking System', 'The Liquor Traffic:

Immoral and Indefensible', and 'The Necessity of a Law to Prohibit the Liquor Traffic, Deduced from the Actual State of the Public-House System in Cornwall', resolved to wage 'uncompromising war' on the traffic,[5] whose legislative suppression 'would be highly conducive to the development of a progressive civilization'.[6]

The emergence of the United Kingdom Alliance was viewed with mixed feelings by many veterans of teetotalism. They had traditionally relied on the method of moral suasion to achieve their objective. Here was a movement which turned its back on that time-honoured, if unsuccessful, method, adopting instead the demand for legislative suppression—and, seemingly paradoxically, encouraging non-abstainers to participate in its agitation. This was intended to forestall the charge that the Alliance was a mere teetotal faction. But many teetotallers failed to see how persons who themselves drank could possibly campaign against the sale of drink. What kind of a movement was it, some of whose leaders were not willing to impose on themselves the law they were asking Parliament to impose on the nation? The National Temperance League, now the principal teetotal organization, was afraid that the Alliance policy of concentrating on the political issue would divert attention from the need to convert public opinion to the wisdom of total abstinence.[7]

Matters came to a head in 1857, when the pioneer teetotaller Joseph Livesey broke with the Alliance because it had put into cold storage its original demand for an immediate nation-wide Maine Law for Britain, bringing forward instead a short-term, less utopian demand—for a 'Permissive Bill', under which the owners and occupiers of property in any locality, by a two-thirds majority, would be able to prevent the granting of public-house licences in that locality (an idea later to be known as 'local option', later still as 'local veto'). Livesey, who did not make his break with the Alliance public until 1861, thought that a Permissive Bill could not be obtained; if it did become law it would do more harm than good; and in any case the agitation for such a Bill was diverting the attention of temperance reformers from other measures, more likely to be carried and of far more practical importance.[8] Livesey also regretted the lack of out and out defence of personal abstinence in the Alliance's publications, and its failure, after some eight years, to introduce a Bill embodying any phase of a Maine Law.[9] The Alliance replied, characteristically, with an ultimatum which made the break permanent. It suggested that its opponents within the temperance movement had dishonourable motives; their flag was lowered; their principles, almost refined away. But 'our truth, and right, and zeal . . . must conquer'.[10]

The ill feeling between the Alliance and the old guard was reflected in a violent quarrel between Dr F. R. Lees, a somewhat pedantic Alliance lecturer, and the ex-alcoholic turned total abstinence lecturer J. B. Gough. Gough had greatly angered Lees and the Alliance by a letter written from America to an English friend in 1856, during a visit to England by Neal Dow, the author of the Maine Law.[11] The cause in the U.S.A., Gough had written, was in a depressed state; the Maine Law was a dead letter everywhere: 'more liquor sold than I ever knew before, in Massachusetts,—and in the other States it is about as bad'.[12] This letter was in due course published, and its publication did no visible good, either to the English prohibitionist cause in general, or to Dow's speaking tour in particular. Lees was soon writing, in a private letter, that Gough had 'been often seen narcotically and helplessly *intoxicated*' and that he was 'as rank a hypocrite, and as wicked a man, as breathes in the Queen's dominions'.[13] This letter, too, rapidly became public property, and Gough sued Lees for libel, testifying that since being given a glass of drugged soda-water in 1845—he woke up in a brothel—he had never tasted spirituous liquors of any kind; and that he had never bought or eaten opium in any form, except on the occasion, before he signed the pledge, when he contemplated suicide by swallowing laudanum. Lees's counsel repudiated his client's allegations and consented to a verdict for the plaintiff —a course which Lees disavowed a day or two later. 'This unpleasant affair . . . had a very damaging effect upon the movement.'[14]

These internecine exercises did not diminish the energy with which Sir Wilfrid Lawson prosecuted the Alliance's battle in Parliament. But, for the most part, he was successful only in attracting alliterative invective. He was called a 'confiscating molly coddle', a 'peregrinating pump handle', 'that old cracked teapot', a 'maudlin mountebank', a 'washed out water party', a 'pop bottle pump orator', and 'the apostle of slops'.[15] His local option Bill, rejected by 294 votes to 37 in 1864, was again defeated in 1869, 1871, 1872, 1873, and 1874. Lesser men might have been daunted; Lawson, when not pressing the merits of local option in lengthy speeches—one covered nearly ten pages of

Hansard—was waging war on the proposal to make Derby Day a holiday and drawing attention to the illegality of the sale of intoxicating liquors within the Commons precincts.[16] This did not make him the most popular figure in the House—or in the country; at one stage his constituents unseated him for three years.

The brains behind the Alliance's parliamentary agitation was its electoral and parliamentary agent, the noted lobbyist and orator James H. Raper. It was to him that prohibitionist M.P.s used to run from the Commons chamber to take down a memorandum from his dictation; running back, they would 'shoot off the powder with which he [had] supplied them'. Alliance supporters were told that Raper took a far greater share in debates than most of them imagined, and that M.P.s, observing that his presence in the lobby not seldom heralded a new burst of anti-drink activity, called him 'the stormy petrel'.[17] One of Raper's rhetorical devices on the public platform was to hold up a sovereign and offer it to anyone who could give him the name of a magistrate who had voted to license a public house next to his own door. After the offer had been repeated several hundred times the sovereign was finally claimed, somewhere in Wales.[18]

Unable to push through its own Bill, the Alliance—though it after-wards always denied with vehemence that it had done so—managed in 1871 to wreck one that in its eyes did not go far enough, even though this Bill did embody a comprehensive revision of the licensing code, and did apply the principle of the ratepayers' veto.[19] A later triumph was the defeat, in 1888 and 1890, of proposals for the compensation of publicans who were refused the renewal of their licences.

Notwithstanding vigorous criticism within the Alliance's own ranks, its General Council decided in 1872 to 'force the pace in the localities' by declaring for 'direct action' in parliamentary elections. This signified support for, and, where necessary, sponsorship of, any candidate favourable to the Permissive Bill, irrespective of party. Eighteen years later 'direct popular veto' was incorporated into the programme of the Liberal Party. Twice in the nineties Liberal governments intro-duced local veto Bills; twice these Bills were unsuccessful. Over a million signatures were collected to petitions against the first one; the second helped to bring about the fall of the Liberals in the 1895 general election. 'In this Election', commented Lawson, 'Drink swept the country more thoroughly than it had ever done before.'[20]

At last, in 1906, a local veto resolution was passed by the Commons, with a majority of 227. Its sponsor was the United Kingdom Alliance's new president, Leif Jones (known to anti-teetotallers as 'T-Leif' Jones). Much to the Liberals' chagrin, however, the Licensing Bill of 1908, incorporating the principle of local option, was thrown out by the House of Lords.

In the nature of things, the Alliance could never hope to win mass support. It threatened too many people with too much thirst. It put travellers' backs up by trying to stop the sale of alcoholic drinks at railway stations. It annoyed the patrons of music-halls by trying to stop the sale of drink at those establishments too. By organizing, immediately before licensing meetings, petitions to magistrates objecting to the issue of additional licences, it offended all who did not see why their rational use of an article should be interfered with simply because there were some who would not, or could not, use it in moderation. As for the publicans, they were traduced year after year, in terms exemplified by a turn-of-the-century pictorial placard showing a landlady, a potboy, 'a degraded drunkard, and a woman with a baby in her arms, and a child at her side. . . . Hung up in shops and halls, or posted on walls or other public places, this Picture [was] sure to attract observation, and give an impressive lesson on the nature and effects of the liquor traffic'. The legend read:

LANDLADY : Turn that drunken rascal out, Jim, or he'll be getting us into trouble.

POTBOY : Please, ma'am, he's got fourpence left.

LANDLADY : Oh! has he? Then ask the gentleman what he'll have to drink.[21]

The brewers and publicans who smarted under this kind of attack were blamed, no doubt justly, for the flour thrown over Bishop Temple and Sir Wilfrid Lawson at Exeter in 1872, and for the yells, catcalls, songs, and horn-blowing which not infrequently broke up Alliance meetings.

16

PUSSYFOOTS WITHOUT CLAWS

Not many people have had the experience of turning, almost overnight, from a national bogy man into something approaching a popular hero. That was what happened to William Eugene ('Pussyfoot') Johnson, leader of the American Anti-Saloon League, when he visited England in 1919 to explain how the U.S.A. had secured national prohibition, and to campaign for Britain to follow the Americans' 'dry' example.

'Pussyfoot' was so nicknamed because of the furtive methods he had used as a special agent in the campaign against liquor smuggling into Indian reservations. In one raid alone he had seized 25,000 bottles of bootleg liquor and dumped them in the Arkansas river. In his opinion the defeat of the British 'wets' was merely a matter of time; it would, he thought, take a decade or so.

When he landed here, following in the footsteps of Dow and Booth, 'Pussyfoot' gave an interview to the *Daily Mail*. The purpose of his visit, he revealed, was to teach the British prohibitionist organizations how to get this country 'dry'. Asked if he was going to butt in on the British elections, he replied, with a candour that sent a thrill of horror through the land: 'Why, yes. Our intelligence service will keep us informed as to when a district is possible, and down we'll send our campaigners. We'll bill the place and buy space in the local newspapers, and show films at the kinemas and give addresses.'[1] And he mentioned the possibility of buying a newspaper in England for propaganda purposes.

Before long, public houses had on their walls a cartoon showing a person whose nose stretched from the United States into John Bull's private premises. It was captioned: 'Pussyfoot Nosey Parker from across the sea. Dollars for dirty work in England. Shall he Pro-boss-us?' Slightly better jokes were told on the music-hall stage. The word 'pussyfoot', as a new synonym for prohibitionist, was in everyone's mouth.

In 1919 a public debate was arranged in London between 'Pussy-foot' and an opponent of prohibition for Britain. About 2,000 students marched on the hall. Having drowned the beginning of Johnson's speech with their singing, they proceeded to smother the speaker him-self with flour. Picked men had been given the task of seizing him; as they carried out his flour-covered form one woman shouted: 'You scoundrels! You cowards! I wish I were a man; I would show you what I would do with you!' At King's College a bottle of Bass was offered to 'Pussyfoot'; he refused to drink, so it was poured over him in a 'christening'. He was then borne along the Strand in a procession headed by a tin trumpet band, with shouts of 'We've got Pussyfoot!' and an assortment of banners, some saying 'Mr Pussyfoot, miaow-wow!', others:

> Pussyfoot, Pussyfoot, why are we here?
> We've come to prevent you from stopping our beer.
> Pussyfoot, Pussyfoot, there'll be a big riot.
> We drink in pubs, but you on the quiet.

Behind the banners, high over the demonstrators' heads, came 'Pussy-foot', smiling and bowing. Near Oxford Circus a force of fifty police-men managed to cut off the front of the procession, and fought the students for ten minutes before rescuing Johnson. At the very moment of the rescue, a hard missile hit him in the right eye, dislocating the lens. 'Pussyfoot' was taken off in a commandeered military vehicle. Though he was in great pain, he pulled a handful of cigars out of his pocket and asked that they be given to his rescuers.

His good sportsmanship, even after his eye was removed in hospital, swiftly endeared him to the public that had earlier been so hostile. On his return to America he made a gramophone record called 'What I See with My Blind Eye', in which he told of the 'dry' world he looked forward to. But the British people's admiration for his courage and cheerfulness—and the students' regret that their rag had got out of hand—did not extend to admiration for his principles.[2] Still another American visitor, Dr Armor, of the Women's Christian Temperance Union (known to her friends as 'Joan of Arc', to others as 'Matchless Mary'), came and went without persuading Britain to go 'dry'.

And yet, from time to time during the first world war, it had looked as though the battle for prohibition in this country was on the verge of success. The King had let it be known that no alcoholic beverages would be served in the royal household for the duration of the war, and Lord Kitchener had followed his example. Over two million adults had signed a petition, presented to Asquith by Leif Jones of the United Kingdom Alliance, calling for the prohibition of the liquor trade until the end of the post-war demobilization. Lloyd George had declared that drink was doing us more damage than all the German submarines put together.[3] The teetotalist agitators had seized on this statement to attack dockers, sailors, and firemen, whose drinking excesses were alleged to be causing serious delay of shipping. A series of near-hysterical booklets by Arthur Mee, the compiler of educational books for children, had besmirched the reputation of soldiers and soldiers' wives, alleging that alcohol was being used as a pro-German poison in the army, and asking who was the degenerate in the War Office that was forcing drink into army camps. The Army Council had quickly banned the export of *Defeat or Victory?* (1917) by Mee and J. Stuart Holden; and G. K. Chesterton had asserted testily that the 'wicked fire-water' fuss made about the rum ration served on certain occasions to British troops in the trenches was neither more nor less than stealing medicine from a sick soldier.[4] In 1916 there had come into existence the Strength of Britain Movement, a small, select circle of business men,[5] which aimed at getting people to follow the example of the King and Kitchener. Mee had soon resigned from it, on the ground that the Movement's committee was not keeping faith with the public, and was no longer serving the cause for which it had collected very considerable funds.[6] The Strength of Britain Movement was revived after the war as a limited liability company, and was eventually incorporated into the National Commercial Temperance League (founded 1891), whose objects included the promotion of total abstinence among professional and business men, propaganda on total abstinence as a business asset, and sociability without liquor.

No little alarm was caused to earnest teetotallers in the twenties by the popularity of an organization known as the Ancient Order of Froth Blowers. Founded by a London ex-service man, this Order promoted nonsensical rituals among the bibulous in order to raise money for charity. Drinkers were asked: 'Do you gollop your beer with zest?' Whoever answered in the affirmative, and paid five shillings for life membership, was unanimously elected a member of the Order, which enjoined a rate of consumption of three gulps to the pint, fourteen to the gallon. The Order's motto was 'Lubrication in Moderation'.[7] A Bradford Primitive Methodist minister, the Reverend Sam Rowley, took up his pen to expose the Froth Blowers, whose Order he denounced as a subtle method of beer propaganda in the guise of charity. It was all very well to be cheery, but decidedly bad to be beery. And in an A.O.F.B. booklet of some sixty-six pages, he found that the hallmark of beer, either by sign, symbol, or word, was stamped on almost every page.[8] The minister took special exception to a passage which said: 'Be damned to all Brachistocephalic Pussyfoot horn-swogglers from overseas . . . T.T.'s and M.P.'s and J.P.'s, and not excluding nosey parkers, mock religious busy-bodies, and suburban fool-hens, all of which are structurally of solid bone from the chin up'.[9] No society, wrote Rowley, could raise the standard of life, even for 'Wee Waifs' (the objects of its charitable efforts), by standard barrels of beer. The Froth Blowers were in danger of dragging down the sacred cause of Charity to the low levels of the beer barrel and the betting ring.[10] This explosion of wrath in Bradford was not heeded; the Froth Blowers went on blowing froth, quaffing beer, displaying emblematic sleeve-links, and collecting for charity, all in their own vigorous, inelegant, and excruciatingly vulgar style.

For by now the pussyfoots of Britain had few, if any, claws left. This was proved by the total failure of a Liquor Traffic Prohibition Bill introduced in 1923 and 1931 by Dundee's prohibitionist M.P., Edwin Scrymgeour. To be sure, an Act of 1923 did make it impossible for young people under eighteen to buy alcoholic drink in a public house, and for children under sixteen to have intoxicants with restaurant meals.[11] But this was a more or less necessary piece of social reform; Scrymgeour's Bill was a piece of bigotry that managed to scrape up only 16 votes in 1923, only 18 in 1931. A few months after its second defeat, Dundee unseated its author in the general election. His efforts had enjoyed the enthusiastic support of one of the most extreme of the teetotalist organizations, the National Prohibition Party. This no-compromise body, founded in 1887, differed from the United Kingdom Alliance in seeing no merit in the local option demand. It aimed at securing the national prohibition of the manufacture, importation and sale of alcoholic liquors as beverages, and opposed the raising of revenue from the liquor traffic in any shape or form. This party, which advised voters in the 1945 general election to write 'A Drink-Free Britain' across their ballot papers, continued to exist till about 1949.

When the brewers met the great depression with a £250,000 advertising campaign behind the slogan 'Beer is best', the teetotallers countered with a poster claiming that 'Beer is—best left alone'. There were fruitless attempts in Parliament to limit liquor advertisements to the manufacturer's name and address, or the name of the product, or the names and addresses of licensed premises; Lord Arnold's Bill for the Regulation of Advertisements on Intoxicating Liquors was negatived without a division in 1935. *Good Housekeeping*, the *Observer*, *Punch*, the *Radio Times*, and the *Spectator* did ban liquor advertisements. Meanwhile the Band of Hope was doing a little advertising on its own account, by selling toy balloons adorned with temperance quotations, for which it charged a penny per balloon.

Some British prohibitionists were given to admiring, a trifle wistfully, the way the Nazis were tackling the drink problem in Germany. In his presidential address to the 1937 meeting of the World Prohibition Federation in Warsaw, Guy Hayler said the fight against inebriating poisons had enjoyed official patronage and leadership since the advent of Herr Adolf Hitler in 1933. Nevertheless there was some disappointment that the example of Herr Hitler as a total abstainer was not more popularly followed, and that breweries and wine dealers had increased their sales. Reich War Minister von Blomberg had given his sympathetic and practical support to the popularization of unfermented grape juice. Reich Minister for Publicity and Propaganda Goebbels had prohibited assertions by advertisers that alcoholic liquors were good for health. . . .[12]

Since the beginning of the second world war the English pussy-foots have thought it best to concentrate on demonstrating a necessary connexion between drinking among adolescents and the rates of illegitimacy and venereal disease. The United Kingdom Alliance's 1940 annual report referred to the moral dangers attendant upon the provision of drinking facilities for young people who were then leaving home for the first time.[13] 'Drink and venereal disease', declared *The Prohibitionist* in 1943, 'are the Siamese twins which are maiming and killing youth faster than the bombs and bullets of the enemy.'[14]

Philocothonista,
OR, THE
DRVNKARD,
Opened, Diſſected, and Anatomized.

LONDON,

Printed by *Robert Raworth*; and are to be ſold at his houſe
neere the *White-Hart* Taverne in *Smithfield.* 1635.

Seventeenth-century drunkards 'Opened, Dissected, and Anatomized'.
From Thomas Heywood's *Philocothonista* (1635)

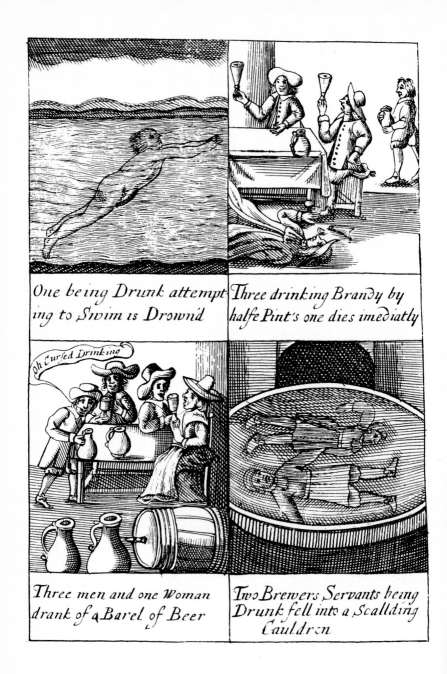

One being Drunk attempting to Swim is Drown'd

Three drinking Brandy by halfe Pint's one dies imediatly

Oh Cursed Drinking

Three men and one Woman drank of a Barel of Beer

Two Brewers Servants being Drunk fell into a Scallding Cauldren

Drinkers meet their fate. Illustrations fr

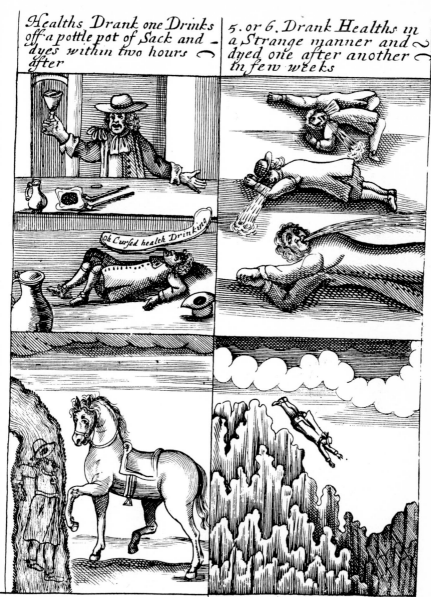

Healths Drank one Drinks off a pottle pot of Sack and dyes within two hours after

5. or 6. Drank Healths in a Strange manner and dyed one after another in few weeks

Oh Cursed health Drinking

One Drownd in a Shallow brook of water being Drunk, his horse standing by.

An exceeding Drunkard in Pembrockshire being Drunk broke himself all to pieces from an high Rock.

A Warning-piece to all Drunkards and Health-Drinkers (1682)

II

'Chemical Experiment in the Tee-total Society' and 'John Bull recovering from his watery humour'. Total abstinence satirized in two sketches by 'Phiz' (H. K. Browne), 1846

The first step in Lucy's downfall.
An illustration from Mrs C. L. Balfour's *The Victim* (1860)

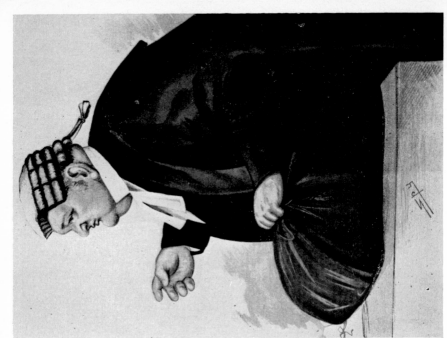

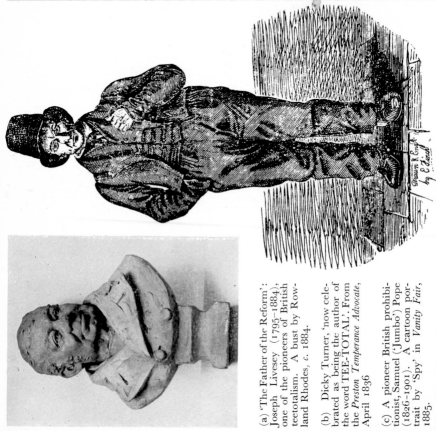

(a) 'The Father of the Reform': Joseph Livesey (1795–1884), one of the pioneers of British teetotalism. A bust by Rowland Rhodes, c. 1884.

(b) Dicky Turner, 'now celebrated as being the author of the word TEE-TOTAL'. From the *Preston Temperance Advocate*, April 1836

(c) A pioneer British prohibitionist, Samuel (Jumbo) Pope (1826–1901). A cartoon portrait by 'Spy', in *Vanity Fair*, 1885.

A modern British teetotaller: Viscount Montgomery refuses a glass of wine.

(a) Teetotal propaganda yesterday ... 'The Temperance Reformation the Fulfilment of Divine Prophecy', 1845

(b) ... and today. 'Beer is—Best Left Alone'

The association of dancing and drinking has been held to be especially dangerous.[15] In 1954 the Alliance noted that the plan to capture youth for beer drinking was being emulated by the wine merchants. Wine-tasting clubs at universities had been accompanied by collective advertising campaigns for wine in general. Cocktail advertisements had increasingly portrayed young women as devotees of this most potent form of alcoholic indulgence.[16] In accents his puritan namesake Stubbes would have approved of, the president of the Alliance, Philip Fothergill, said in 1955 that the rising generation was breaking loose from the restraint and discipline which 'our Temperance forbears' had implanted. Drunkenness and the rate of illegitimate births were rising in the seventeen-to-twenty age group. Not only was the 'young male' indulging in liquor to an increasing extent, but he was using his surplus of earnings to demoralize the young girl as, or before, she left school.[17] Fothergill later described as 'a startling doctrine, with frightful social and moral implications' the Wolfenden Committee's recommendation that the law against soliciting in public houses be invoked only where the whore's conduct gave offence to other users of the premises, or to neighbouring residents. This, he said, would mean that licensed premises would become even more dangerous haunts of vice than in the past. Pubs would become the semi-official rendezvous of prostitutes, their clients, and their dupes. Was it the judgment of Parliament that an eighteen-year-old boy, to some degree disarmed morally by consumption of alcohol, was fair game for the wiles of professional harlots? The Alliance would watch developments with the keenest vigilance.[18]

To our native pussyfoots, 'the national life teems with moral anomalies', one of which is that societies professing to be engaged in social welfare employ the cocktail party or the sherry party as a means of seeking support, popularity, and publicity.[19] Cocktails, incidentally, have a rather special place in the pussyfoots' demonology. These drinks, wrote the late Uncle John (formerly 'the Boy Preacher') of the Lancashire and Cheshire Band of Hope and Temperance Union, were the beginning of the ruin of many young people; 'the person who, under the guise of friendliness in a house or at a party, offers a young person a cocktail is an enemy. . . . Wishing you a happy summer holiday.'[20] But the alternative to alcoholic refreshment is no longer water. The eager reader of the pussyfoot Press is informed that 'the highest mountain in the world has been climbed at last—with the aid of very sweet lemonade!'[21]—and that a similar drink will bring you social success:

> Queenie is Queen of every party
> Her wit so Quick, her laugh so hearty,
> Are not by Quaffing Cocktails made—
> She does it all on orangeade.[22]

The pussyfoots have been venturing into the field of musical criticism. According to a former Board of Education Chief Medical Officer, 'Drunk last night, drunk the night before,/Oh, I was never so drunk before' is 'a really lamentable ditty'.[23] What the pop singer sings is far better, according to Uncle Bill of the Band of Hope:

> We all belong to a great calling, warning others of the dangers of intoxicating drinks. I signed the Temperance Pledge at the age of 9 years. Will you write to me and tell me about yourselves; your meetings; and the sports you are interested in. Send me some jokes. Who is your favourite Pop Singer? Remember Elvis Presley does not drink.[24]

There is opposition to 'a growing incursion of alcohol in the kitchen'. The young and inexperienced cook, especially after a Continental holiday, may think such ingredients as a glass of white wine in the stew, sherry in the cake, and rum in the fruit salad are really essential in her cooking, 'and so start a practice of having alcoholic drinks in the house which otherwise may not have been the case'.[25] At Christmas, we are solemnly advised to 'try a teetotal pudding'.[26]

The dilemma of the pussyfoot, in a country where the worst effects of excessive drinking have long been overcome by improved social conditions, is not an enviable one. The old shibboleths are threadbare. The suggestion that it is impossible to drink in moderation without becoming an alcoholic is disproved in practice by millions of people, despite the British licensing laws' encouragement of 'closing time' insobriety. And the disastrous effects of prohibition in the U.S.A. are fairly widely known.

Let us reserve our sympathy for one teetotaller in particular, whose burden seems a specially cruel and unjust one. He is a vicar. His name is the Reverend Gordon Guinness. He told a temperance meeting in

1962 that he shudders every time he passes a poster with his name on it advertising stout. He is a member of the Guinness family, but

> I am ashamed, drink is a waster and a murderer. . . . I don't see much of the wealthy members of the family. I am proud of the initiative of my grand-father and great grandfather, but if I was offered £10,000 worth of shares in the Company I wouldn't take them. . . . I'm so sick of those posters.[27]

PART IV

UNKINDLING A WANTONNESS

17

THE CREEPING OBSTETRICIAN

A great lady of Middlesex lay in labour. The midwife thought it advisable to call in a physician; so Dr Willughby of Derby was sent for. At the door of the lady's chamber he paused, crouched down—and crept into the room on hands and knees, so as to examine his patient unperceived. His examination over, he crept out again in the same way.[1]

This happened in 1658. Not for another hundred years or more was it thought proper for male physicians to attend women in childbirth. And this conception of modesty, says Havelock Ellis, condemned women to suffer much from the ignorance and superstition of incompetent midwives.[2]

Even when it did become the custom for qualified men to help bring children into the world, such men had to grope in the dark, underneath the bedclothes. Or operations would be performed under cover of a sheet stretching from over the patient on the bed to the doctor, and tied round the latter's neck or otherwise attached to his person.[3] According to a treatise on *The Principles of Midwifery*, published in 1814, it was usual for the room to be darkened, and the bed curtains drawn close, during an obstetric examination. Even so, some women, 'from motives of false delicacy', refused to be examined until the labour pains were severe. Doctors were advised never to propose or make an examination while an unmarried lady was in the room.[4]

Delivering babies blindly in this way was a hazardous undertaking. Operating under the bedclothes on one occasion, the great William Smellie, 'the Master of British Midwifery', accidentally divided the umbilical cord in the wrong place, which resulted in a copious haemorrhage. With notable resource he seized and retied the cord, then won the admiration of the hitherto censorious midwife by telling her that was his way of preventing convulsions in the child. He said afterwards that he had never been so frightened in his life.[5]

Another concession to prudery was the practice, widespread in England but not greatly cared for on the Continent, of examining a pregnant woman from the back. The woman lay on her side, with a pillow between her knees—a position advised by the antiquary Dr John Burton of York (the original of Dr Slop in Sterne's *Tristram Shandy*), who said the accoucheur must not uncover any part of the patient.[6]

Notwithstanding these genuflexions before the taboo on the naked human body in general and the sex organs in particular, the task of the man-midwife was not an easy one. There were some who regarded his calling as intrinsically indecent. For reasons of their own, the female midwives of the second half of the eighteenth century tended to agree, and they indulged in 'the most scurrilous and shameless attacks' on their male rivals.[7] William Smellie himself came under fire from 'a quite peculiarly obnoxious eccentric'[8] named Philip Thicknesse, a man of whom the actor Samuel Foote said: 'He has the stupidity of an owl, the vulgarity of a blackguard, the obdurate heart of an assassin, and the cowardice of a dunghill cock.'[9] Because it contained a description of the anatomy of the female generative organs and of the clinical method of vaginal examination (then known as 'touching'), Thicknesse called Smellie's *Treatise on the Theory and Practice of Midwifery* (1752) 'the most bawdy, indecent and shameful Book which the Press ever brought into the World'.[10] Smellie had written:

> The *Clitoris*, with its *Præputium*, is found between the *Labia* on the middle and forepart of the *Pubis*; and from the lower part of the *Clitoris*, the *Nymphæ* rising, spread outwards and downwards to the sides of the *Os externum*, forming a kind of *Sulcus* or furrow, called the *Fossa magna* or *Navicularis*, for the direction of the *Penis* in coition, or of the finger in touching, into the *Vagina*.[11]

On this passage Thicknesse commented:

> By this shrewd observation on the *wisdom* of Providence, the *modest* Doctor, in his first chapter, shews plainly that *touching* is an essential part of the practice of Midwifery; and that, in his opinion, those parts of a woman were formed by nature, not only for the direction of the Penis in coition, but for the *direction* of the Doctor's finger in *touching*.[12]

Having quoted Smellie's description of the vaginal examination, Thicknesse suggested that its object might be 'to see if any emotions arise in the *touched* lady's breast, that the Doctor may take advantage of'.[13] He went on:

> I know not which to dispise most, the professors of this bawdry profession, or the husbands who tamely submit their wives to be so wantonly and unnecessarily handled by them. . . . I desire every man who loves his wife, or regards his own honour, seriously to figure to himself a smart man-midwife, locked into his wife's apartment, lubricating his finger with pomatum, in order to introduce it into his wife's *Vagina!* nay, if he pleases, two fingers, or one finger in the *Vagina*, and the other into the *Rectum*, according to the *ingenious* Dr. Smellie's direction.[14]

Smellie, with great dignity, refused to reply to this kind of attack—to which the simplest answer is the old Welsh proverb 'Y glaua' ei davod, y butrav ei dîn': 'The more prudish, the more unchaste.'[15]

Later critics of the practice of obstetrics by men emulated both Thicknesse's venom and his prurience masquerading as prudery. The author of *Man-midwifery Dissected* (1793) said the medical profession was guilty of 'actions which the master of a brothel would blush at' and accused doctors of describing, in their cups, the hidden charms of their female patients.[16] Another writer, much exercised by the 'indecent personal examinations' to which doctors unnecessarily subjected their female patients, said most women who abandoned their husbands and families for the society of men of intrigue owed their first contamination to their medical attendants. And one J. R. Pickmere charged lustful medical men with practising 'licentious tricks of enormous depravity'.[17]

This form of prudery is not unknown today. A reader of *Woman's Own* wrote in 1962: 'I have always attended a male doctor but now I have to undergo a rather intimate operation and my husband says it is a job for a woman. . . . This argument is causing trouble between us.'[18]

Between prurient slanderers and prudish patients, the medical profession did not have too enviable a time of it. The lives of innumerable women were lost through what Havelock Ellis called fossilized modesty: 'a kind of pseudo-modesty which, being a convention and not a natural feeling, is capable of unlimited extension'.[19] A coroner wrote in 1908 that he had known several cases of female deaths, reported as sudden and of cause unknown, when the medical man called in during the latter hours of life was quite unaware that his patient was dying of gangrene or of a strangulated femoral hernia, or was bleeding to death from the bowel or from ruptured varices of the vulva. For women would sometimes hide their symptoms, out of a bashfulness 'so great and perverse as to be hardly credible'.[20]

The body taboo often kept husband and wife from seeing each other naked. Ellis mentions the case of a man, married for twenty years, who had never seen his wife completely nude. He cannot have been exceptional. When his wife began to undress for the night, the Victorian husband would retreat into the dressing-room; in households lacking this married man's 'funk-hole' the wife would retire half an hour beforehand, and her spouse would wait 'until a discreet knock on the floor gave him the "all clear" '.[21] Some women not merely found no beauty in man's form, but were positively repelled by the sight of nakedness, even that of a husband or lover. A woman of seventy, the mother of several children, said she had never seen a naked man in her life. And her sister confessed that she had never in the whole course of her life looked at her own nakedness, because it 'frightened' her.[22] It has been known for people, on the recommendation of their religious advisers, to wear a garment in the bath, lest the sight of their own nakedness arouse them sexually, or lest it offend God.[23] This appears to have been a common practice in the middle of the eighteenth century, for when Elizabeth Montagu, the famous blue-stocking, stayed as a girl of twenty-one with the Duchess of Portland at Bulstrode, she wrote to her mother: 'Mary brings me word my bathing tub is ready for use; so tomorrow I shall go in. Pray look for my bathing dress, till then I must go in in chemise and jupon!'[24]

Even today, as Richard Hoggart points out, there is among working-class people 'a great shyness . . . about being seen naked, or even about undressing for the act of sex'.[25]

18

WOMEN, MONSTROUS WOMEN

But the body taboo does not get things all its own way. There is a strong countervailing tendency: the use of clothes to attract, and sustain, the interest of the opposite sex. And the resultant of these two tendencies—towards concealment and towards display—broadly determines the basic fashion of any period.

Each sexually interesting part of the female body is emphasized in turn. It may be partly or completely exposed; or the clothes may be drawn tightly over it; or their lines or ornamentation may be made to point to it, subtly or otherwise; or padding may be used to make it look bigger. In some such way each new fashion seeks to arouse interest in a new erogenous zone to replace the zone which, for the time being, is played out. It is the job of fashion to *chase* the new point of interest, without ever quite catching it up—because 'if you really catch it up you are immediately arrested for indecent exposure'. A particular fashion is indecent ten years before its time, shameless five years before, *outré* one year before. (One year after its time, it is dowdy; ten years after, hideous; fifty years after, quaint; a hundred years after, romantic.) James Laver, who drew up this astonishingly accurate chronology, says it is 'probable that any fashion is slightly indecent *when it is just coming in*'.[1]

It is then that the moralists and satirists are wont to add to their denunciation of clothes as too gorgeous a denunciation of them as too revealing. 'It is both metaphorically and literally true to say that every time woman lifts her skirts'—or lowers her bodice, or makes her buttocks prominent—'the moralists shiver.'[2] Their shivers reflect a clothes prudery which, when we see how constant it remains over many changes of fashion, we come to recognize as, for the masses, an aphrodisiac;[3] for the moralist, a special kind of sexual excitement and satisfaction:

The search for the dreadful fascination becomes by practice an absorbing hobby, and the prude obtains from its pursuit a satisfaction akin to that which the common mind obtains from satisfying the instinct. Indeed prudery may be regarded as a rarified and subtle form of sex-satisfaction whereby a warm glow of moral disapproval can be extracted from quite commonplace spectacles and will even rival the heat of passion itself.[4]

Apart from an early attempt at the bustle, noticed in Chapter 2,[5] there is little to suggest that Englishwomen went out of their way to make themselves unduly attractive to men before the middle of the sixteenth century. Men and women alike wore poulaines, the long, piked, phallic-shaped shoes, generally known in England as crakows, which first came into use here in 1360 and were all the rage from 1395 to 1410 and again from 1450 to 1480. But opposition to these eleven-inch-long forerunners of the modern winkle-pickers seems to have been aimed at confining their use to the upper classes rather than out-lawing them as indelicate. Medieval moralists preferred to select as their targets the habit of washing too frequently and too scrupulously and the practice of changing one's clothes too often; these things were thought unseemly, since they encouraged lust of the eye and pride of life.[6]

Chaucer, in his *Parson's Tale* [c. 1400], found much more to com-plain of in men's clothes than in women's. Men's garments were horribly scanty—too short to cover their shameful members. Some men went about showing the bulge of their genitals; their horrible, swollen members resembled the malady of hernia; their buttocks, the backside of a she-ape at the full of the moon. By dividing their long hose into white and red, they made it appear that half of their shameful privy members was flayed; other combinations of colours made it seem as if half was stricken with erysipelas ('fir of seint Antony') or cancer.[7]

It rather sounds as though Chaucer is here criticizing that remarkable article of masculine attire, the codpiece. In fashion from *c.* 1408 to *c.* 1575, this challenging assertion of virility was 'perhaps the most audacious piece of clothing that has ever been invented'.[8] In the fif-teenth century it was a front flap, forming a pouch, at the fork of the hose; in the sixteenth, this pouch was so padded as to suggest a perma-nent erection. Sometimes it was coloured differently from the rest of the garment; often it was made of silk and decorated with ribbons or even gold and jewels. Not the least remarkable thing about it was the absence of any real outcry against it. Perhaps it would have been inappropriate in the Age of Discoveries to discourage male assertiveness—although the padding of men's shoulders was condemned, in the fifteenth century, as 'a thing exceedingly vain and displeasing in the sight of God'.[9] The codpiece, in fact, 'persisted without provoking as much disapproval, on the score of decency, as, for example, woman's bathing costume has done in modern times'.[10] It was left to later generations to find it 'exceedingly gross and indecent', to record that 'long after a sense of decency had banished this obscene appendage from the common habit, it was retained by the comedians [among them, Shakespeare] as a subject for licentious witticisms', and to declare that 'if any thing can be more ridiculous than the introduction of so filthy a protuberance, it must be the use to which it was sometimes appropriated'[11]—i.e., to stick one's pins into! More recent historians of fashion have been more reticent. 'It is an interesting aspect of our present-day prudery', remarks Pearl Binder, 'that we now regard the codpiece as so indecent that it is hardly ever mentioned in costume books of our time.'[12] But the codpieces that form part of some of the suits of armour on display in the Tower of London usually attract the attention of female visitors, who often seem amused by the ornament's exuberance.

The early christian Church had called the laced openings to women's bodices 'the gates of hell';[13] in the fifteenth century the gates opened a trifle wider, when the upper half of the breasts was exposed; and in James I's time they were thrown wide open, for young unmarried women uncovered the whole of their breasts. In those days girls married at about the age of sixteen, and bare nipples indicated virginity as well as nubility. There were many who not only found this fashion immodest, but failed to view with detachment the less complete décolletage of older women. What 'light housewiues' alone had formerly worn, to attract their customers, was now a habit for chaste and sober matrons.[14] Women were three times as lustful as men, 'for what meaneth els their outward tricking and daintie trimming of their heads, the laying out of their hayres, the painting and washing of their faces, the opening of their breasts, & discouering them to their wastes?'[15] 'Theyr breasts they embuske vp on hie', complained Thomas Nashe, author of The Unfortunate Traveller (1594), 'and theyr round

Roseate buds immodestly lay foorth, to shew at theyr hands there is fruit to be hoped.'[16] John Hall (b. 1529), poet and medical writer, remembered what he had seen as a boy:

> That women theyr breastes dyd shew & lay out.
> And well was y̆ mayd whose dugs then were stoute.
> Which vsance at fyrst came vp in the stues,
> Which mens wyues and daughters after dyd vse.
>
> The preachers at that, then gan out to crye
> And honest men dyd it lothe and defye.[17]

And the anonymous authur of *Quippes for Vpstart Newfangled Gentlewomen* (1595), condemned

> These naked paps, the deuils ginnes,
> to worke vain gazers painfull thrall.[18]

In the *Appendix Containing Divers Reasons and Arguments against Painting, Spots, naked Backs, Breasts, Arms, &c.* (1654), which he added to his work *The Loathsomnesse of Long Haire* (1653), Thomas Hall (whom we have already met as a critic of certain aspects of maypole festivities) said the laying out of naked breasts was a temptation to sin; naked breasts were known provocations to uncleanness; pious matrons were modest—it was only light ones, and such as were for sale, that invited customers by setting open their shop windows. So horribly had sin stained and defiled our bodies that, if it were possible, the whole body, face and hands included, should be covered.[19] Richard Baxter wholeheartedly agreed. In his preface to an English translation of *De l'Abus des nuditez de gorge* (1675) by Jacques Boileau (to which was appended 'An Order of the Vicars General of the Arch-Bishoprick of *Thoulouse* . . . Against naked Arms, Shoulders, and Necks, and the indecency of Maids and Womens apparel') Baxter wrote that if he had his will, four fashions would be altered: the nakedness of women; the monstrous superfluity of cloth that must drag after them; their inordinate pride and laced gaudiness; and the monstrous periwigs of men. He knew God had put some degrees of natural lust into men and women for the propagation of mankind; but if a woman would be desirable to any wise man, it must be most by wisdom, meekness, and a holy frame of mind and life, and not by anything contrary thereto. He went on:

> Will you but think what that *Flesh* is which you are adorning? When the Surgeon shall dissect your Corps, and open your loathsome Entrails, or when it is laid out for the Coffin, or laid to rot in a darksome Grave, where then is Naked Beauty . . . ? What a change will the Small Pox . . . make of that body that you so proudly dress?[20]

These are the authentic accents of the body taboo carried to the point of hatred of the flesh and of life. It is a pleasure to turn from Baxter to the critical but matter-of-fact author of 'Will Bagnall's Ballet' [*c.* 1655], who told the women of his time:

> Your faces trick'd and painted bee,
>   Your breasts all open bare:
> So farr that a man may almost see
>   Unto your Lady ware:
> And in the church, to tell you true,
> Men cannot serve God for looking on you,
>   *Oh Women, monstrous women,*
>   *What do you meane to doe!*[21]

At about the same time 'A Compassionate Conformist', in *Englands Vanity* (1683), termed naked necks and shoulders 'an impudence abominated by the very Light of *Nature*', and cited a divine who held that naked breasts were like a bill fixed to the doorposts telling passers-by that within that place dwelt an unclean heart.[22]

The eighteenth century had hardly begun before *The Guardian*, a daily sheet written by Steele, Addison and others, took up the same theme, chiding the fashionable women of the day for removing the tucker, or neck-piece, thus exposing in its primitive nakedness that gentle swelling of the breast which it had formerly concealed.

> The Neck of a fine Woman at present takes in almost half the Body. Since the Female Neck thus grows upon us, and the Ladies seem disposed to discover themselves to us more and more, I would fain have them tell us once for all how far they intend to go, and whether they have yet determined among themselves where to make a Stop. I am in Pain for a Woman of Rank when I see her thus exposing her self to the Regards of

every staring Fellow. . . . To prevent these sawcy familiar Glances, I would entreat my gentle Readers to sow on their Tuckers again, to retrieve the Modesty of their Characters, and not to imitate the Nakedness, but the Innocence of their Mother Eve.

What troubled *The Guardian* more than anything was that the leaders in this fashion were mostly married women. Why they made themselves bare, the writer could not possibly imagine, for nobody exposed wares that were appropriated—and when the bird was taken, the snare ought to be removed. . . .[23] A few days later he reported that he had received 'great applauses' for having, as he claimed, 'put a seasonable Stop to this unaccountable Humour of Stripping, that was got among our *British* Ladies'. But it had been observed to him, with some concern, that women, besides letting down their stays, were also tucking up their petticoats, which grew shorter and shorter every day. The leg (by which he meant the ankle) discovered itself in proportion with the neck. 'But', he added, 'I may possibly take another Occasion of handling this Extremity, it being my Design to keep a watchful Eye over every Part of the Female Sex, and to regulate them from Head to Foot'.[24]

This guardianship had no effect. Satirical or moralizing comments on the low neckline were frequent in the seventeen-fifties,[25] and Arthur Murphy wrote:

By Advices from *Vaux-hall* and *Ranelagh*, we are informed, that more pretty Legs and Shoulders have been shewn there lately by the Ladies, than has hitherto been attempted in this Country, which causes various Speculations, and it is said a certain *Irish* Gentleman is so pleased with this Phænomenon of the Descent of the Stays, and Ascent of the Petticoat, that he expects shortly to see both Ends meet.[26]

In 1792, not long before women took to wetting their single garments (sometimes weighing only eight ounces, and sometimes worn without underclothes) to make them more diaphanous still, Mary Wollstonecraft quoted, from an educational book, a caution 'against putting your hand, by chance, under your neck-handkerchief; for a modest woman never did so'.[27]

In the period we have just surveyed, other parts of the female body caused far less disturbance than did the neck, shoulders and breasts. There were however murmurings in Elizabethan times against a fashion that gave a woman

> A bumbe like a barrell
> wyth whoopes at the skyrte.[28]

This 'bum-roll' consisted of 'bents of Whale bone to beare out their bûmes',[29] and was taken by some to be a sign of women's lust ('There are boulsters likewise for the buttocks as wel as the breast, and why forsooth? The smaller in the wast, the better handled'[30]), for it swelled out their garments with 'buttocks most môstrously roûd',[31] so that a poet could write (*c.* 1550):

> Downe, for shame, wyth these bottell a[rste] bummes,
>   and theyr trappynge trinkets so vayne!
> A bounsinge packsadel for the devyll to ryde on,
>   to spurre theym to sorowe and payne.[32]

Another writer, forty-five years later, was quite savage:

> If barreld bummes were full of Ale
>   they might wel serue Tom Tapsters turne:
> But yeelding nought but filth and stale,
>   no losse it were if they did burne.[33]

Buttocks did not burn, but dropped out of the picture, returning to prominence with the reappearance of the bustle in the 1690s, the 1770s, the 1830s, 1868–74 and, finally, 1883–89.

The hoops of the early eighteenth century were censured by the devout, who felt that such garments could conceal either a lover or a pregnancy:

> When any *Maid* astray is led
> To lose, poor foolish Girl! her *Maiden head,*
> Then when her Belly doth begin to swell
> A *Hoop* and *Cloak* will serve her Frolick well.[34]

There was some opposition to white stockings when they were introduced a few years later, and there were occasional references to the exciting sight of the female calf:

> Set your hoop, shew your stockings, and legs to your knees,
> And leave men as little as may be to guess.[35]

But, generally speaking, there was little leg taboo during the period of the hoop, whose erotic possibilities were in fact welcomed by a number of writers. The hoop was so light and so liable to be blown about or turned inside out that it gave many a thrilling glimpse of under-petticoats, through which the outline of the legs could be clearly seen. At that time women did not wear drawers; small wonder that Mrs Haywood, describing the way women entered public assemblies 'with a Kind of a Frisk and Jump', throwing their enormous hoops almost in the faces of those who passed by them, quoted a friend who declared: 'The Men of these Days are strangely happy.'[36] Sending young women sky-high on swings was a popular diversion: 'There are very many pretty Shreaks, not so much from fear of falling, as that their Petticoats should unty. . . . The Lover who swings the Lady, is to tye her Cloaths very close together with his Hatband before she admits him to throw up her Heels.' This would prevent his telling the colour of her garters.[37] Yet in this same period a number of portraits of young women painted a hundred or so years before, with the breasts completely or nearly exposed, were brought up to date: the breasts were painted over, so that 'we now see a vague slab of unnatural flesh as an improvement on Nature, and a tribute to the "new look" '.[38]

Prudery has also touched, from time to time, the female ear (there were some in medieval times who held that, since the Virgin Mary had conceived through the ear, women's ears must be covered as sex organs), female arms (at the court of Charles II the upper arm was more carefully hidden from view than the nipples), female hair, and the practice of painting the female face. This form of decoration was to puritans 'the badge of a harlot', since 'rotten posts are painted, and gilded Nutmegs are usually the worst'.[39]

19

THEY EVEN COVERED CUPID

We come now to the time when Mrs Grundy persuades designers
of valentines to put Cupid in a skirt, covers chair legs and pianoforte
legs in decent frills, causes women to bathe in garments that take fully
twelve yards of material, and renders one bride so appalled by the
sight of her husband's legs when he wears his night-shirt that she
spends her honeymoon 'making him nice long night-*gowns* so that I
shan't be able to see any of him'.[1]

It would be wrong however to think of the nineteenth century as
one unbroken period of triumphant prudery. Thus in the eighties the
bodice of women's evening dress was not merely cut very low; being
designed to look like a corset or some other item of underclothing, it
spicily suggested that the wearer was not fully dressed. Again, the
crinoline gave almost as many opportunities as the hoop had done for
delicious revelations of underwear and legs and even buttocks. 'The
girls of our time like to show their legs', wrote Sir William Hardman in
1862. 'I don't see why they should be interfered with; it pleases them
and does no harm to us.' (He added, hastily perhaps: 'I speak for
married, not single, men.')[2] Moreover the century had begun with a
fashion that at times came daringly close to nudity: the vogue of the
revealing 'single garment' (often worn, as we have seen, without
chemise or petticoats), about which a Chester commentator wrote in
1803: 'The only sign of modesty in the present dress of the Ladies is the
pink dye in their stockings, which makes their legs appear to blush for
the total absence of petticoats.'[3] A few years later 'A Lady of Distinction' was reproaching the rest of her sex about the indelicacy of wearing
no chemise. No eye but that of a libertine could look on so wanton a
figure with anything but disgust and contempt; and women who went
about with only a single garment on would be punished with an early
old age, chronic pains and deep wrinkles. The modest fair should hold

the chemise as sacred as the vestal veil. Women should consider this garment as the pledge of honour to shelter them from the gaze of un-hallowed eyes.[4]

The time was not far off when half-naked women would be working in the mines pulling coal-trucks—a practice which attracted, on the whole, fewer and less vehement criticisms than did any nineteenth-century fashion vagary. But then, the female miners were not fashion-able ladies,[5] of whom it was written in 1818:

> When dressed for the evening the girls nowadays
> Scarce an atom of dress on them leave;
> Nor blame them; for what is an evening dress
> But a dress that is suited for Eve?[6]

Under Queen Victoria, evening dress was the exception to the general rule that women's clothes must hide their figures. In evening dress, a woman might exploit the top half of her breasts. 'But always there was the ladylike assumption that any results therefrom were unsought for and were ordained by a Higher Hand. The condemnatory words "bold", "fast" and "immodest" signified that the offender had used her gifts designedly.'[7] According to Mrs Merrifield, when women wore dresses cut low round the bust, men looked on the exposure with unmitigated distaste, and were inclined to doubt the modesty of those young ladies who made so profuse a display of their charms. If the dress were low cut, the bust should be covered, modestly and becomingly, with drapery.[8] This was in the fifties, when such advice had a fair chance of being followed: thus, when Charles Worth, the English founder of the famous Paris fashion house, made an evening dress for one young woman, she had her maid fill in the deep V with a modest fichu of lace and tulle and add short sleeves. 'Nothing remains ex-posed', commented a wit, 'save the fact that she is a virgin.'[9] By 1867 cleavage, as it is called today, was so common that the low-necked dress, and its wearer's bold look, were branded as 'signs of the present fast, frivolous and indecorous age'.[10] Two years later, ball dresses were described as really wicked—'wicked for cost and indecent for cut; with only little gold straps across the shoulders that look as if a good shake would shake them off altogether'.[11] And in the late eighties women's 'full dress' was 'sometimes a pain and more often an embar-rassment' to the observer, since the lowness of the bodice and the total absence of sleeves left an impression of general nakedness.[12] The bodice hung on the shoulders 'by a miracle'.[13]

This cult of the mammary gland apart, the general inconvenience and unmanageability of women's dress at that period led a pioneer sociologist to call it 'the disgrace of civilization'.[14] Layer upon layer of wrappings helped to keep their wearers' minds off what lay under them. Dress reformers had something of a difficult battle, in an age when tennis was played in long, tight gowns that touched the ground (with a short train behind) and black high-heeled canvas shoes; when a riding habit consisting of a top hat and a tight, long-waisted, fitted jacket with a bustle, coming below the knees and worn over breeches and top-boots, was regarded as an affront to womanhood and aroused choleric letters to the daily Press;[15] and when a woman's bathing dress consisted of capacious pantaloons and a thick, roomy, long-sleeved dress reaching to the throat. The frustrations sustained by the most famous dress reformer of all, Mrs Amelia Bloomer, have often been described. It was not until the bicycle craze seized the well-to-do in the early nineties that women at last wore breeches. Even then their new garments were denounced as shameless because they exposed the calf, and the women who wore them were branded as anti-feminine.[16] Stones were thrown by the female inhabitants of at least one village when young women in bloomers cycled through in 1892.[17]

It is sometimes suggested that the extent of the nineteenth-century leg taboo has been exaggerated; or, at all events, that the practice of putting frills round furniture legs was less widespread than is supposed, or that it was confined to the United States. But a French visitor to London, writing in 1851, tells how he asked his hostess why chairs and pianos were more clothed than some of the ladies he saw in the Haymarket or at Covent Garden. 'Wouldn't you be shocked, Monsieur', she replied, 'if you could see the legs of these chairs?'[18] And a German visitor gives an amusing description of the ritual he observed on London omnibuses in the seventies:

I cannot help smiling whenever I think how carefully every man, young or old, sitting opposite each other on the narrow seats of an omnibus, endeavours to straighten the dress of any woman who passes between them, so that on no account shall there be the least glimpse of her foot or still worse of her garter. Each face wears such an earnest look—like a priest who in the morning preaches on the immaculate conception of the Virgin Mary, and in the evening, over a glass of red wine, smiles at the simpleness of the faithful.[19]

This was the time when women's feet caused men such excitement that family photographers erased them from their pictures, making women appear to be floating on air. Men used to enjoy croquet because it afforded them, according to a contemporary account, 'the sight of a neatly turned ankle and pretty boots'.[20] Laver thinks it was the constant side-to-side agitation of the crinoline, with sudden upward shootings of the skirt, which gave mid-Victorian men this ankle complex.[21] Another factor may have been the habit some women had of raising the dress—and sometimes the petticoats too—to protect their garments from the mud. Most men, like Mr Bloom in *Ulysses* ('Watch! Watch! Silk flash rich stockings white. Watch!'[22]), were instinctively alert for such revelations. But it took a certain degree of courage to ask outright: 'Is there anything indecent in showing a neatly-dressed ankle?'[23] Public opinion felt sure there was something, if not exactly indecent, at any rate piquant in it.

The gynaecologist who in 1852 posed this rather daring question about ankles was ahead of his time in another respect too—in advocating that women wear drawers. It is hard to believe now that these garments were at that time considered immodest and unfeminine by Englishwomen, who in consequence almost never wore them. Their advocate, Dr Tilt, felt that their use would preserve women from numberless infirmities, sometimes even from death. They should be made of fine calico, and should not come below the knee. Being worn without the knowledge of the general observer, they would in time be robbed of the prejudice usually attached to an appendage deemed masculine.[24] The subject was a titillating one. In 1855 the British Cabinet enjoyed a hearty laugh over the enthusiasm of a King of Sardinia when he discovered, on a visit to Paris, that the ladies of that city did not wear drawers. Since Victor Emmanuel was to visit London and Queen Victoria, the British ambassador in Paris, Lord Cowley, felt it necessary to warn his government about the visitor's coarseness and outspokenness. One account says that at a State reception a lady-in-waiting tripped over her crinoline and fell; whereupon the King exclaimed to the French Empress: 'I am delighted to see, Madame, that your ladies do not wear drawers, and that the gates of paradise are always open.' 'He'll frighten the Queen out of her senses if he goes on so with her', wrote Cowley. Clarendon replied: 'The anecdotes of the King of Sardinia are *impayable*; pray send more—the roars of laughter in the Cabinet just now about the *caleçons* might have been heard at Westminster Bridge.' In the event, though she found his conversation 'startling in the extreme', Queen Victoria decorated her guest with the Garter.[25]

By 1859 drawers were the latest 'fast' fashion among the aristocracy; and the Hon. Eleanor Stanley, a lady-in-waiting to the Queen, described how the Duchess of Manchester, rushing over a stile, caught a hoop of her cage in it and went head over heels, landing in the ditch with her cage and petticoats over her head, and displaying a pair of scarlet tartan knickerbockers. As the wife of the French ambassador later said to the Duchess of Wellington, 'Ma chère, c'était diabolique!' Sir William Hardman wrote in 1863 that 'women getting into omnibuses, servant girls cleaning door-steps, and virgins at windy sea-side watering places, all show their —— on occasion'.[26]

The permanent possibility of such revelations while one was wearing a crinoline brought a fairly rapid upper- and middle-class acceptance of drawers in the sixties; it took another two decades for them to descend to the working class. Even then, any interesting variation in fabric, colour, or design was viewed as daring and far from wise: Jaeger's woollen drawers in the eighties; the ready-made coloured underclothing made possible by the sewing-machine ('Prudery shuddered; it seemed incompatible with a milk-white mind to wear coloured underclothing. It might lead—in fact it did lead—to wilful exposure of them. And the habit might lead to—who knows what indescribable excesses?'[27]); and the drawers of 1895, twenty inches round the knee, with a ten-inch lace frill ('regarded by many . . . as savouring of the demi-monde'[28]). In the nineties, bicycle skirts were weighted with lead to keep the drawers hidden. 'No nice-minded lady would think of wearing expensive underclothing', wrote a magazine in the same decade.[29] (*Naughty* nineties?) And the century ended with clergymen denouncing as unchristian the nightdresses of 1900, with their accordion pleats and baby ribbon—and with the adoption by the Amateur Swimming Association of the following regulations for bathing costumes:

(a) Only black, red, or dark blue costumes shall be worn.

(b) Drawers shall be worn underneath the costume.

(c) Trimmings may be used *ad lib.*

(d) The shoulder-straps of costumes shall not be less than two inches wide.

(e) All costumes shall be buttoned on the shoulder, and the armhole shall be cut no lower than three inches from the armpit.

NOTE.—*For LADIES a shaped arm, at least three inches long, shall be inserted.*

(f) In the front the costume shall reach not lower than two inches below the pit of the neck.

NOTE.—*For LADIES the costume shall be cut straight round the neck.*

(g) At the back the costume shall be cut straight from top of shoulder to top of shoulder.

(h) In the leg portion the costume shall extend to within three inches of the knee, and shall be cut in a straight line round the circumference of each leg.[30]

20

SHORT SKIRTS
AND LONG FACES

The first world war, in its effects on women's dress, hastened a retreat from prudery that had become apparent in the first decade of the new century. At first the retreat was far from general; and Mrs Grundy did all she could to halt it. But increasing efforts were made both to rationalize and simplify the clothing of women and to transfer erotic interest to the legs; and gradually these efforts succeeded.

As early as 1901 an attempt was made to introduce 'the anti-microbe skirt, daring in its originality'—i.e., a comparatively short walking skirt that no longer swept the streets. Many women preferred however, from motives perhaps not wholly innocent of coquetry, to go on holding up the longer garment.[1] A clearer sign of the times was the fondness of fashionable women for very elaborate petticoats under their rather severe skirts. *Punch* mocked as the 'Pneumonia Blouse' a 1903 attempt to introduce a lower neckline in the daytime, to match the extreme décolletage of evening dress.[2] Evangeline's transparent night-dress, in Elinor Glyn's *The Vicissitudes of Evangeline* (1905), generated pain, shock, suffocation, and perhaps a twinge of envy: 'I consider this garment not in any way fit for a girl—or for any good woman, for that matter . . . I hope my sisters have not seen it . . . What *would* Alexander say if I were to wear such a thing?' Told by Evangeline that the night-dress was becoming, her critic 'almost screamed': 'But no nice-minded woman wants things to look becoming in bed!'[3] Wearers of the harem skirt of 1909–14 were chased off the streets; and a woman sporting transparent sleeves from wrist to shoulder—she had just arrived from New York, where this was the fashion—was chased by a jeering crowd in central London in the summer of 1914.[4] The literary equivalent of these mobs was the fashion writer who, bemoaning 'the passing of our old petticoat modesty', ventured to 'rail indignantly against those greatly daring ladies who, from wearing trousers mentally, so to speak, end at last in clothing their limbs as mannishly as their convictions. . . . We might begin with Turkish Trousers and end—who knows?—with brazen knickerbockers'.[5] And there was an outcry against dresses that showed every movement of the limbs, almost of the muscles, and against stockings so thin as to embarrass the beholder.[6]

The fiercest moralizing was reserved however for *les décolletés du jour* of 1913–14, known in this country as 'V-necks'. Clergymen of all denominations joined in denouncing low necks as indecent; and certain physicians rationalized their prejudices against this new 'Pneumonia Blouse' by forecasting chills and chest diseases for an entire generation of women. 'By some curious aberration', remarks Laver, 'there was no attack upon *les décolletés du soir*, which one would have thought to be infinitely more dangerous both to the health of woman and to the morals of man'.[7] When the *Tatler* recorded in February 1915 that 'the battle that has been raging for several months has ended in a distinct triumph for the high-necked corsage', *Punch* commented sourly: 'Good. Now we can devote our attention to the other war on the Continent.'[8] Women's breasts became more unpopular still—even indecent—during the middle and late twenties and early thirties, and the corset of that period was designed to flatten them and render them inconspicuous.[9] Laver tells how chorus-girls at the Adelphi theatre went on strike in 1933 against having to wear a costume cut 'no lower than would have been worn without embarrassment by an *ingénue* of the eighties when attending her first ball'.[10]

The appearance of immaturity secured by flattening the breasts was heightened by shortening the skirt. Women, abandoning dark stockings for shiny flesh-pink ones visible to the knee or a trifle higher, began to look adolescent or even pre-adolescent. The new zone of erotic interest was not the whole leg; the thigh was excluded (in spite of the generous glimpses of garters, suspenders, bare thighs and drawers which the fashion frequently afforded). The tubular lines of the dress did nothing to accentuate the hips and thighs, but, on the contrary, hid their shape and slimmed them. Attention was focused on the knee and the part of the leg below it—'a region which possesses erotic attraction only to a minor degree'.[11] And this emphasis on the immature, 'little girl' look makes the prudish outcries against short skirts somewhat puzzling, until one detects, in some of them at least, the preoccupations of the voyeur and even the tone of voice of the pornographer.

The man in the street was inclined to see short skirts as the reason for an alleged decline in moral standards —or vice versa.[12] He tended to believe that the style was immodest, that 'the modern girl' was too scantily clad, that the wearers had no right to complain if they caught chills.[13] When Judge Sir Alfred Tobin asked a woman witness, 'Do grown-up married women wear their dress above the knee?', receiving the reply, 'Yes, if they are slim', he snorted: 'Do you mean to say one's grandmother would wear a short skirt? What ridiculous nonsense!'[14] A railway ticket collector said to his wife: 'Oh, I am so heartily *sick* of seeing legs. Every carriage door I open to examine the tickets, I get a vision of legs, legs, legs. Whatever the women of England are coming to, goodness knows!' And a bus conductor remarked as a lady stepped off his bus: 'That is how men are led into sin.'[15] In several towns passengers in tram-cars objected to the amount of leg being shown by young women and asked the conductor to turn them off. In 1924 Birmingham waitresses were forbidden by their employers to wear short skirts. 'We can understand the women of the world dressing like harlots', wrote a citizeness of Liverpool, 'but when professing Christian women, holiness teachers, ministers' wives, dress so, it makes one ashamed of our sex.'[16]

This view was strongly shared by a number of clergymen, one of whom filled up the panels of a pew where girls sat 'because their meagre dress exposed them to the view of boys and men who sat opposite to them'.[17] City men, too, were disturbed. A 'notable business man' started going to town by taxi, for he found it impossible to sit opposite young women; 'one of the most distinguished lawyers in the City' was driven to take refuge in his billiard-room whenever his daughter brought her girl-friends home for dinner and they curled up in armchairs: 'The provocation of silken leg and half-naked thigh, together with little or no concealment of the breasts, was devastating and overwhelming.'[18] Similarly devastated and overwhelmed was 'A Christian Business Man' who went to the extent of writing a twopenny pamphlet describing in some detail the kind of sight he preferred not to see. Thus, at a meeting in the Central Hall, Westminster, some ladies who entered late had to sit on the gallery steps; so short were their dresses that they could not cover themselves, and to those sitting in the body of the hall the sight was frankly indecent.

We cannot open the newspapers of to-day . . . without being confronted with displays of women in semi-nude condition. Particularly noticeable in the summer months are the pictures of women in bathing attire only, posing for the photographer in immodest or indecent positions. All over our beloved land there has of late years been a booming of mixed bathing. . . . Now we are to have 'mixed bathing' for 'the thousands' on the Serpentine, with all its glaring immodesty made more public than ever, with the sexes commingling in semi-nude conditions. How frequently do we see in the Press pictures of women in running shorts and in other ways attired like men. . . . Then there are the drapers' advertisements, with their questionable exhibits; and the horrible cinema adverts. with their 'sex appeal' displays.

Quoting an American prison doctor who felt that rolled stockings had a direct bearing on crime incitation, the author made it clear to good women that they could not copy these unholy styles and be innocent of a share, though indirectly and unconsciously, in the crime wave. He reproached mothers for sending girls of ten into the street with their legs bare except for socks. Nothing could surpass for modesty the plain long sleeve and the lengthened skirt. Modern dress attracted attention to women's arms and legs, and this display day by day on the city streets was a terrible force for evil, and might become a temptation even on Sundays in church. Women had ever been Satan's favourite instrument in introducing evil—and if they were able to walk about unmolested in spite of their suggestive dress, it was due solely to God's restraining power. Christian women should gird up, not their skirts, but 'the loins of the mind'.[19]

The war against short skirts was waged still more energetically, and with a wealth of piquant examples, by the religious writer G. H. Lang in his *Churches of God* (1928). It was, he held, amazing and deplorable that any professing to fear the Lord should wear

skirts so short as to be positively indecent when they are seated or are cycling, or which they must be incessantly twitching down over their knees, so drawing to the matter the more attention. In May, 1926, in a famous English glen, I saw a young woman sitting on a low seat, her knees apart, so that her short skirt was necessarily drawn upward and her white drawers were *entirely* on view. . . . Why should I be compelled to see the garters, and more, of a society girl every time she flung one leg over the other as she sat opposite to me in a train? Surely it is a sign of degenerate moral tone when a hosiery advertisement boldly describes the colour of women's stockings by the term 'nude'. In a large British camp . . . I asked what the men generally thought of the modern short skirt. The reply was: 'Oh! they glory in it: they are all eyes to stare at them!' He must be blind who has not seen this taking place in the streets of any town, and has not read in the eyes of men what kinds of thoughts are passing in their hearts. . . . In February, 1927, on a P. & O. liner on the Mediterranean, there travelled with me an English officer with his young wife and little child. The mother fell asleep in her deck chair, the wind played with her short skirts, and for a quite considerable time some eight inches of bare white thigh, above the stocking, were on view to the troops of young fellows parading the deck. . . . To dress indecently is a sin.[20]

Not the least interesting feature of this passage is that the writer considers it necessary to draw attention to the *colour* of the under-garment and the bare thigh he saw.

The Catholics not only denounced short skirts, but also organized against them. In July 1927 the Mary Immaculate Dress and Deportment Crusade was launched to counteract the demoralizing effect of immodest fashions. Its first rule for adults was:

Not to wear clothes less than four inches below the knee, or so tight-fitting and skimpy as to give undue prominence to the figure, or in any other way bordering on immodesty, such as slit skirts or dispensing with a brassière. . . . Sleeves should be worn not shorter than a few inches above the elbow and better still if they cover the elbow. Stockings should never be dispensed with unless one is too poor to purchase them. When cycling, the knees should be well covered.

As regards deportment, adults were instructed 'not to assume immodest postures and always to cover the knees when sitting in public places'. Nor might they take part in mixed bathing or sun-bathe in exposed public places. There were similar rules for children.[21] A reader of the *Daily Telegraph* signing himself 'British Honour' suggested that town councils and other authorities should post notices requesting all to dress as became ladies and gentlemen.[22]

Some of those who took a different view founded a Sensible Dress Society, whose aim was the retention of the short skirt. But the pendulum of fashion inevitably swung back, skirts descended to the ankles, and, in the thirties, the buttocks became the new zone of erotic interest—so much so that a cotton frock printed with alternate rows of heart and buttock symbols (the former being the latter turned upside down) was voted 'most attractive'.[23]

The most recent vogue of the short skirt has engendered fewer and milder protests than its predecessor in the twenties. And it has found an august defender in the *Sunday Times*. Though skirts, it thinks, have gone about as far as they could go, without charges of indecent exposure, and the only way a skirt *can* go now is downwards, this newspaper believes that short skirts are youthful, becoming, and loved by their wearers and their viewers; it adds a hope that masculine disapproval can this time halt the downward trend.[24] Today's sartorial moralists tend to concentrate their fire on underwear advertisements and women's slacks. In 1956 the Public Morality Council sought an interview with an official of London Transport, to whom they complained that the proportion of underwear posters on the Underground was too high, and that some of them were very near to being indecent. The Council were assured that a considerable measure of restraint was exercised before a poster was accepted for display; that real effort was made to avoid giving offence to the public; but that there would inevitably be some posters which seemed distressingly over the line of acceptability to some, 'whose sensitivity is perhaps more pronounced than others' '.[25]

Sensitivity of this nature is not commonly associated with factory workers. But in 1962 male workers at a Wakefield shirt factory complained when a 23-year-old woman went to work in skin-tight, shocking-pink trousers. A meeting of the directors, having examined the question with some care and from every angle, decided that the trousers were attractive—and gave the young woman permission to go on working in them.[26]

Since 1900, when ladies went skiing in ankle-length skirts, and a corset and stockings were *de rigueur* with a bathing dress, the costumes worn for outdoor sports and for swimming have steadily become more hygienic, less restrictive, and more revealing.

Wimbledon has long been the setting for daring innovations in tennis costume. The celebrated Suzanne Lenglen, in the early twenties, was the first player to wear a one-piece dress instead of a blouse and skirt. It was a low-waisted silk dress with a pleated skirt that came three or four inches below the knee; with it she wore white silk stockings.[27] In 1929 Joan Lycett stirred up strong feelings by playing without any stockings at all. 'The STOCKINGLESS WIMBLEDON CONTROVERSY raged in the Press for weeks. . . . There was talk of bare legs being banned . . . but no ban was imposed, and tennis legs have been bare ever since. . . . Later, shorts were outrageously introduced.'[28] An American, 'Gorgeous' Gussie Moran, practised more recently the arts of gamesmanship and publicity by wearing unusually scanty lace drawers at Wimbledon. In 1962 a countrywoman of hers stitched a Confederate flag to her under-garment; another woman player appeared in 24-carat gold-cloth drawers; and a third scandalized many spectators by wearing shocking-pink drawers under a flapping 'twist dress'. The Wimbledon directors decreed, no doubt in the best interests of the game, that henceforward it would be a condition of entry that all players wear white.[29] A similar colour bar was imposed in 1962 by Miss Mona Mathews, headmistress of a Peterborough girls' grammar school, who sent a circular to parents ruling that 'all panties must be brown' and 'all brassières must be white'. She did so after a surprise physical training session had 'confirmed her worst suspicions'—that 'lots of girls were wearing what she had expressly forbidden. BLACK UNDIES'.[30]

Men's sports costumes have, on the whole, given rise to fewer complaints than those of women. There was a curious exception at Rhyl in the early thirties, when girl members of a hiking club threatened to resign if the men in the club continued to wear shorts, which the young women felt to be indecent. This rather staggered the men, who had been planning to agitate that the girls should themselves adopt shorts and thus come into line with other clubs.[31] Male visitors to public swimming baths in Hull, permitted to wear brief trunks during the war because of the shortage of cloth, were told in 1949 that 'trunks must come to the top of the hip bone and fit snugly, and be straight round the legs'.[32]

The watershed, so to speak, in the evolution of women's bathing dress was 1909, the year when skin-tight one-piece unskirted costumes of woven wool or cotton started to oust serge costumes with long drawers, full skirts, and sleeves down to the elbow. One fashion writer was soon admitting that she had never seen a woman wearing one of the new woven bathing suits without experiencing a slight shock.[33] A Broadstairs by-law of 1910 laid it down that 'for the preservation of decency and order every person above the age of ten years shall wear a suitable costume or dress from the neck to the knees'.[34] Except for the abandonment of stockings with bathing costumes there was little further progress until the early thirties, when a tendency to reveal the flanks through the slashed sides of costumes led a Catholic journal to deplore 'a widespread resolve to lower the standards of modesty still further during any hot weather that 1932 may tardily give us'.[35] Some Protestant opinion was sterner still. One vicar questioned whether seaside resorts were now suitable places to visit:

> No decent-minded person would wish to marry a member of the opposite sex who shamelessly flaunts before the gaze of a sneering public nudities and crudities which might be looked at askance even by the aborigines of the wilds of Africa or Asia. Isn't it about time that so-called civilized people returned to a measure both of sanity and of decency?[36]

Yet, except in the Scottish highlands, where as late as 1946 women bathed in the sea fully clothed in old dresses,[37] Mrs Grundy could no more freeze bathing costumes in pre-Bikini form than she could stop the spread of mixed bathing.[38] Her opposition to the 'nudities and crudities' of sea-bathers and sun-bathers will now be described.

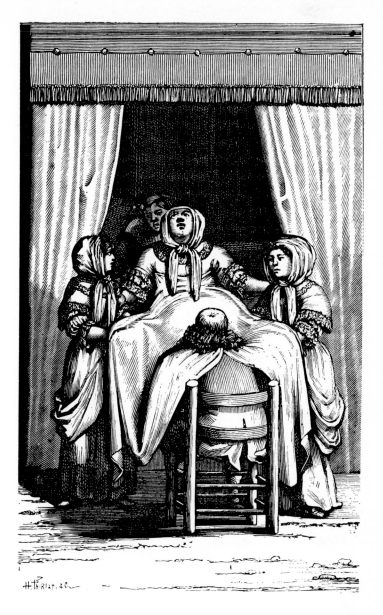

A seventeenth-century male obstetrician operating under a sheet

An English king in a codpiece: Holbein's cartoon for his portrait of Henry VIII

Décolletage in the early seventeenth century. The low neckline of the figure on the left indicates that she is nubile. From a tomb at Lynsted, Kent.

Cupid in a skirt.   A valentine, *c.* 1840

Mid-Victorian tennis costumes

22

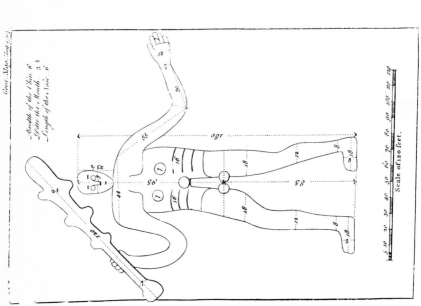

(b) The Cerne giant, as portrayed in an eighteenth-century popular print.

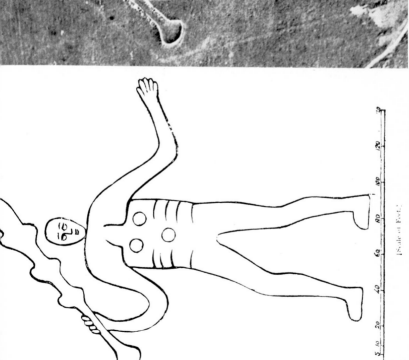

(a) The Cerne giant, as portrayed in the nineteenth century (in John Sydenham's *Baal Durotrigensis* [c. 1842])

(b) The Cerne giant as he really is

(a)   Nudists on the run on the shore of the Serpentine.
A scene from the nineteen-twenties

(b) 'Ban on London sun-bathers', said the caption to this picture in the October 1931 issue
of *Health & Efficiency*. It added: 'Members of the New Health Society on the shores of
the Welsh Harp, Hendon, N. London. Owing to the action of the authorities they have
had to disband.'

NO NUDES IS GOOD NEWS

On the hillside above the Dorset village of Cerne Abbas, the Cerne giant testifies with ithyphallic vigour to the existence of generations of people on this island who defied the body taboo. The origin of the 180-feet-long figure is obscure; its outline trenches, cut through the turf, used to be scoured and filled with fresh chalk every seven years by villagers, who danced each May Day round a fir bole erected just above the giant's head.[1] Not everyone has appreciated the club-swinging giant's virility. He has often been castrated in drawings; and one writer of guide-books called him 'very old and very ugly' before hastily changing the subject.[2] Whether he be Saxon god or Phoenician Hercules, fertility symbol or colossal ribald graffito, the giant is bigger in every sense than his emasculators. He is nine hundred times larger than life; and it is life that he triumphantly affirms.

We have always been fascinated by nakedness. Two contrary facets of the English character are latent in Peeping Tom, the eponymous voyeur who dared to gaze on Godiva, wife of the Earl of Mercia, when she rode naked through the Coventry streets at noonday. Tom, says the legend, was struck blind; that was his punishment for delighting in the pleasure of the eye and for seeing no harm in the unclothed human body. The Peeping Tom who sees a great deal of harm in it has always gone unpunished: whether as a nineteenth-century spinster, binoculars pressed to her eyes, searching the distant sea for naked male swimmers, or as a twentieth-century Press photographer flying low, again and again, over a nudist camp.

Before the nineteenth century nakedness and near-nakedness, generally speaking, were only an occasional, if piquant, phenomenon. In More's *Utopia* (1516) men and women who contemplated marriage were exhibited naked to each other beforehand, to prevent deceit.[3] Fynes Moryson recorded in 1617 that men and women in the wilder parts of Ireland went naked except for a rag of linen round their privy parts and a loose mantle round their shoulders. A Bohemian baron told him that in one place in Ireland he was met at the door by sixteen women, all naked except for their loose mantles; leading him into the house, they sat with crossed legs, like tailors, so low as could not but offend chaste eyes. The local chieftain then came in, naked except for shoes and a mantle which he promptly took off, inviting the baron to follow his example; but the baron was so excited by all this nudity that he was ashamed to take off his own clothes.[4]

Pepys relates that one day in 1667 a Quaker, crying 'Repent! Repent!', passed naked through Westminster Hall, 'only very civilly tied about the privities to avoid scandal, and with a chafing-dish of fire and brimstone burning upon his head'.[5] This strange figure was almost certainly Solomon Eccles, a religious enthusiast of the time. Eccles later exhibited himself stark naked at Cork—he no doubt thought there would be less risk of scandal among the wild Irish—and was flogged through the town and expelled. Pepys also gives an account of the rude behaviour of the poet and playwright Sir Charles Sedley, who, while drunk, defecated into the street from a balcony, then took his clothes off and harangued the populace in profane language while his friends threw down bottles containing urine; the crowd was far from pleased, and he was eventually fined £500, whereupon he told the Lord Chief Justice 'that he thought he was the first man that paid for shiting'. Some years later Sedley and a companion were arrested by the watch after 'running up and down all the night with their arses bare, through the streets'.[6] The Earl of Rochester told his biographer Burnet that he and his friends 'in their Frolicks . . . would have chosen sometimes to have gone naked, if they had not feared the people'.[7]

Two arguments against the body taboo were advanced by Swift and by the 'Gentleman of Great Parts' who wrote *Nakedness Consider'd* (1729). When Gulliver explains the nature of clothes to his master the Houyhnhnm and offers to demonstrate by undressing, 'only desiring his Excuse, if I did not expose those Parts, that Nature had taught us to conceal', Swift puts this reply into the Houyhnhnm's mouth:

> He said my Discourse was all very strange, but especially the last part; for he could not understand why Nature should teach us to conceal what Nature had given. That neither himself nor Family were ashamed of any Parts of their Bodies; but however I might do as I pleased.[8]

The 'Gentleman of Great Parts' set out to 'convince all unprejudic'd Persons of the Absurdity of wearing any Clothes'. He denied that it would be indecent or unbecoming to go without them; men and women were so beautiful that nothing could give more pleasure or be more agreeable to the eye. The covering of our nakedness caused lewdness rather than hindering it. Why one part should be more proper to be concealed than another, he could not find out. And he recommended all that loved their country to set the glorious example of throwing off all sorts of apparel, thus checking luxury and extravagance.[9] William Blake and his wife went further than the mere advocacy of nakedness: a friend claimed to have found them in their garden at Lambeth sitting naked as Adam and Eve and reciting passages from *Paradise Lost* in character.[10]

Men who bathed in the sea or in rivers in the nineteenth century did so quite naked as a rule, though they generally took reasonably good care to be out of sight of women. In 1808 a man who bathed naked at Brighton, undressing and dressing on the beach, was charged with indecently exposing his naked person in the presence of divers of his Majesty's liege subjects. 'The law', observed Chief Baron McDonald, who tried the case, 'will not tolerate such an exhibition. Whatever his intention, the necessary tendency of his conduct is to outrage public decency and corrupt public morals. . . . Whatever place becomes the habitation of civilized men, there the laws of decency must be enforced.' The culprit was convicted, but not punished.[11] In 1831 Joseph Livesey complained in his *Moral Reformer* of the indecencies to be seen at Lea Marsh, a popular swimming place: 'Unrestrained either by principle, custom or authority, the scenes exhibited are just what might be expected from savage nations.'[12] Customs, and the limits of tolerance, seem to have varied greatly from area to area. From Scarborough a member of the Rothschild family wrote in 1858: 'Here is complete absence of costume as in the garden of Eden before the fall of man, and hundreds of ladies and gentlemen look on, while the bathers plunge in the foaming waters, or emerge from them. . . . I really think the police should interfere.'[13] The Reverend Francis Kilvert, when he bathed naked at Seaton, Devon, in 1873, 'set at nought the conventionalities of the place and scandalized the beach'. Nevertheless 'some little boys who were looking on at the rude naked man appeared to be much interested in the spectacle, and the young ladies who were strolling near seemed to have no objection'. Next summer, at Shanklin, he had to adopt 'the detestable custom of bathing in drawers', commenting: 'If ladies don't like to see men naked why don't they keep away from the sight?'[14] Young men of lower social classes than Kilvert would, as they walked up from the sea, grasp their sexual organs with one hand, for concealment.[15] Oxford dons and undergraduates did not need to grasp theirs; they enjoyed 'Parson's Pleasure', the place on the banks of the Cherwell where it was a long-established tradition to swim, and lie in the sun, naked.

Foreign visitors who went bathing had strange experiences sometimes. One who stayed at a quiet seaside place used to take a boat out two hundred yards from the shore, where he would change into a bathing dress and enter the sea. After several days of this a local vicar gravely informed him that two venerable old ladies, whose house faced the sea where he embarked each day, were much distressed in their minds by his proceedings. The swimmer promised that in future he would go a hundred yards further out. Next day however the vicar told him that the old ladies could still see him plainly—by means of excellent binoculars![16] Similar stories have often been told about other hypermetropic ladies, old and young.[17] A Frenchman on a mid-century visit to Brighton bathed naked one Sunday from a wheeled cabin drawn well into the sea. After his swim he found that the tide had gone out, leaving the machine stranded on the beach—and that a lady and her two pretty daughters, holding prayer books, had settled themselves on a bench in his direct line of approach. As he walked up from the sea and passed them they made no pretence of looking away. It turned out that they disapproved of Sunday bathing, and had adopted this method of discouraging delinquents.[18]

It was none other than Gladstone who denied that nakedness had been tolerated among the Greeks, and, in particular, that young women of high rank in ancient Greece had given hospitality to weary male travellers by bathing them and anointing them with oil. 'It is almost of itself incredible', he wrote, 'that habitually, among persons of the highest rank and character, and without any necessity at all, such things should take place. And, as it is not credible, so neither, I think, is it true.'[19] Perhaps a Liberal prime minister could not imagine himself receiving such hospitality without desiring much more. But Gladstone was not the only Victorian who was tempted to attribute his own fantasies to others. When the 'Universal Provider', William Whiteley, built London's first department store, it was said that the ladies of Bayswater stopped going to the public baths for fear of being over-looked; that it was possible to tell from the windows of the store the colour of the ladies' bathing costumes as they swam; and that one lady in her private bath had seen a man on Whiteley's roof peeping in through the window. Whiteley obligingly offered to obscure his windows with paint, fit them with bars, and have them all screwed down. It was argued nevertheless that 'a man of prurient imagination could easily take a screwdriver in his hand in order to realize his desires'.[20]

The ascendancy of the body taboo in Victorian times caused people's natural interest in the human body not merely to be much intensified, but to flow into some fairly odd channels. The Reverend Charles Dodgson, author of *Alice's Adventures in Wonderland* (1865), derived special satisfaction from photographing female children in the nude. Lord Ward's favourite pastime was to gaze for hours on end at his wife as she lay naked—except for her jewels—on a sofa draped with black satin. When Lady Ward complained to her parents of scenes that caused her, first terror, then disgust, they told her that her husband's peculiarity came within the meaning of the marriage vows and that she must submit to his humours. The rest of the story, though not strictly relevant to our immediate theme, is not uninstructive. Lord Dupplin's appreciation of Lady Ward was markedly less passive than her husband's; when the latter discovered her infidelity he turned her into the street at three in the morning. Though she was pregnant, her parents refused to shelter her. She died soon afterwards. Lord Ward, described as 'a pleasant man', wrenched apart the corpse's jaws to show a friend how bad his wife's teeth had been.[21]

A piece of Edwardian science-fiction, Mme F. Blaze de Bury's *The Storm of London* (1904), depicted the results of a sudden destruction of all fabrics and hence of all clothes. The book sold wildly, no doubt because its theme was universal nakedness; within a few years it had gone through five editions.

The ban on nude bathing in swimming baths was questioned soon after the first world war in the magazine *Health & Efficiency*, when a correspondent using the *nom de guerre* 'Purity, not Prudery' complained that, although men might walk round the side of the bath absolutely naked, drying themselves or talking to their friends, they had to don a pair of slips before they could enter the water. In the subsequent correspondence, 'D.C.M.' held that naked bathing was no more degrading than the apparel of ultra-modern women—and not nearly so suggestive.[22] At that stage it was segregated, not mixed, nude bathing that was in question. As a result of this correspondence, it was proposed to start a group or groups for 'Nude-Life Culture and modern-gymnosophy' in England in the summer of 1922; and before long an English Gymnosophist Society was in existence, helped by the publication of English translations of two classics of the German nudist movement: J. M. Seitz's *Back to Nature* (trans. Clifford Coudray, Dresden, 1923) and *Man and Sunlight* (trans. David Arthur Jones, Slough, 1927) by Hans Surén, former commander of the German army gymnastic school. Dean Inge, consulted about the morality of publishing Surén's book, recommended that it be issued with the illustrations, and defended it in a newspaper article.[23]

Until the late twenties there were very few organized nudist groups in England, and the movement attracted correspondingly little publicity. Mrs Nesta H. Webster, in her book *The Socialist Network* (1926) did however reveal that the nudists in the New Gymnosophical Society were part of a vast international German-Russian-Jewish conspiracy directed against christianity and the latter's most remarkable achievement, the British empire. She complained that the police had taken no action against a couple found wandering 'entirely without clothes' on the Sussex downs in the summer of 1925.[24] Within two years the police were on their mettle. They arrested a man for sun-bathing in shorts in Hyde Park (the magistrate said: 'I am going to hold, rightly or wrongly, that to expose the upper part of your body is indecent. I think it is likely to shock persons of ordinary susceptibility'[25]); and they gave the secretary of the New Gymnosophical Society, H. C. Booth, a 'polite but firm hint' that the Society would have to be disbanded.[26]

Members of another group, the Sun Ray Club and New Health Society, began in 1929 to congregate on the shore of the Welsh Harp, a reservoir in Hendon. Though they used a privately owned area invisible from any part of the public footpath, there were indignant letters in the local Press, and next summer the shore of the reservoir was black with hostile spectators shouting ribaldries; mothers brought their offspring, then bewailed the fact that innocent children should have to witness such degrading sights.[27] There were serious disturbances; 'Sun Bath "Riot" at Lake Side', 'Scenes in the Sun Bathing War', and 'Crowd Attacks Sun Bathers' were some of the headlines; police protection had to be obtained. The authorities, by officially throwing open the reservoir shores to the public, were able to compel the wearing of slips or bathing costumes. But the Welsh Harp sunbathers continued to be the subject of sensational articles in the Sunday papers. 'They were so scared at seeing me', wrote one journalist, 'that these madmen and madwomen gathered up their clothes for a speedy departure.'[28] In 1933 a twenty-six-year-old clerk named John Pratt was found guilty at the Old Bailey of an offence against decency at the Welsh Harp recreation ground. 'Unfortunately nowadays', remarked the Recorder, Sir Ernest Wild, 'there are societies and cults who preach the nude, but when they are brought to justice they will be incarcerated in his Majesty's prisons.' He told a detective-sergeant: 'Keep an eye on these nudists, will you? And see if you can bring them to justice.' Pratt was incarcerated for a month. When he next appeared in court, to be bound over for a year, the Recorder slightly changed his tune, saying it must clearly be understood that no attack was being made on sun-bathing, which was an admirable thing if decently conducted.[29]

By this time nudism had ceased to be 'an obscure and secret cult not untouched by that crankiness . . . which characterizes all truly pioneer movements'[30]—a cult whose members often used the names of lesser classical gods, nymphs and heroes as 'camp names'[31]—and had become something of a craze, especially among intellectuals (though its supporters were 'just a little too middle-aged and elderly'[32] to suit all tastes). 'The bulk and mainstay of the movement', wrote William Welby in the peak year of 1938, when 30,000 and even 40,000 adherents were claimed, 'is to be found amongst the middle class concerned with businesses and professions.' It was a family affair. 'Complete families are more the rule than the exception.'[33] Indeed, under its new name of 'naturism',[34] the movement was well on the way to becoming respectable—just one more expression of English eccentricity. Whereas *John Bull* had warned in 1931 that nudist groups were being organized by undesirable extremists, that they had attracted degenerates and unhealthy-minded people, that the movement was a step towards organized orgies, and that the police would have to go into the woods and meadows,[35] the same magazine five years later sent a correspondent to tour the principal nudist clubs in Greater London, where he met clergymen, Harley Street specialists, schoolmasters, civil servants, and B.B.C. officials. 'The leaders of these organizations are, in the main, very intelligent and respectable', *John Bull*'s correspondent reported, adding: 'I have never heard a single reference to sex in an unseemly manner within a nudist club.'[36] And by 1937 the *Daily Mirror* psychologist could write that 'nudism seems to stabilize and normalize neurotic . . . prudist or sex-obsessed people', that it 'takes from sex the unhealthy emphasis which most moderns have to some degree'.[37] Even the Public Morality Council, having made 'very careful enquiry' into advertisements about sun-bathing, admitted that 'no indecent practices can be alleged'.[38] The National Sun and Air Association held its first congress (of naked delegates) in 1932; nudist magazines were available on the bookstalls, though the young women on the covers usually wore bathing dresses; and the final *cachet* of respectability was provided for some by George Bernard Shaw's answer to the question, 'What do you think of nudism?':

> I do not think of it. Now that you call my attention to it I can only say that it seems to me to be a reaction against the doctrine of original sin and against the abuse of clothes to produce an unnatural excess of sexual desire. . . . On these points all my sympathies are with the nudists.[39]

But when 'Critic' of the *New Statesman* visited a nudist camp he found it silly and self-conscious; naked people reading poetry or playing organized games made him laugh.[40]

So respectable, in fact, did some of the nudists become that the servants who brought round the tea wore loin-cloths or aprons to make clear their lower social standing.[41]

All the same, as Ethel Mannin pointed out, the average Englishman preferred to think of sun-bathing camps as places of prurience[42]—places 'organized by old roués as an extension of the Bohemian orgies of German libertines'.[43] And nudism offended social and racial prejudices as well as sexual ones. The Bishop of Ely declared that anyone who visited a nudist camp forfeited the right to be called a gentleman or a lady. 'I wonder', he mused, 'if it is possible . . . to stop this sort of thing. It is intolerable that these things should come along.'[44] Others felt that nudism was not merely ungentlemanly, but positively un-English. 'The cult of nudism', declared a Sussex landowner who objected to a proposal to start a club near his land, 'might be left to the Continentals and not imported into the sylvan glades of England.' And a reader of the *Daily Mirror* felt that 'the white races were certainly never meant to expose themselves in this way'.[45] To the vicar of St Paul's, Shanklin, the ultimate objective of beach undressing was nudism, 'or should it not rather be called lewdism?', and the cult of the body was the cause of world-wide dementia.[46] G. K. Chesterton advised dealing with the nudist by laughing at him and locking him up;[47] one of Chesterton's co-religionists, Father Owen Dudley, took a sterner view. The practice of undressing, he said, was common in asylums with 'the more violent type'. And nudism was an abnormality —an act of violence, a gesture of revolt against the established order of things. The authorities quite rightly interned nudists in fenced camps.[48] Lord Horder agreed: nudist camps were 'stunts that make an appeal to the slightly pathologically-minded among us'.[49]

Other distinguished opponents of nudism in practice included Mahatma Gandhi, who thought it would be a great error to act as though all men and women were pure minded, and George Lansbury, who as Labour's First Commissioner of Works opened the Serpentine to mixed bathing, but who thought a nudist colony in Hyde Park would be crazy, since all London would flock to see the sight and one wouldn't be able to see the park for people.[50] He was no doubt right.

Then there were the numerous local worthies who set their faces resolutely against bare skin on, or off, the beaches. In Sandgate, Kent, a councillor described beach undressing as 'farmyard behaviour'; another said officials were perfectly justified in admonishing a seventeen-stone woman that came out of the water with one of her shoulder-straps off.[51] 'Shall we', demanded a member of Twickenham Ratepayers' Association, 'sacrifice the heritage of a beautiful river bank for a mess of half-naked sun-bathers?' And the chairman of Littlehampton Ratepayers' Association said it was a disgrace to Littlehampton that people with eighty per cent of their clothes missing should be allowed to wander about. 'I have seen girls cycling in our town with next to nothing on, and I don't think it should be allowed', he added.[52] When it was suggested that an open-air swimming pool be built in Bath, Councillor Sam Cook went over to Weston-super-Mare to see what went on there. He reported to fellow councillors that he would never forget what he had seen:

It was disgraceful. I prayed that a tidal wave would come up and wash the whole lot away. It wasn't the bathers so much, though some of their costumes were bad enough. It was the sun-bathers, lying about with as good as nothing on. . . . We do not want that sort of thing in Bath.[53]

Seaside and riparian local authorities that shared this point of view did their best to regulate the display of human flesh. Margate had a policeman patrolling to make sure that bathers were properly dressed, and its entertainments committee heard from one excited councillor that it was 'hot stuff' in Cliftonville.[54] The Hastings authority said nude bathing by men was permitted from a certain part of the beach, but when this ruling was tested the police intervened. And the Sheriff of Chester had the banks of the Dee patrolled by special constables in 1941, to prevent nude bathing.

The attitude of the masses to organized nudism and nudists combined curiosity and hostility in roughly equal measure. When nudists held a summer conference at Harrogate 'the roads in the vicinity were frequently lined with motor cars from the roofs of which young gentlemen and old ladies peered anxiously through opera glasses'.[55] At Haslemere in Surrey the nudists found grounds through which ran a path disused for years—a disputed right of way that no one had championed. A few days after they took over their camp members of the public began to use the path, so that canvas screens had to be put up, and protests were lodged with the police against the affront to decency. In the early days of the movement nudists were sometimes annoyed by aeroplanes and helicopters that flew low over their camps; one newspaper hired an aeroplane to dive on nudists with a high-speed camera. At some camps there were 'overt acts of hostility by a strange alliance of the local "puritans" and "tough eggs"'.[56] Under the heading 'Girl Attacks Nude Male Bathers: Picnickers Applaud Her Action' the *Daily Express* reported an incident where a young woman was so excited by the sight of some naked men bathing that she suddenly rushed up to them and started to flagellate them with a willow-stick, 'a spectacle which seems to have afforded much pleasure to the onlookers'.[57] In the summer of 1939, people living near Woolacombe Sands, Devon, put up barbed wire to stop holiday-makers from reaching the beach. Young people's behaviour had, it was alleged, been shameless; both sexes had gone about together completely unclothed;

and some residents had objected to their children being forced to see such a demoralizing sight.[58] As late as 1953 a parish councillor in Camber, Sussex, was threatening nudists with 'a whiff of buckshot'.[59] A desire to punish had also been the reaction of travellers in Scotland who suddenly saw from the train two nudists lying face downwards on the grass:

> A lady . . . said indignantly that what should be done with such people was to march them up and down Sauchiehall Street just to see how they liked it. This punishment appealed to me as very suitable. I am sure there must be thousands of honest Glesca folk dying to see what nudists look like in their uniforms, just as I did before accident satisfied my curiosity. What do others think?[60]

Press and other printed attacks reflected popular prejudices pretty faithfully. By 1933, nudism was being treated by many papers as a joke. But one Shelagh Gordon, in an article illustrated with a picture of the author shielding her left breast from the avid gaze of *Pictorial Weekly's* readers, said she had seen for herself where nudism ceased and conscious nakedness began. Nudism was sheer bunk . . . yet somehow at the same time an evil and an offence to the civilized world.[61] The *Policewoman's Review* joined in, with what nudists felt to be 'a mean, misleading, unreasoned and dangerous attack'.[62] They were more amused than annoyed by an anonymous pamphlet, entitled *In a Nudist Camp! (Somewhere in England.) or The Naked Truth. By an Eye-Witness. An Exposure of Nudism, The New Menace to Christianity*, which appeared in 1933 over the imprint of the Scottish Protestant League. The author had gone with his wife to a nudist summer conference. By far his most convincing and most feelingly expressed accusations were about 'The Terrible Food', to which he devoted an entire chapter. He did not think much of his dinner:

> Never in my life have I sat down to such a meal . . . what might be called mince-pie . . . coarse brown bread, thickly cut . . . a sort of suet pudding. . . . And that was all! The most outrageous meal which anyone could serve up on the terms of £3 13s. 6d. per week. . . . Some hours afterwards I vomited up the lot!

Nor did the eyewitness greatly care for his tea, 'worse that any "Soirée" stuff we have ever tasted . . . not a piece of white bread to be seen'; and supper was much the same—'a plate of one small sausage, half-cold, with a potato, also half-cold'. Having got the food off his chest, the eyewitness sailed into the nakedness at the bathing-pool, where there was no shyness or coyness or thought of modesty, and even an old granny of about sixty seemed to enjoy having nothing on. But 'there was no sex in that Camp':

> The women threw the ball to the naked men and laughter abounded when the ball happened to hit one of them on a tender spot. It was all so jovial and innocent-like. . . . I have to admit that I saw nothing objection-able . . . in so far as the conduct of the people was concerned, apart . . . from their state of absolute nudity. But had we stayed longer perhaps we would have seen more.

Perhaps. But readers were not wholly disappointed. In place of the promised eyewitness account of nudist goings on, there was abundant innuendo. No female would have refused to go into the woods with any male, 'and this "walk" could have been enjoyed without let or hindrance, both parties being in a state of nakedness all the time. With their clothes off there was no question as to who was married or single. No particular person belonged to any other particular person.' A woman of about thirty did go and sit down about a yard away from the eye-witness, who supposed that 'probably she was after friendship'. Whatever she was after, she did not get it.

The eyewitness concluded that 'no man with a clean mind could be attracted by naked women'; that nudism was unmistakably an effort to get woman to throw aside her modesty (and 'when once your woman strips herself of her clothes . . . she has nothing more to give'); and that nudism was anti-christian ('your Nudist . . . spends his Sundays . . . going about naked among naked women').[63]

This pamphlet contained advertisements for such spicy items as *Convent Life Unveiled, Why Priests Don't Wed, Ligouri the Filthy, The Horrible Lives of the Popes, The Abominal [sic] Confessional*, and *Should Mr Campbell Be Put Out Of The Episcopal Church In Scotland?*

The most thorough-going and extravagantly phrased outburst came from the pen of Captain Reginald Wallis, who held that 'the Devil was the initiator of Nudism'. The fact that there was in existence an organized movement was one of the outstanding signs of the moral deterioration of the age. He went on:

Nudism is from the pit—as profane as the blackest sin, as shameless as the Devil himself, and as heinous as hell. Nudism is a burning and arrogant insult to the modesty of humanity. It is the zenith of human rebellion against God. It is the corruption of the human heart at its culmination. . . . So abased and out of perspective is the natural mind that this nefarious movement is not only defended on ethical grounds . . . but any attack upon it is actually looked upon as a sign of obscenity![64]

Such onslaughts were less frequent and, perhaps, less telling than the jokes the nudists had to put up with. There was Ethel Mannin's delicious satire, *Rolling in the Dew* [1940].[65] And there were songs like one sung by Gracie Fields, called 'What Can You Give a Nudist on his Birthday?'. Some Clapham and Dwyer patter ('I've got a job as attendant in a nudist colony'—'What do you do?'—'I keep the stone seats warm for the members') led to a fine of £10 at Ryde in 1937.[66]

The trouble with the pioneer nudists was that they took themselves far too seriously. They seemed to go out of their way to court ribaldry. This, for instance, was the winning entry in a nursery rhyme parody competition arranged by the *Sun Bathing Review*:

> Little Miss Muffet
> Sat on a tuffet
>   In a naturist sort of way;
> When a Policeman espied her,
> And a Magistrate tried her,
>   And? THE THREE FORMED A 'GROUP' RIGHT AWAY![67]

And when, after a series of articles in the *Sunday Dispatch*, a reader wrote saying that though he was not a nudist he always said his prayers in the nude because it seemed to bring him nearer to God,[68] many nudists must have asked God to preserve them from their friends.

Nudism had to meet an argument a great deal more enlightened—superficially, at any rate—than any we have yet examined. This was the objection raised by non-nudist sun-bathers: that it was hard, if not impossible, for men to contemplate naked females without feeling sexually excited—and equally difficult for them not to have an erection as a result. Challenging the general tendency of the magazine, a reader of *Health & Efficiency* wrote in 1933 that all the nudist men and girls he (or she?) had questioned admitted freely that sex was at the bottom of it and that their main desire was for sexual experience without responsibility. It was practically impossible for a healthy young man and a healthy young woman to be side by side on a summer's afternoon, stark naked and in close physical contact, and not in the end frantically desire sexual connexion. Next month 'Reader No. 2' agreed:

> Dare any man say he never desired sexual relations when courting, what would be his feeling after he had seen his young lady in the nude? . . . I am convinced the nudist societies are nothing but sex. I could not accept [a woman's] statement that she has lain naked with a naked man and felt no sex desire.

The nudists now took up a defensive stand in the magazine's correspondence columns. 'E.L.N.' of Kew, giving 'A Woman's View', affirmed that, though 'comparatively young' and half of Latin blood, she could honestly say she had never for one second felt the slightest sexual urge at a nudist camp. After physical exercise and games she had often lain many an hour beside members of the opposite sex, talking, reading, or even doing crossword puzzles, 'quite as naturally and unselfconsciously as if we were in our own homes'. Another correspondent told of sharing a rug with a married couple, 'both splendid physical specimens . . . full of vitality and, as it happened, both members of a learned profession'. With the lady in the middle, the three of them found that the rug afforded only close quarters; but 'that didn't matter in the slightest'. Discussing the controversy, the three had agreed that 'Reader No. 2' could never have taken part in a reunion of nudists, for 'not once had any person, man or woman, been observed as showing sexual excitement'.

The correspondence went on for months. 'Sceptical' of Kettering insisted that the ordinary decent man could not look on a nude woman without feeling sexual excitement, while 'Semi-nudist' of Southampton believed that he himself would experience excitement until the novelty had worn off. 'Surely', he wrote, 'the basis of sexual allurement is the beauty of form and the touch of smooth, soft flesh.' A man was in the unfortunate position of being unable to experience sexual excitement without showing it; what was a man expected to do in these camps in the event of this unfortunate predicament? Was he looked on as a sensualist and asked to leave, or was it just ignored? There was no very clear reply. 'F.I.O.' of Reading found it inconceivable that the movement could have survived the first experiments if male excitement was not conspicuous by its absence. At length 'Sceptical' of Kettering was driven to providing a solution: a cold douche under the shower.[69]

Apart from the sight, anodyne or risible, of naked people reading poetry or tossing balls about, the nudists in fact possessed a tolerably powerful antaphrodisiac in the shape of their own remarkable prudishness, attested to by many visitors. Most nudists, in the act of taking off their clothes, became virtually sexless. And whoever did not, felt blowing upon his sexuality (whether it manifested itself in a flirtation, a coarse remark, or a timid tumescence) the icy breath of very English, very suburban, disapproval. Nudism, wrote a nudist parson, was completely divorced from 'the all-prevailing curse of Sex'.[70] Prospective members had to convince a group secretary of their sincerity. One group set up a special selection committee of two men and two women, before whom newcomers had to appear—naked. Another group had a woman interviewer who questioned male applicants, made copious notes in a little book, then wagged a divining rod at them.[71] The written consent of husbands, wives or fiancés, if any, had to be obtained. It was virtually impossible for a man to obtain admission unless he took a woman with him. As for flirtations, some of the camps were 'almost painfully austere, forbidding their members to make even the most innocent of contacts with the opposite sex'.[72] The touch of flesh, whether smooth and soft or rough and hard, was not for them. An American couple wrote:

> In many a camp ethics and repressions are still strong, so that taboos strange and suburban are erected, as that no person in the nude may caress, fondle, or even touch another person of the opposite sex under pain of instant expulsion, and in a subtle way most camps are accused of having a faintly prim atmosphere.[73]

Pre-war nudists discussed the compilation of a black list of undesirables, though it is not clear whether it was in fact ever circulated to clubs. A man was asked to leave one club because he had been divorced, another because he used 'bad language'—i.e., words that 'would hardly shock a Sunday School today'.[74]

From time to time in the history of British nudism there have been exotic controversies about the pros and cons of depilation (i.e., the removal of the pubic hair), about the desirability of men and women foxtrotting together while naked, and about indoor nudism, a practice which one veteran of the movement used to describe as 'sex-bathing' since it was not sun-bathing, and of which another wrote: 'A small crowd of people huddled together naked in a tiny sitting-room suggests a meeting of the early Christians in the catacombs.'[75] In 1949 officials of the British Sun Bathing Association actually informed a chief constable that an attempt was being made in his city to form an indoor nudist club at which drinks would be available.

From time to time, also, enthusiasts like 'Starko' of south Devon write to the various nudist magazines complaining that the pictures of nudist activities and of naked young women they publish are retouched, the pubic hair being airbrushed out, more or less skilfully, and the male sexual organs being deleted.[76] Although the *Listener* has been known to use an 'integral' picture of a naked woman,[77] and although foreign nudist magazines imported into this country contain unmutilated pictures, the editorial reply invariably is that to follow suit would be to invite prosecution. This, it may be supposed, is prudence, not prudery.

PART V

DON'T DANCE, LITTLE LADY

BUMPS AND GRINDS
OF LONG AGO

The twist, regarded by some disturbed people as deplorably sexy, if not downright obscene, had its precursors in the middle ages. English girls and women then, like many of their descendants who in their lunch-hour flock to the Lyceum, were passionately fond of dancing in a way that one social historian has called 'rude and boisterous'.[1] And, like the somewhat less influential erotophobes of the present time, medieval moralists lamented the bodily movements, suggestive of those made in coition, which seem to have been a common feature of these dances. There were kissing dances, too, like the cushion dance, in which couples knelt on a cushion and kissed. An eminent English Dominican of Chaucer's day complained of women, decked in bewitching finery, enticing men away to dances from the house of God. Their wanton ways, he said, were a general danger to morality and drew men to sin. Other English preachers told admonitory tales of men and women who disturbed divine service with their dancing and found themselves miraculously compelled to continue, day and night, till some dropped dead from exhaustion and others were finally freed from their torment by an archbishop—but suffered pains in their legs for the rest of their days. Such revellers are thought to have sung coarse songs as well as indulging in rowdy behaviour.[2]

The Church opposed equally the performances of female entertainers who are said to have adopted many of the practices of eastern dancing-girls and to have danced in a way that was 'gross and indecent',[3] amusing their audiences with contortions, leaping through hoops, hand-stands and somersaults. John of Salisbury, in his twelfth-century *Polycraticus*, made disapproving mention of the 'obscene motions of the body' indulged in by these tumblers.[4] And Thomas de Chabham,

Sub-Dean of Salisbury, wrote (*c.* 1213) that some entertainers 'trans-form and transfigure their bodies with indecent dance and gesture, now indecently unclothing themselves, now putting on horrible masks'.[5] If we attempt to define exactly what these obscene motions of the body might have consisted in, we find that the possibilities are limited, the three most likely ones being the forward thrust of the pelvis and its rotation, as in sexual intercourse, and the raising of one leg to an angle of 135 degrees or more, as in Egyptian fertility dances of the sixth dynasty, the *triori* of south Brittany, the *aurresku* of the Basques, the *sardana* of the Catalans, and the cancan. The first two of these three movements are the principal saltatory stock-in-trade of the belly-dancer and the modern strip-tease dancer, who, in America, calls them respectively the 'bumps' and the 'grinds'.

Opposition to dancing under Elizabeth I and the Stuarts is popularly associated with the puritans, who are also thought to have opposed, and ultimately to have abolished, the people's May Day and other festivities. Defenders of the puritans have not been lacking, however, to point out that the kind of dancing they objected to was undisguisedly erotic, and that the festivities they objected to entailed much sexual licence. Frederick J. Furnivall, in one of his forewords to Phillip Stubbes's *Anatomie of the Abuses in England*, asked his readers to recognize how very much there was in the pastimes of Stubbes's day that deserved blame:

> Who . . . now wants to have . . . the *cancan* danced, or drunken jolli-fications going on in Church or Churchyard? Who would let sister, daughter, or maid, be out with a mixt company of men and girls in the woods all night . . . ? Depend upon it, there *were* abuses of the grossest kind in the rough games of Stubbes's and Shakspere's day, abuses even justifying the call that they should in public be put down for a time al-together.[6]

Joseph Crouch, in his *Puritanism and Art* (1910), denied that the objection to May Day celebrations was an example of puritan sourness of temper, and, quoting Furnivall, was at pains to show that the village amusements the puritans suppressed were far from innocent.[7] And Percy Scholes, in *The Puritan and Music* (1934), held that the puritan attitude towards dancing during the seventeenth and early eighteenth centuries was generally tolerant; Cromwell had 'mixt dancing' at the wedding of one of his daughters; the Larger Catechism compiled by the Westminster Assembly of 1643–47 opposed only *lascivious* dancing. Scholes suggested that while in a decent section of society mixed dancing had been unexceptionable, in another section it had customarily been made an opportunity for impropriety. As for May Day celebrations, the puritans—or many of them—had no objection to these, apart from obviously pagan practices 'or practices tending to immorality'.[8]

There is clearly much force in these arguments. The puritan writers were concerned to prevent erotic dancing and to extirpate a tradition in which such dancing had a central place, and in which the coming of spring was greeted with a fertility ceremony evidently carried over from pre-christian religions. On the eve of the first of May each year the villagers would go into the woods, to bring back next day, with great reverence, a garlanded priapic maypole around which they would dance in a ring. Virgins would be deflowered, and there was undoubtedly a great deal of unbridled sex in these 'naïve cults addressed by a primitive folk to the beneficent deities of field and wood and river'.[9]

Long before the advent of puritanism, the Church had been seeking to meet the challenge to its authority implicit in these and similar ceremonies. Between 1236 and 1244, Robert Grosseteste, Bishop of Lincoln, in a series of disciplinary pronouncements, condemned the feast of fools and the May and harvest festivals. In 1240, Walter de Chanteloup, Bishop of Worcester, prohibited another English folk-festival, the play of the king and queen. And William Courtney, Archbishop of Canterbury, is thought to have put a stop to the Lincoln feast of fools in 1390.[10]

One of the earliest puritan onslaughts against lascivious dancing was John Northbrooke's *Treatise against Dicing, Dancing, Plays, and Interludes* [c. 1577]. The author condemned contemporary dancing as wicked, filthy, vain, foolish, fleshly, and devilish. It inflamed men's hearts, which were already evil enough. Lust of the flesh and of the eyes, which ought to be suppressed, was stirred up by the wanton enticement of dances, from which men returned home less good than they had been, and women less chaste in their minds, if not in their bodies. Why did women choose one man rather than another to dance with, if not to declare 'howe they are inflamed eche to other in filthie concupiscence and lust'?

Dancing [Northbrooke continued] is the vilest vice of all. . . . They daunce with disordinate gestures, and with monstrous thumping of the feet, to pleasant soundes, to wanton songs, to dishonest [i.e., lewd] verses: maydens and matrons are groped and handled with unchast handes, and kissed, and dishonestly embraced; and the things which nature hath hidden, modestie couered, are then oftentimes, by meanes of lasciuiousnesse, made naked, and ribauldrie, vnder the colour of pastyme, dissembled.[11]

Stubbes likewise saw dancing as an introduction to whoredom, a preparation for wantonness, a provocation to uncleanness, and an entrance to all kinds of lewdness:

For . . . what kissing and bussing, what smouching & slabbering one of another, what filthie groping and vncleane handling is not practised euery wher in these dauncings? yea, the very deed and action it selfe, which I will not name for offending chast ears, shall be purtrayed and shewed foorth in their bawdye gestures of one to another.

If men and women must dance, let them dance separately. And Stubbes gave a graphic description of the villagers going overnight to the woods and bringing home their maypole ('this stinking Ydol, rather') covered with flowers, hundreds of men, women, and children following it with great devotion. He had heard it credibly reported, by men of great gravity and reputation, that of forty, sixty, or a hundred maids going to the woods overnight, scarcely a third returned home maids, or, as he put it, 'vndefiled'. 'These be the fruits which these cursed pastimes bring foorth.'[12] The author of *A Treatise agaynst Light, Lewde and Lascivious Dauncing* (1583) went one better. He had 'hearde of tenne maidens which went to set May, and nine of them came home with childe'.[13]

The puritan literature regarding erotic dancing is extremely repetitive, often consisting of little more than the same strings of biblical quotations and the same objurgations. The preacher and printer Thomas Lovell, however, in his *Dialogue between Custom and Veritie, concerning the use and abuse of Dauncing and Minstrelsie* [1581], not only puts into the mouth of Veritie a lengthy harangue against the horrible immorality of kissing at the end of a dance—

If that his mate doo seem to like
the game that he would have,
He trips her toe, and clicks her cheek,
to showe what he doth crave

—but actually allows Custom to have quite a reasonable-sounding rejoinder:

> But some reply, what foole would daunce,
>   if that when daunce is doon,
> He may not have at Ladyes lips
>   that which in daunce he won?[14]

And it is only from the puritan Thomas Norton's passing reference in 1578 to 'the unchaste, shamelesse and unnaturall tomblinge of the Italion weomen'[15] that we learn of a performance by a company of Italian players before the Queen in that year.

Among seventeenth-century opponents of the dancing that stirred up lust, we might mention three. William Perkins (notorious in his youth for profanity and drunkenness, but dramatically reformed when he heard a woman in the street threaten her fretful child with 'drunken Perkins') condemned, as the very bellows of lust and uncleanness, 'the mixed daucing of men and women . . . with many lascivious gestures'.[16] The author of *The Anatomy of Melancholy* (1621) regarded dancing, if conveniently used, as a most pleasant recreation of body and mind; if abused, it was 'a furious motiue to burning lust'.[17] And Joseph Bentham condemned, as the fruits and followers of other sins, mixed dancing with wanton gestures and 'the single wanton dance'. Wanton dancing was usually accompanied by a wanton ear given to scurrilous songs; a wanton lip given to wanton kissing, with intention to stir up lust, or for carnal delight between those who were not married; and a wanton hand given to filthy touching.[18] To these three may be added Henry Hingeston, the author of 604 crowded pages of warnings and admonitions to the inhabitants of England and expostulations to the clergy—a work which, though published in 1703, belongs spiritually to the preceding century. Dancing, wrote Hingeston, was the Devil's procession, 'and he that entereth a good and wise Man into the Dance (*if it can be that such a One is either good or wise*) cometh forth a corrupt and a wicked Man'.[19]

A dissenting voice was that of John Stow, who recalled in his *Survey of London* (1598) how young girls used to dance for garlands hung across the streets, 'which open pastimes in my youth, being now suppressed, worser practices within doores are to be feared'.[20]

Of more practical import than any declarations was the Long Parliament's decree, in 1644, that

> all and singular May-Poles that are, or shall be erected, shall be taken down and removed by the Constables, Borsholders, Tything-men, petty Constables, and Churchwardens of the Parishes, and places where the same be: And that no May-pole shall be hereafter set up, created, or suffered to be within this Kingdome of England, or Dominion of Wales.[21]

23

SIN IN THE BALL-ROOM

One evening in the year 1711 a man took his wife and sixteen-year-old daughter to a ball. Before long he took them home again, lest the girl's skirts fly up and reveal more leg than he thought proper. He had been amazed to see his daughter handed by and handing young fellows with so much familiarity. This was how he described the scene in Steele's and Addison's *Spectator*:

> They very often made use of a most impudent and lascivious Step called Setting . . . the very reverse of *Back to Back*. At last an impudent young Dog bid the Fidlers play a Dance called *Mol. Pately*, and after having made two or three Capers, ran to his Partner, locked his Arms in hers, and whisked her round cleverly above ground in such manner, that I, who sat upon one of the lowest benches, saw further above her Shoe than I think fit to acquaint you with. I could no longer endure these Enormities, wherefore just as my Girl was going to be made a Whirligig, I ran in, seized on the Child, and carried her home.

This correspondent would have been more annoyed still, said an editorial note, if he had seen 'one of those *kissing Dances* in which . . . they are obliged to dwell almost a Minute on the Fair One's lips'. In country dancing, too, the great familiarities between the two sexes might produce very dangerous consequences, the ladies' hearts being melted by a handsome young fellow who was continually convincing them that he had the perfect use of all his limbs.[1]

John Wesley disapproved of public dances—unless men and women were to dance in separate rooms. And in 1791 the methodists decided to expel schoolmasters and schoolmistresses that received dancing-masters into their schools, as well as parents employing dancing-masters for their children.[2]

Though the upper classes had their dances (and some of them, as we

shall see, their orgies), the 'threepenny hops' of the lower orders in-
curred official disapproval, and there is a description of a raid by
constables and their assistants on a gathering of this kind in Piccadilly,
attended by 'footmen, servant-maids, butchers, apprentices, oyster and
orange-women, common w——s, and sharpers'.[3]

By the early part of the nineteenth century many English husbands
were forbidding their wives to go dancing—and at least one mother,
towards the end of her life, expressed gratitude to her beloved daughters
for never having asked permission to enter a ball-room.[4] Possibly they
went sometimes without permission. Such husbands and mothers shared
the view of the congregationalist minister George Burder, to whom
the dancing of both sexes together was bound to awaken improper
passions, and was a frequent cause both of adultery and of imprudent
and unhappy marriages.[5] Another preacher, Rowland Hill (who wrote
Cow-pock Inoculation, vindicated and recommended (1806) and who
personally vaccinated thousands), deplored mad, wanton, foolish
revels, with their promiscuous intercourse (the expression had not
yet acquired its present meaning) and their next to filthy conversation
calculated to kindle every dangerous and impure flame.[6] And, in a
little tract entitled *Folly's Advocate* (1827), Mrs Prudence tells Monsieur
Fribble that those who practised dancing did so either in the degrading
worship of idols or for other purposes not fit to be named. She herself
would rather see her children hobbling or crawling in the paths of
virtue than gracefully skipping and dancing in the flowery paths of
vice.[7]

The waltz came to England from Germany in 1812 and, as everyone
knows, was immediately opposed as indecorous—largely because the
dancers embraced as they danced. Mothers forbade their daughters to
dance in this improper way; many people viewed the waltz as an
attempt to shake the foundations of society; and there was talk of getting up a petition to Parliament for its prohibition as a national danger.
Nevertheless the new dance, 'an outright romp . . . as destitute of
figure or variety as the motion of a horse in a mill',[8] became a national
craze. One of its earliest advocates, General Thornton of the First
Regiment of Guards, was vehemently attacked by Mr Theodore Hook,
who held that the dance was 'calculated to lead to the most licentious
consequences'. The two men fought a duel, as a result of which the

General had to resign his commission.[9] In the *Sporting Magazine* a correspondent signing himself 'Hop' denounced this 'will-corrupting dance' as a compound of immodest gesture and infectious poison, and recommended that the 'disgusting interloper' be sent back to Germany.[10]

One of the first anti-waltzing satires was written by Byron, though how far his tongue was in his cheek may be judged from the pseudonym he adopted: Horace Hornem, Esq. The new dance, he wrote, 'wakes to wantonness the willing limbs'. Not even Cleopatra had 'displayed so much of *leg*, or more of *neck*', while

> Round all the confines of the yielded waist,
> The strangest hand may wander undisplaced.

And Byron warned that

> The breast thus publicly resigned to man
> In private may resist him—if it can.[11]

In some lines written in a friend's scrap-book, Sheridan referred to 'waltzing females with unblushing face' who 'disdain to dance but in a man's embrace'; and he mourned that 'modesty is dead'.[12] And from an anonymous satirist's pen came these verses:

> With timid steps and tranquil downcast glance,
> Behold the well-paired couple now advance;
> One hand holds hers, the other grasps her hip,
> But licensed to no neighbouring part to slip.
> * * *
> In such pure postures our first parents moved,
> While hand in hand through Eden's bowers they roved,
> Ere Beelzebub with meaning foul and false
> Turned their poor heads, and taught them how to waltz.[13]

The author of *The Ladies' Pocket-Book of Etiquette* (1840) devoted ten stern pages to 'the pollution of the waltz', which she characterized as an anti-English dance, 'the most degenerating . . . that the last or present century can see'.

> Ask the mother . . . can she consent to commit her daughter promiscuously to the arms of each waltzer . . . ? . . . Ask the lover . . . could he

endure the sight of the adopted of his heart half-embraced and all but reclining in the arms of another? ... Ask the husband ... Will you suffer your wife to be half-embraced by every puppy who can turn on his heel or his toe?[14]

A decade later, Mary Fitz George, in *Ball Room Refinement* [1851], was repeating the charge that pollution had entered the ball-room. It was a new and still more daring variety of the waltz that she objected to: the waltz *à deux temps*, in common time (a solecism for *à deux pas*, or two-step waltz). Once again we read of husbands forbidding their wives to perform a new dance. Propriety, it seems, was lost sight of in this maelstrom of the ball-room; modesty was sent to the lowest depth in— Miss Fitz George did not lack wit—double quick time. She did not lack imagination, either:

> If the dance *deux temps* actually requires the gentleman's entire posses-
> sion of the lady's waist, and that her head should really repose on his
> shoulders, let me ask anyone in this nineteenth century, *this age of moral
> refinement,* whether *this* is a becoming position to be exhibited in a ball
> room? ... The great velocity of this dance, and proximity of the partners,
> make it graceless and vulgar. It gives the spectator the idea of a double
> teetotum, or Siamese twins of a new genus, or the offspring of a two faced
> Janus looking both ways ... presenting to the imagination a novel kind
> of quadruped with an enormous beak and single wing, formed by the
> lady's high flowing robe, sometimes whirling round with the greatest
> rapidity. ... A fine exhibition truly for the zoological gardens ... but not
> for the select ball room.[15]

Two-backed beast or not, by the eighteen-sixties the waltz was being spoken of as an old favourite; but many still took the view that a lady should never come into contact with any gentleman not a near relative or an actual or probable husband. No dance, it was thought, exercised so great an influence over the senses as did the waltz.[16] Another relatively liberal view was that *if* immodesty, coarseness, vulgarity, gesticulation, extravagance in posture or style, boisterousness and indecorum were all banished from the ball-room—then dancing *could* be an innocent pleasure.[17]

Later, diehard, opposition to the waltz came from members of the clerical and medical professions. At the age of eighty-seven the Reverend James Davies, already the author of a tract 'specially and entirely on the gross immorality of the rapid round dance', returned to the attack in *Our Morals* (1873), in which he stigmatized modern dancing as coarse and vulgar and a dark spot that ought never to have been imported from the Continent, and denounced the immodest way they danced 'in those dreadful London dancing saloons'.[18] And Dr J. H. Kellogg, in a section of his *Ladies' Guide* (1890) headed 'The Immoral Dance', declared that dancing was in the highest degree demoralizing. This was particularly true of the waltz. He quoted with approval the views of a Philadelphia dancing-master who regarded the waltz as immoral because the ladies that danced it were hugged by gentlemen hitherto unknown to them; who had seen couples so closely interlocked that the man's face was in contact with that of the palpitating girl in his arms; and who had watched kisses being exchanged amid the whirl of the maddening waltz. Dr Kellogg did not even approve of dances where the participants were members of the same family. Many innocent young women had begun the downward course to shame and utter ruin in the dancing-school. Respectable christian people everywhere ought to discountenance this form of amusement, which was harmful not only on account of its immoral tendencies, but also on account of the physical injury it frequently caused. . . .[19]

24

THE ABOMINABLE
COPULATIVE BEAT

Just before the First World War it became apparent to many in England that the old order was changing rapidly. Young people were no longer so respectful to their elders as they had been under Queen Victoria; they had begun to dress with appalling casualness; they lounged in their club arm-chairs instead of sitting decorously; above all, they had started to dance an immodest dance with a suggestive lateral movement of the hips—a dance called the tango—and other dances, still worse, whose very names were alarming portents of the new, 'rag-time' era.

The arrival of the tango from the Argentine (via Deauville) in 1912 was the signal for a violent Press attack on this depraved dance. People who had obviously never seen it performed wrote to the newspapers protesting against its indelicacies, and some papers invented the story that Queen Mary had banned it.[1] The spiritual director of the Catholic Women's League, Father Bernard Vaughan, a Jesuit much in the public eye, warned of the dangers lurking at social gatherings known as 'tango teas'. 'It is not what happens at a Tango tea that so much matters, as what happens after it', he said. 'I have been too long with human nature not to know that, like a powder magazine, it had better be kept as far as possible fireproof.'[2]

Whatever fires the tango lit, the turkey trot and the bunny hug poured oil on. These latter dances were so unruly—or so it was claimed —that mothers were frightened to let their daughters accept invitations, and some forbade them to, taking their lead from a letter signed 'A Peeress' which was published in *The Times*. Its author, describing herself as one of the many matrons on whom devolved the task of guiding a girl through the mazes of a London season, sought the powerful aid of *The Times* in a matter of grave perplexity. Her grandmother,

she recalled, had often told of the shock she experienced on first beholding the polka. But what would her grandmother have said had
she been asked to introduce a well-brought-up girl of eighteen to the
'scandalous travesties of dancing which are, for the first time in my
recollection, bringing more young men to parties than are needed'?
'A Peeress' went on:

> I need not describe the various horrors of American and South American
> negroid origin. I would only ask hostesses to let one know what houses to
> avoid by indicating in some way on their invitation cards whether the
> 'Turkey Trot', the 'Boston' (the beginner of the evil), and the 'Tango' will
> be permitted.

This letter attracted much attention, both in Britain and the U.S.A.
The correspondence it provoked lasted for nearly three weeks. Many of
the contributions might have been written in the eighteen- (or even
the nineteen-) sixties. One, from 'A Parent', declared that modern
dances were a natural corollary of the licence and vulgar impropriety
which had become only too patent in modern life; another, that the
turkey trot was 'frankly symbolic of those primitive instincts of human
nature which it is the aim of civilization to suppress'.[3]

The view that the Boston waltz had been the beginning of the evil
was shared by Mrs C. E. Humphry ('Madge' of *Truth*, and author of
How to be Pretty though Plain (1899), *Manners for Girls* (1901) and
Points Worth Noting for Women [1918])—though she told the *Daily
Express* that the Boston's successors had far exceeded it in extravagance
and indecency.[4] William Boosey, the music publisher, wrote to the
Daily Telegraph about the 'vulgar and decadent "one-step" '.[5] The
Dancing Times sat uncomfortably on the fence by carrying one article
defending the turkey trot ('a much-abused and generally misunderstood
dance') and another declaring that its wild hopping and swaying and
wriggling were not suitable for any ball-room.[6] And *Punch* called on
dramatic critics to devote their energies to keeping our ball-rooms
clean.[7]

This herculean task devolved however upon the editor of the
Dancing Times, Philip Richardson, who, soon after the end of the war,
was struck by the way that Continental dancing had become objectionable, so that Catholic prelates had started warning their flocks
against the dangers lurking in modern dances. To Richardson it

seemed highly desirable that something should be done in this country to call a halt to freakish dancing before it became something worse.

Jazz, and the style of dancing then associated with it, had just hit London with a collectively improvised roar, and for a few months people went jazz crazy: some pro-, others anti-. As early as December 1917, a writer in the *Dancing Times* called for the stamping out of a discreditable and repulsive innovation: certain objectionable Negroid movements that were being exploited in European ball-rooms even before the war. What was permissible in an African kraal became disgusting when exhibited in a British ball-room.[8] The teacher of dancing employed by the Aberdeen School Board agreed that under the spell of the Negroid dance the ball-room shed the manners of a civilized age and reverted to the customs of the totem and the witch-doctor (this, at the height of the first world war!).[9] The same issue of the *Dancing Times* recorded that 'a fearsome thing called "Jazz music" has reached us. . . . What its effect will be, time alone can show'. Those who disagreed with the jungle theory blamed undesirable dancing on the influence of musical comedy, where the man flung his partner about with apache wildness, she clutching him by the neck and being swung off her feet. Young people went into the ball-room and tried to imitate this. . . .[10] In the spring of 1919 the air was vibrant with denunciations of jazz. One paper, asking 'Is Jazz an orgy of immorality?', said it was impossible to describe the dancers' motions in print, 'for obvious reasons'.[11] The eminent 79-year-old physician Sir Dyce Duckworth (chiefly celebrated for his *Treatise on Gout* (1889)), said he had not seen 'the Jazz' himself, but, from what he had heard of it, it was not likely to be continued by decent people.[12] And Canon Drummond of Maidenhead said he had no personal experience of jazz dancing, and only knew of it by what he had read and heard, but it seemed to him most degrading to encourage a dance so low, so demoralizing, and of such a low origin—'the dance of low niggers in America, with every conceivable crude instrument, not to make music, but to make a noise'.[13]

And so, in 1920, Philip Richardson summoned a conference of about two hundred dancing-teachers, to whom he announced that there was a tendency towards an artistic bolshevism in the ball-room. M. Maurice, the most famous ball-room dancer in the world, went further. He protested against the admission of jazz music and dubious steps into

'Steps the teachers wish to abolish. M. Maurice and Miss Leonora Hughes showing two of the steps which it is hoped will be banished from the ball-room.' From the *Daily Mail*, 1920

THE LAST NEW CAN-CAN.—MELLE. COLONNA AND HER PARISIAN TROUPE AT THE ALHAMBRA PALACE.

The cancan that caused the Alhambra to lose its licence. From *The Day's Doings*, 1870

(b) 'Wiry Sal' (Sarah Wright), the most famous of the Alhambra cancan dancers

(a) 'Who Is to Draw the Line: the Magistrate or the Ballet-Master?' From *The Day's Doings*, 1870

27

The future Lady Hamilton posing as Hygeia, goddess of health, at Dr James Graham's Temple of Æsculapius. A satirical drawing by Thomas Rowlandson, *c.* 1800

Women entertainers of the middle ages

(b) 'Paphian Revels' in a London brothel: strippers of the eighteen-forties. From *The Swell's Night Guide through the Metropolis* [1841]

A DIVORCE CASE.   BEFORE THE "LORD CHIEF BARON."

(c) The Judge and Jury Society at the Coal Hole in the Strand, with Renton Nicholson, 'Lord Chief Baron', presiding

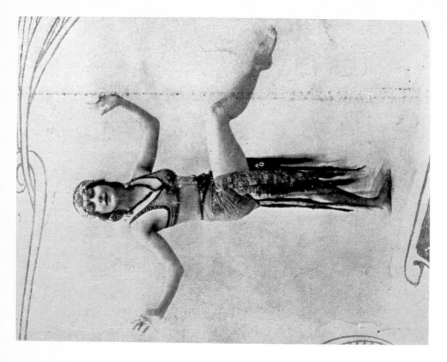

(b) Stasia Napierkowska in her disrobing 'Dance of the Bee', 1911

(a) Maud Allan as Salome, 1908

30

(b) Strip-tease in the nineteen-sixties

(a) Lady Constance Stewart-Richardson

In 1916 the Lord Chamberlain was shocked by these *Bystander* impressions of C. B. Cochran's *Half-past Eight*, since the artist 'seemed deliberately to have created the effect of feminine garments being blown up'. He ordered the removal of a framed copy from the outside of the Comedy theatre decent places, pointing out that they had originated in low Negro haunts and had *au fond* a prurient significance. In particular, M. Maurice objected to men putting their right hands on their partners' sides. The conference passed a unanimous resolution pledging the dancing-teachers to do their very best to stamp out (i.e., abolish) freak steps—'particularly dips and steps in which the feet are raised high off the ground'.[14]

Despite these well-meaning efforts, matters went from bad to worse. Or so it seemed to the Countess of Limerick, who, in an article entitled 'Delirious Dancing', told readers of the *Weekly Dispatch* that dancing had become a means of arousing passion, young girls dancing with men they hardly knew 'in such a manner that in the streets they would be arrested for improper behaviour. The very steps of the dances are suggestive.'[15] There were, for instance, the toddle and the shimmy; the name of the latter alone made the older generation shudder almost as tremulously as the movement it described. A further conference of dancing-teachers spent a great deal of time discussing this movement, finally setting up a shimmy committee, which eventually ruled that the knees must be kept together.[16]

Then, in 1925–26, came the Charleston, more delirious still. Its furious backward and upward kicking of the leg from the knee turned ball-rooms, in the opinion of those who objected to it, into beargardens. In many dance-halls the letters P.C.Q. were displayed, standing for 'Please Charleston Quietly'; and a London hotel banned the dance because so many of those who danced it were injured by the kicks of their fellow dancers.[17] Terpsichore in an ultra-short skirt, with her vigorous black bottom, even brought dissension into the heart of the temperance movement: eight Bands of Hope refused to take part in a fête arranged by the Lincoln Temperance Society because dancing was included in the programme, and dancing had done so much to damn the lives of young people.[18]

This was precisely the opinion of a number of religious writers. One, in his *Words of Help for Christian Girls*, wondered how girls with any self-respect could yield themselves, especially when attired in flimsy ball-room costume, to the embraces of strange men, whose morals might be worse than doubtful.[19] The Reverend Herbert Lockyer quoted, at some length, an American's opinion that as long as the schools were used to teach the first rudiments of prostitution (i.e., dancing) there would be prostitutes. According to Lockyer, nearly all prostitutes were graceful dancers, and perfect in the art. The waltz had originated in Parisian brothels, and was therefore no amusement for a child of God to engage in. But the lure of dancing would be gone if, by Act of Parliament, women were allowed to dance only with women and men only with men.

> The bodily contact demanded by the present modes of dancing are [*sic*] most unseemly. . . . Is it a comely thing to see a man's wife pressed to the bosom and whirled round in the arms of another man? . . . Is it a pleasant thing to see a Christian girl in the embrace of a young man who has no thought of God?[20]

It was left to the *Border Standard* to reveal some interesting facts (discovered, or so it claimed, by none other than Henry Ford) about the conspiratorial origins and subversive function of jazz. The editor of the *Dancing Times*, with his talk of artistic bolshevism, had nothing on Henry Ford and the *Border Standard*. To begin with, the word jazz was a central African word meaning public fornication.

> The dance, and the music, with its abominable rhythm and copulative beat, was imported from Central Africa by a gang of Bolshevists in America, their aim being to strike at Christian civilization throughout the world. They laid their plans carefully, they employed mass suggestion. In the 'music' they knew they had something which would make an appeal to the most debased sexual instinct. By superlative syncopation allied with the copulative beat, beat, beat of the drum, they stirred up forces all over the world. . . . These extremely cunning Bolshevists in America . . . were acting with full knowledge of what damage immoderate syncopation and the copulative beat had done in the days before the Greeks were strong enough to rear their civilization on the foundation of 'moderation in all things'. They knew perfectly well the part this abominable 'music' had played in bringing the austere Roman civilization into the dust. And they deliberately (and with what success everyone knows) employed this engine of Hell to do the Devil's work.[21]

There has been nothing quite so fierce as this in the more recent outcries against jitterbugging, jive, the creep, rock 'n' roll, and the twist, though each of these has had vociferous detractors. Once again, Mrs Grundy gives the impression of having been fighting a rearguard action in recent years; but in this field, too, it must be admitted that her influence is by no means dissipated.

Dances of virtually sexless calm—in comparison with those we have just mentioned—were the palais glide and the Lambeth walk. Yet the first was banned as rowdy by Bridlington dance-halls, and the second was attacked, quite seriously, as owing much to 'the savage rituals of the Congo river'.[22]

An interesting variation was the refusal by Wallasey magistrates in 1932 to grant a dancing licence to the town's new bathing-pool. The chairman said it was not in the interests of the borough that young people in bathing costumes should start embracing and dancing.[23]

Rock 'n' roll stimulated its adolescent devotees to an unusually high degree of audience participation, which cinemas, being full of seats, tended to frustrate. In 1956 there were disturbances in some cinemas, and in the streets outside, while the film *Rock around the Clock* was being shown; crowds of young men and young women sang and danced. This behaviour tended to get the dance a bad name. More than a dozen towns and cities knocked the rock by banning the film; in the first half of September over sixty youths appeared in magistrates' courts charged with rowdyism. *The Times* reminded top people that the Lambeth walk, in its day, had set citizens dancing in many a London street.[24] By the end of the following year rock 'n' roll was no longer immoral, subversive or non-U. 'Taught on television by the great Silvester himself', it had become 'U in polite society'.[25]

The twist is too much with us to need more than a mention. An example of the early opposition to it has already been given, on page 15. Popular enthusiasm for it was carefully fostered, and the dance energetically plugged; and it soon became too fashionable and too profitable for opposition to seem worth while. Anti-twist prejudices did linger on in such odd backwaters as the High Court, one of whose luminaries suggested that a young man might meet a better type of partner waltzing or doing the slow fox-trot than he would doing the twist.[26] Such a statement is rather surprising, for the twist is manifestly the least erotic of the long series of dances brought to Britain from America. Eager female jitterbugs and rock-'n'-rollers thought nothing of displaying thighs, backsides, and undergarments as they were tossed upside down in the air by their partners; eager female twisters display nothing more titillating than their knees and their ability to execute, with excruciating monotony, a basic step and a 'backscratcher'. The bodies of the dancers do not touch. Whoever believes, with *Komsomolskaya Pravda*, that this is an indecent and hysterical dance[27] possesses an enviable capacity for being stimulated by what its inventor called the grinding out of a couple of cigarette butts and the towelling of the back after a bath.[28]

25

KICKING AGAINST
THE HIGH-KICKS

The compiler of *The Slang of Venery* probably had his tongue in his cheek when, in 1916, he described the cancan as 'an eccentric dance, and one of rather questionable character'.[1] For by 1916 the cancan's main features were as well known, and as tolerated, as they are today. The executants' costume had become conventionalized in that faded, though still evocative, stereotype of Edwardian eroticism: those black stockings, garters and suspenders, those frilly petticoats and drawers, are the eighteen-nineties idealized in the imagination of the succeeding generation. The outfit, for all the nostalgia that clings about it, is not that in which the dance first seized public consciousness in Britain (where the women who pioneered it were attired either as men or as ordinary ballet girls of the eighteen-sixties and -seventies). And this outfit is very different from the costume of the original Parisian cancan, which was at least as much a grotesque dance as an erotic one. In short, the cancan has been frozen as a period dance—but in the wrong period, and with the usual errors of detail besides.

Nevertheless the essential movements of the cancan as we know it are probably much the same today as they were in the late sixties and early seventies, when its pioneers were disgusting and fascinating London theatre-goers and giving the stout officers of the Metropolitan Police, C Division, an assignment demanding keen observation and close attention to detail. The woman cancan dancer raises her skirts at the front and kicks one leg high in the air; for variation, she bends the raised leg and rotates it, thus moving the thigh and the pelvis in a manner mildly suggestive of coition. All this recalls the 'women's rite of exposing the genitalia by drawing up the skirts—a rite which in Greece was specially associated with Demeter'.[2] In France these movements are (or were) known as *le poirier* (the pear-tree) and *la tulipe orageuse* (the agitated tulip). When the dancer throws her leg straight up in the air, it is called *le présentez-armes*. Other steps are *le passage du guet* (the passing of the patrol), *le coup du lapin* (the charge of the rabbit), *la chaloupe en détresse* (the launch in distress)[3] and *le pas du hareng saur* (the red herring step). The cartwheel and the raising of the skirts at the back while bending forward (the display of backside that so shocked Khrushchev while he was in the U.S.A.) seem to be twentieth-century embellishments.

It was in the late eighteen-forties and early fifties that rumours first crossed the Channel about the boisterous dancing to be seen in Paris dance-halls. In 1851 an American journal complained of the obscene dances that were being introduced from Paris, and quoted the Paris correspondent of an unnamed London magazine, an Englishman who found the cancan and its sister-dance the *chahut* 'far worse than . . . the most lascivious of Spanish dances of Andalusia'. If obscenities were tolerated in public places, a blow was struck at the very foundations of society. 'I may not, even in a letter, enter into a minute description of these dances', the correspondent added. 'Suffice it to say, they would not be endured in England, even by women who had fallen from the paths of virtue, unless their minds and hearts were wholly debauched.'[4]

One gathers that at this stage the cancan was still a social dance, albeit a rowdy one. In 1854 the proprietor of a kind of dance-hall in Soho told a parliamentary committee that he did not permit people to dance improperly: 'Sometimes young men do not care how they dance; they have a nasty manner of dancing in the French style, called "Cancan".' Respectable people did not like to see this bad dancing.[5] Within a few years Offenbach, closely followed by Hervé and Lecocq, had brought the dance on to the stage; and a London critic observed in 1867 that the end of the second act of Offenbach's *The Grand Duchess* at Covent Garden was singularly weak and ineffective, whereas in Paris the curtain had come down on 'a wild and characteristic dance well-known and highly-prized in the French capital'. The critic went on: 'We must not be understood to advocate the importation of this dance to our saint-like shores, even if there were anybody in England who could dance it (which we incline to think there is not)'.[6] This critic was not well informed; the first cancan seen on the English stage had already been danced at the Princess's theatre in 1866, in Watts

Phillips's *The Huguenot Captain.*[7] The performance, says one historian of the theatre, 'does not seem to have created much alarm in the breast of Mrs Grundy and her followers'.[8] The reason is quite simple: this was a cancan danced by *men*—MM. Clodoche, Flageolet, Comète and Normande, 'the grotesque dancers from the Théâtre Impérial du Chatelet', who had come over from France at a salary of £320 per month.

In 1867 G. F. Hollingshead, stage director of the Alhambra, Leicester Square, was visiting Paris in search of novelties for his theatre when he saw 'a very handsome gypsy-like woman' dancing the cancan at the Café du Helder. This was Josephine Durwend, a Creole whose stage name was Finette; she was a former mistress of Whistler.[9] Hollingshead wished to engage her, but knew that in England, where names excited more horror than things, the cancan was not a welcome sound to the licensing authorities.[10] He therefore took the prudent step of having her dance at the Lyceum, under the Lord Chamberlain's licence, before putting her on at his own theatre, where the Middlesex magistrates were the arbiters of propriety. Accordingly, on Boxing Day 1867, Finette danced in a pantomime by W. S. Gilbert entitled *Harlequin Cock Robin and Jenny Wren; or Fortunatus! The Three Bears; the Three Gifts; the Three Wishes; and the Little Man Who Woo'd the Little Maid.* Those who had been looking forward to exciting glimpses of the lady's undergarments found, to their disappointment, that her pants were just about as long as the title of the pantomime. In fact, as *The Times* recorded, Finette wore a man's costume, 'and, therefore, much of the objection which an English audience would have to the French dance was removed'. The performance was well received, the dancer repeated it 'amid loud manifestations of approbation',[11] and before long the Prince of Wales took Princess Alexandra to see it.

The *cachets* of the Lord Chamberlain, the Lyceum audience and the royal family having been secured, Finette appeared next summer at the Alhambra, in *Mabille in London.* Once again, however, her costume was that of a man. As Hollingshead put it: 'She was dressed as effectively as and a little more decently than a "burlesque prince", and her dance had none of the offensive features of the can-can in petticoats. The most that could be said against it was that it was not a hornpipe.'[12]

A year later, in July 1869, patrons of the St James's theatre got their money's worth when a cancan danced, at last, by women in women's clothing was performed in the tempestuous finale of Offenbach's *Orphée aux Enfers*. The watchful *Times* stigmatized this dance as 'the most outrageous "can-can" ever seen on any London stage'. It was danced by the whole company and rapturously encored; but *The Times* strongly advised all fastidious persons to take leave of *Orphée* at the end of the third tableau, though 'perfectly aware that by this very advice we are only recommending a large majority of the audience to remain in the theatre till the final descent of the curtain'.[13]

This first sally into the underworld having passed off without incident, *Les Nations*, produced at the Alhambra by the Belgian Henri Dewinne, was expanded to feature the Parisian Troupe of Mlle Colonna. The *noms de théâtre* and the dancing of these four young women were Parisian enough; but Mlle Colonna herself was by birth a Miss Newnham, and her colleague Sarah Wright, soon to achieve eminence as 'Wiry Sal', was the daughter of a waiter at the Oxford music-hall. Still, the dancing was the thing, and one enthusiastic critic welcomed France's national dance, 'more vigorous than ever in Leicester Square' while the French capital was 'in sackcloth and ashes' (at the height of the Franco-Prussian war). For go, dash, and acrobatic convolution, this dance was unlike anything of the kind yet seen in London: 'That Madlle. Colonna will one evening arrive with her head upon the boards is, we believe, only a matter of time.' The cancan, this critic explained to such of his readers as did not already know, 'is simply a quadrille, with the most eccentric and extravagant figures, which are devised by the fertile imaginations of the dancers themselves. . . . Puritanically-disposed personages will never cease condemning it, of course.'[14]

On the evening of the day these words appeared in print, two such personages, Inspector J. E. Perry and Sergeant John Pope, of the Metropolitan Police, C Division, visited the Alhambra in plain clothes. The dancers' imaginations proved far too fertile for these guardians of public order. When the Middlesex magistrates held their next licensing session a few days later, the following special report, signed by Perry and Pope, was handed in:

> Mdlle. Colonna and *troupe* (four in all) appeared and danced the Pari-
> sienne Quadrille, or ordinary Can-Can. Two of them personated men
> dressed in bodices and trunks to match, and flesh-coloured hose; the others,
> as females, dressed as ordinary ballet girls, except that more of the thigh is
> visible in consequence of wearing very scanty drawers.

The dance on the whole is indecent, especially on the part of one dressed as a female, who raises her foot higher than her head several times towards the public, and which was much applauded. There was a loud influx of visitors shortly before the ballet commenced, but which decreased immediately after.

The other performances were carried on principally by females dressed as males, but there was nothing objectionable observed.

The two officers had assured their superintendent that the whole of the dance was objectionable, 'but appears a paying proposition, numbers of persons visiting to witness this alone and leaving immediately the dance is over'. And they attached to their report a copy of a drawing of the *Les Nations* cancan that had appeared in *The Day's Doings*. The justices were told that to take away the Alhambra's dancing licence would throw about 400 people out of work, to which a Mr Pownall acidly replied that if persons undertook employment to pander to the depraved tastes of a certain small section of the public, they must take the consequences. The licence was unanimously refused.[15] It was not to be restored for fourteen years. For a time the gap was filled with 'nightly scenes . . . far more dangerous to the public *morale* . . . than the cancan could have been': the band played 'The Watch on the Rhine' and the Germans roared approval; then it played the Marseillaise and the French counter-demonstrated.[16]

The female mentioned in the police report as being much applauded for raising her foot higher than her head, was the celebrated Wiry Sal, 'a product of a juvenile ballet, where her limbs must have acquired fiendish suppleness'.[17] A 'wispy slip of a girl', she had been the sensation of the performance; 'the verb "to kick" had never been so actively conjugated before', wrote Emily Soldene, who had the bright idea of engaging the Colonna troupe for the Philharmonic music-hall, Islington. For the Philharmonic had a theatrical licence and was therefore independent of Mr Pownall and his fellow magistrates.

We put on 'The Parisian Quadrille', and boomed it with a mighty boom. . . . 'Mdlle. Sara' (who had shorter skirts and longer legs than most girls), to the great delight and satisfaction of herself and all London, kicked up her agile heels a little higher than had previously been deemed possible, and was equally successful in dusting the floor with her back hair. Goodness knows what awful suffering was endured by the Middlesex

magistrates, for while the Alhambra languished in outer and inner darkness . . . in merrie Islington, safe under the shield of the Lord Chamberlain's
licence, that wicked, wicked dance was danced every night. The theatre
was crammed, and 'Wiry Sal' was the toast of the London clubs.[18]

Was the cancan in fact indecent? A writer in *Notes and Queries*
insisted that it had no more connexion with obscenity than had the
waltz or the bolero. It could of course, like any other dance, be rendered indelicate and immoral; but there were many cancans that might
be danced in any domestic circle. The genuine cancan of France was
less liable to objection than were many German waltzes and Scotch
reels. 'A Frenchman' hastened to point out that indecent cancans *were*
danced in Paris—but, admittedly, never in public places.[19]

The Anglo-Saxons were ambivalent about the dance. Just as Mark
Twain, visiting Paris, put his hands before his face for very shame, but
peeped through his fingers,[20] so English families of untarnished
respectability came to regard a trip to Paris as incomplete without at
least one visit to a place where high-kicking was the chief attraction.
One such family was observed at the turn of the century, watching the
dancers curvetting without drawers; the husband smiled, while his
wife gazed gravely at them through her *lorgnette* and remarked:
'Shocking perhaps, but amusing certainly.'[21] It was people like this that
fell foul of Mrs Lilly Grove, a writer on dancing who found it highly
deplorable that Parisians should imitate the antics of a dancing monkey;
who noted that such ugly and vulgar forms of the art lived solely by the
applause they received and would soon die out if ignored; and who
roundly scolded her compatriots: 'It is to be regretted that British . . .
who sermonize so strongly on the evils of the *Cancan* should give the
sanction of their presence to its performance.'[22] But by 1905 it was
possible to write that what Mlle Colonna's troupe had done in the way
of high-kicking 'would doubtless appear to many nowadays as of no
particular altitude'.[23]

Four years after the Alhambra affair the whole question of the
cancan's alleged indecency had been ventilated in the courts. The
dance had been gaining rapidly in popularity. It had become the rage of
the music-halls, where ladies with French-sounding names (Fadette at
Highbury, Fanchette at the Marylebone) drew attentive and apprecia-
tive audiences. There had been a cancan in Hervé's *Chilpéric* at the
Lyceum in 1870. The Alhambra's proprietor, Frederick Strange, had

without difficulty secured a regular theatre licence from the Lord Chamberlain, and in 1871 engaged Esther Austin, 'whose "Quadrille du Grand Opéra de Paris" was not so very different from the dance that had caused him so much trouble twelve months before'.[24] Half way through the 1871-72 run of Offenbach's comic opera *Geneviève de Brabant*, the Colonna dancers had returned to the Alhambra. When the 'Dancing Quakers', Mr Riley and Miss Barnum, had danced a cancan at the Gaiety in 1872, the Lord Chamberlain, Lord Sydney, had been pestered with letters asking him to stop this improper performance; he had gone to see for himself, 'and being a man of the world, he saw no just cause for interference'.[25] Of *The Black Crook* at the Alhambra (1872-73), *The Times* had written: 'Any merits the piece may have as a spectacle are neutralized so long as the manager retains the "Cancan" in the performance.'[26] The offending French dancers had been withdrawn before the authorities could take any action. And in the 1873 production of *La Belle Hélène* Wiry Sal had taken her own troupe to the Alhambra, where she was once again a great favourite (till one winter evening she kicked too high, even for her, and injured her leg). Then, in May 1874, Offenbach's *Vert-Vert* had opened at the St James's theatre, with the Orpheon troupe dancing a cancan to end all cancans (as indeed it did, for a time): the outrageous *ripirelle*.

'This astounding Terpsichorean Revel' was, according to the advertisements, 'rapturously re-demanded nightly'.[27] The *Vanity Fair* critic, however, a Mr Mackay, was moved to something less than rapture. He summed up the performance as 'introducing the worst orchestra, some of the flattest singing, and one of the most indecent dances in London'.[28] This harsh judgment was repeated in subsequent issues, till it was changed to 'improved and the singing less flat, but the dance uncalled-for and indecent'; the week after that there was a further retreat to 'a rather improper dance'.[29] What had happened in the mean time?

First, the skirts of the *Vert-Vert* dancers (already half an inch longer than the normal ballet skirts of the period) had been lengthened—and it may be that *Vanity Fair* was the agent of this change, for the journal was, if truth be told, a shade obsessive about short skirts (its comment on *Flick and Flock* at the Alhambra in the same month was: 'Ballet, with everything lengthy but the dresses'[30]). At all events, the maximum publicity was squeezed out of the change. When criticisms were made, the Lord Chamberlain was consulted for a suggestion as to how the dresses should be altered—and the ballet was then coolly advertised as danced in costumes designed by the Lord Chamberlain! This was calculated to annoy that official very much, with what results we shall see in a moment.

The second factor that induced *Vanity Fair* to moderate its criticisms was an action for libel brought against its publisher by the manager of the St James's theatre, Francis Charles Fairlie.

The hearing was immediately preceded by a number of stern Press pronouncements about 'Stage Decorum', as the *Saturday Review* headed its slashing attack on 'a vicious French dance' that imitated the crude and shameless profligacy of the lowest savages. This dance had now been added to the stock of mentionable subjects; the next step would be the cancan in the drawing-room. A French gentleman with any pretensions to good breeding would be ashamed to utter the word 'cancan' in society, 'and it would be an insult to a [French] lady to suppose that she could possibly ever have heard of it'; yet in the capital of moral, respectable England, which shook its head at French vice and mourned at French grossness, this dance might until recently have been seen almost any night at half a dozen theatres. That the dance should even be talked of was evil, because it led to coarseness even where it did not stimulate vice. It was satisfactory to know that the censor had, for the present at least, cleared the stage of this pollution.[31] This tirade set the tone for the court proceedings the following week, as it was no doubt intended to.

The case, which lasted two days, was opened by Serjeant Ballantine, who called the *Vanity Fair* article cruel and rancorous. If the critic was shocked by what he saw he ought to have looked away. (Laughter.) He ought to be paid pretty well for being exposed to such naughtiness. (Renewed laughter.) Fairlie told the jury that the dresses were by the best-known costumier in London, and not at all indecent. By accident they were longer than usual—and the costumier's forewoman came into court to confirm this. One witness said he took his wife to *Vert-Vert*, and she saw no harm in the dance; another's wife had liked it so much that she had gone a second time. The dramatic critic of the *Weekly Dispatch* said the *ripirelle* was an agile and athletic dance: 'I mean the ladies were agile and the dance athletic.' (Laughter.)

Then it was the turn of the defence, who called the Lord Chamberlain, the Marquis of Hertford, to describe his own visit to *Vert-Vert*.

His lordship said the dance was in his opinion neither graceful nor artistic, but decidedly and purposely indecent. He had given instructions that all dances of a cancan character should in future be interdicted. After seeing this one he had wished to have it withdrawn altogether; but he was advised that this might do more harm than good, since it was going to the provinces, where his jurisdiction did not apply.

The Lord Chamberlain's evidence virtually settled the case; but the defence had three more witnesses to call. *Vanity Fair*'s proprietor and editor, Thomas Gibson Bowles, testified that the *ripirelle* was simply a cancan, with all of the indecency and none of the art of the French original. *The Times* told its readers that Bowles then described the details, intention and meaning of the dance 'in a way the details of which are unfit for publication'. The report in *The Era* was a shade less reticent:

> I shall ask you to describe to the Jury what the 'Can-Can' is. (Laughter.) —It could only be done by dancing it, which I could not do. The word Can-Can cannot be translated into English without indecency; and the dance is suggestive of the most indecent acts.

In cross-examination, Bowles said he had known the dance in Paris and London, and had gone to see it several times, 'partly for information and partly for amusement'. He was examined, 'with some severity', as to why he had gone to see it after discovering its disgusting nature. There was laughter when he told Ballantine: 'The basis of the dance is no doubt disgusting; but I went to see it again for the same reason as you would have gone, and did go, to the St James's theatre several times.'

A Mr Stevens, a member of the *Vanity Fair* staff, thought the dance was the most indecent and suggestive he had ever seen. Since he was a former foreign correspondent of *The Times*, he, too, had perhaps had a good deal of experience. Finally, a Mr Vaughan said he considered the dancing was most disgusting, but more so in the attitudes and gestures than in the dress. This witness, who was an employee of the Inland Revenue Office, caused roars of laughter by throwing about his coat tails in the manner of ballet skirts.

Impressed by this weight of expert evidence, the jury had little alternative but to find for the defendant, which it did without retiring.[32]

Vanity Fair carried no report of the case, but modestly celebrated its victory with a letter from 'The Public Chorus' (i.e., no doubt, the editor himself). This reminded critics that they had a duty to condemn 'a disgusting dance', so that one might take one's wife, mother or sister to the theatre certain that their eyes would not be shocked by the appearance of naked females and lewd dances.[33]

A few days later the Lord Chamberlain issued a manifesto against the 'present degraded state' of the English stage, and the 'indecent dances and immodest dresses which now form so prominent a part of the entertainment at some theatres', and appealed to all managers to assist in abating and putting a stop to the scandal, 'which has now reached a climax'.[34]

And so the cancan went underground for a time, into such places as the Gardenia club, Leicester Square, where one of the favourite Paris dancers, La Goulue, with three other 'high-kicking damsels', gave performances later described as consisting of 'disgusting and wholly indescribable antics'.[35] A 'drawers ballet' was performed at places in Maidstone, Greenwich, and Gravesend, but no details seem to be known about it. The tradition of high-kicking was carried on by such dancers as Lottie Collins, whose anglicized version of the cancan, which she executed after singing 'Ta-ra-ra-boom-de-ay', aroused some protests—though, in truth, it was 'never even in its wildest moments very shocking'.[36] In the eighteen-nineties there was an abortive campaign for the Lord Chamberlain to prevent stage performances by women in 'visible tights', or whose skirts were more than four inches above the ground, or whose bust was partly exposed, or whose skirts opened at the side.[37] And there were occasional complaints that young women could not get their living on the music-hall stage if they could not do high-kicking.[38] But gradually the cancan ceased to shock anybody but a residuum of prudes: as late as 1936, protests against cancan performances were among twenty-six complaints sent to the authorities by the stage plays committee of the Public Morality Council.[39] It continued however to exercise a powerful fascination over each new generation of men, so that no edition of the Windmill theatre's *Revudeville*, for instance, is complete without its cancan.

What is the secret of this dance's appeal? The psycho-analysts have a remarkable explanation. 'The great popularity of the cancan', we read, '. . . was primarily based on the *unconscious* "reassurance" provided by frequent glimpses of the buttocks, and the continuing sight of one leg waving in the air. Symbolically, the dance attested to man that woman "possesses" a penis.'[40]

So *that* is why the prudes have been unable to kill it! One feels certain that Wiry Sal herself, not to mention Lord Hertford, would have found this a most surprising statement.

26

THE SHOCKING HISTORY
OF STRIP-TEASE

The first strip-tease act presented on the English stage was, like the first cancan, performed by a man. It occurred in Mrs Aphra Behn's most popular play, *The Rover* (1677), in an amorous scene where Blunt, an English country gentleman, undresses and 'goes towards the Bed in his shirt, Drawers, &c.'. The Cunningtons, in their *History of Underclothes*, say this was evidently accepted, at the time, as highly attractive to the female part of the audience.[1] From the time of Mrs Behn till the police intervened against a more recent all-male show, entitled *Call Me Mister*, at a London strip-tease club, the art of taking one's clothes off as a form of collective entertainment appears to have been confined to the female sex.

At private gatherings, however, from the end of the eighteenth century onwards, naked dancing by men and women together seems to have been fairly popular among people who earned their living by prostitution, robbery and begging. In 1693, in Rosemary Lane, near East Smithfield, a constable who was a member of a Society for the Reformation of Manners heard 'a great *Revel rout*, with many *Oaths* and *Cursings*' at the house of one Mistress Smith ('who was known to entertain Whores and Theives'). Forcing his way in, after the manner of the national reformers, he found three naked men and three naked women, who had been dancing and revelling. They were arrested and carried to the watch house, and next morning committed to the Bridewell house of correction and whipped, 'with one more'—a pleasant touch—'who came to vindicate them'.[2] A few years later, it was claimed that members of the Societies had been instrumental in putting down 'several Musick-houses which had degenerated into notorious Nurseries of Lewdness and Debauchery', where 'some of both Sexes had shamelessly danced naked'—and where over twenty murders had been committed in a very short time.³ This type of dance was known to its participants as a 'buff-ball', or 'buttock-ball'. As late as the eighteen-seventies these gatherings were said to be popular among the down-and-out dwellers in the lodging houses of Golden Lane, Finsbury: 'The most favourite entertainment . . . is known as a "buff ball", in which both sexes—innocent of clothing—madly join, stimulated with raw whisky and the music of a fiddle and a tin whistle.'⁴

Our concern however is not with naked balls. Something much more akin to modern strip-tease was witnessed at Bartholomew Fair at the beginning of the eighteenth century, where Ned Ward, the 'London Spy', saw

> a couple of Plump-Buttock-Lasses, who, to show their Affection to the Breeches, wore 'em under their Petticoats; which, for decency sake, they first Danc'd in: But to show the Spectator how forward a Woman once warm'd is to lay asider Modesty, they doft their Petticoats after a gentle Breathing, and fell to Capering and Firking as if Old *Nick* had been in 'em.⁵

Bartholomew Fair seems to have enjoyed relative immunity from reformers. But in the same period there were numerous lamentations over the increasing degeneracy of the stage because vulgar dancing and panto-mime were part of the entertainment; and when a French dancer, Mlle Rose, first wore fleshings on the English stage, a moralist declared that France, despairing of conquering John Bull, was trying to corrupt him.⁶

Strip-tease, in the literal sense of both 'strip' and 'tease', was a regular part of the entertainment provided in London brothels in the eighteenth century. There is a detailed description of a performance by 'posture girls' in an erotic work entitled *The History of the Human Heart; or The Adventures of a Young Gentleman* (1749). The women, who included 'Miss M—— the famous Posture Girl', stripped stark naked and climbed on the table.

> They each filled a Glass of Wine, and laying themselves in an extended Posture placed their Glasses on the Mount of Venus, every Man in Com-pany drinking off the Bumper, as it stood on that tempting Protuberance, while the Wenches were not wanting in their Lascivious Motions, to heigh-ten the Diversion. Then they went thro' the several Postures and Tricks

made use of to raise debilitated Lust. . . . Their last Exploit inflamed these Sons of Debauchery so much, that they proposed, as a Conclusion of the Scene, that each Man should chuse his Posture, and go through what they had seen only imitated before. But this was a Step the Nymphs would not comply with, it being the Maxim of these Damsels, never to admit of the Embraces of the Men, for fear of spoiling their Trade.

One of the women assured the visitors that she had 'as great an Aversion to Whoring . . . as some Women who are nicely scrupulous in every other Respect'.[7]

Higher up the social scale, admirers of the naked female body could command the services of the prettiest members of the *corps de ballet*, who, after the opera, were taken in closed carriages to the secluded house in Regent's Park of the third Marquis of Hertford (a predecessor of the Lord Chamberlain we met in the last Chapter).

> Scandal said that once there the ladies discarded the conventional attire of the ballet and waited on Lord Hertford and his friends at supper wearing less than what is now [1909] considered good form to appear in as Salome. . . . The guests were among the best-known members of the *haut monde*, and the lovely houris played their part.[8]

In 1780 or 1781, the sixteen- or seventeen-year-old Emily Lyon, who afterwards became Lady Hamilton, is said to have posed, lightly draped, as Hygeia, goddess of health, at the Temple of Æsculapius of Dr James Graham, the 'Emperor of Quacks'. She is supposed to have stood for an hour at a time on a dais, 'alike to her own satisfaction and the delight of the doctor's visitors',[9] pretending to feed a serpent out of a cup. Graham later opened a Temple of Hymen in Pall Mall, with a *tableau vivant* of Hebe Vestina, goddess of health and beauty, as living advertisement and high priestess. Graham would sit naked in an earth-bath together with an equally naked young woman; their protruding heads, 'beautifully dressed and powdered', appeared 'not unlike two fine, full-grown cauliflowers'.[10]

Lacking our present-day opportunities for inspecting the female body on the beach or in the pages of popular newspapers (though sensational sheets like *The Day's Doings* sailed as near to the wind as they dared with semi-nudes based on paintings and statues), the men of the Victorian age were enthusiastic gazers at *poses plastiques* and *tableaux vivants* (the precise distinction between these is far from clear); and many of them were assiduous visitors to brothels and near-brothels where women could be looked at in a state of undress. The 1841 edition of *The Swell's Night Guide through the Metropolis* informed the amateur of such entertainments that at the Union, 'under the very nose of the Magistrates in Bow Street, Covent Garden', the visitor was 'often indulged with a lewd song or half-naked dance, to the great delight of the degraded lot who nightly assemble'; while in the Waterloo Place and Waterloo Road district there were two 'temples of voluptuousness' where girls, mostly French, 'in every possible state, from complete nudity to the half-dressed, go through the most voluptuous exhibitions—imitate the classic models—and perform the most spirit-stirring dances'.[11] In the 'Hall of Rome' at the Windmill Saloon, Windmill Street, there were *tableaux vivants*: 'The ladies go entirely naked, and the gentlemen dress without clothes.'[12]

The most famous of these entertainments were those provided by Renton Nicholson, the self-styled 'Lord Chief Baron', who in 1841 established his Judge and Jury Society at the Garrick's Head hotel in Bow Street. This was a Monday night song-and-supper-room entertainment, where recent divorce cases, with all their wealth of titillating detail, were rehearsed; they were popular with members of both Houses of Parliament, who often formed part of the 'jury'. In 1846 Nicholson expanded the programme to include *poses plastiques* illustrating lectures, which he himself delivered, on poetry and song. The girls, attired in flesh-coloured costumes simulating nakedness, sang choruses behind the curtains before appearing in the *tableaux*.[13] Nicholson himself had friends in high places; his imitators were less fortunate, and were prosecuted for presenting obscene performances.

Despite such prosecutions, and despite the gradual increase of opposition by vigilantes, *poses plastiques* flourished in London and provincial music-halls; and in some cases 'particular patrons', we are told, were 'welcome to the dressing-room'.[14] 'The Sultan's Favourite Returning from the Bath' and 'Diana Preparing for the Chase' were featured at the Parthenon Rooms, Liverpool, in 1850;[15] other popular titles included 'Daughters of the Deep' and 'Greeks Surprised by the Enemy'. Nicholson introduced *poses plastiques* at the Cider Cellar, Maiden Lane, in 1853, and at the Coal Hole in the Strand five years later.[16] Living pictures became a mania; and around the time of the cancan *brouhaha* a section of the Press seized the opportunity to raise the question of stage nudity too. The principal *arbiter elegantiarum* was the *Saturday Review*, which disclosed that the manageress of one theatre had set an example by the free and unabashed display of her undraped figure: 'This exhibition of a big woman who appears to be wholly unclothed except for about a foot and a half round her middle is one which may be commended to the attention of the Censor. It is impossible to imagine anything more outrageously disgusting.' The following Saturday the *Review* was at it again:

> We observe that one of the theatres has put forth a special appeal to the gentlemen from the country who come up for the Cattle Show. They are invited to regale themselves in the evening with an exhibition very similar in character to that which has engaged their attention during the day. 'VENUS, the goddess of material love,' is offered for inspection, and our country friends will have an opportunity of enjoying the unreserved exposure of her 'points' and those of her companions. It is obvious that, if this sort of show is to become common, the eloquent and picturesque writer who does the Smithfield Show for the *Times*, and who describes so graphically the 'beast of ample size, level form, but somewhat weak in rib and rump', and 'the perfect beauty, with superb bosom, neck, shoulders, and flank', may be expected to turn his attention to dramatic criticism. It is sometimes remarked at Islington that an animal 'reveals to the hand a want of solidity not at once discerned by the eye'; but it is to be hoped that country visitors will be made to understand that at the theatre—as yet— their curiosity cannot be indulged to quite the same extent.[17]

These sentiments, minus only the ponderous humour, were shared a few years later by the National Vigilance Association, whose vigilance was rewarded with actions and songs that were 'very vile, and increasing in audacity', the sight of 'indecent attire', and the spectacle of large numbers of semi-nude girls who 'had to perform every afternoon in the broad daylight . . . at the Italian Exhibition'.[18] In 1890 the Association distinguished itself by its campaign against a poster showing Zæo, a 25-year-old female acrobat appearing at the Aquarium. The poster consisted of an enlargement of a photograph of Zæo in her gymnast's costume. In the course of the campaign it was alleged that Zæo suffered from severe excoriation as a result of falling to the net from a great height. A solemn deputation of London county councillors visited the Aquarium, and 'sanctimonious creatures eyeing Zæo's back filled the comic papers'. The L.C.C.'s licensing committee at length had the poster withdrawn;[19] and a Bill Posters' Association was formed to censor bills submitted for posting. The National Vigilance Association also wrote to the Crystal Palace authorities begging them to alter the dresses in a pantomime there, to avoid 'breaches of decorum' which were 'injurious to the young girls who are thus exhibited' and which exercised a demoralizing influence on the spectators—largely young men and boys.[20]

Meanwhile the campaign against living pictures went on, well into the new century. Perhaps the most artistic ones were the Kilani troupe, presented 'on an heroic scale—with perfect mechanism and naughty daring'. The management of the Palace theatre booked them in 1893 with a certain uneasiness, and there was trouble with the authorities. But an arrangement was come to, for the troupe in fact wore sub-stantial fleshings laced at the back.[21] Their nakedness was only a clever illusion. The needs of foreign immigrants were catered for by what a royal commission in 1902 heard described as 'terrible' dancing places: 'There were *poses plastiques*—there were girls half naked, and it is the sort of thing existing right the way round Cannon Street, and it is not fit to bring up a family round there.'[22] By 1906 such exhibitions were known as 'living statuary'. One was stopped at the Hull Hippo-drome in that year, and next year a joint crusade by the National Vigilance Association and the London Council for the Promotion of Public Morality, including a deputation to the L.C.C.'s theatres and music-halls committee, succeeded, not without severe controversy, in driving living statuary out of London. The deputation, claiming to represent thirty-six organizations, was headed by the Bishop of London, who told the committee that efforts to raise the spirit of purity and self-control among boys and girls were being seriously impeded by such exhibitions; that the proper places to study sculpture were the museums and art galleries; and that the people who went to music-halls ought to be protected against anything that might deprave or corrupt them. These arguments did not greatly impress the com-mittee; but when the matter was debated at a full council meeting a resolution banning living statuary was carried by 66 votes to 45.[23]

There were other mild strip-tease sensations for theatre-goers. There was the serpentine dance of Loie Fuller, for instance, which allegedly owed something to the influence of Lady Hamilton. A lady called Charmion, at the Alhambra, used to climb to her trapeze in an elaborate walking dress, with picture hat and parasol, and take her clothes off in the air, eventually appearing in the ordinary tights of the acrobatic performer. And Stasia Napierkowska's 'Dance of the Bee' at the Palace in 1911 consisted in the lady tearing off her clothes in search of a bee that was supposed to have crawled beneath them.[24] Censorship then, as now, was prone to do rather ridiculous things. Maeterlinck's *Monna Vanna* was banned because the heroine appeared on the stage naked *under a cloak*, a fact that was indicated in the dialogue.[25] And when a picture of an episode from *The Arabian Nights* was submitted to the film censor in the early days of the cinema, it was returned with an official letter: 'Passed for adult distribution provided that all dancing scenes showing the dancing-girl's navel are cut out.'[26]

By 1908 public opinion was just about ready to tolerate two women dancers, one from the U.S.A., the other from Canada, who exposed more of their bodies than had hitherto been customary. Isadora Duncan's costume, in her classical dances at the Duke of York's theatre, was a flowing tunic that left bare the unshaven axillary hair; this was thought by many to savour of impropriety. She claimed to be the first western dancer to dance with bare feet. But Maud Allan usually danced barefoot, too, in a loose Greek gown ('a wisp of chiffon'[27]) designed by herself. Her performances at the Palace theatre were boosted by a pamphlet written by Augustus Moore and distributed beforehand to the critics. This document was one long purple passage telling how Miss Allan was in artistic sympathy with those Latin races whose fair bodies and acute passions had brought about the greatest *crimes passionnelles*; how she was perfectly made, with slender wrists and ankles; how each of her rose-tipped fingers was instinct with intention; how her skin was satin smooth, crossed only by the pale tracery of delicate veins that laced the ivory of her round bosom and slowly waving arms; how her naked feet, slender and arched, beat a sensual measure while the pink pearls slipped amorously about her throat and bosom; how the desire that flamed from her eyes and burst in hot gusts from her scarlet mouth infected the very air with the madness of passion; how she was such a delicious embodiment of lust that she might win forgiveness for the sins of such wonderful flesh.[28] Not altogether surprisingly, the London public was dubious about Miss Allan—till she had tea with Mr Asquith.[29] That made her dances respectable—even the one in which, portraying Salome, 'she was all but naked and had St John's head on a plate and kissed his waxen mouth (a business later forbidden on the Covent Garden stage, where a dish of gravy was substituted)'.[30]

But what had become respectable in London remained, as is often the case, scandalous in Manchester. When Miss Allan signed a contract to appear there, the chief constable of the city and certain members of the not inappropriately named watch committee were sent to London to watch her dance. The chief constable could not see everything he wanted to, and said he wished to go back-stage to inspect the dancer's costume more closely and find out whether she was really as naked as she seemed to be. The manager refused this request; to grant it, he said, would be an insult to the performer. The Mancunians thereupon decided that Miss Allan's dancing would not be tolerated in their city—or, at least, that the licence of any theatre where she danced would be withdrawn. But the opposition collapsed when she threatened legal action.[31] 'Miss Maud Allan', quipped Punch, 'cannot understand why the Manchester Watch Committee should make so much fuss about such a trifle as her dress.'[32]

Isadora Duncan and Maud Allan soon had an imitator of noble birth in the shape of Lady Constance Stewart-Richardson, already famous as a swimmer, sportswoman and traveller, whose classical dances at the Palace on behalf of a scheme to start a school for small boys were severely criticized as audacious and inartistic. 'She just made her costume possible by her obvious sincerity of purpose', wrote The Times. 'But it was difficult to associate it in thought with the school for little boys.'[33]

Several brushes with the Lord Chamberlain's department enlivened the early career of Sir Charles Cochran. When his 'musical thing' Half-past Eight went on at the Comedy theatre in 1916 an official who saw the show on the first night agreed that the costumes and general presentation were beyond reproach. Approval extended, apparently, to the popular scene in a Turkish bath on ladies' day, where some prudish ladies gradually removed their own clothing in order to cover their sisters' nakedness. The Bystander published a page of caricatures of the show, and Cochran reproduced this as an advertisement, so boosting business greatly. But the Lord Chamberlain, Lord Sandhurst, protested against this pictorial advertisement and ordered the removal of a framed copy from the outside of the theatre, complaining that the artist 'seemed deliberately to have created an effect of feminine garments being blown up'. Lord Sandhurst often objected to photographs in the illustrated papers of scenes from Cochran revues. A bishop once showed him, in their club, a picture in the *Sketch* and asked him whether that was the sort of thing to allow in theatres. His lordship went to see the show and found no harm in it; but he still objected to the photograph.[34] The dresses worn by Alice Delysia in Cochran's *As You Were* (1918)—particularly a close-fitting black silk costume that she wore as Lucifer—were attacked in the Press, the main complaint being that too much of her back was visible. The dresses worn by the ladies of the Court of Hunzollern in the same show were also objected to, and the Lord Chamberlain compelled some changes.[35]

The thirties were a period of renewed anxiety for the Public Morality Council. First, there were the stage revues in which women wore scanty attire consisting merely of 'breastlets' and slight covering of the loins. In 1930 objection was taken to the movements of performers (sometimes in pairs, often in groups of twelve or sixteen) 'which cannot be described as dances in any sense, but are simply means of exhibiting all parts of the body which are quite nude save for the slight covering referred to'. In six instances alterations were made to the costumes, and this gave encouragement to the Council's stage plays committee and to that committee's chairman, Miss Edith Neville, and vice-chairman, the Reverend Clarence May.[36] By now static nudity was permitted on the stage, though nudes might not move. This did not satisfy the Bishop of London, and a protest of his against the scantiness of stage costumes brought a letter to *The Times* from Marie Tempest—a letter that came like a breath of fresh air:

If an ankle in the nineties thrilled one . . . what must a whole leg do in 1934? Well, the answer is that there is no thrill at all. . . . The modern young boy and girl are so used to the sight of practically naked bodies that I am confident nudity and indecency have nothing in common. . . . I believe that some girls have objected to the costumes they have to wear, but that later they got used to them. . . . I remember that when I first wore tights in *The Red Hussar*, showing about as much leg as a lift girl at Selfridges, I wept for about an hour and then went on in a large cloak to hide my shame. In a few days I realized how silly I was and discarded the cloak. . . . I do protest strongly at any attempt to revive the activities of the Prudes on the Prowl, the spying of the Stigginses, and the chortling of the Chadbands.[37]

This letter seems to have made things appreciably easier for London theatres; but again the provinces lagged behind. The credit for educating provincial watch committees was claimed by 'the girl with the most perfect figure in Britain', known to music-hall audiences as Rosemary Andrée. She 'made history' by appearing naked (under specially arranged lighting) at provincial music-halls in an act based on the legend of Pygmalion and Galatea. At first her costume had consisted of rhinestones mounted on net, and could be carried in an envelope. Then she had the brainwave of dispensing with the envelope—and its contents. Local watch committees would ask for details of her performance, then say that 'this sort of thing' could not possibly be allowed in their towns. Whereupon Miss Andrée would invite them to a special performance, after which—if her account is to be believed —they generally gave in. Birmingham however remained adamant, insisted on her being covered, and, 'after a lot of persuasive talking', compromised on a piece of net, minus rhinestones.[38]

But the Public Morality Council's worries about stage nudity as such were nothing to the effect that modern strip-tease, imported from America in the late thirties, produced on its collective imagination. The Council claimed that it had been kept well informed of strip-tease activities in America; its reading may have included Gorer's *Hot Strip Tease* (1937), which cited a passage in James T. Farrell's *Studs Lonigan* where a young man has an orgasm while watching a shimmy dancer in a cheap American burlesque theatre. 'The whole section', commented Gorer, '. . . shows to my mind as accurately as possible the effect that burlesque is intended to provoke.'[39] When the Council heard in 1937 that an act called 'Strip-teasing You' was to be presented in a London theatre and restaurant, it wrote to the police and licensing authorities giving a description of the act; this was before any performance whatever had taken place in Britain. Then, when performances started, 'repeated visits were paid to ascertain exactly what transpired'. Mr Sydney W. Carroll wrote to the *Daily Telegraph* protesting against strip-tease shows; the Bishop of London weighed in with a letter to the Press endorsing this protest; and the Lord Chamberlain arranged a conference on strip-tease at which licensing authorities and theatrical interests were represented. It was decided that greater strictness was essential, and there were prosecutions and heavy fines.[40] In 1939 the Public Morality Council's vigilance led to two men being fined £60 each for improper management of a club where 'it was proved that the "strip-tease" act was performed by more than one girl'. At another club, where 'most disgusting and obscene behaviour' took place, the court was informed that 'among those present were women in male attire, effeminate men and coloured people': clearly a place of uncommon iniquity, and the court disapproved to the tune of £201 in fines and costs.[41] The Council also noted, in the same year, a police raid on a night-club during a strip-tease competition. By 1940 the National Vigilance Association was getting in on the act, registering satisfaction at the Lord Chamberlain's summoning yet another conference to get rid of stage nudity and improprieties in gesture and word. There would, it vowed, be no lessening of the Association's determination to preserve the moral health of the community.[42]

By that stage of the war most people had other things to be determined about, and moralizing on the subject of stage nudity was muted. The Reverend Leslie D. Weatherhead however, addressing the 1943 annual general meeting of the Association on 'The Christian Answer to the Lure of Sex', did inform delegates that the sex stimulation created at some theatres was enormously powerful, especially to soldiers 'keyed up to the apex of physical fitness'. The exploitation of female nudity resembled 'what it must be to a starving man to be forced to witness a parade of appetizing delicious foods before his very eyes without being able to eat'.[43]

It was another decade before the appetizing parade of strip-teasers once again excited the Public Morality Council's hunger for prohibitions and prosecutions. In 1952 its stage plays sub-committee hailed as 'most timely' an L.C.C. decision prohibiting the removal of garments while the performer was within sight of the audience.[44] The Council protested that the country had been inundated with a spate of revues whose chief feature was blatantly advertised nudity; its vigilance defeated an attempt to flout the L.C.C.'s anti-strip-tease regulations; and in 1957 it opined that nudity on the stage could do nothing but harm, whether it were to the elderly roué patronizing the front rows, or to the adolescent receiving a totally false and debasing idea of sex from this source.[45] Observers from the Public Morality Council were presumably immune from harm.

Strip-tease now began to flourish as never before, in clubs supposedly free from police interference, so that the Council wrote agitatedly in 1959 about London's having become the Mecca of the strip-tease industry, outstripping Paris and the Continent and debauching the public: 'What we fear is what tolerance of this kind of thing will lead to.'[46] By the summer of 1960 there were an estimated two hundred strip clubs in London and about a hundred more in the provinces. One club was boasting ten M.P.s, eight millionaires, over sixty knights, and thirty-five peers among its members. And some of the hundreds of young women who nightly undressed in central London were replying to complaints about the unhealthy nature of their work by carrying through Soho placards that declared: 'WE ARE NICE GIRLS' and 'WE ARE STRIPERS [sic]—SO WHAT?'

What seems to have sparked off the series of prosecutions that closed, first five clubs, then many more, and thus brought about the collapse of the great strip-boom, was not so much the work of the Public Morality Council (though that body naturally found these develop- ments 'most enheartening'[47]) but an article in the Spectator. 'I have news for the Public Morality Council', wrote Kenneth Allsop. 'I confess that it surprises me finding myself supplying evidence for this body which, while doubtless worthy in intention, has never excited my support.' His article (from which, as he later revealed, 'several factual sentences were excised—no doubt for sound reasons of propriety'[48]) seems to have encouraged the police to crack down on the kind of entertainment he described: a brunette, for instance, thrusting her hands inside her panties, kneading her breasts, and presenting 'a solitary sexual charade of half a dozen postures and speeds' for the benefit of what was apparently a board meeting of company directors. Allsop went on to describe flagellation acts, girls bare to their pudenda, and girls 'drawing phallic inferences from objects in a dozen different ways just short of hanging a label on them'. And he mentioned that audiences included 'solitaries in raincoats and spectacles seeking nourishment for their sad and obscure preoccupations';[49] whether these were solitary company directors or just ordinary shareholders was not made clear. An editorial note in the same issue spelled out the nature of the performances in another way: 'It is not . . . possible for a writer to set down, however clinically, exactly what can be seen on these club stages: no printer would print it, no publisher publish it, for fear of exciting the attention of the Director of Public Prosecutions.'[50] This was no doubt a reference to highly realistic representations of the movements of coition, including the spasms of orgasm, and to the practice adopted by some performers of manipulating, or pretending to manipulate, the clitoris. Ours is a culture in which most people say they find such exhibitions disgusting; though there are many who, if they had an opportunity of witnessing them without incurring opprobrium, would do so. Why it is less disgusting for men to enter marriage ignorant of the clitoris, or of its role in women's sexual pleasure, than for men to witness a demonstration of the clitoris being used to secure pleasure (from which they might conceivably learn how to give more pleasure to their wives) is not immediately apparent.

At all events, neither Kenneth Allsop nor the police saw any merit, therapeutic or otherwise, in bumps, grinds, and kindred movements; and the police lost little time in putting a stop to the pleasures of company directors, whether solitary or attending by the board, so to speak. In all fairness, it should be admitted that the police were conscientious in gathering evidence. Before proceeding against one club, which had a membership of nearly 50,000, a painstaking police-sergeant attended a performance of 'Bonnie Belle the Ding-Dong Girl' no fewer than five times. Asked by the magistrate why he had to visit the club so many times before he was satisfied, the officer explained that he felt obliged to make quite certain the exhibition was obscene as it was done 'in I must say an artistic way'.[51]

The closing down of clubs, with heavy fines and imprisonment for some proprietors, was hailed—need we add?—by the Public Morality Council as a warning that indecency would not be tolerated. Nevertheless, 'vigilance must be maintained and every watchful care exercised'.[52] No doubt the vigilantes are still watching with care.

Let us round off our survey with three recent instances of opposition to the display of the female body.

Miss Liz Mayo was chairman of the Young Conservatives in Chesham, Buckinghamshire, when she performed a strip-tease act at a party in a local church hall. Though she ended the act in an overcoat, her conduct was deemed unusual in a Young Conservative, unbecoming to a chairman, and unworthy of a resident of Chesham. She apologized to the vicar, vacated the chair, and refused an offer of £100 a week to repeat her act in a West End club. Having purged her offence, she was re-elected to office.[53]

An eleven-year-old schoolgirl, of Fifield, Berkshire, danced in a Persian slave-girl costume at a show for old people in a Slough church hall. Though she wore not one, not two, but three pairs of pink drawers under her black net Turkish trousers, the vicar called out, 'This act must be stopped', and it was. The girl, explained the vicar, looked 'completely naked' under her trousers, and her dance was 'sinful and indecent'. 'The act couldn't corrupt our minds', said a 67-year-old woman spectator. 'There was nobody at the party under sixty.'[54]

When five women undergraduates at Girton agreed to appear with uncovered breasts in a Cambridge University production of *Expresso Bongo*, the proctors gave their permission. But the young women backed down under pressure from the college authorities. 'The girls have realized', said an official, 'that they would bring nothing but shame upon themselves by appearing with nothing on.'[55]

At this rate, Mrs Grundy's obsequies look like being long delayed.

NOTES

1 The original Mrs Grundy was the neighbour, in Thomas Morton's play *Speed the Plough* (1798), of whom it was continually asked: 'What will Mrs Grundy say?'

2 *Guardian*, Jan. 5, 1962, p. 16.

3 *Daily Mail*, Jan. 4, 1962, p. 5.

4 Commander D. Vaudreuil told the rural district council that, after nudists had been reported on the beach, roads to the coast were jammed by cars and coaches 'filled with curious visitors' (*The Times*, Jan. 10, 1962, p. 6).

5 Haynes [and others], *English Review*, Dec. 1913, pp. 123–34. See also Himes, *Medical History of Contraception* (1936), p. xv ('Even the British Museum has a special cabinet for certain books; and to secure access to these requires not only serious purpose but tact, patience, and persistence'); [Haynes], *A Lawyer's Notebook* (1932), pp. 120–2; Craig, *Above All Liberties* (1942), p. 166; Craig, 'B.M. Catalogue', *Times Literary Supplement*, no. 2,870, p. 129, Mar. 1, 1957; Craig, *Banned Books* (1962), pp. 205–7; Terence Deakin, 'B.M. and B.N.', *Times Literary Supplement*, no. 3,191, p. 295, Apr. 26, 1963, and subsequent correspondence.

6 Letter to the author from Mr R. A. Wilson, Principal Keeper, Department of Printed Books, British Museum, Dec. 20, 1961.

7 Cunnington, *Feminine Attitudes* (1935), p. 275.

8 Andrew Sinclair, *Prohibition: the Era of Excess* (London, 1962).

9 An observation I owe to Cunnington, *Looking Over My Shoulder* (1961), p. 138.

PART I

PLAIN WORDS, PRUDE WORDS, AND RUDE WORDS (pp. 27–85)

1 A CURE FOR GOOSEFLESH

1 Cicero, *Ad Famil.* ix. 22. The Romans avoided saying *cum nobis*, because it sounded like *cunnibus*.

2 Cf. *Registration and Licensing Authorities* (1961). The Devon list jumps from ROD to TOD, Hampshire from ROT to TOT, Salop from EUX to GUX, Wiltshire from CAM to EAM, Birkenhead from MBG to OBG, Birmingham from AOG to COG. Birmingham also omits POX, Leeds BUB and BUG, West Ham MAN, and Aberdeenshire LAV. Grimsby however includes PEE. 'Index marks are allotted to Councils by Regulations made from time to time by the Minister of Transport, and any combinations of letters which might cause offence are avoided at the time of making such Regulations. The responsibility for making the Regulations is the Minister's.

There are no regulations laying down which words or initials are to be avoided' (Letter to the author from an official of the Information Branch, Ministry of Transport, Dec. 7, 1961). The University of California Language Department was recently asked to make a study of possibly objectionable three-letter combinations, not merely in English, but in seven commonly used foreign languages too! As a result the following prefixes, among others, were banned from Californian motor-car licence plates: SEX, WED, BRA, ALE, BAD, BAG, BAH, BED, CAN, DAM, DUD, FAT, GOD, HAG, NAG, NUN, RAG, RAT, RAW, RUM, RUT, SAD, SAG, SAP, and SOT (*Daily Telegraph*, Jan. 17, 1963, p. 17).

3 Carnoy defines dysphemism as the putting of things in an astonishing, funny, vulgar (*triviale*) or provocative (*irritante*) way (*La Science du mot* (1927), p. 337).

4 *The Gentleman's Magazine: and Historical Chronicle*, vol. lxi, pt 2, no. 6, pp. 1099–100, Dec. 1791.

5 *AL* (1936 edn), p. 303. Cf. Webster, *Holy Bible* (1833), *passim*, and p. xvi: 'Many words and phrases are so offensive, especially to females, as to create a reluctance in young persons to attend Bible classes and schools, in which they are required to read passages which cannot be repeated without a blush.' Cf. also Webster, *Mistakes and Corrections* (1837), pp. 3–6.

6 *AL* (1936 edn), p. 300.

7 Eliot, *Survey*, June 15, 1922, p. 390. The same writer, Associate Professor of Sociology at Northwestern University, Illinois, also proposed calling punishment 'treatment' and communists 'industrial neurotics'.

8 The full list appears in *AL* (1936 edn), pp. 305–6. Mencken comments (p. 306 n. 1): 'I suspect that the prohibition of *bum* is due to the fact that the word is obscene in England.'

9 Read, *American Speech*, Dec. 1934, pp. 264–78.

10 *Ibid.* pp. 264, 277.

11 [Bache], *Vulgarisms* (1868), p. 35.

12 Read, *op. cit.* p. 274. Cf. Richard Hoggart's evidence at the *Lady Chatterley's Lover* trial: 'We have no word in English . . . which is not either a long abstraction or an evasive euphemism, and we are constantly running away from it, or dissolving into dots, at a passage like that. He wanted us to say "This is what one does. In a simple, ordinary way, one fucks", with no sniggering or dirt' (Rolph [*sc.* Hewitt] (ed.), *Trial of Lady Chatterley* (1961), p. 99).

13 Carnoy, *op. cit.* pp. 337–50.

14 Partridge, *Words, Words, Words!* (1933), p. 96.

15 Read, *op. cit.* pp. 264, 277.

16 Wyld, *History of Modern Colloquial English* (1920), p. 387.

17 Weekley, *Romance of Words* (1917), p. 99.

2 THE NUDE TRUTH (pp. 31–55)

1 Popular English synonyms for nakedness, and for parts of the body with sexual significance, are listed in three monumental works on slang. The first is the *Slang and its Analogues* (1890–1904) of Dr John S. Farmer and W. E. Henley. Only 750 copies of this seven-volume work were printed. The second is an anonymous and painstaking compilation, privately printed in Chicago in 1916: *The Slang of Venery*. It is almost certainly the work of Henry N. Cary. The third is the indispensable slang dictionary of Eric Partridge, a very rich source of information, and a work on which I have leaned heavily. Throughout this Part I have selected from all three, reproducing such notes as seemed useful, and taking the dates in most cases from *DS*. Partridge distinguishes slang words from colloquialisms, etc., and states which words are obsolescent or obsolete. I did not think it necessary to give these details, which are readily accessible in his *Dictionary*. On the other hand, he does not make the distinction between plain words, euphemisms, and dysphemisms that I have made, and, in the case of many slang expressions, would perhaps disagree with such a subjective cross-classification.

2 Mencken's study, 'The Interior Hierarchy', was reprinted in *A Book of Burlesques* (1923), pp. 190–8.

3 Vancouver (B.C.) *Daily Province*, June 9, 1936, cited, *AL* Supp. I (1945), p. 647.

4 Here and elsewhere the date in parentheses after a word is the date given in *OED*, or *DS*, or Craigie and others (ed.), *Dictionary of American English* (1938–44), or *AL* Supp. I (1945), for its first known or conjectured use in the sense referred to; except in a few cases where Cunnington, *History of Underclothes* (1951), gives an earlier quotation, or where I have taken an antedating from *Notes and Queries*, or have myself discovered one.

5 Wycherley, *The Country-Wife* (1675), II. i. 420–1; p. 27.

6 *SV*, vol. iii, p. 85, gives *all face* and *on the shallow* as popular synonyms of *naked*. Others are the (originally) cant term *ballocky* (c. 1905), as in *Ballocky Bill the Sailor* (euphemized into 'Barnacle Bill the Sailor'); *ballock-naked* (C. 20; of both men and women); *stark-bol(l)ux*, used in Australia from c. 1890; *in morocco* (C. 19), a gypsy slang term.

7 *AL* (1922 edn), p. 150.

8 Cited, Bloch, *History of English Sexual Morals* (1936), p. 11.

9 Craig, *Sex and Revolution* (1934), p. 122 n.

10 Wilde, *Salome* (1894), pl. 7, facing p. 40. And Partridge (*DS*, vol. i, p. 834) gives *stomach-timber* (1820; 'food') as 'a nonce-variation of *bellytimber*' (c. 1600; Standard English in C. 17).

11 And to delete *foul breathing*. See Sadleir, *Trollope* (1927), pp. 165–6.

12 Partridge (*DS, passim*) gives *victualling office* (1751), *dumpling-depôt* (C. 19), *porridge-bowl* (mid-C. 19), *victualling department* (1878), and *bread-*

room as other pugilistic slang terms for the belly. A clearly dysphemistic term is *shit-bag* (mid-C. 19).

13 Cf. *AL* (1936 edn), p. 304.

14 Natasha Lytess, 'Marilyn Monroe: Her secret life', *People*, July 15, 1962, p. 2: 'It was cut *that* low I could see her waist dimple.'

15 Cf. *AL* Supp. I (1945), p. 651. The novelist Susan Ferrier complained in 1810 that she had been 'held . . . up to the scorn of the virtuous and the detestation of the pure in heart' for having written a letter to a man 'on the subject of *corn cutting*. You will allow I must have had some ingenuity if I could extract either immorality or indecency from a corn! But so it was. I was reprobated . . . as one of the abandoned of my sex' (Ferrier, *Memoir and Correspondence* (1898), p. 91).

16 Cf. Marryat, *Diary in America* (1839), pt i, vol. ii, pp. 246–7. And see p. 181 below.

17 [Bache], *Vulgarisms* (1868), pp. 34–5.

18 Marryat, *op. cit.* pt i, vol. ii, p. 246.

19 [Bache], *op. cit.* p. 35.

20 Dingwall, *American Woman* (1956), p. 82, citing A. M. Gow, *Good Morals and Gentle Manners for Schools and Families* (Cincinnati, New York, 1873), p. 199. One traveller observed however that 'ladies who have been in Europe do not shrink from saying "legs" almost as freely as they talk of "limbs" ' (Grattan, *Civilized America* (1859), vol. ii, p. 53).

21 Longfellow, *Kavanagh* (1849), p. 46. Italics added. Cf. *SV*, vol. iii, p. 64.

22 And a Welsh colloquial euphemism for women's legs was *underneaths* (late C. 19).

23 [Marryat], *Peter Simple* (1834), vol. ii, p. 202. *The white meat* was also used; cf. Grattan, *op. cit.*

24 F & H, vol. ii, pp. 247; *SV*, vol. iii, p. 87–8; *DS, passim*. Other popular synonyms for *breasts* include: *chest and bedding* (before 1785; nautical), *top ballocks* (C. 19; military), *cabmen's rests* (*c.* 1870; rhyming slang), *upper works* (*c.* 1870), *Berkeleys* (*c.* 1875), *Langtries* (*c.* 1880–1900; Society slang; from the actress Lily Langtry), *thousand pities* (late C. 19; rhyming slang), *towns and cities* (late C. 19; rhyming slang), *Bristol cities* (rhyming slang; hence the C. 20 *Bristols*), *toora-loorals* (before 1909; theatrical), *ooja(h)-pips* (*c.* 1920), *baby's bottom, breastworks, butter bags, butter boxes, half-way house, milk route, milk shakes, nursing bottle, other parts*, and *saddle bags*. Two Australian slang terms are *nubbies* (late C. 19) and *elders* (*c.* 1920).

25 Marcy, *Prairie Traveler* (1863), p. 109 n.

26 *DS*, vol. i, p. 247.

27 F & H, vol. ii, p. 247; *SV*, vol. iii, p. 88, *DS, passim*. Other colloquial terms for the nipples include *dairy* or *dairies* (*c.* 1780), *cream-jugs* (before 1891) *cat-heads* (C. 18; nautical), *charleys* or *charlies* (*c.* 1840), and *poonts* (*c.* 1870).

28 Wright, *Vocabularies* (1884), vol. i, col. 159, l. 44.

29 Partridge, *Origins* (1961), p. 27. The presumed Indo-European root is *ars-*, with *ers-* and *ors-* as variants.

30 Brie (ed.) *The Brut* (1906–08), pt ii, p. 297, ll. 7–9.

31 [Butler], *Hudibras* (1663–78), I. iii. 964; p. 236.

32 Scott (ed.), *Prose Works of Swift* (1897–1908), vol. i, p. 169. In the line above, however, *damned* is given as *d——d*!

33 [Grose], *Classical Dictionary* (1785 edn), sig. A3 recto.

34 [Manning], *Her Privates We* (1930), p. 54. This was 'an ordinary edition . . . but with certain prunings and excisions' of the same author's *The Middle Parts of Fortune* (1929), of which a limited edition of 520 copies was issued to subscribers by Peter Davies. *Fuck, fuckin'*, and *bugger* in the limited edition became ——, *muckin'*, and *beggar* in the 'ordinary' one.

35 *Putnam's Monthly*, vol. v, no. 27, p. 295, Mar. 1855, in an article entitled 'Sensitive Spirits'. Cf. however *ibid.* p. 284, where *asses* is spelt in full.

36 Cf. *AL* (1922 edn), p. 154. In the 1920s even *aster* was sometimes considered suggestive in the Ozark mountains of south-west Missouri and north-west Arkansas, Cf. Randolph, *Dialect Notes*, vol. vi, pt i, pp. 62–3, 1928.

37 [Grose], *op. cit.* (1785 edn), sig. O verso.

38 *OED*, vol. i, p. 1173. Cf. F & H, vol. i, p, 373.

39 Johnson, *Dictionary* (1755), vol. i, sig. 3S recto.

40 Callender, *Deformities* (1782), p. 36. In the New York *Organ* (a 'family journal devoted to temperance, morality, education and general literature') of May 29, 1847, the word *seat* was adopted in place of *chair* (cf. *AL* (1922 edn), p. 149).

41 *DS*, vol. i, p. 106.

42 *AL* Supp. I (1945), p. 644 n. 3. As a verb however *bum* is now 'perfectly acceptable' and 'in regular use in colloquial English, as in "can I bum a cigarette off you?" ' (Wallace Reyburn, 'The Americanisation of the English Language', *Sunday Times*, July 8, 1962, colour section, p. 23).

43 In proceedings against the American magazine *Esquire* in 1943–44 the 'snoopers and smut-snufflers' of the U.S. Postmaster General objected to its use of the words *backside, behind*, and *bawdy-house* (*AL* Supp. I (1945), p. 646).

44 Ware, *Passing English* [1909], p. 134.

45 Cunnington, *History of Underclothes* (1951), p. 121.

46 Graves, *Lars Porsena* [1927], p. 19.

47 F & H, vol. i, pp. 231, 373; *SV*, vol. iii, pp. 108–9; *DS*, passim. *Cracker* refers to the expulsion of wind from the anus. *Dilberries* are deposits of faecal matter on the anal hairs. Other popular synonyms for the buttocks are: *butt* (C. 15; Standard English till C. 17), *camera obscura* (before 1900), *West-*

phalia (before 1904), *afternoon, douglas, fanny* (very common in the U.S.A.), *juffs, moon, parts behind, skue,* and *twist.* An Australian slang term is *quoits* (*c.* 1925); *hinnie* and *sitty-billies* are American (students?).

48 F & H, vol. i, p. 231; *SV*, vol. iii, pp. 109–10; *DS, passim.* Other popular synonyms for the anus are *blind eye* (C. 18), *brown* (mid-C. 19), *monocular eye-glass* (*c.* 1860–1910), *eye sore, cul, nether eye, nether throat, postern* (*door*), *single O, stage door, tib,* and *tewel* or *tuel.*

49 Cf. Middle Dutch *pric, pricke,* Low German *prick, pricke.* See Partridge, *Origins* (1961), p. 525.

50 Akin to Old Norse *kokr,* Old Slavic *kokotŭ,* Old French and French *coq* and Late Latin *coccus,* 'app[arently] deriving from L[atin] *coco coco,* the cock's cry.' 'The sense-development of the n[oun] seems to be: male bird; faucet or tap, and then, very soon, a cocking mechanism; finally, prob[ably] from the "faucet" sense, the true C. 18–20 S[tandard] E[nglish] word for "penis" ' (Partridge, *op. cit.* p. 108).

51 Shakespeare, *Romeo and Juliet,* II. iv. 120–1; *King Henry V,* II. i. 51–2. Cf. Partridge, *Shakespeare's Bawdy* (1947), pp. 171, 88.

52 Florio, *Worlde of Wordes* (1598), p. 76.

53 Fletcher and Massinger, *The Custom of the Country* [*c.* 1619], III. iii; Glover (ed.), *Works of Beaumont and Fletcher* (1905–12), vol. i, p. 341.

54 [Bache], *op. cit.* pp. 35–6. Buckingham, *Slave States* [1842], vol. ii, p. 134, cites a preacher who did in fact read: 'Before *a certain fowl* shall crow, thou shalt deny me thrice.'

55 De Vere, *Americanisms* (1872), p. 380.

56 For *he-biddy* cf. *ibid.*: 'There is little harm, perhaps, in calling a hen a *biddy* . . . but to make from it a *he-biddy* for the cock . . . is a somewhat violent proceeding.' In the Ozarks, in the 1920s, grown men sometimes used such terms as *girl-birds* and *boy-birds,* blushed and stammered, when women were present, at the mere mention of *stop-cocks,* and, instead of describing a gun as *cocked,* would say '*she's ready t' go*' or '*th' hammer's back*'. 'When a hillman says "*I pulled back both roosters*" he means only that he cocked both barrels of his shotgun. The word *peacock* is very bad, since it is supposed to suggest micturition as well as the genitalia. Even *cock-eyed, cock-sure* and *coxcomb* are considered too suggestive for general conversation, and many natives shy at such surnames as *Cox, Leacock, Hitchcock* and the like' (Randolph, *op. cit.* pp. 58–9).

57 For *crower* cf. Farmer (comp. and ed.), *Americanisms* (1889), p. 186. This, says Farmer, is not the only instance in which certain sections of Americans 'fall from the frying-pan of squeamishness into the fire of indelicate suggestiveness'.

58 [Haliburton], *The Clockmaker,* 2nd ser. (1838), pp. 272–4.

59 Bartlett, *Dictionary of Americanisms* (1877), p. 243. Cf. Davenport,

Curiositates Eroticæ Physiologiæ (1875), pp. vi–vii: 'What is to be said of those would be *linguistic purists* who recommended mutilating the brave old English word *cock*, and thus metamorphose it into *co.*, on account of its indecency, a sentence which is to be extended to all the unfortunate words compounded of it, as Turncock, which must be read Turnco, &c., &c. The absurdity of this proposed change, as well as its injustice to poor Chanticleer, the husband of Dame Partlet, is the greater, since it is well known that hens are fecundated, not by intromission but by compression.'

60 F & H, vol. ii, pp. 208–9, vol. v, pp. 288–90; *SV*, vol. iii, pp. 90–9; *DS*, *passim*. *Customs officer*, also given by F & H, is defined by Partridge as 'a cathartic pill'. Their *kennel-raker* is, he says, Standard English for 'scavenger', their inclusion of *knack* 'almost certainly an error'. *Milkman* he defines as 'a masturbator'; F & H's *tickle-faggot*, *tickle-gizzard*, and *tickle-piece* were almost certainly Standard English nonce-words; their *tug-mutton* is a whore-monger; their *twanger* 'anything very fine or . . . large'.

61 *DS*, vol. i, p. 229.

62 *DS*, vol. ii, p. 1267.

63 Except for (*Old*) *Hornington* (C. 19) and (*Old*) *Horney*, both probably dysphemistic.

64 There are many more euphemisms for the penis than have been given in the text. They include: *verge* (before 1400), *pintle* (Standard English until *c.* 1720), *pil(l)cock*, *pil(l)icock* and *pillock* (C. 14–18; used by Shakespeare, etc.), *pizzle* (of animal, from *c.* 1520; of man, from C. 17; Standard English until *c.* 1840), *jockum* or *jockam* (mid-C. 16–early 19), *rubigo* (late C. 16–17; Scots), *strunt* (1608), *tantrum* (1675–? 1800), *plenipo* (C. 18–19), *indelicacy* (1758), *may-pole of love* (1758), *impudence* (*c.* 1760–1900; lower-middle- and lower-class women's), *The Electrical Eel; or, Gymnotus Electricus* (*c.* 1774), *Mimosa: or, The Sensitive Plant* (1779), *barometer of health* (in Timothy Touchit [pseud.], *La Souricière* (1794), vol. ii, p. 1), *dibble* (C. 19; Scots), *dolly* (C. 19), *eye-opener* (C. 19), *fool-sticker* (C. 19) and *fool-maker*, *pecker* (C. 19), *pecnoster* (C. 19), *sucker* (C. 19), *Irish root* (*c.* 1830–1914), *langolee* (mid-C. 19; Irish), *gooser* (*c.* 1871), *almond (rock)* (*c.* 1880; shorter form *c.* 1890; rhyming slang; mostly Cockneys'), *bean-tosser* (late C. 19), *Hampton (Wick)* (late C. 19; rhyming slang), *sting* (C. 19), *red cap* (*c.* 1918), *whang* or *wang* (C. 20), *corey* or *corie* (C. 20; Cockneys' and Kentish dialect), *beak, blueskin, chanter* (Scots), *devil, dong, donger, doodah, enemy, father confessor, father-of-all, fee to women's virtue, fiddle-diddle, freeman, gadzooks, genuine article, gong-beater, horn of flesh, horn of plenty, jargonelle, king-member, linchpin, love's nectar-laden stalk, morsel, nature, nature's masterpiece, O-for-shame, organ of lust, partner, phallic glory, pillar of ivory, pioneer of nature, pup, quarter-master, quickener, rogue, root of evil, shaft of Cupid, shaft of flesh, snapper, solicitor-general, sword of pleasure, tag, tent, terror of virgins, that, third leg,*

tinker, titbit, tree of love, trifle, trombone, wand of love, what's-his-name, what's-its-name, wimble, yelper, and *Zadkiel.* Nursery euphemisms, in addition to those mentioned in the text, are *doodle* (mid-C. 18) and *nippy* (*c.* 1850); schoolboys' terms include *tallywag* (occasionally *tarriwag*; late C. 18), *diddle* (*c.* 1870), *tosh* (1870s), *plonk* (C. 20), and *tallywhacker* (C. 20). *Person* is much used by policemen giving evidence. Common in the armed forces are *bell-end* (C. 20), *blunt end* (C. 20), *red end* (C. 20), and *small arm. Crab-tree* (*c.* 1750) was a dysphemism alluding to *Phthirus inguinalis.* A *donkey's* (late C. 19) is a large penis. Terms for parts of the penis include *bobstay* (mid-C. 18), *bridle (-string)* (late C. 19), and *G-string* (C. 20) for the fraenum, *crest* for the head, *skin* (mid-C. 19) and *sheath* for the prepuce, *eye-hole* (late C. 19) for the *introitus urethrae,* and *reins* and *ribbons* for the muscles of the penis.

65 Wright, *op. cit.* vol. i, col. 265, l. 34.

66 *Lev.* xxii. 24, in Wycliffe, *Holy Bible* (1850), p. 346: 'Al beeste, that outher with al tobrokun, or crippid, or kitt and taken awey the ballokes is, ȝe shulen not offre to the Lord.'

67 And was consequently avoided, even in its primary meaning, in the U.S.A., where it was 'thought indelicate to use the word stone' (Buckingham, *op. cit.* vol. ii, p. 133). Cf. De Vere, *op. cit.* p. 554, quoting S. S. Haldeman: 'A young lady, who was so refined that she avoided saying *stone,* spoke thus: I took up a ground-seed (stone) and threw it at a he-biddy (cock) sitting on a turn-about (grinding-stone) and killed him *stone-*dead.'

68 In the sense of 'nonsense', *balls* was held to be obscene in February 1929, but had become permissible in print by 1931. Cf. *DS,* vol. i, p. 29. *Testicles to you!* (*c.* 1920) is an interesting semi-euphemism for this sense.

69 F & H, vol. ii, p. 149; *SV,* vol. iii, pp. 132–3; *DS, passim.* A common oath among London costermongers, says Davenport, *Aphrodisiacs and Anti-aphrodisiacs* (1869 [*sc.* 1873]), pp. 8–9, was '*S'elp my taters*'. Other popular synonyms for the testicles or scrotum are *lurn* (*c.* 1910), *beauties, (bird's) eggs, bullets, bum-balls, clock-weights, dependences, dornicks, dowsetts, jewels, (k)nick-(k)nacks, knockers, love-apples, magazines, marbles, ornaments, oval reservoirs, purse, shot pouch, trinkets, whennymegs,* and *witnesses of one's virility. Cobblers* (C. 20) is rhyming slang (*cobblers' awls*).

70 *AL* (1936 edn), p. 301.

71 *AL* (1922 edn), p. 152. For the same reason, a paper bag was always a *sack* or a *poke* in the Ozarks in the 1920s (Randolph, *op. cit.* p. 60).

72 *AL* (1936 edn), p. 302. In the Ozarks the 'innocent verb *alter* [was] never used in the presence of women' (Randolph, *op. cit.*).

73 *AL* Supp. I (1945), p. 658.

74 *DS,* vol. ii, p. 1054.

75 *DS,* vol. ii, p. 1055.

76 Partridge, *Origins* (1961), p. 135.

77 Rattray, *Quarterly Review*, Jan. 1961, p. 14.

78 Partridge, in Grose, *Classical Dictionary* (1931 edn), p. 111.

79 *Ibid.* Cf. Lawrence, *Lady Chatterley's Lover* (1960), p. 185.

80 Charles, *Sexual Impulse* (1935), p. 31. Cf. [Potter and others], *Romance of Lust* (1873–76), vol. iii, pp. 5–6: 'To the true votaries of these love orgies grossness of language is a stimulant to passion. Fuck—frig—bugger—cunt —prick—bollocks—bubbies—arse-hole—are all sacred words only to be pronounced when in the exercise of love's mysteries.' Cf. also Kronhausen, *Pornography and the Law* (1960), pp. 219–20; and the section on what he terms 'erotolalia' in MacDugald, 'Language and Sex', Ellis and Abarbanel (ed.), *Encyclopædia of Sexual Behaviour* (1961), vol. ii, pp. 588–9.

81 Cf. *DS*, vol. i, p. 198.

82 Ekwall, *Street-Names of the City of London* (1954), pp. 164–5; Gelling, *Place-Names of Oxfordshire* (1953–54), pt i, p. 40; Smith, *Place-Names of the East Riding* (1937), p. 289 (citing Drake, *Eboracum* (1736), pp. 346–7: '[The] name tending not a little to obscenity, as it is wrote very plain in some antient writings, I shall not pretend to etymologize. We know our ancestors used to call a *spade* a *spade*; but custom has prevailed upon their descendants to be more modest in expression, whatever they are in action. However, that the plainness and simplicity of our predecessors may have all due regard paid to it, I have given some authorities for the antient name of this lane in the appendix. It is very probable that this place was of old a *licenced brothel*; though so near the cathedral church as to be exactly opposite to the great gates of the *deanery*'); Gover and others, *Place-Names of Northamptonshire* (1933), p. 8; Reaney, *Place-Names of Essex* (1935), p. 457. There was a Gropelane in Peterborough and Grope Lanes in Chipping Barnet, Herts., Bristol and Worcester; these were euphemistic variants.

83 Gelling, *op. cit.*

84 Robinson (ed.), *Works of Chaucer* (1957), p. 49, l. 3276. Other spellings were *quaint* and *quaynt(e)*. This pronunciation 'survived in the North Country till 1890 at least' (Partridge, in Grose, *op. cit.* (1931 edn), pp. 111–12).

85 Shakespeare, *Twelfth Night*, II. v. 88–92. Cf. *country matters* (*Hamlet* [c. 1603], III. ii. 125).

86 Fletcher, *The Spanish Curate* (1622), IV. v; Glover (ed.), *Works of Beaumont and Fletcher* (1905–12), vol. ii, p. 120.

87 Palsgrave, *L'Éclaircissement de la langue française* (1852), p. 209. *Shap*, *shape*, or *shappe* for sexual organs dates from before 1000, and was used by Chaucer.

88 Cotgrave (comp.), *Dictionarie* (1611), sig. T iij verso.

89 Minsheu, *Guide into Tongues* (1617), p. 112.

90 [Grose], *op. cit.* (1788 edn), sig. H4 verso. But the Greek κόννος, meaning 'trinket', 'beard' was not related semantically to the Latin *cunnus*.

91 *Ibid.* (1796 edn), sig. Ee verso.

92 *DS*, vol. i, p. 198. 'Yet', he adds, 'the *OED* gave *prick*: why this further injustice to women?'

93 F. L. G. [*sc.* Gower?], *Swell's Night Guide* [1841], 'The Stumer's'.

94 Forman (ed.), *Letters of Keats* (1931), vol. i, p. 82.

95 [Kopernicky and others (ed.)], Κρυπτάδια (1883–1911), vol. iv, pp. 394–5.

96 'Whether or Not', *Collected Poems of D. H. Lawrence* (1932), p. 89.

97 Barth, *The Sot-Weed Factor* (1961), jacket. Diminutives of *cunt* are *cunnicle*, *cunnikin*, *cuntkin*, and *cuntlet*. *Tenuc* (*c.* 1860) is back slang; *sharp and blunt* (late C. 19), *grumble and grunt* (C. 20), *Berkshire Hunt, Lady Berkeley Hunt*, and *(Sir) Berkeley Hunt* (C. 20; not one in a thousand who uses the word *berk* realizes that it is an abbreviation of one or all of these) are rhyming slang. *Sluice (cunt)* (C. 17) was a name for a large one, as were *bushel cunt* (C. 19) and *cow cunt* (C. 19), terms applied to a woman deformed by child-bearing or prostitution.

98 *OED*, vol. xi, pt 2, p. 519. A mid-C. 17–early 19 diminutive of *twat* was spelt variously *twachel*, *twachil*, *twachyle*, and *twatchell*. *Trot* is a C. 18 synonym. *Twittle* and *twam(my)* (C. 20) may be similarly derived.

99 *Vanity of Vanities* [1659]. The editor having 'considered it his duty to expunge as much as possible the gross expressions which sometimes occur in the originals, and which were less obnoxious to the ears of our forefathers than to those of our contemporaries' (Wright (ed.), *Political Ballads* (1841), p. xiii), these lines appeared in one nineteenth-century edition in the following bowdlerized form (*ibid.* p. 197):

> They talk't of his having a cardinall's hat,
> They'd send him as soon, I know not what!

100 Kenyon (ed.), *Works of Browning* (1912), vol. ii, pp. 156–7. Professor Basil L. Gildersleeve, however, did not think Browning innocent, accusing him of salacity in using that 'notorious word which smirches the skirt of *Pippa Passes*' (*American Journal of Philology*, vol. xxxii, no. 2 [126], p. 241, Apr., May, June, 1911).

101 Variants are *queme*, *quim-box*, *quimsby*, and *quin*.

102 [Pinkerton], *Ancient Scotish Poems* (1786), vol. ii, p. 384.

103 I am indebted to Mr T. B. Thompson for this version of 'It'.

104 *SV*, vol. i, p. 82. Cf. Κρυπτάδια (1883–1911), vol. iii, p. 364; vol. iv, p. 396, where the rhyme is said to be a parody of a song by Dr Arnold. A somewhat different version ('sung by Mr Edwin in *The Agreeable Surprise*') appears in Farmer (comp. and ed.), *National Ballad and Song* (1897), vol. ii, pp. 266–7. There is a description of *The Agreeable Surprise*, an eighteenth-century musical farce, in *Travels of Moritz in England in 1782* (1924), p. 73, where the rhyme is quoted in what is apparently the original version:

Amo, amas,
I love a lass,
She is so sweet and tender,
It is sweet *Cowslip's* Grace,
In the Nominative Case,
And in the feminine Gender.

It is also quoted by Marryat in *Jacob Faithful* (1834), vol. i, p. 223, but here

she laid me flat,
Though of the feminine gender.

105 Other cultured euphemisms for the female sex organ include: *axis, beauty (spot), carnal part, centre of attraction, centre of love, centre of sensibility, Cupid's shrine, domain of love, domain of Venus, end of the Sentimental Journey* (from the last sentence of Sterne's *A Sentimental Journey through France and Italy* (1768): 'So that when I stretch'd out my hand, I caught hold of the Fille de Chambre's   '; this space is replaced by a dash in many later editions), *hallowed spot, ineffable, instrument, ivory gate, jewel, keystone of love, laboratory of love, lady star, lamp of love, little beauty, little darling, little one, little pet, name-it-not, nameless, nature, nature's privy seal, nature's treasury, nature's tufted treasure, ornament, part, parts* ('a hyper-euphemism', says Partridge, *Slang* (1933), p. 191 n. 1), *parts more dear, person, point of attraction, privates, privities, privy council, promised land, pudend, sanctuary of love, seat of desire, seat of love, secret charm, sex, sex's pride, sexual treasure, shrine of love, temple of connubis, temple of love, that, thing, treasure, undeniable, undertaker.*

106 Other terms coined by Cleland include: *(burning) spot, centre of desire, centre of sense, centre of the senses, centre spot, channel, cloven spot, conduit, (right) door, (little) fairy, garland, gate, greasy landscape, main joy, main spot, nether lips, parting, passage, rift, sheath, strait, stricture.*

107 [Grose], *op. cit.* (1785 edn), sig. D3 verso, D4 recto.

108 Farmer (comp. and ed.), *National Ballad and Song* (1897), vol. i, p. 224.

109 Other terms of this kind include: *quarry* (C. 18–19), *blind alley* (C. 19), *(Cupid's or one-ended) furrow* (C. 19), *gate of life* (C. 19), *horse collar* (C. 19), *pouter* (C. 19), *gully-hole* (C. 19), *gully* (c. 1850), *long eye* (c. 1850), *Marble Arch* (c. 1850), *Holloway* (c. 1860), *Upper Holloway, hatchway* (c. 1865; nautical), *amulet, aperture of bliss, bonne bouche, box, breach, cave of love* (or *harmony*), *cavity, (under) dimple, entrance, fore door, gateway, love's channel, love's harbour, niche, (single) O, opening, orifice, portal (of love), postern door, rent, slot, tail-gap, tail-gate, tail-hole, trench, tunnel, velvet sheath, wallet, wicket,* and *wrinkle (of love).* All these, together with those in the text, are more or less euphemistic. Included among the dysphemisms of this group are: *dark hole* (1613), *black hole, black joke* (late C. 18–early 19), *black ring,*

dumb squint (C. 19), *gaper (over the garter)* (C. 19), *red ace* (mid-C. 19), *red C* (mid-C. 19), *coral sheath, vermilion sheath, quack, (upright) grin, upright wink, winker,* and *rough O.* A sub-class, mostly dysphemistic, names the pudenda by referring to the pubic hairs: *mossy face* (late C. 18–mid-19), *moss-grown glen, mossy bank, mossy cell, mossy lips* and *mossy vale; crown and feathers* (C. 19); *Hairyfordshire* (c. 1865), *hairy oracle* (c. 1870), *hairy prospect, hairy ring* (c. 1870), and *bit of hair.*

110 Others in this group are: *forecourt* (C. 19), *forehatch* (C. 19), *forewoman* (C. 19), *front window* (C. 19), *belly dale, belly dingle, belly entrance, bottom cavity, cellar door, central furrow, central office, County Down, door of the inner temple, Downshire, downstairs, down there, fore room, front passage, middle gate, middle kingdom, middlings, parts below, South Pole, under belongings, under entrance, unders* and *underworld* (euphemisms); *a bit on a fork* (C. 19), *front gut* (C. 19), and *gut entrance* (c. 1840) (dysphemisms).

111 *Old ling* (mid-C. 18–mid-19) is clearly dysphemistic.

112 Other euphemisms in this category include: *Paphian grove* (1792), *Jack Straw's castle* (C. 19), *locker* (C. 19; mainly nautical), *(front) parlour* (C. 19), *premises* (C. 19), *kitchen* (c. 1860), *alcove, (cyprian* or *Cupid's) arbour, Bluebeard's closet, bower, cabinet of love, corner cupboard, Cupid's cupboard, Cupid's cloister, cyprian cave, fort, fortress, grotto (of pleasure), harbour (of hope), inglenook, kennel, love's pavilion, mystic grotto, reception hall, Venus's (secret) cell,* and *vestry.* Cf. the dysphemistic *Fornicator's Hall* (C. 19).

113 *Dripping pan* seems definitely, *till* possibly, dysphemistic.

114 But Partridge calls this term 'more coll[oquial] than euphemistic' (*DS*, vol. i, p. 353).

115 Partridge however thinks this may be a ' "dubious" euphemism, the double pun being indelicate' (*DS*, vol. i, p. 304).

116 Cf. [Grose], *op. cit.* (1785 edn), sig. E recto: 'A woman, who was giving evidence in a cause . . . made use of the term cauliflower, for which the judge on the bench, a peevish old fellow, reproved her, saying she might as well call it artichoak; not so, my lord, replied she, for an artichoak has a bottom, but a * * * * and a cauliflower have none.'

117 Pyles, *Modern Language Notes,* Jan. 1949, p. 2 n. 5. The Barrison sisters, advertised as the wickedest girls in the world, used to perform a song and dance entitled 'Do You See My Little Pussy?' while holding kittens in front of them at the level of the *mons veneris* (see Wall, *Sex and Sex Worship* (1919), p. 473, fig. 278). Other feline euphemisms are *malkin* (c. 1540; Scots), *civet* (C. 18), *pussy-cat* (C. 19), *cat* (C. 19), *chat* (C. 19), *mouser* (C. 19), and *kitty. Rough malkin* (C. 16; Scots) may have been dysphemistic.

118 As are *tench* (mid-C. 19), *periwinkle* (mid-C. 19), *whelk* (c. 1860; working-class Cockney), *clam, dormouse, monkey,* and *mule.* Cf. also *bun* (C.

17–19), from the Scottish and northern dialect sense, 'tail (of a hare)'.
119 For *grandmother* cf. Nell Dunn, 'Out with the Girls', *New Statesman*, vol. lxiii, no. 1627, p. 708, May 18, 1962. Other personifications are *brown madam* (late C. 18–early 19) and *Black Bess*.
120 *Quoniam* (C. 17–18), *modicum* (*c.* 1660–1840), *tu quoque* (late C. 18–early 19), *quid* (C. 19), *omnibus* (*c.* 1840), *factotum, trincum,* and *vade-mecum*. There is also a French name, *qui vive*.
121 *(K)nick-(k)nack, whim(-wham)* (from *quim?*), *tuʒʒy-muʒʒy* (*c.* 1710; occasionally *tuʒʒi-muʒʒy* or *tuʒʒimuʒʒy), crinkum-crankum* (*c.* 1780–1870), and *tirly-whirly* (late C. 18; Scots).
122 Cf. *jiggambob, thingum(m)y, thingam(m)y, thingumbob, thingambob* (all C. 19).
123 [Grose], *op. cit.* (1788 edn), sig. D2 verso.
124 *Ibid.* (1788 edn), sig. O4 recto.
125 Cf. p. 47 above.
126 G. A. Stevens, cited, F & H, vol. iv, p. 337.
127 And *Jacob's ladder* (C. 19), *pleasure boat* (C. 19), *altar of love* (or *Hymen* or *pleasure), hall of pleasure, haven of bliss, mine of pleasure, object of enjoyment, palace of pleasure, place of amusement, pleasure-ground, pleasure-conduit, (portal of the) temple of pleasure, road to heaven, road to paradise, seat of pleasure, way to heaven.*
128 Dysphemisms alluding to the penis are *touch-hole* (C. 17), *cock-alley* (C. 18), *cock-hall* (C. 18), *cock-lane* (C. 18), *cockpit* (C. 18), *Cockshire* (C. 18), *niche-cock* (C. 18), *doodle-sack* (mid-C. 18), *Miss Laycock* (late C. 18–19), *cockchafer* (C. 19), *Cock Inn* (C. 19), *never out* (C. 19), *skin-the-pizzle* (C. 19), *suck-and-swallow* (C. 19), *tickle-Thomas* (C. 19), *goat milker* (*c.* 1840), *penwiper* (*c.* 1850), *cockholder, eel pot, eel skinner, eel trap, prick-holder, prick-purse, prick-scourer, prick-skinner,* and *tool chest.*
129 Cf. the dysphemistic *jelly bag* (C. 17), *milk jug* (C. 18), *milk pan* (C. 18), *milking pail* (C. 18), *gravy-maker* (C. 19), *lather-maker* (C. 19), *milker* (C. 19), *milt-market* (and *-shop*) (C. 19), *butter boat, oyster catcher, sperm sucker,* and *spew alley.*
130 Euphemisms: *pump(-dale)* (late C. 17), *leak* (C. 18), *water box* (C. 19), *watercourse* (C. 19), *water-gate* (C. 19), *water-engine, water-mill, waterworks, Streams Town* and *s.t.* (all *c.* 1820–90), *P-maker* (mid-C. 19) and *make-water.* Dysphemisms: *pisser* (C. 19), and *waste pipe.*
131 *Drain* (C. 19) and *jam pot* (C. 19), both dysphemisms.
132 Euphemisms: *generating place* (C. 19), *the nursery* (C. 19), *storehouse* (1901), *bath of birth, birth place, brat-getting place, certificate of birth,* and *road to a christening.*
133 Dysphemisms: *custom-house goods* (mid-C. 18–early 19), *money-box* (C. 19), *money-maker* (C. 19), *money-spinner* (C. 19), *free fishery* (C. 19), *meat*

market (C. 19), *bum-shop* (mid-C. 19), *butcher's shop, bazaar, breadwinner*. 134 F & H, vol. iv, pp. 336–40; *SV*, vol. iii, pp. 142–57; *DS, passim*. Other euphemisms, in addition to those given in the text and in notes above, include: *fiddle* (*c.* 1800) and *lute*; the nursery word *pee-wee* (C. 19) and the schoolgirls' *fie-for-shame* (*c.* 1820); *Botany Bay* and *Cape of Good Hope*; and the following: *leather* (C. 16), *princock* (or *princox* or *princy-cock*; C. 16–mid-19; from the Standard English sense, 'a pert, forward, saucy boy or youth'), *sear* or *sere* (late C. 16–17), *whetting-corn(e)* (? C. 17–mid-19), *conundrum* (*c.* 1640–1830), *gig(g)* (later C. 17–early 19), *gyvel* (C. 18; Scots), *leather lane* (C. 18), *mill* (C. 18), *non(e)such* (C. 18), *lock* (mid-C. 18), *The Torpedo* (*c.* 1774), *money* (*c.* 1780; of a young girl), *coffee-house* (late C. 18–19; from the popularity of such places at that period), *regulator* (late C. 18–19), *broom* (C. 19), *caze* or *kaze* (C. 19), *Cupid's Arms* (C. 19), *funny bit* (C. 19), *gal(l)i-maufr(e)y* (C. 19), *gimcrack* (C. 19), *jigger* (C. 19), *limbo* (C. 19), *lobster pot* (C. 19), *machine* (C. 19), *Mons Meg* (C. 19), *mumble-peg* (C. 19), *number nip* (C. 19), *old ding* (C. 19), *open C* (C. 19; originally printers'), *patch* (C. 19), *pigeon-hole* (C. 19), *poor man's blessing* (C. 19), *prat* (C. 19), *sampler* (C. 19), *teazle* (C. 19), *tiv(v)y* (C. 19), *valve* (C. 19), *milliner's shop* (*c.* 1840), *naf* (*c.* 1845; ? back slang on *fan*), *ace* (*of spades*) (mid-C. 19), *funniment* (mid-C. 19), *naughty* (mid-C. 19), *pen* (mid-C. 19), *roasting-jack* (mid-C. 19), *(bee-) hive* (*c.* 1850), *diddly-pout* (*c.* 1860; ? rhyming slang on *spout*), *grummet* (*c.* 1860; nautical), *leaving shop* (*c.* 1860), *home, sweet home* (*c.* 1870), *minge* (late C. 19; cant), *punse* (late C. 19), *growl* (*c.* 1890; cant), *Abraham's bosom, Adam's own, alpha and omega, arsenal, awful gate of life, bed-fellow, bit, bit of fat, bit of stuff, boat, bore, budget, busby, catherine wheel, clock, cloth, clouds, confessional, cornucopia, cradle, crooked way, Cupid's anvil, Cupid's corner, cushat, cushion, dark, dear morsel, dike, double oracle, duck pond, dumb oracle, dummelhead, duster, Dutch clock, elastic folds, everlasting wound, Eve's custom house, Exeter Hall, fancy bit, faucet, firelock, fireplace, firework, flap, forecaster, fountain of love, gusset, hogstye of Venus, House of Commons, juncture, keifer, land of rest, link, love's fountain, maddikin, miraculous cairn, Mount Faulcon, naggie, narrow, ninepence, open charms, padlock, parenthesis, pillie, pretty, pulpit, pulse, scratch, seal, (sensitive) quiver, shady spring, skin, slipper, spinning jenny, spit fire, star, straits, tile, toy shop, trick, trinket, twicket, vacuum, ware, wayside ditch, wayside fountain, wonderful lamp*, and *workshop*. Dysphemisms (probable or certain) other than those given in the text and in earlier notes, are: *bottomless pit* (late C. 18–early 19), *dumb glutton* (mid-C. 18–19), *cut-and-come-again* (C. 19), *fly-catcher* (C. 19), *fly-cage* (C. 19), *fly-by-night* (C. 19), *fly-trap* (C. 19), *gutter* (C. 19), *melting-pot* (C. 19), *Molly's hole* (C. 19), *prannie* or *pranny* (C. 19; term of contempt among men), *puddle* (C. 19), *sportsman's gap* (C. 19), *sportsman's hole, rough and tumble* (*c.* 1850), *catch-'em-alive-o* (*c.* 1864), *better (h)ole* (1916–19; mostly military), *bit for the finger, bit of rough, cab mat, Cape Horn, chuff-box, doddle case,* and *wanton ace.* The dysphemisms *burning bower, burning passage,* and *claptrap* apparently refer to a diseased vagina.

135 *SV*, vol. iii, p. 14; *DS*, vol. ii, pp. 1024, 1170. According to Partridge, *little boy in the boat* is 'a mostly Canadian variant (since *c.* 1908)' (*DS*, vol. ii, p. 1170). *Harris's List of Covent-Garden Ladies . . . For . . . 1788* [1788], p. 30, gives *coral headed tip.* [Potter and others], *The Romance of Lust* (1873–76) vol. iii, p. 140, has *clitty,* which is no doubt a literary attempt to be colloquial. Edmund Wilson uses *little bud* in *Memoirs of Hecate County* [1951], p. 221. The relative paucity of popular terms for the clitoris in European languages is discussed in articles by Blau and Kanner, *Psychoanalytic Quarterly,* 1943 and 1945.

136 *SV*, vol. iii, p. 166; *DS, passim.* Other synonyms are *maid's ring* (C. 19; Cockney), *hidden mine, (imaginary) jewel, jewel without price, keep, membrane, pearl without price, tail-fence, titbit,* and *toy.* Note also *cockles* (C. 18) for the *labia minora, double sucker* (*c.* 1870) for abnormally developed *labia maiora,* and *milk and water* for the breasts and pudenda.

137 *DS*, vol. ii, p. 1022.

138 F & H, vol. iii, pp. 18–19; *SV*, vol. iii, pp. 123–4; *DS, passim.* Other synonyms are: *bandoliers, bearskin, belly bristles, belly thicket, belly whiskers, boskage of Venus, catskin, cunny skin, Cupid's arbour, damber bush, grove of Eglantine, Hebe, lady's low toupee, lower wig, motte (carpet), moustache, mustard and cress, nether eyebrow, nether (eye)lashes, nether whiskers, pubic floss, pumpkin cover, rug, sweet briar, tail feathers, tufted honours* and *whin bush. Pillicock Hill* (cf. *King Lear,* III. iv. 76), *Mount Pleasant* (*c.* 1880), and *Shooter's Hill* (late C. 19) are terms for the *mons veneris.*

3 THEY SHOCKED MRS BEETON (pp. 56–59)

1 [Wolcot], 'Ode to Affectation', *Works of Pindar* (1794–1801), vol. ii, p. 425. The Cunningtons, *English Costume in the Eighteenth Century* (1957), p. 25, cite a writer who in 1756 remarked ironically that the word *breeches* was so outrageously indecent that a modest woman could not bring herself to pronounce it even when alone. They also cite a poem of 1791 in which a mother says to her daughter:

> Heydey! What lady e'er of *bitches* heard?
> E'en *breeches,* Sukey, is an odious word.
> She-dogs and small-clothes more polite appear,
> Breeches and bitches suit a barb'rous ear.

2 Calverley, in *Carmen Saeculare* (1853), wrote satirically of '*crurum non enarrabile tegmen*' ('that leg-covering which cannot be told') (*Complete Works* (1901), p. 54, l. 6). For *conveniences,* see McMillan, *American Speech,*

Apr. 1943, p. 122. *Farting-crackers* (late C. 17–18) was a dysphemism for breeches; cf. the C. 20 *diarrhoea-bags* for plus-fours. The old-fashioned trousers with a flap in front were known popularly and dysphemistically as *fornicators* (obsolete by 1880); *bags* (1853), *bum-bags* (*c.* 1860) and *trollywags* (*c.* 1870) are other slang terms for trousers; a working-class term was *round-mys* (before 1909; for *round my houses*, rhyming slang).

3 Cunnington, *History of Underclothes* (1951), p. 121; Davenport, *Curiositates Eroticæ Physiologiæ* (1875), p. vii.

4 Beeton, *Book of Household Management* (1861), p. 978.

5 In *Crofutt's Trans-Continental Tourist's Guide*, 1871, cited, M. Meredith, *American Speech*, Apr. 1930, p. 287.

6 R. H. Newall, *The Orpheus C. Kerr Papers*, 2nd ser. (1865), cited, M. Meredith, *op. cit.* p. 286.

7 Brooks, *As Others See Us* (1908), p. 11.

8 Trollope, *Domestic Manners of the Americans* (1832), vol. i, p. 221.

9 Cunnington, *op. cit.*

10 'Americanisms', *Blackwood's Edinburgh Magazine*, vol. lxxxix, no. 546, p. 436, Apr. 1861.

11 *Ladies' Home Journal*, cited, Lyall, *Future of Taboo* (1936), p. 99.

12 Cunnington, *op. cit.* p. 12.

13 Congreve, *Love for Love* (1695), II. i; p. 27.

14 *Academy*, Oct. 14, 1911, cited, Weekley, *Romance of Words* (1917), p. 99.

15 Hunt, *Autobiography* (1850), vol. iii, pp. 217–18. The *chemise* became the *vest* in 1924, though it survived under its original name till *c.* 1938. *Chemivest* is recorded from 1928.

16 Bartlett, *Dictionary of Americanisms* (1859 edn), p. 204.

17 A speaker's choice between these two terms is said to be a linguistic class indicator. Cf. Ross, *Neuphilologische Mitteilungen*, 1954, p. 43.

18 Trollope, *op. cit.* vol. i, p. 190.

19 Cf. Cunnington, *op. cit.* pp. 16–17: 'The nineteenth century endowed the word "drawers" with extraordinary qualities, and on the comic stage veiled allusions to the garment were greatly appreciated by (masculine) audiences. When in the nineties an actress with a bicycle sang a ditty about:

> Just a little bit of string—such a tiny little thing,
> Not as tightly tied as string should be;
> So in future when I ride, I shall wear things that divide,
> Or things that haven't strings, you see!

the verse was hailed as a daringly witty allusion to a closely guarded secret.'

20 *Whereabouts* (*c.* 1920) is an Australian euphemism for men's drawers.

21 Women's *pantaloons*, longer than ordinary drawers, were soon renamed

pantalet(te)s—to give the name a more feminine sound, say the Cunningtons (*op. cit.* p. 114).

22 Cunnington, *op. cit.* p. 14.

4 JUST BROWSING (pp. 60–65)

1 Untermeyer (ed.), *Albatross Book of Living Verse* (1933), p. 43. Cf. Dickins and Wilson (ed.), *Early Middle English Texts* (1952), p. 118 and glossary.

2 G. Meredith, *Ordeal of Richard Feverel* (1859), vol. ii, pp. 197, 198. Cf. Ericson, *Modern Language Notes*, Feb. 1938, pp. 112–13. 'Editorial prudishness', he writes, 'has kept that fine little Middle English poem, the *Cuckoo Song*, out of many a school-book, all because the old poet was familiar with English barnyards and meadows and in his poem recalled those sights and sounds. He knew that bullocks and bucks feel so good in the springtime that they can hardly contain themselves, and he set down what he saw and heard, leaving it to squeamish editors to distort one of his innocent folk-words into a meaning that he would not recognize' (p. 112). Thus Chambers and Sidgwick, *Early English Lyrics* (1907), p. 4, insist that *verteth* means 'harbours in the green'. 'One suspects', comments Ericson, 'that scholarly ingenuity has been overworked by [these] scholars to save the children of England from indecency' (*op. cit.*).

3 Nineteenth-century diminutives of *fart* were *fartick* and *fartkin*. *To wind up one's* (or *the*) *horn* (C. 18–mid-19) meant to break wind.

4 Cf. the dysphemistic *snot-box* (mid-C. 19) and *snotter* (c. 1830) for *nose*.

5 For *nose spasm*, see McKnight, *English Words* (1923), p. 269.

6 Weekley, *Romance of Words* (1917), pp. 98–9. 'In 1829', he adds, 'the use of the word *mouchoir* in a French adaptation of *Othello* caused a riot at the Comédie Française.' *Snotter* (c. 1820), *nose-wipe* (c. 1820), *nose-wiper* (c. 1894), and *snot-rag* (late C. 19) are popular (and the first and last, dysphemistic) terms for *handkerchief*.

7 *Gentleman's Magazine*, vol. lxi, pt 2, no. 6, p. 1099, Dec. 1791. Except that she said 'oxen' for 'horses', the chestnut 'Horses sweat, men perspire and young ladies glow' has been attributed to a woman teacher in a girls' finishing school (Steadman, *English Studies*, Apr. 1935, p. 86). When, in 1885, the wearing of 'wool next the skin' was held to be necessary 'to absorb perspiration', a writer complained: 'But surely a gentlewoman rarely does anything to cause such an unpleasant thing!' (cited, Cunnington, *History of Underclothes* (1951), p. 194).

8 Cf., e.g., Sue Sheridan, 'What Every Gal Should Know', *Roxy*, Nov. 18, 1961: 'Real smart kookies know that B.O.—or body odour—is a year-round problem that affects everybody. We all perspire, but it is stale perspiration which is so offensive.'

9 Drs Eberhard W. and Phyllis C. Kronhausen, 'The Smell of Love', *Esquire*, vol. l, no. 2 (297), p. 67, Aug. 1958. I am indebted to Mr Trevenen Peters for this reference.

10 C. 20 Australian slang terms are *lose a meal* and *make a sale*.

11 Cf. Steadman, *American Speech*, Apr. 1935, p. 97.

12 For *burp* see Dwight L. Bolinger, 'Among the New Words', *American Speech*, vol. xvi, no. 2, p. 145, Apr. 1941.

13 Cf. Fowler, *Modern English Usage* (1954 reprint), p. 159: 'The mealy-mouthed American must be by this time harder put to it with *expectorate* than the mealy-mouthed Englishman with *spit*; his genteelism has outgrown its gentility & become itself the plain rude word for the rude thing; it must be discouraging to have to begin the search for decent obscurity all over again—with so promising a failure behind one, too.'

14 Cf. Pyles, *Modern Language Notes*, Jan. 1949, p. 7: 'It is certain that the ladies of our grandmothers' generation had no idea of the significance of the word [*shitepoke*] when they used it jocularly and endearingly to their children and grandchildren as the equivalent of "little rascal".'

15 Cf. F & H, vol. i, pp. 389–90. Slang terms that are not euphemistic are *crap* (C. 18), *do* (or *have*) *a crap* (C. 19), and *cack* (C. 19; originally Standard English). *Poop* (C. 19) is mostly a children's word, says Partridge (*DS*, vol. i, p. 648). *Tom-tit* (late C. 19) and *pony and trap* (late C. 19) are rhyming slang. *To leave its visiting-card* (of an animal) is 'non-U', writes Ross *Neuphilologische Mitteilungen*, 1954, p. 23.

16 [Bache], *Vulgarisms* (1868), p. 37.

17 Cf. the second-world-war Forces variant, *shake hands with the bloke one enlisted with*.

18 *DS*, vol. ii, p. 1356.

19 Cf. also *pump ship* and *squeeze the lemon*. I have heard it suggested that the colloquialism *piddle* (late C. 18) caused a vowel-change in the name of the most celebrated town on the Dorset river Piddle, so that we speak of the Tolpuddle martyrs, though of Piddle Hinton and Piddletrenthide. But the form Pudele is recorded as early as 1325.

20 The modern indoor privy with flushing arrangement was invented in 1596 by a godson and courtier of Queen Elizabeth I, Sir John Harington, who announced it in a work with the doubly punning title *A New Discourse of a Stale Subject, called the Metamorphosis of Aiax* (n.p. [London], 1596; a new edn, annotated by Elizabeth Story Donno, was published in 1962). *Ajax* was pronounced *age aches*; in *Wit's Academy* (1656) the question 'Which of the valientest Greeks had the fowlest name?' is answered 'Ajax' (cited, Jespersen, *S.P.E. Tract No. XXXIII* (1929), p. 424).

21 Cf. *AL* (1922 edn), p. 155. During a public health campaign in the thirties, medical advice to the public about washing the hands after evacuation

of the bowel had to be withdrawn because the newspapers dared not print the word *water-closet*.

22 Charlton, *Recollections* (1949), p. 140. She added: 'Neither of them ever availed themselves of such a convenient appliance, alleging that *suchlike whims bred pestilence and fevers*. In all weathers they preferred to take their walks abroad, their aim and object being located in a shrubbery at the back' (*ibid.* p. 141).

23 Or *Johnnie*. Mencken (*AL* Supp. I (1945), p. 640) says this arose in American women's colleges in the 1930s. Like *George*, it is widely used by British students. It may be a modernization of *jakes*.

24 Cf. *Evening Standard*, Jan. 25, 1962: 'The bear had broken into a house and the woman occupier rushed into the smallest room and locked herself in.'

25 F & H, vol. iv, p. 369, list English synonyms for *privy*. Popular synonyms, in addition to those given in the text, include *Quaker's burying ground* (C. 19), *forakers* (C. 19; Winchester College slang), *colfab(i)as* (*c.* 1820; Latinized Irish), *fourth* (before 1860; Cambridge slang; a man would pin a note on his door with the message: 'Gone⁴'), *casa* and *case* (before 1864), *rear(s)* (*c.* 1880; university slang), *dunnekin* (late C. 19; many other spellings), *cacatorium, chapel, house* (or *place*) *of ease, letter-box, the Long, the temple of health*. In the U.S.A. '*B.O.* (bad odor) is a popular designation for the latrine in boys' camps' (I.T., 'Aliases for the Latrine', *American Notes and Queries*, vol. i, no. 8, p. 121, Nov. 1944). Two Australian slang terms are *lavo* (*c.* 1920) and *trizzer* (*c.* 1922). *Shit-house* (in C. 19 also, mostly among furniture removers, a commode) seems usually dysphemistic—today, at any rate—rather than a plain term; other dysphemisms are *crapping-casa*, *-case* and *-ken* (all C. 18), *crapping-castle* (C. 19), *spice island* (*c.* 1810–50), and *crapping-house*. For an excellent discussion, see Pudney, *Smallest Room* (1954), pp. 20–37. And for illustrations, see R. W. Symonds, 'Of Jakes and Close Stools. Their Place in English Social History', *The Connoisseur*, vol. cxxix, pp. 86–91, May 1952.

26 Keun, *I Discover the English* (1934), p. 164. This account does not quite carry conviction.

27 *Western Mail*, cited, *New Statesman*, vol. lxv, no. 1667, p. 266, Feb. 22, 1963.

28 Lyall, *Future of Taboo* (1936), p. 50.

29 Cf. *AL* Supp. I (1945), p. 640: 'During the days of Prohibition some learned speak-easy proprietor in New York hit upon the happy device of calling his retiring-room for female boozers a *powder-room*.'

30 *OED*, vol. ii, pt 1, p. 258.

31 Other terms are *rogue with one ear* (late C. 17–early 18), *Jordan* (C. 18), and *master-can* (Scots).

32 Cf. *flower-time* and the dysphemistic *tail-flowers*.

33 Cf. *AL* (1922 edn), p. 152: 'American women use *unwell* in a certain indelicate significance, and hence avoid its use generally.'

34 Other popular synonyms include: *the road is up for repairs* (mid-C. 19), *be at Number One, London* (mid-C. 19), *there is a letter in the post office* (late C. 19), *Tommy* (late C. 19), *little Audrey's come for a few days* (C. 20), *have one's auntie* (or *grandmother*) *with one, my country cousins have come,* and *see one's auntie* (or *grandmother* or *little friend*). *Fly the (red) flag* (c. 1850), *the flag* (or *danger-signal*) *is up* (c. 1850), *have the rags on* (1860), and *flash the red* are dysphemisms. Cf. *SV*, vol. iii, pp. 82–3.

35 For a brief but valuable survey of 'The Vernacular of Menstruation', see Joffe, *Word*, Dec. 1948, pp. 181–6.

5   THE 'BLOODY' TABOO (pp. 66–68)

1 Partridge, *Words, Words, Words!* (1933), p. 87. Cf. *AL* Supp. I (1945), p. 680: 'The known history of the term [does not] show any relation to any physiological process.'

2 Scott (ed.), *Prose Works of Swift* (1897–1908), vol. ii, p. 173.

3 Dana, *Two Years before the Mast* (1841 edn), pp. 2, 53. The word was never tabooed in America. Cf. Semper, *English Journal* (college edn), Apr. 1929, p. 309: 'The American is frankly puzzled by the attitude of the refined Englishman toward this word, and inquiry generally elicits the information that the word is frightfully vulgar, not because of any hidden meaning attached to it, but because it is used by frightfully vulgar people.'

4 Cook and Wedderburn (ed.), *Works of Ruskin* (1903–12), vol. xxxiv, p. 294.

5 Matthews, *Parts of Speech* (1916), p. 199.

6 *Beeton's Manners of Polite Society* [1876], p. 34.

7 This is the date given by Partridge. That *ruddy* was in use much earlier is suggested by the story told in *AL* Supp. I (1945), p. 682: 'When, on January 22, 1887, a new operetta, *Ruddygore*, by Gilbert and Sullivan, was presented at the Savoy theatre, London, the title caused a considerable raising of eyebrows. . . . The more queasy Savoyards raised such a pother against it that it was changed to *Ruddigore* after the fourth performance. Even then, there were murmurs, and letters of protest flowed in on the authors.' To one of these letters, Gilbert replied: 'I do not know what there is to complain of. *Bloodigore* would have been offensive, but there can be no offence about *Ruddygore*. *Ruddi* is perfectly harmless; if, for example, I were to talk of your *ruddy* cheek you could not be angry with me, but if I were to speak, as well I might, about your—well—' (cited from a series of letters in the *Sunday Times*, May 24, 31, June 7, 14, 1936).

8 Generally in the catch-phrase *not Pygmalion likely* (1912).

9 Matthews, *op. cit.* p. 200.

10 Masefield, *Everlasting* Mercy (1911), p. 3.

11 *New York Times*, Apr. 14, 1914, cited, *AL* (1922 edn), p. 155.

12 Withington, *American Speech*, Oct. 1930, p. 29.

13 *Red Peppers*, one of his *To-night at 8.30* plays. See *Collected Plays of Noël Coward*, vol. iv (1954), p. 95.

14 Lyall, *Future of Taboo* (1936), p. 83.

15 *Hansard*, 5th ser., vol. 355, col. 421, 656.

16 D. B. Wyndham Lewis, 'Standing By', *Tatler and Bystander*, vol. clx, no. 2082, p. 280, May 21, 1941. The poem referred to appeared in *The Times*, May 6, 1941, p. 5.

17 *Gorton Reporter*, Oct. 30, 1942, cited, *AL* Supp. I (1945), p. 679.

18 'Post Office Object to Six-Letter Word', *The Times*, June 1, 1962, p. 6.

19 Cf. Weekley, *Words Ancient and Modern* (1926), p. 16.

6 SEX, PREGNANCY, AND PROSTITUTION (pp. 69–85)

1 Finley, *The Lady of Godey's* (1931), pp. 205–7.

2 *AL* (1922 edn), p. 152.

3 Cf. [Bache], *Vulgarisms* (1868), p. 37: 'When some little girls from the city were spending their summer vacation at a farm-house, one of them, happening to speak of her being afraid of a bull in the neighbourhood, was frowned out of countenance by the mistress of the house, who, taking her aside, chid her for using the word, telling her that it was *indecent*.'

4 Yelverton [*sc.* Longworth], *Teresina in America* (1875), vol. i. p, 313.

5 Cited, Rowe, *American Speech*, May 1957, pp. 111–12, from Hans Kurath (ed.), *Linguistic Atlas of New England* (Providence, R.I., 1939–43). The others: *male beast, toro, gentleman ox, top cow, roarer, masculine, bison, he animal, short horn, he critter, top ox, he ox, male ox, kooter, cow critter, he creature, top steer, male critter, man cow, bullock, cow topper* ('probably an innovation used by children'), *doctor, bullit, paddy* and *bungy.* Tacey, *American Speech*, May 1959, p. 146, added *heifer bull, Jumbo, he,* and *him.* Other American terms, given in Berrey and Van den Bark (ed.), *American Thesaurus of Slang* [1943], p. 138, are *buttermilk cow, cow's husband, duke, he thing, surly, bullette* ('a young bull'), and *he stuff* ('male cattle'). Mencken gives *Jonathan* (*AL* (1936 edn), p. 302). And 'even today in Labrador a woman will warn someone of the dangerous "big animal" in a pasture instead of saying "bull" ' (Halpert, *Journal of American Folklore*, July–Sept. 1962, p. 191).

6 Rowe, *op. cit.* p. 116.

7 Randolph, *Dialect Notes*, 1928, pp. 57–8. He adds: 'A tourist's casual reference to *shirt-studs* once caused considerable embarrassment to some very estimable hill-women of my acquaintance.'

8 *Journal of the American Medical Association*, Nov. 17, 1917, advertising p. 24, cited, *AL* (1922 edn), p. 149.

9 *Pensacola Journal*, cited, *Literary Digest*, vol. cxii, no. 12 (2187), p. 48, Mar. 19, 1932.

10 Cf. *AL* (1922 edn), p. 149.

11 *She*, May 1962, p. 23.

12 [Grose], *Classical Dictionary* (1785 edn), sig. B3 verso. *Dog's lady*, *dog's wife*, *dogess*, and *puppy's mama* were 'jocular ways of calling a woman a bitch' (*ibid.* sig. H2 verso). In 1760 the Archbishop of Canterbury forced the Drury Lane management to delete from the play *The Minor* the line: 'You snub-nosed son of a bitch' (Cunnington, *English Costume in the Eighteenth Century* (1957), p. 25).

13 S. T. Coleridge, *Christabel* (1816), p. 3.

14 [Allsop (ed.)], *Letters of S. T. Coleridge* (1836), vol. i, p. 206.

15 E. H. Coleridge (ed.), *Christabel* (1907), p. 61 n. 2; *Poetical Works of S. T. Coleridge* (1828), vol. ii, p. 43. The change was made 'for some reason, good or bad, to preserve the *ordonnance* of the verse, or to satisfy the scruples of an "honoured friend" ' (E. H. Coleridge, *op. cit.*). The word *bitch* twice occurs later in the poem, but here Coleridge did not change it.

16 Cited, Lyall, *Future of Taboo* (1936), pp. 81–2. Since *c.* 1920, says Partridge, *witch* has been a common euphemism for *bitch* in this sense (*Swift's Polite Conversation* (1963), p. 167).

17 Partridge, *Origins* (1961), p. 239. Cf. *DS*, vol. i, p. 305; vol. ii, p. 1099; Read, *American Speech*, Dec. 1934, pp. 264–78.

18 James Barke, 'Pornography and Bawdry in Literature and Society', [Burns and others], *The Merry Muses* (1959), p. 18.

19 Mackenzie (ed.), *Poems of Dunbar* (1932), pp. 53–4.

20 Hamer (ed.), *Works of Lindsay* (1931–36), vol. i, p. 103.

21 Bannatyne (comp.), *Bannatyne Manuscript* (1896), vol. ii, p. 363.

22 *Ibid.* vol. iii, pp. 400–1.

23 Cranstoun, *Satirical Poems* (1891–93), vol. i, p. 202. *Sempill Ballates* (1872), p. 141, spells it *fakking*.

24 *Merry Wives of Windsor*, IV. i. 53–65. Cf. Partridge, *Shakespeare's Bawdy* (1947), p. 118.

25 See [Burns and others], *The Merry Muses* (1959).

26 In which it appears with monotonous frequency. See, e.g., [Potter and others], *Romance of Lust* (1873–76), *passim*.

27 *The Times*, Jan. 23, 1882, p. 7, col. 4; Jan. 27, 1882, p. 9, col. 6.

28 *Ibid.* Jun. 12, 1882, p. 8, col. 2.

29 Fraxi [*sc.* Ashbee], *Catena Librorum Tacendorum* (1885), p. lv, n. 83. The Edwardian era, too, produced a jester at Printing House Square. In 1905 the *Times Literary Supplement* reviewer of a book by Oscar Wilde wrote: 'It is impossible, except very occasionally, to look upon his testament as more than a literary feat. Not so, we find ourselves saying, are souls laid bare'

('De Profundis', *Times Literary Supplement*, no. 163, p. 64, Feb. 24, 1905).
30 Read, *American Speech*, Dec. 1934, p. 274.
31 The other being *iape, sard, swiue* and *occupy*. Florio, *Worlde of Wordes* (1598), p. 137.
32 Skinner, *Etymologicon* (1671), sig. Tt2 verso. Skinner, a Lincoln physician, died before his dictionary was ready for the press, and the work was completed by Thomas Henshaw, a Fellow of the Royal Society and the King's under-secretary of the French tongue. The article on *fuck* was one of Henshaw's additions.
33 Coles, *English Dictionary* (1676), sig. A2 recto.
34 Marchant and Gordon, *New Complete English Dictionary* (1760), p. iv.
35 Bailey, *Universal Etymological English Dictionary* (1721), sig. Zz3 recto; Bailey, *Dictionarium Britannicum* (1730), sig, Oooo verso.
36 Ash, *New and Complete Dictionary* (1775), vol. i, sig. Aaa4 recto.
37 [Grose], *op. cit.* (1785 edn), sig. K2 recto, H4 recto.
38 Read, *op. cit.*
39 Rattray, *Quarterly Review*, Jan. 1961, p. 16; Bernard (ed.), *Rimbaud* (1962), p. 188 (for Fr. *piner*); Wentworth and Flexner, *Dictionary of American Slang* (1960), pp. 203–4, etc.; Loth, *The Erotic in Literature* (1962), p. 83 (citing Rochester's 'The Wish'), etc.; McCullers, *Clock without Hands* (1961), p. 183, etc.; Lessing, *The Golden Notebook* (1962), p. 111, etc.; Murdoch, *An Unofficial Rose* (1962), p. 63. Cf. also Wilson, *Old Men at the Zoo* (1961), pp. 16, 276.
40 The reviewer of the third edition of *Webster* in the *New Yorker* (Mar. 10, 1962, p. 140) pointed out that 'all the chief four- and five-letter words are here, with the exception of perhaps the most important one [i.e., *fuck*]. [The editors] defend this omission not on lexical grounds but on the practical and, I think, reasonable ground that its inclusion would have stimulated denunciation and boycotts. There are, after all, almost half a million other words in their dictionary—not to mention an investment of three and a half million dollars—and they reluctantly decided not to imperil the whole enterprise by insisting on that word.' What Craig calls 'the voice of established obscurantism' was heard when it was announced that the words would not appear in the Oxford dictionaries—'in spite of the fact that they are used in a novel now widely read throughout most of the English-speaking world' (Craig, *Banned Books* (1962), p. 168).
41 Cf. F & H, vol. iii, pp. 206–9; vol. vi, pp. 21–2; *SV*, vol. iii, pp. 15–34; *DS, passim*. Direct derivatives are: *goose and duck* (*c.* 1870; rhyming slang; Irish?; hence *go goosing* (*c.* 1870) and *to goose* (*c.* 1875; also signifies 'to prod someone between the buttocks with the thumb, unexpectedly')), *push in the truck* (C. 20; rhyming slang; 'the term has great currency among long-distance lorry drivers', says Franklyn, *Dictionary of Rhyming Slang* (1960),

p. 120), *trolley and truck* (C. 20; rhyming slang), *cattle* (from *cattle-truck*, rhyming slang), *Colonial Puck* (U.S. rhyming slang), *Friar Tuck* (rhyming slang), *lame duck* (U.S. rhyming slang), *eff* (C. 20; commonly used in courts of law; note also the working-class *effing and blinding* for 'swearing'), and *fuckle*. The 'low pedantic' *fulke* (c. 1820–1900) was, say F & H (vol. iii, p. 83), from the first and last words of Byron's *Don Juan*: 'I' and 'Fulke'.

42 Partridge, in Grose, *op. cit.* (1931 edn), pp. 155–6.

43 Howell, *Proverbs* (1659), p. 17. Tilley, *Dictionary of Proverbs* (1950), p. 273, G406, glosses *sard* as 'to get children'.

44 Presumably because of this, the word was notably avoided in any sense in C. 17 and most of C. 18. Against 194 quotations for C. 16, the editors of *OED* found only eight for C. 17, outside the 1611 Bible, and only 10 for C. 18, all for the last third of that century. 'The verb occurs only twice (equivocally) in Shakespeare, is entirely absent from the Concordances to Milton and Pope, is not used by Gray' (*OED*, vol. vii, pt ii, p. 48). Cf. *2 Henry IV*, II. iv. 144–5: 'as odious as the word "occupy".'

45 Cant. Often spelt *nygle* (C. 16–early 17) or *nigle* (C. 17–18). Used by Dekker.

46 *DS*, vol. i, p. 696.

47 Cf. the later *enjoy the conjugal embrace* and *enjoy the pleasures of love*.

48 Cf. the rare noun *coit* (1671).

49 Cf. *bestow* (or *lavish*) *one's favours on, grant the favour*, and *yield one's favours* (all of women).

50 Usually in *have sexual* (or *carnal* or *improper*) *intercourse (with)*.

51 A writer in *Punch*, vol. ccxlii, no. 6350, p. 790, May 23, 1962, has recalled 'that sick Fleet Street story of the girl who was beheaded, chopped into pieces, and placed in a trunk but "was not interfered with" '.

52 Cf. also *do the act of love, do the work of increase, have it off (with), have one's way with, have one's will of* (both suggesting some resistance), *mate with, oblige* (of women), *perform connubial rites, phallicize, scale the heights of connubial bliss, solace, stay with* (as in an American daily newspaper of 1915, cited, *SV*, vol. ii, p. 137: 'pick up a man and stay with him to get money'), *surrender* (or *give*) *the enjoyment of one's person* (of women), *use benevolence to*. *Tread* (before 1250) is used of birds; *cover* (1535; mostly of horses), *tup* (1549; mostly of sheep), *serve* (1577), and *mount* (1592; originally of human beings) are used of animals.

53 Note also Rochester's dysphemistic *rub one's arse on* (of women).

54 Cf. also *be where uncle's doodle goes, get a handle for the broom* (of women), *go doodling, to pole, to spike, strip one's tarse in, draw a cork* (of women), and *give standing room for one* (of women). Dysphemisms of this kind include: *to cock* (C. 19), *cure the horn* (C. 19; of women, *give a cure for the horn*), *do* (or *have*) *a bit of beef* (or *take in beef*) (C. 19; of women), *have a hot pudding*

(or *live sausage*) *for supper* (C. 19; of women), *give a hot poultice for the Irish toothache* (C. 19; of women), *peel one's (best) end (in)* (long form, C. 19), *go pile-driving* (mid-C. 19), *slip* (usually *her*) *a length* (late C. 19), *to ballock*, *go* (or *do a*) *ballocking*, *go* (or *have a bit of*) *cock-fighting*, *go prick-scouring*, *have a bit of cock* (usually of women?), *have a bit* (or *taste*) *of (the) gut-* (or *cream-*, or *sugar-*)*stick*, or *get a go at the cream-stick*, or *suck the sugar-stick* (all of women), *get a pair of balls against one's butt* (of women), *get* (or *have*) *a flesh injection* (of women), and *to prick*.

55 Cf. also *be in Abraham's bosom*, *be on the spot*, *bird's nesting*, *bush-ranging*, *cunny-catching*, *have a bit of curly greens*, *open a clam*, *a shot at the bull's eye*, *take a turn in Cupid's Alley* (or *Cupid's Corner*). Dysphemisms referring to the female pudenda or pubic hair include: *go beard-splitting* (late C. 17–early 19), *have a plaster of warm guts* (late C. 17–mid-19), *have a bit of split-mutton* (C. 18?), *to split* (C. 18), *take a turn in Cock Alley* (or *Lane*) (C. 18), *feed the dumb glutton* (mid-C. 18–19), *be in a woman's beef* (late C. 18–mid-19), *do* (or *have*) *a wet 'un* (C. 19; of women), *give* (or *lend*) *a hole to hide it in* (C. 19; of women), *go to Hairyfordshire* (C. 19), *go working the dumb* (or *double* or *hairy*) *oracle* (C. 19 or earlier), *have a bit of cunt* (C. 19), *hole (it)* (C. 19), *have* (or *get*) *a bit of hole*, *take a turn in Hair Court* (or *the stubble*) (C. 19), *feed* (or *trot out*) *one's pussy* (mid-C. 19; of women), *grease the wheel* (mid-C. 19), *do a slide up the straight* (c. 1870), *have a slide up (the board)* (c. 1870), *have a bit of sharp-and-blunt* (late C. 19; rhyming slang), *block a woman's passage* (C. 20), *get a shove in one's blind eye* (of women), *get one's chimney swept out* (of women), *to quim*, *quim-sticking*, *quim-wedging*, *twat-raking*, *twatting*, and *a wipe at the place*.

56 Cf. the dysphemistic *to tail* (C. 18), *join giblets* (late C. 18), *do* (or *have*) *a bit of giblet-pie* (C. 19), *do* (or *have*) *a jumble-giblets*, *give a bit of snug (for a bit of stiff)* (C. 19; of women), *make (a) settlement in tail* (C. 19), *give mutton for beef* (of women), *go prick-chinking*, *have a game in the cock-loft*, *play cock-in-cover*, and *go tail-twitching* (or *-tickling*).

57 *Play at itch-buttocks* (late C. 16–19), *buttock-ball* (late C. 18–early 19), *go buttocking*, *get a wet bottom* (C. 19), *do* (or *have* or *perform*) *a bottom-wetter*, (C. 19), *play at tops and bottoms* (mid-C. 19), *to (go) rump(ing)* (c. 1850), *go rump-splitting*, *to bum*, *go bum-faking* (or *-tickling* or *-working*), *play at brangle-buttock*, and *play at buttock-and-leave-her*.

58 *Rub-belly* (C. 18), *belly-bump* (C. 19), *tummy-tickling* (C. 19), *have a belly-warmer*, *have a bit on a fork* (C. 19), *to fork* (mid-C. 19), *get on the old fork* (late C. 19), *wriggle navels* (C. 19), *play couple-your-navels*, and *do a spread* (c. 1840; of women).

59 Of *put it in*, Partridge writes: 'Perhaps rather an S[tandard] E[nglish] approximation to euphemism than a coll[oquialism]: when, however, there is no thought, intention or subconscious impulse towards euphemism, it may

be considered a coll., and not, from the psychological nature of the case, S.E.' (*DS*, vol. i, p. 672). I have not followed Partridge in considering colloquialism and euphemism mutually exclusive terms. Dysphemistic, or leaning towards dysphemism, are *drive into* (C. 19), *cram* (mid-C. 19), *stuff* (mid- or late C. 19), *slip into* (c. 1870), *block* (C. 20), *be up to one's balls, to bung, put it in and break it,* and *wollop it in* (or *have a wollop-in*).

60 And *do a backfall* (of women), *have a drop in, have* (or *do*) *a dive in the dark,* the American *lay,* and the Australian *lay off with* (C. 20).

61 *DS,* vol. i, p. 326.

62 And *turn up* and *vault. Whack it up* (mid-C. 19), *have a hoist-in* (c. 1850), and *hoist* seem dysphemistic.

63 *Grind* (noun, late C. 16; verb, before 1811), *grind one's tool* (mid-C. 19), *scour* (C. 17), *rub-off* (late C. 17–early 19), *push (on)* (C. 18), *do a push* (late C. 19), *screw* (before 1785), *stitch* (late C. 18), *(have a) poke* (C. 19), *(have or do a) rasp* (C. 19), *sew up* (C. 19), *jiggle* (c. 1845), *chuck* (or *do*) *a tread* (c. 1860), *do a ride* (c. 1860), *go through* (c. 1870), *bounce* (late C. 19), *go tromboning* (late 1880s), and *bore*.

64 *Do* (or *have*) *a squeeze-and-a-squirt* (C. 19), *give juice for jelly* (C. 19), *whitewash* (C. 20), *catch an oyster* (of women), *to lard, squirt one's juice, take in cream* (of women).

65 And *do a turn on one's back* (of women), *get on top of, lie under* (of women) and *look at the ceiling over a man's shoulder* (of women). Note also the dysphemistic *polish one's arse on the top sheet* (late C. 19).

66 *Horse* (C. 17), *bull* (C. 18), *hog* (C. 19), and *tom* (late C. 19; north country).

67 *Be up a woman's petticoats* (C. 18), *have a bit of skirt* (C. 19), *be among a woman's frills* (c. 1860–1914), *go under-petticoating* (c. 1870–1920), *have a bit of smicket* (i.e., smock; usually pronounced *smigget*), *pull up one's petticoats to* (of women), *to smock,* and *take off one's stays* (of women).

68 Cf. the C. 20 Australian *get one's oats from.* Corresponding dysphemisms are *a bit of mutton* (c. 1670), *a bit of meat* (C. 18), *a bit of giblet pie* (C. 19), *a bit of fish* (c. 1850), *have a banana with* (c. 1905–30), *a bit off the chump end.*

69 *Play (at):* push-pike (late C. 17–18), *lift-leg* (or *lift one's leg*) C. 18–mid-19), *hey-gammer-cook* (C. 18–early 19), *two-handed put* (C. 18–early 19), *hooper(')s hide* (C. 18–mid-19), *pully-hauly* (late C. 18), *mumble-peg* (C. 19), *thread-the-needle* (C. 19), *the ace against the jack* (or *one's ace,* etc.) (C. 19; of women), *squeeze-'em-close* (mid-C. 19), *horses and mares* (c. 1850; school-boys'), *Irish whist (where the jack takes the ace)* (c. 1850). *Have fifty* (or *a hundred) up* (C. 20). *Play (at): Adam and Eve, all-fours, fathers and mothers, put-in-all, the first game ever played,* and *the same old game.*

70 Cf. *the cushion dance, the married man's cotillon, the mattress jig, dance to the tune of 'The Shaking of the Sheets',* and the dysphemistic *buttock jig, dance with your arse to the ceiling,* and *have* (or *do*) *a bit of bum-dancing.*

71 Cf. however the still very common *fiddle (about) (with)* (C. 17; 'to caress familiarly').

72 This however was at least influenced by *to nock*. The U.S. *knock up* signifies 'to impregnate accidentally'.

73 In C. 16 occasionally *swynge*, in C. 16–18, *swindge*. Literally, 'to castigate'. Used by Fletcher and Dryden.

74 Rudy Vallee's Music Notebook, *Radioland*, Mar. 1935, p. 35, cited *AL* (1936 edn), p. 306, 306 n. 2.

75 *DS*, vol. i, p. 348. Other euphemisms used of and by women are: *do what Eve did with Adam, do what mother did before me, draw a man's fireworks, get the best and plenty of it, lose the match and pocket the stakes, show* (or *give*) *a bit, take* (both transitive and intransitive), and *take in and do for. Take the starch out of* (mid-C. 19) refers, seemingly dysphemistically, to erection or to semen or to both.

76 *Have* (or *do*) *a bit of business* (C. 17–18), *lap-clap* (C. 17–mid-18), *to poop* (C. 17–18; cf. *poop-noddy*, C. 17), *smoke* (C. 17), *ride below the crupper* (mid-C. 17–18; literary), *be at clicket* (late C. 17–18; from a term used of foxes), *jock* (late C. 17–19), *shoot between* (or *betwixt*) *wind and water* (late C. 17), *huddle* (C. 18), *quiff* (C. 18), *spit* (C. 18), *go face-making* (mid-C. 18– early 19), *hump* (c. 1760–1800), *trim the buff* (1772), *(have a) shag* (verb, late C. 18; noun, C. 19), *(have a) touch-up* (verb, late C. 18–mid-19), *come about (one)* (C. 19; said of men by women), *cross* (c. 1790), *cully-shaggy* (C. 19), *dibble* (C. 19), *frisk* (C. 19), *gay it* (C. 19), *get one's hair cut* (C. 19), *go jottling* (C. 19), *(have a* or *do a) jottle, jack* (C. 19), *make* (or *do*) *nookie* (C. 19), *man* (C. 19), *perform (on)* (C. 19), *plowter* (or *plouter*) (C. 19), *snug* (C. 19), *do a bit of ladies' tailoring* (c. 1815), *hustle* (c. 1830–1910), *chauver* (c. 1840; cant?), *do* (or *have*) *an inside worry* (c. 1840), *horizontalize* (c. 1845), *have* (or *do*) *a bit of flat* (mid-C. 19), *have a go (with)* (mid-C. 19), *(go and) post a letter* (mid-C. 19), *have* (or *get* or *give*) *one's greens* (c. 1850; 'derived by some', say F & H, vol. iii, p. 206, 'from the old Scots' *grene* = to pine, to long for, to desire with insistence: whence *greens* = longings, desires.' They add: 'But in truth, the expression is a late and vulgar coinage. It would seem, indeed, to be a reminiscence of *garden*.'), *(have a) rootle* (verb, c. 1850; noun, c. 1880), *do a bit* (c. 1860), *chaws* (c. 1860), *hive it* (c. 1860), *horizontal refreshment* (c. 1870), *rack (someone) off* (1873), *get about her* (or *it*) (c. 1880; properly, 'to effect intromission'), *charver* (late C. 19; theatrical), *have a bit* (late C. 19), *have a blow-through* (late C. 19), *have it (in)* (longer form, late C. 19), *have one's cut* (late C. 19), *qualify* (late C. 19), *bate up* (C. 20), *a bike ride to Brighton* (C. 20; barmaids'), *dirty work at the cross-roads* (C. 20), *flop* (C. 20; U.S.), *get* (or *have*) *one's (h)oggins* (C. 20), *myrtle* (C. 20; Australian), *nattum* (noun; C. 20; Australian), *nurtle* (noun; C. 20; Australian), *the other* (C. 20), *have a bunk-up* (1939; Forces'), *a trip up the Rhine*

1945; Forces'), *Adamize, Adam and Eve it, be in the act, be on the job, compress, ease, flap, gender, give a lesson in simple arithmetic* (i.e., addition, division, multiplication and subtraction), *go molrowing, go to Durham, handle, have a bit of rough, have a blindfold bit, have* (or *do*) *a jumble-up, have a touch-off, iounce, lerri(com)poop, put the devil into hell* (from Boccaccio), *rig, muddle, mump, muss, stoat* (U.S.) *strain, towse,* and *work*. Miscellaneous dysphemisms are: *go through (a woman) (like a dose of salts)* (shorter form, C. 19; longer form, C. 20), *frig* (mid-C. 19; originally, from *c*. 1590, 'masturbate'), *make (a woman) grunt* (C. 20), and *exchange spits* (C. 20; workmen's).

77 *Play handy-dandy* (or *handie-dandie*) (C. 16–18), (*do* or *have a*) *mow* (C. 16–early 19), *jobbing* (C. 17), *dance the reel o' bogie* (C. 18), *dance the reel o' stumpie* (C. 18), *dance the miller's reel* (C. 18), *supple both ends of it* (late C. 18; of women), *tether one's nag* (C. 19), *snib* (*c*. 1810), *hogmagundy* (*c*. 1820–90), *jink, labour-lea, nidge, nodge, nail twa wames thegither, slip in Daintie Davie, slip in Willie Wallace,* and the dysphemistic *dance with your arse to the kipples.*

78 *Dock* (*c*. 1560–*c*. 1840), *cavault* (or *cavolt*) (C. 17–early 19), *twang* (C. 17–18), *nug* (late C. 17–mid-19), *prig* (late C. 17–early 19), *strap* (late C. 17–19), *nig* (C. 18), *nub* (C. 18–early 19), and *see* (C. 19; whores').

79 *Blow(-off) the groundsels* (C. 17–18; cant) = on the floor. *Have a buttered bun* (C. 17) = with a whore who submits to the sexual embrace in quick succession with different men. *To milk* (C. 17), *huffle* (C. 18), *bagpipe* (late C. 18–19), *gamahuche* (or *gamaroosh* or *gamaruche*) from (French *gamahucher*; 1867; frequently shortened to *gam*), *play the clarinet* (or *flute* or *trombone*), *suck (off),* and *suck gristle* (or *the sugar-stick*) = penilingism. *Riding St George* or *the dragon upon St George* (late C. 17–mid-19) = with the woman on top. *Tip the velvet* (late C. 17; cant), *bark in the muff* (theatrical?), *blend wigs, eat hair pie* (U.S.), *eat one's middlings, go down for the honey* (theatrical?), *go south, lap, lick, plate,* and *tongue* = cunnilingism. *French tricks* (mid-C. 19), *Frenching* (*c*. 1918; U.S.), *French way* (*c*. 1918; U.S.), *do the French, go down,* and *taste* = either cunnilingism or penilingism. *Sixty-nine* and *soixante-neuf* = simultaneous cunnilingism and penilingism. *Lie in state* = 'in bed with three harlots' ([Grose], *op. cit.* (1785 edn), sig. Y4 verso). *Dog's rig* (mid-C. 18–19) = 'sexual intercourse, to exhaustion, followed by back-to-back indifference' (*DS*, vol. i, p. 232). *Take a flourish* (mid-C. 18–19) = hastily. *Take a flier* (*c*. 1780) and *snatch-fuck* = without undressing. *Threepenny upright* (or *bit*) (late C. 18 and mid-C. 19 respectively) = with a whore. *Upright* (late C. 18), *fast-fuck* (C. 19; whores' slang), *perpendicular* (mid-C. 19), *knee-trembler* (*c*. 1850), and *upright grand* (*c*. 1925; Australian urban) = a standing embrace. *To dog* (C. 19) = on all fours. *Flat-fuck* (C. 19; noun and verb) = rub the genitals together (of women). *To soak (it)* (C. 19) = to linger. *Have a bit of brown* (mid-C. 19?), *to rim*

(C. 20) and *to bottle* = buggery. *Make a dog's match of it* (or *have a dog's marriage*) = by the wayside. *Have* (or *do*) *a back-scuttle* (mid-C. 19), and *dogways* (late C. 19; workmen's) = from the back. *(Have a) rush up the frills* (or *petticoats* or *straight*) (*c.* 1850) = without preliminaries. *Make the chimney smoke* (mid-C. 19), *please,* and *satisfy* = cause the female to experience orgasm. *A matrimonial (polka)* (*c.* 1850) = in the usual European position (as opposed to others). *To be caught with rem-in-re* (*c.* 1860) = to be surprised in the act of copulation. *Do* (or *have*) *a flutter* (*c.* 1870; cf. *flutter a judy, c.* 1850) = for pleasure rather than passion. *Go to see* (or *sit up with*) *a sick friend* (*c.* 1880) = an excuse for absence all night from the conjugal bed. *Partie carrée* (before 1873) = two couples participating. *(Play* or *act) postil(l)ion* (1873) = insert a finger in the anus. *Circus* (before 1916; U.S.), *daisy chain, gang shag* (or *gang shay*) (U.S.) = several persons participating. *To spoon* = lying 'spoon-fashion'. For other American terms see Justinian [pseud.], *Americana Sexualis* (1939), and Wentworth and Flexner, *Dictionary of American Slang* (1960).

80 But there is a fair number of dysphemistic and semi-dysphemistic terms: *cock-stand* (C. 18; cf. *stand* (C. 19), *standing ware* (mid-C. 19), *have a stand on, standing* and *on the stand*); *horn-colic* (mid-C. 18–mid-19; a temporary erection), *the jack* (C. 19), *Irish toothache* (C. 19), *hard-on* (adjective, *c.* 1860; noun *c.* 1890), *get a rise (on)* (late C. 19), *bar* (C. 20), *beat* (C. 20), *fixed bayonets, hidden tumor* (U.S.) *lance in rest, in one's best* (or *Sunday*) *clothes* (cf. *the old man has got his Sunday clothes on*), *lust-pride, prick-pride* (cf. *pride of the morning* (late C. 19) or *morning pride*: a morning erection, supposedly due to retention of urine), *on, on prod, on prop, prick-stand, the spike,* and *stiffened up. Keep one's pecker up* = 'maintain an erection'. Cf. F & H, vol. iii, p. 351; *SV*, vol. iii, p. 57.

81 Similar popular terms include *(melted) butter* (C. 18), *ointment* (C. 18), *(white) honey* (C. 19), *hot milk* (C. 19), *lather* (C. 19), *milt* (C. 19), *roe* (*c.* 1850), *fetch* (late C. 19), *come* (before 1923), *baby-juice, buttermilk, home-brewed, jam, love-liquor, the oyster, seed, soap, spendings, spume, starch, stuff,* and *the tread.* Literary terms are: *thrice-decocted blood* (Marlowe), *Cypris sap* (1611), *spermatic juice* (Rochester, who also coined *snowball* for a single drop), *father-stuff,* and *white-blow* (Whitman). Dysphemisms are *letchwater* (late C. 18), *fuck* (C. 19), *lewd infusion, tail-juice,* and *tail-water.* Cf. F & H, vol. ii, pp. 207–8; *SV*, vol. iii, pp. 127–8.

82 The story that the condom was invented by, and named after, Dr Condom (or Conton), a physician at the court of Charles II, is discussed by Himes, *Medical History of Contraception* (1936), pp. 191–4. He is 'inclined to think it a myth' (p. 193).

83 *AL* (1936 edn), p. 296, n. 4. Cf. Lyall, *Future of Taboo* (1936), p. 59: 'The English and the French each attribute to the other a simple and wide-

spread malthusian device; and the English even bestow the name "French" on a variation of the common kiss which must be as old as kissing itself.' A *French tickler* is a condom with a sharp protuberance at the tip, designed to afford additional stimulation to the vagina during coition.

84 Cited, *AL* (1936 edn), p. 310. The same authority laid down the usage *was cited as co-respondent* for *committed adultery* (cf. the *News of the World*'s *association* for *living in adultery*, cited, *AL* Supp. I (1945), p. 646). *SV*, vol. iii, p. 126, lists popular synonyms, euphemistic and dysphemistic, for *seduced*, including *to have broken one's knee* and *sprained one's ankle* (which are closely paralleled in French and German). Cf. also *she made a slip*.

85 Associated Press dispatch, Sept. 11, 1933, cited, *AL* (1936 edn), p. 305.

86 Cf. p. 28 above.

87 White, *Words and their Uses* (1871), pp. 178–9.

88 'Euphemisms', *Chambers's Journal of Popular Literature, Science and Arts*, vol. xi, no. 285, p. 405, June 18, 1859.

89 For other popular synonyms, see *SV*, vol. iii, pp. 113–15.

90 Lyall, *op. cit.* p. 88.

91 Laws of 1925, ch. 515, cited, *AL* (1936 edn), p. 293.

92 Cf. *SV*, vol. iii, p. 3. A dysphemism is *hasty pudding* (c. 1870). Baltimore Negroes used *single child* in the 1940s (cf. *AL* Supp. I (1945), p. 658, which adds: '*Bastrich* is used in the Duluth [Minnesota] region as a happy compound of *bastard* and *son-of-a-bitch*.') *SV*, vol. ii, p. 8, defines *niece* as 'a priest's illegitimate daughter, or concubine'.

93 Cf. *AL* (1936 edn), p. 305.

94 Bloomfield, *Language* (1935), p. 401.

95 *AL* (1936 edn), p. 304.

96 Graves, *Future of Swearing* (1936), p. 22.

97 Cf. F & H, vol. vii, pp. 77–80; *SV*, vol. iii, pp. 117–18. Other popular euphemisms include: *puttock* (C. 16), *bat* (C. 17–early 19), *gamester* (C. 17), *girl of ease* (1756), *blowen* (= a showy whore; late C. 17–early 19), *fancy piece* (before 1823), *gay bit* (c. 1830; cf. *gay woman*), *Columbine* (c. 1845; theatrical), *barrack-hack* (= soldiers'; c. 1850) *flutter a skirt* (c. 1850), *be on the turf* (c. 1860), *princess of the pavement* (C. 20; Australian), *Totty* (or *Tottie*) *fie* (C. 20; Londoners'), *nymph of darkness*. Some dysphemisms are: *cat* (C. 16–19), *mutton* (1518–1900), *open-arse* (rarely, *open-tail*) (C. 17–mid-18), *ploll-cat* (C. 17; from *poll-cat*), *light horse* (c. 1620–1700; originally Society slang), *trading dame* (1678), *(she-)trader* (c. 1680–1820), *(female) screw* (shorter form, c. 1720–1870; longer form, c. 1780–1850), *bed-fag(g)ot* (C. 19), *on the grind* (C. 19), *split-arsed mechanic* (C. 19), *tumble-a-bed* (C. 19 or earlier), *loose fish* (1809–c. 1895), *on the batter* (late 1830s), *shake* (before 1860), *flagger* (before 1865), *flash-tail* (before 1868), *bit of meat* (late C. 19),

ferry (C. 20; Australian). *Traffic* (late C. 16–early 17), *wapping-dell* (or *-mort*) (C. 17–18), *onicker* (*c.* 1880), and *caso* (C. 20) are cant words.

98 *AL* (1922 edn), p. 150.

99 Cited, *AL* (1936 edn), p. 311.

100 For other popular synonyms, see *SV*, vol. iii, pp. 7–9. Euphemisms include *vaulting-school* (*c.* 1605–1830), *cavaulting-school* (late C. 17–early 19), *hummum(s)* (late C. 17–18; 'Turkish bath', from an Arabic word meaning 'bath'), *coupling-house* (C. 18–19), *gay house* (C. 19), *pheasantry* (C. 19), *dress-house* (*c.* 1820), Dysphemisms include *cunny-warren* (before 1785), *buttocking-shop* (or *-ken*) (C. 19), *button-hole factory* (C. 19), *meat-house* (or *-market*) (C. 19), *whore-shop* (C. 19), *knocking-shop* (or *-house*) (mid-C. 19), *girlery* (*c.* 1870), *girl-shop* (*c.* 1870), *moll(y)-shop* (before 1914), and *cat-house* (U.S.). *Warren* (late C. 17) and *caso* (*c.* 1910) are cant terms.

101 Cf. *SV*, vol. i, p. 4.

102 Jones, *Adrasta* (1635), pp. 10–11.

103 *AL* Supp. I (1945), p. 597.

104 *SV*, vol. iii, pp. 51–3, gives popular synonyms for these diseases. Syphilis was also known as *(the) great pox* (1529; Swift has *the greater pox*). *Flap(-)dragon* (late C. 17–early 19), *sauce* (C. 18–early 19), and *pintle fever* (C. 19) were names for either disease; *double event* (*c.* 1870) signifies both at once.

105 McKnight, *English Words* (1923), p. 269.

106 *AL* (1922 edn), p. 152.

107 Cf. *AL* Supp. I (1945), pp. 648–9.

108 Cited, *ibid.* p. 648. When the Catholic Press started hinting at a boycott of sponsoring advertisers and of the newspapers that used the advertisements, 'there was some abatement of the initial enthusiasm' *(ibid.)*.

109 Cf. Steadman, *American Speech*, Apr. 1935, p. 103.

110 Cited, Read, *American Speech*, Dec. 1934, p. 271, from an MS. note by Sir Herbert Croft, a friend of Johnson's, in the front of his copy of the second (1755) edition of the *Dictionary*. 'Inasmuch as Croft disposed of his copy in 1795', writes Read, 'this antedates considerably the first appearance of the anecdote in print known to me, in H. D. Best, *Personal and Literary Memorials* (London, 1829), pp. 11–12, where it is told of two sisters.'

111 Rowe, *American Speech*, May 1957, p. 115 n. 15.

PART II

THE GRUNDY SUNDAY (pp. 89–125)

7 MERRY ENGLAND'S REVELLING DAY

1 Cf. Neale, *Feasts and Fasts* (1845), pp. 111–15; Coulton, *Medieval Pano-*

rama (1949), pp. 181–3. The letter, supposed to have been written by Jesus Christ, had been turning up in various places from time to time throughout the middle ages; see Priebsch, *Letter from Heaven* (1936).

2 Cf. Whitaker, *Sunday in Tudor and Stuart Times* (1933), pp. 12–13; Baker, in Lennard (ed.), *Englishmen at Rest and Play* (1931), p. 81. For pre-Conquest laws against Sunday work, travelling and trading, from Ine, seventh-century King of the West Saxons, onwards, see Hessey, *Sunday* (1889), p. 89. Coulton points out (*Medieval Village* (1925), pp. 254–6) that it is wrong to suppose sabbatarianism came in with the Reformation. It was 'to the distress of good Churchmen' that people made merry after mass.

3 *The Dialogue of Dives and Pauper* (1493), cited, Coulton, *Medieval Village* (1925), p. 256. The same writer (probably a friar) approved of honest dances and plays performed in a good manner after mass, provided they did not stir men and women to lechery and other sins, or to 'ouir longe wakinge on nightes'—adding, however, 'as it is righte likly yᵗ they do in our daies' (cited, Manning, *The People's Faith* (1919), p. 136).

4 *A Necessary Doctrine and Erudition for any Christian Man* (1543), in Lloyd (ed.) *Formularies of Faith* (1825), p. 309. Cf. John Frith, in Russell (ed.), *English Reformers* (1831), vol. iii, p. 295: after going to church, people 'may return unto their houses, and do their business as well as any other day. He that thinketh that a man sinneth which worketh on the holy day . . . ought better to be instructed.' Cf. also notes 14 and 26 below, pp. 289, 289–90.

5 Jenkyns (ed.), *Remains of Cranmer* (1833), vol. iv, p. 336.

6 Ayre (ed.), *Catechism of Becon* (1845), p. 80.

7 *Ninth Report of the Royal Commission on Historical Manuscripts*, pt i (1883), p. 155, col. 1.

8 Whitaker, *op. cit.* p. 25.

9 Strutt, *Glig-Gamena Angel-Ðeod* (1801), p. xxxii.

10 See Furnivall (ed.), *Robert Laneham's Letter* (1890), pp. 20–33. Cf. Nichols (ed.), *Diary of Henry Machyn* (1848), p. 206: at Lord Arundel's on a Sunday night in 1559 the Queen was given 'soper, bankett, and maske, with drumes and flutes, and all the mysyke that cold be, tyll mydnyght; and as for chere has nott bene sene nor hard'.

11 Neale, *op. cit.* p. 189.

12 D'Ewes, *Journals* (1682), pp. 322–3.

13 Wilkins, *Concilia Magnae Britanniae* (1737), vol. iv, p. 255. Parliament and the Privy Council often sat on Sunday in the reign of Elizabeth I, and she received foreign ambassadors on that day. The puritan Mr Fuller wrote to her complaining that she swore and blasphemed; was too slack in punishing murderers, adulterers and fornicators; and did too little to sanctify the sabbath, which resulted in her people, without punishment, offending God more on

that day than on any other day of the week (Peel (ed.), *Seconde Parte of a Register* (1915), vol. ii, pp. 49–64).

14 Henry Brinklow, *c.* 1542, had found it absurd to permit Sunday games while forbidding Sunday work. After a Latin service the people 'depart the church as empty of all sprytual knowlege as thei came thether. And the rest of the day thei spend in all wanton and vnlawful gamys, as dyse, cardys, dalyeng with wemen, dansing, and such lyke. But if any man do any bodyly worke . . . he shal be punysshed, and called heretycke to' (Cowper (ed.), *Henry Brinklow's Complaynt of Roderick Mors* (1874), pp. 62–3).

15 *Certain Sermons* (1850), pp. 343–4.

16 Kethe, *Sermon* (1571), f.8 verso, f.16 recto.

17 Anglo-phile Eutheo [pseud.], *A second and third blast of retrait from plaies and Theaters* (1580), [Hazlitt (ed.)], *English Drama and Stage* (1869), pp. 134–5. Cf. Roberts, *An earnest Complaint* (1572), p. 51: places of Sunday amusement 'are become yonge Helles, such is their wickedness. So that, the tendre Yonglynges, beynge come of good Houses . . . are as it were, translated, or chaunged into Monsters . . . spendynge their Money lewdly, and also learnynge to practice ungodlynes.' In 1555 Bishop Bonner, though a Catholic, issued an injunction against young people and others resorting to taverns or going into the country on Sundays and holy days (Frere and Kennedy (ed.), *Visitation Articles and Injunctions* (1910), vol. ii, pp. 366–7). The justices at Bury, in February 1579, laid it down that boys who were found 'evill occupied or idle' in the streets, churchyard or elsewhere on Sundays should be whipped by their parents, 'the constable seeinge the performance thereof' (Furnivall (ed.), *Stubbes's Anatomy of Abuses* (1877–82), pt i, p. 370 n.).

18 Furnivall, *op. cit.* pt i, p. 137.

19 *Ibid.* pt i, p. 184.

20 *Ibid.* pt i, p. 179. Cf. Field, *A godly exhortation* (1583).

21 Strype, *Annals* (1824), vol. ii, pt 2, p. 397. Cf. A. Golding, *A Discourse vpon the Earthquake* (1580), in L. T. Golding, *An Elizabethan Puritan* (1937), pp. 184–98.

22 *Workes of More* (1557), p. 208.

23 John Stockwood, preaching at St Paul's Cross, Aug. 24, 1578, Chambers, *Elizabethan Stage* (1923), vol. iv, pp. 199, 200.

24 Collier, *History of English Dramatic Poetry* (1879), vol. i, pp. 270–1; Chambers, *op. cit.* vol. iv, pp. 284–5, 295–6. Sunday plays were forbidden at Canterbury in 1595 and Norwich in 1597.

25 Roberts, *op. cit.* p. 36.

26 *Ibid.* p. 37. Cf. Crowley, *One and thyrtye Epigrammes* (1550), sig. Avi verso:

How hallow they the Saboth
that do the time spende,
In drynking and idlenes
tyll the daye be at an ende?
Not so well as he doeth
that goeth to the plowe
Or pitcheth vp the sheues
from the carte to the mowe.

27 *The Vnlawfull Practises of Prelates Against Godly Ministers* [c. 1584], cited, Cowper (ed.), *Select Works of Crowley* (1872), p. xxiv.
28 Hall (ed.), *Transactions of the Royal Historical Society*, 3rd ser., vol. i (1907), p. 270. Another sinner had to confess publicly 'that I haue offended Allmightie God and by my euill example you all, for that I did plaie at Cardes vppon the Sabboth daie in Eveninge praire time for which I am hartelie sorie' *(ibid.)*.
29 W[hite], *A Sermon Preached at Pawles Crosse* (1578), pp. 45–6. Thomas White was the founder of Sion College, London.

8 NO MORE CAKES AND ALE? (pp. 95–102)

1 Bates (ed.), *Somerset Quarter Sessions Records* (1907–19), vol. i, p. 211.
2 Ley, *Sunday a Sabbath* (1641), sig. c3 verso.
3 Eleven years before, a Member of Parliament called Shepherd had been expelled for opposing, on these grounds, a Bill 'for punishment of divers abuses on the Sabbath day, called Sunday'.
4 [T. Rogers], *Faith, Doctrine, and religion* (1607), preface, sect. 22.
5 Furnivall (ed.) *Stubbes's Anatomy of Abuses* (1877–82), pt i, p. 139. One version says that the Earl of Gloucester, hearing that the trapped man did so great reverence to his sabbath day, thought he would do as much to his own holy day, 'and so kepte hym there tyll Monday, at whiche season he was foundyn dede' (Fabyan, *New Chronicles* (1811), p. 347).
6 H. Burton, *Divine Tragedie* (1636), pp. 6, 9, 11.
7 Bownd, *Sabbathum Veteris et Novi Testamenti* (1606), pp. 211–12. This was an expanded edition of his *Doctrine of the Sabbath* (1595), which Archbishop Whitgift and Lord Chief Justice Popham had tried to suppress in 1599.
8 Heylyn, *History of the Sabbath* (1636), pt 2, p. 251. This work, undertaken by royal command, was written and printed in four months.
9 *Ibid.*
10 Fuller, *Church-History* (1655), bk ix, pp. 227–8.
11 Cf. Chambers, *Elizabethan Stage* (1923), vol. iv, p. 335. Nevertheless, Sunday performances of plays went on at Court until 1637, and the Bishop of

London had a play (probably *A Midsummer Night's Dream*) acted in his house one Sunday night in 1631 (see Baker, in Lennard (ed.), *Englishmen at Rest and Play* (1931), pp. 113–14, 113 n. 6).

12 Cf. the warning by some of the Somerset clergy in 1633 that if people were debarred from their lawful recreations they would resort to alehouses 'and there talk of matters of church and state' (cited, Baker, in Lennard (ed.), *op. cit.* p. 126 n. 2); cf. also the Earl of Newcastle's advice to Charles II, p. 100 below.

13 Govett, *King's Book of Sports* (1890), pp. 35–40. Exercises, he pointed out, 'may make their bodies more able for warre' (*ibid.* p. 37).

14 Heylyn, *op. cit.* pt 2, pp. 260, 261.

15 Bruce (ed.), *Calendar of State Papers, Domestic Series, 1634–35* (1864), p. 2.

16 See Peyton (ed.), *Churchwarden's Presentments* (1928), pp. 139, 194, 205, 206, 208, 283, 288, 289, 291.

17 Lowth, *Letter to Stillingfleet* (1687), p. 56. See also Pocklington, *Sunday no Sabbath* (1636) and *Petition and Articles* (1641).

18 Firth and Rait (ed.), *Acts and Ordinances* (1911), vol. i, p. 81.

19 *Ibid.* vol. i, pp. 420–2.

20 *Ibid.* vol. ii, pp. 383–7. John Evelyn, returning to England from France in 1650, found that 'Next day being *Sonday*, they would not permit us to ride post' (De Beer (ed.), *Diary of Evelyn* (1955), vol. iii, p. 13).

21 Firth and Rait, *op. cit.* vol. ii, pp. 1162–70.

22 *Diary of Thomas Burton* (1828), vol. ii, p. 262.

23 *Ibid.* vol. ii, pp. 264–5.

24 [Jeremy Taylor], *Rule and Exercises* (1650), pp. 277–8. There must be no unlawful games, nor anything scandalous or dangerous 'and apt to mingle sin with it', nor any 'games prompting to wantonnesse, to drunkennesse, to quarrelling, to ridiculous and superstitious customs' (*ibid.* p. 279).

25 Firth and Rait, *op. cit.* vol. i, p. 599.

26 See Baker, in Lennard (ed.), *op. cit.* pp. 122–5.

27 John Taylor, *Short Relation* [1653], pp. 26–7.

28 See, e.g., Cotton and Woollcombe, *Gleanings* (1877), pp. 123, 165. For the common people's resentment of the puritan hysteria that had ruined what used to be the best day of the week, see *The Lamentable Complaints of Nick Froth the Tapster* (1641).

29 Harris, *Transactions of the Royal Historical Society*, 4th ser., vol. iii (1920), p. 113. 'It grieved me', wrote the mayor, 'that this poore deluded people should undergoe punishment of this nature.'

30 Historical Manuscripts Commission, *Report on Manuscripts in Various Collections*, vol. i (1901), p. 113.

31 *Ibid.* p. 126.

32 Cited, Strong, *Catalogue of Letters* (1903), pp. 223–7.

33 Baker, in Lennard (ed.), *op. cit.* p. 127.

34 Hockliffe (ed.), *Diary of Josselin* (1908), pp. 137, 145.

35 Atkinson (ed.), *Quarter Sessions Records*, vol. vi (1888), pp. 125, 141.

36 Wheatley (ed.), *Diary of Pepys* (1903–04), vol. i, p. 206.

37 *Ibid.* vol. vi, p. 185.

38 *Ibid.* vol. vii, pp. 311–12. He afterwards burnt the book, 'that it might not be among my books to my shame' (*ibid.* vol. vii, p. 312).

39 *Parliamentary History*, vol. iv (1808), col. 285.

40 Strickland, *Lives of the Queens*, vol. xi (1847), p. 78; Whitaker, *Eighteenth-Century English Sunday* (1940), p. 24.

41 Hardy (ed.), *Calendar of State Papers, Domestic Series, 1690–91* (1898), pp. 437–8.

42 Cox, *Literature of the Sabbath Question* (1865), vol. ii, p. 13.

43 Wells, *Practical Sabbatarian* (1668), pp. 684–5, 688, 690, 694.

44 Baxter, *Dreadful Warning to Lewd Livers* [*c.* 1682]. The first story is taken from Stubbes, who says the incident happened in Swabia. See Furnivall (ed.), *op. cit.* pt i, pp. 111–13.

9   INFORMERS AND REFORMERS (pp. 103–108)

1 *Short View of the Religious Societies* (1703), p. 7; *Account of the Societies for Reformation of Manners* (1699), p. 4; Woodward, *Account of the Rise and Progress of the Religious Societies* (1698), p. 31.

2 *Representation of the State of the Societies for the Reformation of Manners* (1715), p. 7.

3 *44th Account of the Progress made . . . By the Societies for Promoting Reformation of Manners*, Smith, *Sermon* (1738), p. 26. By 1720 the Societies had given away 400,000 books (*26th Account* [1721], p. 1). Similar societies were active in Gloucester, Leicester, Coventry, Shrewsbury, Hull, Nottingham, etc. (*Account of the Societies* (1699), p. 18).

4 [Bolton], *Letter to a Lady* (1748), p. 36.

5 Webster, *Two Sermons* (1751), p. 21.

6 *Works of Porteus* (1811), vol. ii, p. 217.

7 [Bolton], *Letter to an Officer* (1757), pp. 27–8.

8 *Short View* (1703), p. 9.

9 Cf. Disney, *Essay* (1710), pp. 205–6.

10 See *Account of the Progress of the Reformation of Manners* (1705).

11 *Short View* (1703), pp. 7, 11.

12 Disney, *Second Essay* (1710), p. 172. Elsewhere he denied that the members of the Societies received any pecuniary advantages from informing (*ibid.* p. 105).

13 *Ibid.* pp. 206–23.

14 Woodward, *op. cit.* p. 78.

15 See Portus, *Caritas Anglicana* (1912), table facing p. 254. For some other details of the Societies' activities, see pp. 240–1 below.

16 *The Heaven-Drivers* (1701), pp. 1, 5–6, 9. De Foe protested in 1698 against the repression of poor men's amusements, while those of the rich were uncurbed.

17 *Sermon Preached before the Former Societies for Reformation of Manners* (1760), pp. 35, 36.

18 See De Coetlogon, *Nature, Necessity, and Advantage* (1776), pp. 43–7.

19 Newton, *Memoirs of Grimshaw* (1799), pp. 110–11.

20 See Laker, *History of Deal* (1917), pp. 247–51.

21 [Newte], *Tour* (1785), pp. 40–1.

22 Cf. Hamersley, *Advice to Sunday Barbers* (1706), p. 20.

23 In 1745 the Rector of Bushey, Herts., complained to the Bishop of London about Sunday coach-racing. See Fairbrother, *Notes and Queries*, Feb. 24, 1917, p. 145.

24 Wendeborn, *View of England* (1791), vol. ii, pp. 269–70. Another German visitor, in 1782, was rebuked by his London landlady's son for humming a lively tune on Sunday (*Travels of Moritz* (1924), p. 24).

25 *Lettres philosophiques, Œuvres complètes de Voltaire*, tom. xxii (1879), p. 99.

26 Cited, Hodgson, *Life of Porteus, Works of Porteus* (1811), vol. i, pp. 72–3. In one of his sermons the Bishop expressed the view that some Sunday evening places of amusement were 'nurseries of popery, infidelity and vice' (*Works of Porteus* (1811), vol. ii, p. 215 n.).

27 See Hodgson, *op. cit.* pp. 73–6. For the debates on the Bill, see *Parliamentary History*, vol. xxii (1814), col. 262–90.

28 Kennicott, *Sabbath* (1781), p. 39.

29 *Sabbath-keeping* (1767), pp. 9–10. Every horse should pay 2s. at every turnpike, and pedestrians should pay 6d.—except physicians, midwives, sick people, and persons going to their parish churches.

30 Archenholtz, *Picture of England* (1797), p. 167.

31 Young, *Annals* (1890), p. 223. 'Cursed be those *Sunday Barbers*', wrote Hamersley, 'that live and allow themselves in that known sin of following their Callings on the Lord's Day without Repentance' (*op. cit.* p. 3). A barber was working on Sunday when one of his children came in from play and fell down dead; the father did not trim on the Lord's day any more (*ibid.* pp. 49–50).

32 Webster, *op. cit.* p. 16.

33 Cited, Pickard, *Sabbath* [c. 1857], p. 30. A judge commented in a similar case: 'The laborious part of the community are entitled to some indulgence for the labours of the week past; and ought not to fare harder on a Sunday

than on any other day. They must be fed, and many of them had not the means of dressing their dinners at home' *(ibid.)*.

34 Whitaker, *Eighteenth-Century English Sunday* (1940), pp. 151–3.

35 *Ibid.* pp. 161–2.

36 Stonhouse, *Admonitions* (1800), p. 7. A sabbatarian of the present day—who omits, no doubt inadvertently, the word 'Coffee-houses'—holds that these words are 'as applicable to modern times as they were to the days in which they were written' (Hansford, *Champions* (1951), p. 11).

37 W[illison], *Treatise* (1745), pp. 168–9.

38 Beresford (ed.), *Diary of a Country Parson* (1924–31), vol. i, p. 20.

39 W. Wilberforce, *Practical View* (1797), p. 196.

40 La Combe, *Tableau de Londres* (1784), p. 18.

10 DAY OF GLOOM (pp. 109–117)

1 *London Gazette,* June 2–5, 1787, p. 269.

2 See *Report of the Committee of the Society for Carrying into Effect His Majesty's Proclamation* [1800], pp. 16–18.

3 *Ibid.* p. 13.

4 *Annual Register,* 1798, p. 229. Whitaker thinks this account is exaggerated; see *Eighteenth-Century English Sunday* (1940), pp. 181–3.

5 R. I. and S. Wilberforce, *Life of Wilberforce* (1838), vol. ii, p. 272.

6 [Bowles?], *Address to the Public from the Society for the Suppression of Vice,* pt ii (1803), pp. 5–13.

7 It asked to be informed of Sunday trading, work, riotous conduct, swearing, acts of lewdness or indecency, public games and gambling (*Address of the Society for Promoting the Observance of the Christian Sabbath* [1809], pp. 7, 10–11).

8 Prentice, *One Day's Rest* (1855), p. 1.

9 *3rd ARLD* (1834), pp. vii–viii.

10 *7th ARLD* (1838), p. 39.

11 Cited, M'Crie, *Memoirs of Agnew* (1850), p. 123.

12 *Hansard's Parliamentary Debates,* 3rd ser., vol. xxxiii, col. 12. These lines were adapted from Richard Brathwait's *Barnabæ Itinerarium, or Barnabee's Journal* (1638).

13 M'Crie, *op. cit.* p. 310.

14 Cited, *ibid.* p. 129.

15 *Ibid.* pp. 132–3. See *Report from Select Committee on the Observance of the Sabbath Day* (1832).

16 Cited, M'Crie, *op. cit.* pp. 177–8.

17 Cf. *70th ARLD* (1901), p. 21.

18 A Scotchman, *Letter to Joseph Locke* (1849), p. 15.

19 *Sermons in Glass* (1854), pp. 12, 13.

20 *Ibid.* p. 11. A fellow minister, half-shaved when the clock's striking twelve announced that the sabbath had begun, was glad to be told that the clock was a few minutes fast, 'which solved the difficulty without a breach either of propriety or of the Sabbath' (Fyfe (ed.), *Scottish Diaries* (1942), p. 561). Earlier, there was controversy about the right of clergymen to make horses work by going to church in coaches.

21 *Some Account of the Lord's Day Conference Meeting Held at . . . Derby* (1861), pp. 4–5.

22 *22nd ARLD* (1853), p. 12.

23 *45th ARLD* (1876), p. 14.

24 *Quarterly Publication*, no. 50, p. 508, July 1855.

25 Strachey and Fulford (ed.), *Greville Memoirs* (1938), vol. vii, pp. 203, 229.

26 *Occasional Paper*, no. 82, p. 77, Oct. 1869.

27 In the latter part of the 1870s there were five other anti-sabbatarian organizations in existence: the Sunday Society, which published the *Sunday Review* (1876–90), the Sunday Lecture Society, Sunday Evenings for the People, the Sunday Shakespeare Society, and the Social Sunday Union.

28 Cf. *Occasional Paper*, no. 75, p. 923, Feb. 1866.

29 *65th ARLD* (1896), p. 9.

30 *Ibid.* pp. 21–2. The sabbatarians had reading rooms at Derby and Dunstable closed (*22nd ARLD* (1853), p. 11) and prevented their being opened in many other places, including Leeds and Sheffield.

31 Arthur, *'The People's Day'* (1855), p. 28. Cf. Parkinson, *Two Addresses* (1857), p. 17: 'I doubt whether the study of science or art has such a morally refining and purifying influence as many assume.'

32 The letter went on: 'More or less all men at such sights do "think evil". . . . Such exhibitions must tend to corrupt the sight-seers, and especially so the young of both sexes' (*Occasional Paper*, no. 98, pp. 618–19, Oct. 1877).

33 *22nd ARLD* (1853), p. 27. Earlier, the Society had bemoaned 'the number of the better class of society who frequent the Parks and Zoological Gardens in London' on Sundays (*8th ARLD* (1839), p. 34) and had prevented the Sunday opening of public gardens in Manchester and Sheffield (*9th ARLD* (1840), p. 11).

34 'There is nothing in all this but the mere indulgence of the animal nature! This man does not *rest* in any sense of the word. . . . The man who spends his Sundays in mere amusements is less prepared for business on the Monday than he was on the Saturday' (Parkinson, *op. cit.* pp. 16–17).

35 Unfortunately I have not been able to trace a copy of these *Hints.*

36 'He has done that in a foreign country which he dare not do here', declared the protester (see *Quarterly Publication*, no. 36, pp. 265–7, Jan. 1852).

37 Baines, *Value of the Sabbath* (1855), p. 7.

38 Kirtland, *Voice of Truth* (1857), pp. 22 n., 23.

39 *Some Account of the . . . Meeting . . . at Derby* (1861), p. 28. For the stopping of 'sinful' Sunday concerts at Eastbourne, see Domville, *Sunday Band* (1856).

40 *Occasional Paper*, no. 59, p. 636, July 1858. The Lord's-day Society wrote to the Chief Commissioner of Works in 1877 complaining that whereas they had been told that permission had been granted only for 'To Thee, Great Lord' and the Hallelujah Chorus to be played in Regent's Park one Sunday, the programme in fact included a quick step, a selection from *Faust*, a galop, a selection of *Sea-side Echoes*, and the Grand March from *Tannhaüser* (*46th ARLD* (1877), pp. 31–2).

41 *68th ARLD* (1899), p. 12.

42 *8th ARLD* (1839), pp. 41–2. Since the wakes attracted 'men and women . . . of loose habits', the Derbyshire publicans were persuaded to close their houses on wake Sundays (*Some Account of the . . . Meeting . . . at Derby* (1861), p. 30). See also the letter from the Vicar of Steventon, Berks., *Quarterly Publication*, no. 10, pp. 79–80, Oct. 1849: 'The concourse of people who used to come on our Feast Sunday has, I am told, greatly diminished, so that now scarcely any but children collect, and they only in the evening.'

43 Taine, *Notes sur l'Angleterre* (1872), p. 16.

44 *51st ARLD* (1882), p. 7.

45 *Quarterly Publication*, no. 44, pp. 432–3, Jan. 1854. In 1882 the Society complained about 'loose women going about in a state of drunkenness, shouting [and] singing ribald songs' on Sunday evenings near a military camp on Wimbledon Common (*51st ARLD* (1882), pp. 22–3).

46 *Occasional Paper*, no. 66, p. 771, July 1861. The Palace was 'a monster opposition temple to compete with, and to draw from, the temples of Jehovah' (*ibid.* p. 770).

47 *65th ARLD* (1896), p. 16. The Act was invoked by the Society in 1866 to stop a series of lectures by Huxley and others, sponsored by the National Sunday League. See *Occasional Paper*, no. 75, pp. 926–9, Feb. 1866.

48 *48th ARLD* (1879), pp. 38–40.

49 *45th ARLD* (1876), pp. 21–2.

50 Osborn, *Moral and Physical Evils* (1875), pp. 8–9.

51 Along with the travelling of stage-wagons and stage-coaches and the operation of breweries on Sundays. These 'infringements of the ordinances of heaven' would 'produce a most fatal effect on the principles and morals of the people' (*Works of Porteus* (1811), vol. vi, pp. 326, 328).

52 *3rd ARLD* (1834), p. viii.

53 'Sunday Newspapers in America', *The Times*, May 24, 1899, p. 6. The article was reprinted by the Society (*68th ARLD* (1899), App.).

54 Cf. *Post-Office and the Sabbath Question* (1850), p. 15: 'Where . . . is the infallible judge who is to decide what is necessary, or what is an act of mercy? . . . There may be no perdition in potted pilchards, though hot hake be a damnable heresy. . . . We knew a milkman who would readily supply the greatest possible quantity of cream to the greatest possible number of customers on a Sunday; but, on the meekest requisition for a junket, would solemnly pronounce on us, with a judicial air of unlimited confidence, a sentence of eternal damnation!'

55 *51st ARLD* (1882), pp. 23–4.

56 Clifford, *Sabbath Question* (1856), letter x, p. 6 n.

57 *Sermons in Glass* (1854), p. 11.

58 Baines, *Value of the Sabbath* (1855), p. 5.

59 Baines, *On the Attempt to Change the Character of the Christian Sabbath* (1853), p. 7. Martha Browning, executed for murder in 1846, was one of them, according to the Ordinary of Newgate (see *Quarterly Publication*, no. 11, pp. 87–8, Apr. 1846).

60 *7th ARLD* (1838), p. 35.

61 *Todd's Lectures to Children* [1860], pp. 121, 122.

62 Cf. Hamilton, *Letters* (1801–02), vol. i, pp. 123–4.

63 Kirtland, *op. cit.* p. 22.

64 Harrison, *Sundays and Festivals* (1867), pp. 13–14.

11 'MISERY' MARTIN VERSUS THE TWENTIETH CENTURY (pp. 118–125)

1 See, e.g., *Lord's Day*, no. 1, p. 3, Jan. 1902; *75th ARLD* (1906), p. 7; *76th ARLD* (1907), p. 8. King Edward VII had already been reproached, in rather more veiled terms, while Prince of Wales.

2 *71st ARLD* (1902), p. 5.

3 *Abraham Duquesne* [1905], p. 4.

4 *81st ARLD* (1912), p. 6.

5 *79th ARLD* (1910), p. 13.

6 *83rd ARLD* (1914), p. 11. In an earlier protest against Sunday rifle practice the Society pointed out that military training on the Lord's day had not saved the sabbath-breakers—i.e., the cavaliers—from 'decisive defeat at the hands of their more scrupulous brethren' in the civil war (*75th ARLD* (1906), p. 11).

7 *84th ARLD* (1915), p. 6.

8 *86th ARLD* (1917), p. 7. See also *Lord's Day*, no. 62, pp. 492–3, Apr. 1917; no. 63, pp. 500–1, July 1917 ('In a certain district where the farmers abstained from agriculture on the Lord's Day . . . the crops at the end of May were full of promise. Near by a thunderstorm brought very heavy rain, washing (it is said) potatoes out of the ground, but in the former area there was a gracious and refreshing rain'); no. 64, pp. 507–9, Oct. 1917. In

July 1917 *The Lord's Day* began to carry the injunction 'Eat less Bread' on the inside of its front cover.

9 *88th ARLD* (1919), p. 3; *90th ARLD* (1921), p. 5.

10 *93rd ARLD* (1924), p. 7.

11 The Working Men's Lord's Day Rest Association was formed in 1857, the League against Sunday Travelling (as the Anti Sunday-Travelling Union) in 1884. The League published *Our Heritage* (1895–1914).

12 *Lord's Day*, vol. iii, no. 19, p. 145, July 1925.

13 *Manchester Evening News*, Jan. 5, 1940.

14 Martin, *Happy Man* [1921], p. 16.

15 Martin, *Shall We Copy the Continental Sunday?* [1923], p. 10.

16 *Ibid.* p. 19.

17 *Ibid.* p. 14.

18 *Lord's Day Magazine*, no. 116, p. 33, July–Sept. 1930.

19 This was seen as the precursor of 'jazz dances' in the parks on Sundays; the proof was a quotation from the *Sunday Chronicle*: 'Who can hear this music without his or her toes beginning to have a light, fantastic, fox-trot feeling?' (cited, *Lord's Day*, vol. iii, no. 19, p. 149, July 1925).

20 *Our Year Book* [1926], p. 6.

21 *Lord's Day*, no. 99, pp. 36–7, July–Sept. 1926.

22 *Our Year Book* [1928], p. 17; *Lord's Day Magazine*, no. 108, p. 46, July–Sept. 1928.

23 *Our Year Book* [1928], p. 16.

24 *Our Year Book* [1926], pp. 14–16. One Sunday in 1927 some people at Towyn, Merionethshire, paraded through a golf course to prevent play. The Chancery Division granted an injunction against them.

25 *Let Your Summer Holiday Help the Sunday Cause!* Leaflet included with *Our Year Book* [1928].

26 *Our Year Book* [1929], p. 23; *Lord's Day Magazine*, no. 109, pp. 51–2, Oct.–Dec. 1928.

27 *Lord's Day Magazine*, no. 194, pp. 2–3, Jan.–Mar. 1950.

28 *Our Year Book 1933*, p. 5.

29 *Our Year Book 1934*, p. 15. A typical verse ran:

> Adam was the first man that is what we all believe,
> One morning he was filleted and introduced to Eve;
> He had no one to tell him, but he soon found out the way,
> And that's the only reason why we're sitting here today.

The song (better known as 'The Darkies' Sunday School') was soon deleted from the publishers' catalogue.

30 *News Review*, June 18, 1936 ('Where agitation arises for the Sunday opening of Cinemas down goes an experienced Organiser from the Red Lion

Square Headquarters, frequently with complete success in quashing the proposals'); *Daily Express*, Jan. 22, 1934.

31 *Our Year Book 1939*, p. 4.

32 And in *Lord's Day Magazine*, no. 149, p. 63, Oct.–Dec. 1938, which asked: 'What next . . . will the mongers of so-called Sunday Sport think of purveying for the delectability [*sic*] of their patrons?'

33 *Our Year Book 1941*, p. 5. A post-war complaint about Sunday wireless programmes took exception to 'Murder Trials, Detective Stories, Novel Reading, Jazz, Tangos, Waltzes, Stage Plays, Musical Comedies, Variety Turns, and the like' (*Our Year Book 1947*, p. 3).

34 *Our Year Book 1940*, p. 2.

35 The apologies appeared in the *Sunday Dispatch*, Jan. 16, 1944 and the *Ely Standard*, Feb. 18, 1944.

36 *Lord's Day Magazine*, no. 174, p. 5, Jan.–Mar. 1945.

37 See *Hansard*, 5th ser., vol. 481, col. 530–638.

38 See *Hansard*, 5th ser., vol. 510, col. 1335.

39 *Joy and Light*, no. 209, p. 133, Oct.–Dec. 1953.

40 *Ibid.* no. 220, p. 182, July–Sept. 1956.

41 *Ibid.* p. 181. 'Britain not only insulted her Queen by arranging for these criminals to be received by her, but caused an affront to the King of Kings by misusing the hallowed hours of His Day in entertaining and conferring with these infidel men of blood-stained hands' (*ibid.* no. 222, p. 226, Jan.–Mar. 1957).

42 *Ibid.* no. 240, p. 63, July–Sept. 1961.

43 *Ibid.* no. 243, pp. 149–50, Apr.–June 1962.

44 In a memorandum submitted to the Departmental Committee on Sunday observance law appointed by the Home Secretary. See *The Times*, Jan. 5, 1962, p. 7.

45 Morrish, *To Whom Ye Yield* (1959), p. 134.

46 *Joy and Light*, no. 209, p. 133, Oct.–Dec. 1953.

PART III

THE TEETOTALITARIANS (pp. 129–163)

12 OUR DIZZY ISLAND

1 Cited, Rae (ed.), *National Temperance League's Annual for 1882* [1881], p. 108.

2 Furnivall (ed.), *Stubbes's Anatomy of Abuses* (1877–82), pt i, p. 107.

3 Downame, *Foure Treatises* (1613), pp. 80, 83, 104.

4 This was the title of works by Thomas Young, later Master of Jesus College, Cambridge, and Edward Bury, an ejected minister who dabbled in astrology, published in 1613 and 1677 respectively.

5 Reeve, *God's Plea for Nineveh* (1657), p. 130.

6 Prynne, *Healthes: Sicknesse* (1628). An eighteenth-century Bishop of Cork took 217 pages to prove the same thing ([Browne], *Discourse of Drinking Healths* (1716)), and devoted another work, in two parts, to a demonstration that drinking to the memory of the dead was 'Sacrilegious, Profane, and Idolatrous' ([Browne], *On Drinking to the Memory of the Dead* (1713); Browne, *A Second Part of Drinking in Remembrance of the Dead* (1714)).

7 Hall, *Funebria Floræ* (1660), p. 3.

8 *Warning-piece* (1682), sig. A3 recto.

9 Multibibus [*sc.* Brathwait], *Solemne Ioviall Disputation* (1617), pp. 20–1, 45–6.

10 Junius, *The Drunkard's Character* (1638), p. 38.

11 Freman, *Dehortation from all Sinne* (1663), p. 2.

12 [Darby], *Bacchanalia* (1680), pp. 12–13.

13 See, e.g., his diary entry for Sept. 9, 1771, commenting on Dr William Cadogan's *Dissertation on the Gout* (London, 1771): 'Why should he condemn wine *toto genere*, which is one of the noblest cordials in nature?' (Curnock (ed.), *Journal of Wesley* [1909–16], vol. v, p. 430). The wesleyan preacher Adam Clarke, however, is supposed to have declared that strong drink was 'not only the way to the devil, but the devil's way into you' (cited, Hudson, *Temperance Pioneers of the West* (1887), p. 47).

14 Trotter, *Essay on Drunkenness* (1804), p. 134.

15 *Ibid.* p. 156.

16 Burns, *Juvenile Temperance Catechism* [1873], p. 15.

13 INTEMPERATE TEMPERANCE (pp. 132–143)

1 Cited, Winskill, *History of the Temperance Reformation* (1881), p. 5.

2 Published posthumously as *Facts Authentic in Science and Religion* (Salford, 1818–20).

3 Hicks, *Temperance Pioneers* [1957], p. 4.

4 Brotherton, *First Teetotal Tract* (1890), p. 9. Brotherton's tract, entitled *On Abstinence from Intoxicating Liquors* (*Letters on Religious Subjects*, no. 8, Salford, May 1821), was forgotten until 1890, when it was reprinted with an introduction by William Axon, a temperance advocate whose works include an anonymous booklet listing *The Names of God in 405 Languages* (Manchester, 1870).

5 See H[amilton], *Temperance Reformation in Scotland* (1929), p. 18.

6 Dunlop, *Philosophy of Drinking Usages* (1839), p. 287.

7 See *Report from the Select Committee on Inquiry into Drunkenness* (1834).

8 Engels, *Condition of the Working-Class* (1936 reprint), pp. 102–3.

9 Baker, *Historical Syllabus* [1900], p. 14.

10 A facsimile appears in *Life and Teachings of Livesey* [1886], p. 109.

11 Cf. Mounfield, *Beginnings of Total Abstinence* [1903], p. 4.

12 Burns, *Temperance in the Victorian Age* (1897), p. 10 n. Cf. *London Alliance Review*, no. 11, p. 5, Oct.–Dec. 1901.

13 Winskill, *Temperance Movement and its Workers* (1892), vol. i, p. 4.

14 Cited, *Life and Teachings of Livesey* [1886], p. cxxvii.

15 Catlin, *Liquor Control* (1931), p. 21.

16 Cited, Winskill, *Temperance Reformation* (1881), p. 54. The adverb 'tee-totally', an emphasized form of 'totally', was in use in the U.S.A. in 1832. Lees (*Text-Book of Temperance* (1871), p. 12) says 'tee-total', as an empha-sized form of 'total', was in common use in Ireland and Lancashire from *c.* 1770. 'Teetotal(l)er' and 'teetotalism' were at first regarded as vulgar; an Edinburgh professor tried, without success, to substitute 'neephalist' and 'neephalism', from a Greek word meaning 'I drink not'.

17 Cited, Carter, *English Temperance Movement* (1933), p. 43.

18 See 'They do it slyly', *Preston Temperance Advocate*, no. 5, p. 40, May 1837.

19 A later historian had a felicitous sentence about this phenomenon: 'Upon the principle indicated in the old proverb, "Set a thief to catch a thief", it has been fully proved that the best method of teaching temperance principles to a certain section of the working population ... is to bring them under the influence of men of their own class' (Winskill, *Temperance Movement and its Workers* (1892), vol. ii, p. 256).

20 Cf. Killen, *Memoir of Edgar* (1867), p. 94; *Preston Temperance Advocate*, no. 5, p. 36, May 1837.

21 *Temperance Penny Magazine*, vol. viii, no. 96, p. 174, Nov. 1843; Reid, *Temperance Memorials of Kettle* (1853), p. lix.

22 *Life and Teachings of Livesey* [1886], pp. 69–70.

23 For specimens of 'short' and 'long' pledges in use in London in 1837, see Carter, *op. cit.* p. 253. One man who did not wish to seem inhospitable appeased his conscience by putting intoxicating liquors on his table in vessels marked 'poison' (Burns, *op. cit.* p. 30).

24 Draper, *Jubilee Sketch* (1889), p. 16.

25 Baker, *op. cit.* pp. 61 n. 1, 62–3.

26 Church of England Temperance Society, *Enforcement Committees* [1900]; *idem, Enforcement of the Licensing Laws* [1900], pp. 2, 9–10.

27 Cf. Kimball, *Blue Ribbon* (1894), p. 227.

28 See Kerr, *Stimulants in Workhouses* [1882].

29 *Preston Temperance Advocate*, no. 4, p. 31, Apr. 1837.

30 Cf. Hudson, *Temperance Pioneers of the West* (1887), pp. 37–40.

31 Cited, Russell (ed.), *Lawson* (1909), p. 141.

32 *Preston Temperance Advocate*, no. 3, p. 17, Mar. 1837.

33 Burns, *Temperance History* [1889–91], vol. i, pp. 304–5, 305 n.

34 Cited, Gourlay, *'National Temperance'* (1906), p. 105.

35 Atkin, *Philosophy of the Temperance Reformation* [1874], p. 34.

36 Ward, *The Poisoning Conqueror, Alcohol* [1883].

37 Mudge, *Guide to the Treatment of Disease* (1863), p. 48.

38 Burns, *Juvenile Temperance Catechism* [1873], p. 16.

39 Ridge, *Band of Hope Catechism* [1894], p. 10.

40 Jakeman, *Some Fallacies* [1908], p. 5.

41 Ridge, *op. cit.* p. 9.

42 *Ibid.* p. 8.

43 Ackroyd, *History and Science of Drunkenness* (1883), p. 86.

44 Smith, *Nuts to Crack* [1890], pp. 15, 16. Cf. Catlin, *op. cit.* p. 30: 'A social worker of considerable experience in London has remarked that, in his observation, most serious criminals habitually commit their crimes on cocoa.'

45 *Life and Teachings of Livesey* [1886], p. cxxv, citing *The Temperance Almanac for 1839.*

46 Sabbaforry [pseud.], *Social Viper* (1869), p. 9. 'The strong arm of the law must enter this house of Baal, and break in pieces its images, and destroy its witchcraft and trickery' (*ibid.* p. 41).

47 Edmunds (ed.), *Life of Baker* (1865), p. 50.

48 Inward, *Pictures of the Traffic* [1881], pp. 7, 9, 30–1. See also Evans, *Picture Gallery of Bacchus* [1883].

49 Roaf, *Pastor's Pledge* (1861), p. 36.

50 Ward, *op. cit.* pp. 39–40.

51 See Burroughs, *Medical Substitute* [1890].

52 *Temperance Drinks for the Harvest and Home* [c. 1913].

53 'Teetotal Recipes: Domestic and Medical', *Ipswich Temperance Tracts*, vol. i [c. 1853], no. 19, pp. 1–2.

54 See Freedom Association, *Handbook* (1920 edn), pp. 58–60.

55 Burns, *Temperance History* [1889–91], vol. i, p. 107 n.; *Preston Temperance Advocate*, no. 2, p. 16, Feb. 1837.

56 Atkin, *Reminiscences* (1899), p. 93. See also two publications of the Joint Committee on the Employment of Barmaids, *The Barmaid Problem* [1904] and *Women as Barmaids* (1905). This Committee sought legislation to limit the barmaid's calling to those already in it, and thus gradually to abolish it.

57 Burns, *Temperance History* [1889–91], vol. i, p. 293.

58 Hopkins, *Rise and Progress of the Temperance Movement* [1905], p. 25.

59 Baker, *op. cit.* p. 12.

60 Dearden, *Brief History of Tee-totalism* [1840], p. 25.

61 Livesey, *Staunch Teetotaler*, no. 1, p. 16, Jan. 1867.

62 Moffat (ed.), 'The Times' Drinking Bout [1892], p. 28.

63 Blackwell, Booth (1883), pp. 250–5. At Swansea, employers led the way to the pledge-table at the head of their employees, and six months after Booth's visit three large breweries were shut down (ibid. pp. 215, 217).

64 Cf. Kimball, op. cit. p. 226.

65 Alcohol versus Teetotalism (1863), p. 13.

66 [Young], Blue Ribbon v. the Cross (1883), p. 10.

67 Farquharson, Case for Moderate Drinking (1892), p. 12.

68 Democritus [pseud.], Reply to the Teetotal Pamphleteers (1840), pp. 40–1.

69 G. B. H., Teetotalism Unmasked (1845), p. 49.

70 [Young], op. cit. pp. 9–10.

71 G. B. H., op. cit. pp. 53–5, 55 n. Most of the chartists declared for temperance; Feargus O'Connor, after first opposing 'Teetotal Chartism', became a total abstainer; for Ernest Jones's attitude, see Saville, Ernest Jones: Chartist (1952), pp. 42–3.

72 Haynes, Interesting Account [1840], p. 2. Later, there was a strong teetotal trend in the British socialist movement, two of its most prominent representatives being Keir Hardie and Philip Snowden.

73 Correct Outline (1839), p. 34.

74 Daniell, Via Media [1840?], p. 15.

75 C. P. H., Teetotalism Examined and Exposed (1872), p. iv.

76 Smeeton, Confessions (1849), pp. 7–8.

77 Lucas, Wine Bad and Good (1894), p. 5.

78 Winslow, Come out from among them [1882], p. 51.

79 Ridge, op. cit. p. 5.

80 Cf. Killen, op. cit. p. 94.

81 Cf. Kempster, The Dean and the Drink [1892], pp. 4, 6–9.

82 Bromley, Observations on Totalism (1841), p. 19.

83 Shaw, Life of Gregson (1891), pp. 132–3.

84 Cited, Hudson, op. cit. pp. 199–200.

85 Cf. Shaw, op. cit. ch. xii, xiii, xiv.

14 FOR SOTS AND TOTS (pp. 144–150)

1 Complete Catalogue [1887].

2 Gourlay, Oinosville (1902), pp. 167–8.

3 Ibid. pp. 250, 257.

4 Bateman, Tippling and Temperance (1890), p. 9.

5 Punch, vol. v (1843), p. 223.

6 Cited, G. B. H., Teetotalism Unmasked (1845), p. 58 n. Hudson, Temperance Pioneers of the West (1887), pp. 222–3, attributes these lines to a Mr Gavid of St Maybyn, and says they were regarded in Cornwall as a stroke of poetical

genius: 'the injunction to clap their hands and fan the blaze was literally and vigorously responded to'.

7 Beardsall (comp.), *New Selection of Hymns and Songs* [1836?], p. 85.

8 Burns, 'A Teetotaller—Why?', *Temperance Ballads* [1884], p. 39.

9 *Ibid.* pp. 25, 26.

10 Andrew Kemp, 'Physical Foes', *The 'London' Temperance Entertainer*, no. 5, p. 51, n.d. [1901].

11 Edward Johnson, M.D., 'Song of the Water Drinker', *Ipswich Temperance Tracts*, vol. i [c. 1853], no. 15.

12 'St George and the Dragon', Burns, *op. cit.* p. 22.

13 *Onward Reciter*, 'For the Child', Campaign No. XC, 1920, p. 23.

14 *Illustrated Temperance Reciter*, vol. i [1894], p. 166.

15 'Alcohol's place is out of the body', *Band of Hope and Children's Circle Message*, n.s., no. 17, p. [3], Nov. 1948.

15   THE BRITISH PROHIBITIONISTS (pp. 151–155)

1 Cited, Carter, *English Temperance Movement* (1933), p. 64. An Association for the Suppression of Beer-Shops had been formed in Liverpool in 1848, with the aim of procuring an Act of Parliament to prohibit both the granting of new licences to beershops and the renewal of existing licences.

2 Cited, Burns, *Temperance History* [1889–91], vol. ii, p. 288.

3 *The Times*, July 2, 1906, p. 6.

4 Agg-Gardner, *Some Parliamentary Recollections* [1927], pp. 225–6.

5 M. Hayler, *Vision of a Century* (1953), p. 30.

6 Cited, Carter, *op. cit.* p. 81.

7 Cf. *ibid.* pp. 109, 99.

8 Livesey's views were set forth in his pamphlet *Free and Friendly Remarks upon the Permissive Bill, Temperance Legislation, and the Alliance* (1862), which is summarized in Carter, *op. cit.* pp. 103–11.

9 *Temperance Spectator*, vol. iii, no. 7, p. 99, July 1, 1861.

10 The Alliance's reply, *A Vindication of the Principles and Policy of the United Kingdom Alliance, in Reply to Recent Objections* (reprinted from *Alliance News*, 1862), is summarized in Carter, *op. cit.* pp. 111–21.

11 After this visit, the first of three, Dow (a general on the northern side in the American civil war) predicted for prohibition in Britain 'a still more rapid and complete triumph than it has yet accomplished in America' (cited, Carter, *op. cit.* p. 85).

12 Cited, Martyn, *John B. Gough* (1893), p. 175.

13 Cited, 'Impressions on the "Gough-Lees Controversy" by an Outsider', App., p. 53, *Final Words in Gough versus Lees* (1860).

14 Winskill, *History of the Temperance Reformation* (1881), p. 137.

15 Cited, Luke, *Lawson* (1900), p. 54.

16 See *37th Annual Report (for 1898) of the Executive Committee of the London Auxiliary of the United Kingdom Alliance* (1899), p. 7. The authorities did not close the bars, so a summons was taken out against one of the attendants. When the Bow Street magistrate dismissed the summons the Alliance took the case to the Queen's Bench Division, where it was dismissed on a technicality, the Lord Chief Justice saying that he was far from satisfied that no offence had been committed.

17 *United Kingdom Alliance. A Full Report of the Speeches* [1870], p. 29.

18 Hilton, *Memoir of Raper* (1898), p. 29.

19 The role of the Alliance in relation to the 1871 Bill is discussed by Carter, *op. cit.* pp. 155–64.

20 Russell (ed.), *Lawson* (1909), p. 229.

21 *London Alliance Review,* no. 6, p. 6, July–Sept. 1900.

16 PUSSYFOOTS WITHOUT CLAWS (pp. 156–163)

1 *Daily Mail,* July 10, 1919.

2 There are accounts of the kidnapping and rescue of 'Pussyfoot' Johnson in *The Times,* Nov. 14, 1919, p. 12, and Nov. 15, 1919, p. 9; McKenzie, *'Pussyfoot' Johnson* [1920], ch. x, xi; Malins, *Wilson Stuart* (1935), pp. 104–7.

3 At Bangor, Feb. 28, 1915.

4 In Crichton-Browne and others, *Liberty* (1917), p. 38.

5 *The Prohibition Bulletin,* no. 45, p. 2, May 1930.

6 Cf. *Daily Mail,* July 25, 1917.

7 *A.O.F.B.* [1925], p. ii of cover; *ibid.* [1928], pp. 3, 5.

8 Rowley, *Who Are the Frothblowers?* [1927], pp. 4, 3.

9 *A.O.F.B.* [1928], p. 20. The words 'T.T.'s and M.P.'s and J.P.'s' do not appear in the two editions of this work I have been able to trace. Rowley (*op. cit.* pp. 5–6) omits the word 'Brachistocephalic'.

10 Rowley, *op. cit.* p. 14.

11 This Act was largely due to the efforts of Lady Astor, who called A. P. Herbert 'the playboy of the drink world', and who, in her maiden speech in 1920 (reprinted, Astor, *Problem for Women* [1920]), accused the drink trade of having profiteered during the war to the tune of many millions.

12 G. Hayler, *Towards World Sobriety* (1937), pp. 5–6.

13 *Annual Report of the Executive Committee of the United Kingdom Alliance for the Year Ending September 30th, 1940* (1940), p. 14.

14 *The Prohibitionist,* no. 147, p. 1, Dec. Quarter 1943.

15 See, e.g., James Hudson, *Hansard,* 5th ser., vol. 447, col. 1398.

16 *Ann. Rep. of the … U.K.A. for … 1954* (1954), p. 15.

17 *Ann. Rep. of the … U.K.A. for … 1955* (1955), p. 9.

18 *Ann. Rep. of the … U.K.A. for … 1958* (1958), p. 14.

19 *Ann. Rep. of the … U.K.A. for … 1948* (1948), p. 8.

20 *Band of Hope and Children's Circle Message*, Summer 1962, p. [1].

21 *The Wide-Awakes' Own*, vol. xiv, no. 8, p. [1], [Aug. 1953].

22 *Ibid.* vol. xxiii, no. 9, p. [1], [Sept. 1962].

23 MacNalty, *Mirage of Alcohol* [1946], p. 4.

24 *Band of Hope and Children's Circle Message*, Autumn 1962, p. [2].

25 Jane Sheldon, in *Christian World*, cited, *Alert* (journal of International Temperance Assn, Northern European Region), vol. i, no. 2, p. 19, Oct.–Dec. 1956.

26 *The Wide-Awakes' Own*, vol. xiv, no. 12, p. [2], [Dec. 1953].

27 *Band of Hope and Children's Circle Message*, Autumn 1962, p. [3].

PART IV

UNKINDLING A WANTONNESS (pp. 167–208)

17   THE CREEPING OBSTETRICIAN

1 Willughby, *Observations* (1863), pp. 135–6. According to Georgiana Hill (*Women in English Life* (1896), vol. ii, p. 281), '150 years later a famous midwifery professor more than once, it is said, had to use similar secrecy'.

2 Ellis, *Studies* (1936 edn), vol. i, pt 1, p. 29.

3 See Johnstone, *Smellie* (1952), p. 36.

4 Burns, *Principles of Midwifery* (1814), pp. 284–5.

5 See Spencer, *History of British Midwifery* (1929), pp. 43, 51.

6 Burton, *Essay* (1751), pt i, p. 108.

7 Spencer, *op. cit.* p. 146.

8 Johnstone, *op. cit.* p. 34 n.

9 Cited, *ibid.*

10 Cited, *ibid.* p. 35.

11 Smellie, *Treatise* (1752), pp. 91–2.

12 [Thicknesse], *Man-midwifery Analysed* (1764), p. 5.

13 *Ibid.* p. 7.

14 *Ibid.* pp. 10, 21.

15 A reviewer (Smollett, perhaps) of Thicknesse's *Letter to a Young Lady on her Marriage* (1764) said it turned on two points. The first was a severe invective against man-midwives, the second a most excellent receipt for a young lady to keep her teeth clean, by the help of a butcher's skewer. The latter was by far the most valuable part of the performance. The author, who pretended to take up the pen in favour of decency, was perhaps the most indecent creature that ever handled one, the reviewer added (*The Critical Review: or, Annals of Literature*, vol. xvii, p. 66, Jan. 1764).

16 Blunt [*sc.* Fores], *Man-midwifery Dissected* (1793), pp. 76, 88–9.

17 *Observations on the Impropriety of Men Being Employed in the Business of Midwifery* (1827), pp. 6–7; Pickmere, *Address to the Public, The Pamphleteer*, vol. xxviii, p. 67, 1827.

18 *Woman's Own*, Nov. 24, 1962, p. 93.

19 Ellis, *op. cit.* vol. i, pt 1, p. 65 n. 2; vol. iv, p. 101.

20 Westcott, *British Medical Journal*, Feb. 29, 1908, p. 492.

21 Cunnington, *Feminine Attitudes in the Nineteenth Century* (1935), p. 221.

22 Ellis, *op. cit.* vol. i, pt 1, pp. 33–4.

23 See Bertrand Russell's account of 'the nuns who never take a bath without wearing a bathrobe all the time. When asked why, since no man can see them, they reply: "Oh, but you forget the good God." Apparently they conceive of the Deity as a Peeping Tom, whose omnipotence enables Him to see through bathroom walls, but who is foiled by bathrobes' (Russell, *Unpopular Essays* (1950), p. 100).

24 Climenson, *Elizabeth Montagu* (1906), vol. i, p. 89.

25 Hoggart, *Uses of Literacy* (1957), p. 83.

18 WOMEN, MONSTROUS WOMEN (pp. 171–178)

1 Laver, *Taste and Fashion* (1945), pp. 201, 202; Laver, *Clothes* (1952), p. xiv. Italics in the original.

2 Dunlap, *Journal of General Psychology*, vol. i (1928), p. 65.

3 Cf. Flügel, *Psychology of Clothes* (1930), p. 192: 'Modesty is essentially correlated with desire. Its purpose is to fight desire, but in doing so it rekindles it, so that a circular process is inevitably set in motion.'

4 Cunnington, *Art of English Costume* (1948), p. 196.

5 See p. 35 above, quotation from *The Chronicles of England*.

6 Cf. Laver, *Clothes* (1952), p. 32.

7 Robinson (ed.), *Works of Chaucer* (1957), p. 240.

8 Flügel, *op. cit.* p. 148.

9 Cunnington, *op. cit.* p. 22.

10 *Ibid.* p. 207.

11 Strutt, *Dress and Habits* (1796), p. 258.

12 Binder, *Muffs and Morals* (1953), p. 19.

13 Cf. the garters on sale in London in the 1920s, adorned with a silver representation of a gate bearing such inscriptions as 'Go warily', 'This gate is private' and 'Private ground' (Flügel, *op. cit.* p. 27 n. 2).

14 Furnivall (ed.), *Harrison's Description of England* (1877), p. 170.

15 Averell, *A meruailous combat of contrarieties* (1588), sig. B2 recto.

16 Nashe, *Christs Teares* (1593), p. 71.

17 J. Hall, *Court of Virtue* (1961 edn), p. 351.

18 *Quippes* (1595), sig. A4 recto. In roughly the same period French moralists were fulminating against the immodest dress of their young country-

women, with their 'abominable collars, gaping and ruffed [*goudronnez*]' and their breasts open to the public view—'O intolerable crime, O pernicious scandal' (see Dingwall, *Girdle of Chastity* (1931), p. 30 n. 3).

19 T. Hall, *Loathsomnesse of Long Haire* (1653), pp. 107, 109–10.

20 [Boileau], *Just and Seasonable Reprehension* (1678), Preface, sig. A4 verso, A5 recto, A6 recto–A6 verso.

21 *Wit Restor'd* (1658), pp. 40, 39.

22 A Compassionate Conformist, *Englands Vanity* (1683), p. 61.

23 *The Guardian*, Numb. C, July 6, 1713.

24 *Ibid.* Numb. CIX, July 16, 1713.

25 Cf. Cunnington, *English Costume in the Eighteenth Century* (1957), p. 28. A good example is *A Vindication of the Reformation, On Foot among the Ladies, to Abolish Modesty and Chastity, and Restore the Native Simplicity of going Naked*, by 'Adam Eden', a second edition of which appeared in 1755. It declared that 'the Conduct of the Ladies in appearing in Publick quite Naked, from the Top of the Head, almost to the Waist, discovering their Neck, Shoulders, Breast, and part of their Waist quite bare, and shortening their Petticoats almost to the Knees, sufficiently shew their Intention of returning to the original Custom of going stark-naked' (pp. 1–4). The writer had not observed any lady uncover more of her legs than the calf, and had therefore invented some new-fashioned garters (a sort of bracelet to adorn and set off a well-shaped leg) that would tempt them to diminish the length of their petticoats (p. 25). And so on, in the same vein.

26 Murphy, *The Gray's Inn Journal* (1756), vol. ii, p. 244.

27 Wollstonecraft, *Rights of Women* (1792), p. 289 n.

28 Crowley, *One and thyrtye Epigrammes* (1550), sig. D viii recto.

29 Averell, *op. cit.*

30 [Lodge], *Wits Miserie* (1596), p. 15.

31 J. Hall, *op. cit.* p. 350.

32 Bansley, *Treatyse* [1841], p. 7.

33 *Quippes,* (1595), sig. B verso.

34 *Female Folly* (1713), p. 3. Cf. *Quippes, loc. cit.*:

> I not gainsay, but bastards sprout,
>   might Arses greate at first begin:
> And that when paunch of whoore grew out,
>   these hoops did helpe to hide their sinne.

35 'A-la-Mode, 1754', *The Universal Magazine of Knowledge and Pleasure*, vol. xv, p. 31, July 1754.

36 [Heywood], *The Female Spectator* (1745 [1744–46]), vol. i, bk v, p. 298; vol. ii, bk xii, p. 376.

37 *The Spectator*, Numb. CCCCXCII, Sept. 24, 1712.

38 Cunnington, *History of Underclothes* (1951), p. 70.
39 T. Hall, *op. cit.* p. 101.

19 THEY EVEN COVERED CUPID (pp. 179–184)

1 Cunnington, *History of Underclothes* (1951), p. 185.
2 Ellis (ed.), *Mid-Victorian Pepys* (1923), pp. 103–4.
3 *Chester Chronicle*, 1803, cited, Cunnington, *op. cit.* p. 112.
4 *The Mirror of the Graces* (1811), cited, Laver, *Clothes* (1952), pp. 223–4.
5 The employment of half-naked women in the pits was defended by James Moodie, a Scottish surgeon, in *Principles and Observations on Many and Various Subjects, for the Health of Nations and Individuals* (Edinburgh, 1848), [pt ii,] pp. 32–5. Their dress, he wrote, was not noticed or thought of by their male fellow workers.
6 Cited, Cunnington, *Feminine Attitudes* (1935), p. 42.
7 Cunnington, *Art of English Costume* (1948), p. 199.
8 Merrifield, *Dress as a Fine Art* (1854), pp. 13–14.
9 C. Hall, *From Hoopskirts to Nudity* (1938), p. 43.
10 Cited, Cunnington, *Feminine Attitudes* (1935), p. 181.
11 Cited, Cunnington, *Art of English Costume* (1948), p. 96.
12 Cited, *ibid.* p. 201.
13 Cited, Cunnington, *Why Women Wear Clothes* (1941), p. 148.
14 Ward, *Dynamic Sociology* (1907), vol. i, p. 643. Tight-lacing in particular aroused opposition, on the ground that it was injurious to health. An American phrenologist, in a book published in London in 1849, condemned tight-lacing on the ground that it inflamed all the organs of the abdomen, 'which thereby EXCITES AMATIVE DESIRES'. It was high time that men who wanted virtuous wives knew this fact; it was also high time that virtuous women should blush for shame to be seen laced tight, just as they should blush to be caught indulging impure desires (Fowler, *Intemperance and Tight Lacing* (1849), p. 32).
15 Cf. Binder, *Muffs and Morals* (1953), pp. 70–1.
16 Cf. Laver, *Taste and Fashion* (1945), p. 73.
17 See Peel, *Hundred Wonderful Years* (1926), pp. 151–2.
18 Texier, *Lettres sur l'Angleterre* (1851), p. 39.
19 Rasch, *London bei Nacht* (1873), p. 24.
20 Cited, Cunnington, *Art of English Costume* (1948), p. 228.
21 Laver, *op. cit.* pp. 52–3. According to a former superintendent of the British Museum reading room, two or three young men among the readers started dropping pieces of paper on the floor in order to peep, while retrieving them, at the ankles of young women sitting on the other side. 'Their game . . . was very soon stopped' (Barwick, *Reading Room of the British Museum* (1929), p. 153).

22 Joyce, *Ulysses* (1954 reprint), p. 66.

23 Tilt, *Elements of Health* (1852), p. 194.

24 *Ibid.* pp. 192–3.

25 Cunnington, *English Women's Clothing in the Nineteenth Century* (1937), p. 21; Wellesley (ed.), *Paris Embassy* (1928), pp. 84–5; [Harris], *Memoirs of an Ex-Minister* (1884), vol. ii, p. 37.

26 Erskine (ed.), *Twenty Years at Court* (1916), pp. 343, 345; Ellis (ed.), *op. cit.* p. 262.

27 Cunnington, *History of Underclothes* (1951), p. 153.

28 *Ibid.* p. 196.

29 Cited, Cunnington, *English Women's Clothing in the Nineteenth Century* (1937), p. 20.

30 Amateur Swimming Association, *Handbook for 1899* [1899], p. 43.

20   SHORT SKIRTS AND LONG FACES (pp. 185–192)

1 Cf. Cunnington, *English Women's Clothing in the Present Century* (1952), p. 40.

2 Cited, Adburgham, *A* Punch *History of Manners and Modes* (1961), p. 227.

3 Glyn, *Vicissitudes of Evangeline* (1905), pp. 99–101.

4 Kennedy, *Forum*, June 1926, p. 829.

5 Cited, Cunnington, *op. cit.* p. 102.

6 Cited, *ibid.* p. 87.

7 Laver, *Taste and Fashion* (1945), p. 97. The exposure of one other part of the female body—the head—caused concern during the Edwardian period. In 1905 Cranstock church in Newquay, Cornwall, was closed on account of the 'irreverence of numbers of women, who, walking uncovered, presume to enter God's house with no sign of reverence or modesty upon their heads' (cited, Sumner, *Folkways* (1907), pp. 455–6).

8 Cited, Adburgham, *op. cit.* p. 256.

9 'After the holocaust of the Great War motherhood was at a discount, and the attributes of motherhood, so far from being admired, as they had been in most ages, were treated as something to be rigorously concealed' (Laver, *op. cit.* p. 103).

10 *Ibid.* p. 201 n.

11 Cunnington, *op. cit.* p. 148.

12 Cf. Sanborn, *American Journal of Psychology*, Jan. 1926, p. 1.

13 Cf. Flügel, *British Journal of Medical Psychology*, vol. ix (1929), p. 115.

14 Cited, *These Tremendous Years* (1938), p. 82.

15 Cited, Lang, *Churches of God* (1928), p. 149 n.

16 Cited, A Christian Business Man [*sc.* T.I.W.], '*Modest Apparel*' [1931], p. 5. Women operators at a London telephone exchange were warned in the summer of 1927 that serious disciplinary measures

would be taken if they did not wear sleeves at least four inches long.

17 *The Gospel Magazine and Protestant Beacon*, no. 779, n.s., p. 503, Nov. 1930. The Reverend J. D. Jones, chairman-elect of the Congregational Union, declared that modern women's attire made it harder for the men in his Bible class to 'keep straight' (cited, *H & E*, vol. xxiii, no. 284, p. 525, Nov. 1924).

18 Collier and Lang, *Just the Other Day* (1932), p. 155, citing A. Corbett-Smith.

19 A Christian Business Man [*sc.* T.I.W.], *op. cit.* pp. 17, 10–11, 15–16, 13, 14, 15, 16, 17, 19.

20 Lang, *op. cit.* pp. 148–9. Cf. Cunnington, *Why Women Wear Clothes* (1941), p. 154: 'You had only to sit opposite a woman to be informed of the colour of her knickers and bus journeys were relieved of some of their monotony. We needs must love the highest when we see it and we certainly saw it then.'

21 Cited, St. Clair, *Vice of To-day* [1943], pp. 45, 46. A chapter of a confraternity known as the Little Flower of Jesus was established in London in 1931. Somewhat late in the day, it opposed skirts which failed to cover the knee. It was also against blouses cut lower than two inches below the hollow of the throat, dresses with sleeves ending above the elbows, and transparent stockings, especially flesh-coloured ones. Young women were forbidden to take part in public gymnastic displays lest they showed their legs.

22 Cited, Barry (ed.), *This England* (1933), p. 40.

23 Cf. Cunnington, *Art of English Costume* (1948), p. 26.

24 'At the drop of a . . .', *Sunday Times*, Dec. 3, 1961, p. 12.

25 Public Morality Council, *Public Morals* (1957), p. 21.

26 *News of the World*, Sept. 23, 1962, p. 9.

27 Cf. Adburgham, *op. cit.* p. 301.

28 *Ibid.* p. 322.

29 *Time* (Atlantic edn), vol. lxxx, no. 18, p. 36, Nov. 2, 1962.

30 *Daily Mirror*, Dec. 21, 1962, p. 2. I am indebted to Mr Trevenen Peters for this reference.

31 *Manchester Evening News*, cited, Barry (ed.), *op. cit.* pp. 40–1.

32 Cited, *SBR*, vol. xvii, no. 67, p. 67, Oct.–Dec. 1949.

33 Cited, Cunnington, *English Women's Clothing in the Present Century* (1952), p. 40.

34 Cited, Adburgham, *op. cit.* p. 248.

35 *Tablet*, cited, Barry (ed.), *op. cit.* p. 40.

36 *Seale and Sands Parish Magazine*, cited, Barry (ed.), *op. cit.*

37 Naomi Mitchison, 'Tabu in the Highlands', *SBR*, vol. xiv, no. 55, p. 50, Autumn 1946.

38 By the early thirties Bournemouth, for instance, no longer tried to define

the 'regulation costume' exactly, but left it to 'the good sense of the bathers' (cited, Barry (ed.), *op. cit.* p. 56).

21   NO NUDES IS GOOD NEWS (pp. 193–208)

1 Colley March, *Proc. Dorset Nat. Hist. Club*, vol. xxii (1901), p. 106. Since 1920 the giant has been in the care of the National Trust.
2 Mee (ed.), *Dorset* (1939), p. 55.
3 Lupton (ed.), *Utopia of More* (1895), p. 225.
4 *Itinerary Written by Fynes Moryson* (1617), pt iii, bk 4, pp. 180–1.
5 Wheatley (ed.), *Diary of Pepys* (1903–04), vol. vii, p. 44.
6 *Ibid.* vol. iii, p. 191; vol. viii, p. 129; Wood, *Athenæ Oxonienses* (1813–20), vol. iv, p. 731; Johnson, *Lives of the Poets* (1905), vol. ii, pp. 303–4. In 1927, Sedley's parting shot at his trial was regarded as 'amusing but unfortunately unquotable' (Pinto, *Sedley* (1927), p. 66).
7 Burnet, *Rochester* (1680), p. 23.
8 [Swift], *Gulliver's Travels* (1726), vol. ii, pt iv, pp. 40–1.
9 *Nakedness Consider'd*, By a Gentleman of Great Parts (1729), pp. 3, 4–5, 7.
10 Gilchrist, *Life of Blake* (1863), vol. i, p. 115. John Linnell, who knew Blake intimately later in his life, doubted the truth of this popular legend.
11 'The Law—and You!', *SBR*, vol. vii, no. 25, p. 9, Spring 1939.
12 Livesey, *Moral Reformer*, vol. i, no. 9, p. 280, Sept. 1, 1831.
13 Cited, Cohen, *Lady de Rothschild* (1935), p. 93.
14 Plomer (ed.), *Kilvert's Diary*, vol. ii (1939), p. 358; *ibid.* vol. iii (1940), p. 37.
15 Ellis, *Studies* (1936), vol. i, pt 1, p. 39.
16 O'Rell [*sc.* Blouet], *John Bull's Womankind* [1884], pp. 49–50.
17 And in 1941 a 'dear old gentleman' complained that he could see a nudist camp at Macclesfield from a distance of several miles with the aid of binoculars (*SBR*, vol. ix, no. 35, p. 62, Autumn 1941).
18 Wey, *Les Anglais chez eux* (1856), pp. 301–3.
19 Gladstone, *Studies on Homer and the Homeric Age* (1858), vol. ii, p. 514. Cf. *ibid.* pp. 516–17: 'The statement that water was poured over [Ulysses'] head and shoulders, as he sat in the bath, evidently implies that what may be called essential decency was preserved. . . . Even if it were not so, we could not in this point argue from the manners or morals of a Phoenician goddess to those of a Greek damsel. . . . The statements of Homer give no ground whatever for sinister or disparaging imputation.'
20 Lambert, *Universal Provider* (1938), pp. 112–13.
21 [Lancastre Saldanha,] Countess of Cardigan, *My Recollections* (1909), pp. 45–50.
22 *H & E*, vol. xx, no. 247, p. 336, Oct. 1921; vol. xxi, no. 253, p. 146, Apr. 1922.

23 'Costume and Custom', *Evening Standard*, Oct. 19, 1927.

24 Webster, *Socialist Network* (1926), p. 122.

25 Cited, *H & E*, vol. xxvi, no. 318, p. 429, Sept. 1927.

26 *SBR*, vol. xvii, no. 68, pp. 91, 94, Jan.–Mar. 1950.

27 Cf. A. Harper, 'The Nudist Movement in England: A Brief History', *Illustrated Sun Bathing News*, vol. i, no. 3, p. 8, Autumn 1935.

28 Cited, Clifford Coudray, 'Hiking à la Nature', *H & E*, n.s., vol. i, no. 3, p. 86, Oct. 1931.

29 *The Times*, Sept. 20, 1933, p. 7; Oct. 19, 1933, p. 4.

30 Craig, *Plan*, vol. x, no. 6, p. 3, Jun. 1943.

31 Cf. 'How It All Began', *SBR*, vol. xvii, no. 67, p. 71, Oct.–Dec. 1949.

32 'The Future of British Nudism', *H & E*, n.s., vol. iii, no. 7, p. 228, July 1933.

33 William Welby, 'Is Nudism "Just a Craze"?', *The Naturist*, vol. i, no. 2, p. 37, Jan. 1938.

34 Cf. *H & E*, n.s., vol. iv, no. 2, p. 37, Feb. 1934: 'The word "naturism" . . . was coined by this magazine. And, according to us, the originators, it means a sane and healthy practice of nudism.' The precise distinction (if any) between nudism and naturism, though much discussed, is exceedingly obscure. In 1961 the British Sun Bathing Association, at its seventh annual conference, disowned the term 'nudist'; in future, to avoid confusion with strip-teasers, the word 'naturist' would be used in all official publications or communications. Similarly, 'sun club' has replaced the expression (now taboo within the movement) 'nudist colony'.

35 John Walsh, 'Sun-Bathing Societies—A Warning', *John Bull*, Aug. 15, 1931.

36 *John Bull*, Nov. 28, 1936.

37 Cited, *SBR*, vol. v, no. 20, p. 98, Autumn 1937.

38 Public Morality Council (London), *33rd Annual Report (1932)*, p. 32.

39 *Dress and Beauty*, 1935, cited, *H & E*, n.s., vol. v, no. 12, p. 414, Dec. 1935. Shaw however had somewhat earlier taken the view that communal nudism was impractical, since few naked men could look on a naked woman without being moved. This passage was suppressed when a letter of Shaw to the founder-editor of the *SBR*, N. F. Barford, was published in that journal in 1933. See *SBR*, vol. i, no. 2, p. 6, Summer 1933; vol. xxiv, no. 95, p. 59, Oct.–Dec. 1956).

40 *New Statesman and Nation*, vol. x, no. 235 (n.s.), p. 244, Aug. 24, 1935.

41 Graves and Hodge, *Long Week-end* (1940), p. 274; Evans, *Sensible Sun-Bathing* (1935), pp. 27–8. One man was asked to leave a club because he was a manual worker (*SBR*, vol. xxiv, no. 93, p. 7, Apr.–June 1956). It is claimed that nudism is nowadays less snobbish though no less respectable. In 1958 the sixth world naturist congress was held at Woburn Abbey, where dele-

gates shared the park with the Duke of Bedford's prize cattle. 'The whole thing is rather dreary—like meat in a butcher's shop', said the Duke (cited, *H & E*, vol. xxx, no. 7, p. 30, July 1960).

42 Cited, Clifford Lewis, 'The Morals of the Modern Nudist', *H & E*, n.s., vol. iii, no. 2, p. 39, Feb. 1933.

43 Gordon, *London Roundabout* (1933), p. 240.

44 Cited, *SBR*, vol. iii, no. 12, p. 142, Winter 1936.

45 Cited, 'A Conscientious Objector—to Sun Bathing', *H & E*, n.s., vol. i, no. 10, p. 338, May 1932; cited, *SBR*, vol. iv, no. 14, p. 64, Early Summer Number, 1936.

46 Cited, *SBR*, vol. iv, no. 17, p. 178, Winter 1937, Cf. the view of the Vicar of Bognor Regis twenty years later that there is no medical evidence in favour of nudity: 'It is an excuse for something worse' (cited, *SBR*, vol. xxiii, no. 92, p. 89, Jan.–Mar. 1956).

47 Chesterton, *All Is Grist* (1931), p. 16.

48 Cited, *SBR*, vol. v, no. 18, p. 27, Spring 1937.

49 Cited, *SBR*, vol. v, no. 20, p. 99, Autumn 1937.

50 Cited, Mr Clothes, *Modern Review*, Jan. 1936, p. 17; cited, William R. Lucas, 'A Plea for Sane Nudism', *H & E*, n.s., vol. ii, no. 2, pp. 41–2, Sept. 1932.

51 Cited, C. E. M. Joad, 'The Alleged Wickedness of the Body', *SBR*, vol. i, no. 3, p. 8, Autumn 1933.

52 Cited, *SBR*, vol. iv, no. 15, p. 106, Second Summer Number, 1936; cited, *SBR*, vol. iv, no. 14, p. 65, Early Summer Number, 1936.

53 Cited, *SBR*, vol. iii, no. 12, pp. 142–3, Winter 1936.

54 Cited, *H & E*, n.s., vol. ii, no. 1, p. 2, Aug. 1932.

55 Alec Craig, 'Looking Back', *SBR*, vol. iii, no. 11, p. 88, Autumn 1935.

56 *H & E*, vol. vii, no. 8, p. 208, Aug. 1937.

57 Lyall, *Future of Taboo* (1936), p. 60 n. 1.

58 *SBR*, vol. viii, no. 29, p. 19, Spring 1940.

59 Cited, *SBR*, vol. xxi, no. 82, p. 39, July–Sept. 1953.

60 Letter in *Glasgow Evening News*, cited, *Illustrated Sun Bathing News*, vol. i, no. 2, p. 32, Summer 1935.

61 Cited, *Gymnos*, vol. i, no. 11, p. 3, Dec. 1933.

62 *Policewoman's Review*, June 1933, cited, *Gymnos*, vol. i, no. 6, p. 13, July 1933.

63 *In a Nudist Camp! . . . By an Eye-Witness* (1933), pp. 6, 7, 9, 13, 20.

64 Wallis, *New Adorning* [1938], pp. 18–19.

65 Other novels wholly or partly inspired by nudism include Anthony Gibbs's *The New Crusade* [1931] and George C. Foster's *Sunwards* (1931) and *Rahab and Rachel* (1933). *The Bare Idea* by 'Gordon Sherry' (H. B. Sheridan) had a long run at the Comedy theatre, followed by a long tour.

66 Cf. *SBR*, vol. v, no. 20, p. 96, Autumn 1937.

67 *SBR*, vol. v, no. 18, p. 16, Spring 1937.

68 Cited, *SBR*, vol. xvii, no. 68, p. 82, Jan.–Mar. 1950.

69 *H & E*, n.s., vol. iii, no. 8, p. 266, Aug. 1933; no. 9, p. 309, Sept. 1933; no. 10, pp. 352, 355, Oct. 1933; vol. iv, no. 2, p. 50, Feb. 1934; no. 6, p. 198, June 1934; no. 8, p. 270, Aug. 1934.

70 *Illustrated Sun Bathing News*, vol. i, no. 3, p. 31, Autumn 1935.

71 Evans, *Sensible Sun-Bathing* (1935), p. 28; *H & E*, vol. xxx, no. 11, p. 11, Nov. 1960.

72 Evans, *op. cit.* p. 29.

73 Gordon, *op. cit.* p. 238.

74 *SBR*, vol. xxiv, no. 93, p. 7, Apr.–June 1956.

75 *SBR*, vol. xiii, no. 49, p. 7, Spring 1945; Gordon Spencer, 'Is there a case for Indoor Nudism?', *SBR*, vol. xvi, no. 64, p. 76, Jan.–Mar. 1949.

76 The letter of 'Starko' appeared in *Gymnos*, vol. i, no. 12, p. 18, Jan. 1934.

77 A nude by Adolf Ziegler, *Listener*, vol. xviii, no. 454, p. 607, Sept. 22, 1937.

PART V

DON'T DANCE, LITTLE LADY (pp. 211–253)

22 BUMPS AND GRINDS OF LONG AGO

1 Wright, *History of Domestic Manners* (1862), p. 111.

2 Owst, *Holborn Review*, Jan. 1926, pp. 35, 34. For references, see Chambers, *Mediaeval Stage* (1903), vol. i, p. 162 n. 1. The legend was first told of the people of Kölbigk in Anhalt, Saxony; see the extract from Robert Mannyng's *Handlyng Sinne* (1303–38) in Ford (ed.), *Age of Chaucer* (1954), pp. 262–70.

3 Wright, *op. cit.* p. 228.

4 John of Salisbury, *Polycraticus*, i. 8, cited, Nicoll, *Masks Mimes and Miracles* (1931), pp. 151, 167.

5 Cited, *ibid.* p. 152.

6 Furnivall (ed.), *Stubbes's Anatomy of Abuses* (1877–82), pt i, pp. 46*–47*. He went on (pp. 47*–48*): 'There are two sides to great gatherings for amusement now. . . . I was saying to a faithful-working curate-friend . . . how pleasant all lookt at the fair that morning. "Yes", he answered, "I suppose one oughtn't to grudge the people their gathering; but our annual crop of bastards 'll be sown to-night. We had twelve last year, and eleven the year before; and many of the girls get ruind for life."' And an easy-going acquaintance told him, apropos of the races on Runnymede: 'If you

want to know when the harm's done, and what it is, come with me to the booths the nights before and after, and then take a turn about the grass, and see what's going on there. I'm not one of the strait-laced lot; but knowing what I do, I don't wonder at people trying to stop the whole affair.'

7 Crouch, *Puritanism and Art* (1910), pp. 290–1, 292 n.

8 Scholes, *Puritans and Music* (1934), pp. 58, 60, 70, 89.

9 Chambers, *op. cit.* vol. i, p. 94. The maypole was 'nothing less than a great phallic emblem' (*Phallism* (1889), p. 26). 'The Puritans were deeply impressed with the belief that the maypole was a substantial relic of Paganism; and they were no doubt right. . . . The maypole had taken the place of the phallus. The ceremonies attending the elevation of the two objects were identical. . . . Both [English and Roman] festivals were attended with the same licentious-ness' ([Wright and others], *Essay on the Worship of the Generative Powers*, Knight, *Discourse on the Worship of Priapus* (1865), p. 163). Cf. Davenport, *Aphrodisiacs and Anti-aphrodisiacs*, (1869 [*sc.* 1873]), p. 6.

10 Chambers, *op. cit.* vol. i, pp. 91, 322.

11 Northbrooke, *Treatise* (1843 reprint), pp. 145, 146, 155–6, 161, 171.

12 Furnivall (ed.), *op. cit.* pt i, pp. 154–5, 166, 149.

13 Christopher Fetherstone, *A Dialogue agaynst Light, Lewde and Lascivious Dauncing* (1583), cited, Chambers, *op. cit.* vol. i, p. 93 n. 2.

14 Thomas Lovell, *A Dialogue between Custom and Veritie, concerning the use and abuse of Dauncing and Minstrelsie* [1581], cited, Collier, *Bibliographical Account* (1865), vol. i, p. 491.

15 Thomas Norton, 'An Exhortation or Rule set downe by Mr. Norton, sometyme Remembrauncer of London, wherebie the Lord Maior of London is to order himselfe and the Cittie' [*c.* 1574], cited, *ibid.* vol. ii, p. 59.

16 Perkins, *Cases of Conscience* (1608), bk iii, p. 119.

17 Democritus Iunior [*sc.* Burton], *Anatomy of Melancholy* (1621), p. 589.

18 Bentham, Χοροθεολογον (1657), pp. 55–6.

19 Hingeston, *Dreadful Alarm* (1703), p. 75.

20 Stow, *Survey of London* (1908 reprint), vol. i, p. 95.

21 Firth and Rait (ed.), *Acts and Ordinances* (1911), vol. i, p. 421.

23 SIN IN THE BALL-ROOM (pp. 217–221)

1 *Spectator*, Numb. LXVII, May 17, 1711.

2 Wesley, *Works* (1878), vol. vii, p. 34; Davis, *Thoughts on Dancing* (1791), p. [iii].

3 Malcolm, *Anecdotes* (1808), p. 163.

4 [Lemercher de Longpré,] Baron d'Haussez, *La Grande-Bretagne* (1833), vol. i, p. 90; Darton (ed.), *Life and Times of Mrs. Sherwood* (1910), p. 15.

5 Burder, *Lawful Amusements* (1805), pp. 17–18.

6 Hill, *Warning to Professors* (1833), p. 46.

7 B.E., *Folly's Advocate* (1827), pp. 17–25.

8 Yates, *The Ball* (1829), p. 55.

9 Stirling (comp.), *Letter-Bag of Spencer-Stanhope* (1913), vol. ii, p. 182.

10 Hop, *Sporting Magazine*, Aug. 1812, pp. 213–14.

11 Hornem [*sc.* Byron], *Waltz* (1813), pp. 10, 14, 23, 24.

12 Cited, Rae, *Sheridan* (1896), vol. ii, p. 210 n.

13 Cited, Stoddard (ed.), *Personal Reminiscences by Knight and Raikes* (1875), pp. 285–6.

14 A.F., *Ladies' Pocket-Book* (1840), pp. 67, 74, 70, 67–8.

15 Fitz George, *Ball Room Refinement* [1851], pp. 15, 12–13, 12, 16–19.

16 Cited, Cunnington, *Feminine Attitudes* (1935), p. 188.

17 *Dancing, in a Right Spirit* [1865], pp. 16, 10.

18 Davies, *Our Morals* (1873), pp. 3–7, 20.

19 Kellogg, *Ladies' Guide* (1890), pp. 212–14.

24 THE ABOMINABLE COPULATIVE BEAT (pp. 222–228)

1 Cf. Richardson, *History of English Ballroom Dancing* [1946], p. 25.

2 Cited, Slonimsky, *Music of Latin America* (1946), p. 61.

3 *The Times*, May 20, 1913, p. 9; May 21, 1913, p. 11; May 22, 1913, p. 11.

4 Cited, *Dancing Times*, n.s., no. 33, p. 548, June 1913.

5 Cited, *ibid.* no. 30, p. 352, Mar. 1913.

6 Cecil Hewitt, 'The Turkey Trot', *ibid.* no. 26, pp. 80–2, Nov. 1912; *ibid.* no. 33, p. 548, June 1913.

7 Adburgham, *A* Punch *History of Manners and Modes* (1961), p. 244.

8 E. Scott, *Dancing Times*, Dec. 1917, p. 66.

9 *Ibid.* no. 88, p. 128, Jan. 1918.

10 *Ibid.* no. 90, p. 179, Mar. 1918.

11 Cited, *ibid.* no. 102, pp. 190–1, Mar. 1919.

12 *Evening News*, Mar. 18, 1919.

13 *Daily Mail*, Mar. 15, 1919.

14 Richardson, *op. cit.* pp. 41–4. For a report of the conference, see *Dancing Times*, n.s., no. 117, pp. 697–703, June 1920.

15 Cited, *ibid.* no. 124, p. 306, Jan. 1921.

16 Richardson, *op. cit.* pp. 46–7. The shimmy was first mentioned in the *Dancing Times* in Nov. 1918: 'It is still very, very crude—and it is called "Shaking the Shimmy". . . . It's a nigger dance, of course, and it appears to be a slow walk with a frequent twitching of the shoulders' (no. 98, p. 35, Nov. 1918). Cf. *ibid.* no. 125, p. 413, Feb. 1921: 'What is the origin of the name "shimmy"? One Parisian wag connects it with the word "chemise", but his explanation will not bear repeating in the chaste columns of the

Dancing Times'; and *ibid.* no. 146, p. 225, Dec. 1922: 'The shoulder shimmy was taboo from the moment it was seen.'

17 Richardson, *op. cit.* p. 64; Short, *Fifty Years of Vaudeville* (1946), p. 221.

18 *Daily Mail*, July 11, 1927.

19 B. Meyer, *Words of Help for Christian Girls*, cited, Lockyer, *Dancing, Ancient and Modern* (1930), p. 35.

20 Lockyer, *op. cit.* pp. 22, 31, 25, 26, 35.

21 *Border Standard*, Aug. 1927, cited, Lockyer, *op. cit.* pp. 53–4.

22 Graham, *Millgate*, Jan. 1940, p. 235.

23 Cited, *H & E*, n.s., vol. i, no. 11, p. 362, June 1932.

24 'Stimulus behind "Rock 'n' Roll" Disturbances', *The Times*, Sept. 15, 1956, p. 4.

25 'Rocking the Ballroom', *ibid.* Dec. 27, 1957, p. 7.

26 *Evening Standard*, Jan. 14, 1963.

27 *Guardian*, Apr. 16, 1962.

28 Cited, 'New Twist to an Old Story', *Weekend*, Feb. 7–11, 1962, p. 5.

25   KICKING AGAINST THE HIGH-KICKS (pp. 229–239)

1 *SV*, vol. iii, p. 50.

2 Thomson, *Studies in Ancient Greek Society*, [vol. i,] *The Prehistoric Ægean* (1949), p. 206. Demeter was the goddess of the corn-bearing earth and of agriculture.

3 The French name is probably a play on words. *Une chaloupe* is also a rowdy dance and a loudly dressed woman; *chalouper* = to sway or swing like a boat while dancing, and *chalouper une danse* = to turn a dance into a vulgar romp.

4 'Scandalous Dances', *International Monthly Magazine*, Feb. 1, 1851, p. 133.

5 *Report from Select Committee on Public Houses* (1854), qq. 1649–52.

6 *The Tomahawk*, no. 30, p. 311, Nov. 30, 1867.

7 And not, as Pearl says (*Girl with the Swansdown Seat* (1955), p. 220, following *The Times*, Dec. 27, 1867, p. 7) by Finette at the Lyceum on Boxing Day, 1867; hers was the first cancan danced on the English stage *by a woman*.

8 Sherson, *London's Lost Theatres* (1925), p. 159.

9 Pearl, *op. cit.*

10 Hollingshead, *My Lifetime* (1895), vol. i, p. 224.

11 *The Times*, Dec. 27, 1867, p. 7.

12 Hollingshead, *op. cit.* vol. i, p. 225.

13 *The Times*, July 15, 1869, p. 10.

14 *The Day's Doings*, vol. i, no. 11, p. 10, Oct. 8, 1870.

15 *The Times*, Oct. 14, 1870, p. 12. The Alhambra's managing director complained that the illustration in *The Day's Doings* was 'highly overdrawn

and exaggerated'; the paper retorted that the management had bought over eighty copies of the issue containing it, for the purpose of advertising the performance (*The Day's Doings*, vol. i, no. 13, p. 2, Oct. 22, 1870).

16 Hibbert, *Fifty Years* (1916), p. 105.

17 Rendle, *Swings and Roundabouts* (1919), p. 115.

18 Soldene, *Recollections* (1897), pp. 94–5.

19 *Notes and Queries*, 4th ser., vol. vi, p. 455, Nov. 26, 1870; p. 556, Dec. 24, 1870.

20 Twain [*sc.* Clemens], *Innocents Abroad* (1869), p. 136.

21 Witkowski and Nass, *Le Nu dans le théâtre* (1909), p. 248.

22 Grove and others, *Dancing* (1895), p. 287.

23 Morton and Newton, *Sixty Years' Stage Service* (1905), p. 85. Cf. Rendle, *op. cit.* p. 113: 'The "wickedness" of it was much exaggerated'; and Hibbert, *op. cit.* p. 222: 'The indecency of the dance . . . began when women, or men dressed as women, addressed themselves to an increase of its antics.'

24 Guest, *Alhambra Ballet* (1959), p. 15.

25 Hollingshead, *Gaiety Chronicles* (1898), p. 228.

26 *The Times*, Dec. 27, 1872, p. 8.

27 *Ibid.* May 7, 1874, p. 8, advertising.

28 *Vanity Fair*, vol. xi, p. 249, May 9, 1874.

29 *Ibid.* p. 277, May 23, 1874; p. 292, May 30, 1874.

30 *Ibid.* p. 276, May 23, 1874.

31 *Saturday Review*, vol. xxxviii, no. 997, p. 726, Dec. 5, 1874.

32 *The Times*, Dec. 9, 1874, pp. 10–11; *The Era*, vol. xxvii, no. 1,890, p. 4, Dec. 13, 1874; *Saturday Review*, vol. xxxviii, no. 998, p. 758, Dec. 12, 1874.

33 *Vanity Fair*, vol. xii, p. 331, Dec. 12, 1874.

34 Cited, *ibid.* p. 347, Dec. 26, 1874.

35 Hibbert, *op. cit.* p. 126.

36 Flitch, *Modern Dancing* (1912), p. 96.

37 See Sims, *Glances Back* (1917), p. 192.

38 Burton, *Drunkards, Moderate Drinkers, Teetotalers* (1902), p. 25.

39 Public Morality Council (London), *37th Annual Report* (*1936*), p. 21.

40 Bergler, *Fashion and the Unconscious* (1953), p. 125.

26 THE SHOCKING HISTORY OF STRIP-TEASE (pp. 240–253)

1 [Behn], *The Rover* (1677), III. ii; p. 39; Cunnington, *History of Underclothes* (1951), p. 54.

2 *Proposals for a National Reformation of Manners* (169¾), pp. 31–2.

3 Woodward, *Account of the Rise and Progress of the Religious Societies* (1698), p. 79.

4 Greenwood, *In Strange Company* (1873), p. 26. Cf. Barrère and Leland, *Dictionary of Slang* (1889–90), vol. i, p. 191.

5 [Ward], *The London-Spy* (1704), p. 241. The word 'Firking', which has no sexual connotation—it means 'moving about briskly'—is omitted, with much else, from the 1927 edition, edited by Arthur L. Hayward.

6 See Avery, *Studies in Philology*, July 1934, pp. 417–18; Witkowski and Nass, *Le Nu au théâtre* (1909), p. 265.

7 *History of the Human Heart* (1749; reprinted 1885), pp. 103–6. The original of the passage attributed to *The Midnight Spy* (1766) in Partridge, *History of Orgies* (1960), pp. 138–9, does not in fact refer to a 'posture girl', but to a drunken woman accidentally exposing herself. This passage is retranslated from the German in Bloch, *History of English Sexual Morals* (1936), p. 327, and in Bloch, *Sexual Life in England* (1938), p. 327, without, apparently, having been checked against the original. Bloch, and Partridge, have: 'A beautiful woman . . . *offers to the view* just those parts of her body that, were she not without all *shame*, she would most zealously seek to conceal. . . . Look, she is *on all fours* now, like an animal.' (Italics added.) The original is quite different: 'A fine woman . . . *exposing* those parts, which, was she not *thus* deprived of all *sense*, she would labour *on such occasion* to conceal. . . . See, she is *carried out* like a beast' (*Midnight Spy* (1766), p. 63; italics added).

8 [Lancastre Sardanha,] Countess of Cardigan, *My Recollections* (1909), p. 10.

9 Jeaffreson, *Lady Hamilton and Lord Nelson* (1888), vol. i, p. 30.

10 Cited, Hamilton and Stewart, *Emma in Blue* (1957), p. 22.

11 F. L. G. [*sc.* Gower?], *Swell's Night Guide* [1841], 'Union', 'Paphian Revels'.

12 Lord Chief Baron [*sc.* Nicholson], *Swell's Night Guide* (1846), p. 36.

13 Nicholson, *Autobiography* [1860], pp. 286, 345–6.

14 Hibbert, *Fifty Years* (1916), p. 83.

15 Short, *Fifty Years of Vaudeville* (1946), p. 136.

16 The Cider Cellar was where W. G. Rose sang *Sam Hall*, with its daring refrain 'Damn your eyes', in the 1840s.

17 *Saturday Review*, vol. xxxviii, no. 997, p. 726, Dec. 5, 1874; no. 998, p. 758, Dec. 12, 1874.

18 National Vigilance Association, *Third Annual Report of the Executive Committee* (1888), pp. 6, 22, 23.

19 Hibbert, *op. cit.* p. 191; Nat. Vig. Assn, *Work Accomplished* (1906), p. 5.

20 *Vigilance Record*, vol. ii (n.s.), no. 11, p. 123, Dec. 15, 1888.

21 Hibbert, *op. cit.* p. 165; Short, *op. cit.* p. 136.

22 *Minutes of Evidence, Report of the Royal Commission on Alien Immigration* (1903–04), vol. ii (Cd 1742), p. 307, q. 9312.

23 London Council for the Promotion of Public Morality, *Report . . . for . . . 1907*, pp. 3–5; Nat. Vig. Assn, *23rd Ann. Rep. of the E.C.* (1908), p. 8. Another complaint was made in 1909, when the Council had 'a short sketch of a most objectionable character' removed from a music-hall programme

(London Council for the Promotion of Public Morality, *Rep. . . . for . . . 1909*, p. 9).

24 Hibbert, *op. cit.* p. 110; Cochran, *Cock-a-Doodle-Do* (1941), p. 203.

25 *Report from Joint Select Committee . . . on the Stage Plays (Censorship)* (1909), p. 161, q. 2815; p. 255, q. 4687; p. 314, qq. 5621–2; Maeterlinck, *Monna Vanna* (1902), p. 54. A protest was signed by Meredith, Swinburne, Hardy and many others.

26 Cited, Langdon-Davies, *Future of Nakedness* (1929), p. 76.

27 Cooper, *Rainbow Comes and Goes* (1958), p. 87.

28 Cited, Hibbert, *op. cit.* p. 111.

29 Cf. Cochran, *Secrets of a Showman* (1925), p. 93.

30 Cooper, *op. cit.* p. 88.

31 Witkowski and Nass, *op. cit.* pp. 265–8; *Rep. . . . on the Stage Plays (Censorship)* (1909), p. 182, q. 2312; p. 254, q. 4674.

32 *Punch*, vol. cxxxiv, p. 451, June 17, 1908.

33 *The Times*, Jan. 18, 1910, p. 13.

34 Cochran, *Secrets of a Showman* (1925), pp. 219–20.

35 Cochran, *I had almost Forgotten* (1932), p. 233; Graves, *Cochran Story* [1951], p. 72.

36 Public Morality Council, *31st Ann. Rep. (1930)*, p. 21.

37 *The Times*, Jan. 5, 1935, p. 6.

38 Andrée [pseud.], *My Life Story* (1945), pp. 4–6.

39 Gorer, *Hot Strip Tease* (1937), p. 69. The passage referred to was omitted from the English edition of *Studs Lonigan* (London, 1936); it appears in James T. Farrell, *Judgment Day* (London, 1959), pp. 289–90.

40 Public Morality Council (London), *38th Ann. Rep. (1937)*, pp. 22–4.

41 *Idem, 40th Ann. Rep. (1939)*, pp. 24–5.

42 Nat. Vig. Assn, *54th Ann. Rep. of the E.C.* (1941), p. 8.

43 *Idem, 57th Ann. Rep. of the E.C.* (1944), p. 5.

44 Public Morality Council (London), *53rd Ann. Rep. (1952)*, p. 11.

45 *Idem, 54th Ann. Rep. (1953)*, p. 9; *Public Morals in 1954* (1955), p. 13; *Public Morals* (1957), p. 15.

46 *Public Morals* (1960), p. 12.

47 *Public Morals* (1961), p. 12.

48 *Spectator*, no. 6896, p. 307, Aug. 26, 1960.

49 Allsop, *Spectator*, Aug. 12, 1960, pp. 240–1.

50 *Ibid.* p. 236.

51 Cited, Binder, *The English Inside Out* (1961), p. 87.

52 *Public Morals* (1961), p. 13.

53 *Daily Mail*, Jan. 25, 1963, p. 3.

54 *Daily Mirror*, Jan. 17, 1963, p. 4.

55 *Daily Mail*, Jan. 25, 1963, p. 9.

LIST OF WORKS CONSULTED

This is not intended as a comprehensive bibliography. It lists those works to which reference is made in the text or notes, together with the more important of the other works consulted. Where a work is referred to in more than one Part, it will be found in this list under the heading of the first Part in which reference is made to it. Authors' names and titles of works are reproduced as they appear on the title-pages of the copies consulted.

INTRODUCTION (pp. 15–24)

CALVERTON, V. F. *Sex Expression in Literature.* New York, 1926.

CRAIG, ALEC. *Above All Liberties.* London, 1942.

CRAIG, ALEC. *The Banned Books of England and Other Countries. A Study of the Conception of Literary Obscenity.* London, 1962.

CRAIG, ALEC. *Sex and Revolution.* London, 1934.

CUNNINGTON, C. WILLETT. *Feminine Attitudes in the Nineteenth Century.* London, 1935.

CUNNINGTON, C. WILLETT. *Looking Over My Shoulder.* London, 1961.

[HAYNES, E. S. P.] *A Lawyer's Notebook.* London, 1932.

HAYNES, E. S. P. [and EDWARD CARPENTER and HAVELOCK ELLIS]. 'The Taboos of the British Museum Library.' *English Review,* vol. xvi, pp. 123–34. Dec. 1913.

HIMES, NORMAN E. *Medical History of Contraception.* London, 1936. Medical Aspects of Human Fertility ser.

TAYLOR, GORDON RATTRAY. *The Angel-Makers. A Study in the Psychological Origins of Historical Change 1750–1850.* London, 1958.

TAYLOR, G[ORDON] RATTRAY. *Sex in History.* London, 1953.

PART I

PLAIN WORDS, PRUDE WORDS, AND RUDE WORDS (pp. 27–85)

ASH, JOHN. *The New and Complete Dictionary of the English Language.* London, 1775. 2 vol.

Fraxi, Pisanus [pseud., *sc.* HENRY SPENCER ASHBEE]. *Catena Librorum Tacendorum: Being Notes Bio- Biblio- Icono- graphical and Critical, on Curious and Uncommon Books.* London, 1885.

[BACHE, RICHARD.] *Vulgarisms and Other Errors of Speech.* Philadelphia, 1868.

BAILEY, N[ATHANIEL]. *An Universal Etymological English Dictionary.* London, 1721.

BAILEY, N[ATHANIEL]. *Dictionarium Britannicum.* London, 1730.

Bannatyne, George (comp.). *The Bannatyne Manuscript.* Ed. Jas Barclay Murdoch. n.p. [Edinburgh], 1896 [1873–1901]. 4 vol.

BARTH, JOHN. *The Sot-Weed Factor.* London, 1961.

BARTLETT, JOHN RUSSELL. *Dictionary of Americanisms.* 2nd edn, Boston and London, 1859. 4th edn, Boston, 1877.

Glover, Arnold (ed.). *The Works of Francis Beaumont and John Fletcher.* Cambridge, 1905–12. 10 vol.

BEETON, Mrs. ISABELLA. *The Book of Household Management.* London, 1861.

[BEETON, SAMUEL ORCHART.] *Beeton's Manners of Polite Society.* London, n.d. [1876].

BERREY, LESTER V. and VAN DEN BARK, MELVIN. *The American Thesaurus of Slang.* London, n.d. [1943].

BLAU, ABRAM. 'A Philological Note on a Defect in Sex Organ Nomenclature.' *Psychoanalytic Quarterly,* vol. xii, no. 4, pp. 481–5. 1943.

BLOCH, IVAN. *A History of English Sexual Morals.* Trans. William H. Forstern. London, 1936. [Reprinted as:] *Sexual Life in England Past and Present.* London, 1938.

BLOOMFIELD, LEONARD. *Language.* London, 1935.

Brie, Friedrich W. D. (ed.). *The Brut or The Chronicles of England.* London, 1906–08. 2 pt. Early English Text Soc. Original ser., 131, 136.

BROOKS, JOHN GRAHAM. *As Others See Us.* New York, 1908.

Brophy, John and Partridge, Eric (ed.). *Songs and Slang of the British Soldier: 1914–1918.* 3rd edn, London, 1931.

Kenyon, F. G. (ed.). *The Works of Robert Browning.* London, 1912. 10 vol.

BUCKINGHAM, J. S. *The Slave States of America.* London and Paris, n.d. [1842]. 2 vol.

BURKE, W. J. *The Literature of Slang.* New York, 1939.

[BURNS, ROBERT, and others.] *The Merry Muses of Caledonia.* Ed. James Barke and Sydney Goodsir Smith. Edinburgh, 1959.

BURTON, RICHARD. *Why Do You Talk Like That?* Indianapolis, 1929.

[BUTLER, SAMUEL.] *Hudibras. The First Part.* London, 1663.

[CALLENDER, JAMES THOMSON.] *Deformities of Dr Samuel Johnson. Selected from his Works.* Edinburgh, 1782.

CALVERLEY, C. S. *The Complete Works.* London, 1901.

CARNOY, A. *La Science du mot. Traité de sémantique.* Louvain, 1927.

CHAMBERS, E. K. and SIDGWICK, F. *Early English Lyrics.* London, 1907.

CHARLES, EDWARD. *An Introduction to the Study of the Psychology, Physiology and Bio-Chemistry of the Sexual Impulse.* London, 1935.

CHARLTON, BARBARA. *The Recollections of a Northumbrian Lady. 1815–1866.* Ed. L. E. O. Charlton. London, 1949.

Robinson, F. N. (ed.). *The Works of Geoffrey Chaucer.* 2nd edn, London, 1957.

[CLELAND, JOHN.] *Memoirs of a Woman of Pleasure.* London, 1749. 2 vol.

Clitorides, Philogynes [pseud.]. *The Natural History of the Frutex Vulvaria or Flowering Shrub.* London, 1741.

Coleridge, Ernest Hartley (ed.). *Christabel.* London, 1907.

COLERIDGE, S[AMUEL] T[AYLOR]. *Christabel: Kubla Khan, a Vision: The Pains of Sleep.* London, 1816.

[Allsop, Thomas (ed.).] *Letters Conversations and Recollections of S. T. Coleridge.* London, 1836. 2 vol.

COLES, E[LISHA]. *An English Dictionary.* London, 1676.

CONGREVE [WILLIAM]. *Love for Love: A Comedy.* London, 1695.

Cotgrave, Randle (comp.). *A Dictionarie of the French and English Tongues.* London, 1611.

The Collected Plays of Noël Coward. Play Parade. vol. iv. London, 1954.

Craigie, Sir William, and others (ed.). *A Dictionary of American English on Historical Principles.* Chicago, 1936–44. 4 vol.

Cranstoun, James (ed.). *Satirical Poems of the Time of the Reformation.* Edinburgh, 1891–93. 2 vol. Scottish Text Soc.

CUNNINGTON, C. WILLETT and PHILLIS. *Handbook of English Costume in the Eighteenth Century.* London, 1957.

CUNNINGTON, C. WILLETT and PHILLIS. *The History of Underclothes.* London, 1951.

DANA, R. H., Jun. *Two Years Before the Mast.* 2nd edn, London, 1841.

DAVENPORT, JOHN. *Aphrodisiacs and Anti-aphrodisiacs: Three Essays on the Powers of Reproduction.* London, 1869 [or rather, 1873].

DAVENPORT, JOHN. *Curiositates Eroticæ Physiologiæ; or, Tabooed Subjects Freely Treated.* London, 1875.

DE VERE, M. SCHELE. *Americanisms; the English of the New World.* New York, 1872.

DE VOTO, BERNARD. 'The Easy Chair.' *Harper's Magazine,* vol. cxcvii, no. 1183, pp. 98–101. Dec. 1948.

Dickins, Bruce, and Wilson, R. M. (ed.). *Early Middle English Texts.* Cambridge, 1952.

DINGWALL, ERIC JOHN. *The American Woman. A Historical Study.* London, 1956.

DRAKE, FRANCIS. *Eboracum: or The History and Antiquities of the City of York*. London, 1736.

Mackenzie, W. Mackay (ed.). *The Poems of William Dunbar*. Edinburgh, 1932.

EKWALL, EILERT. *Street-Names of the City of London*. Oxford, 1954.

ELIOT, THOMAS DAWES. 'A Limbo for Cruel Words.' *The Survey*, vol. xlviii, no. 10, pp. 389–91. Jun. 15, 1922.

ERICSON, ESTON EVERETT. 'Bullock Sterteþ, Bucke Verteþ.' *Modern Language Notes*, vol. liii, no. 2, pp. 112–13. Feb. 1938.

[Cotton, Charles?] Ερωτοπολις. *The Present State of Betty-land*. London, 1684.

Farmer, John S. (comp. and ed.). *Americanisms Old and New*. London, 1889.

Farmer, John S. (comp. and ed.). *National Ballad and Song. Merry Songs and Ballads Prior to the Year A.D. 1800*. n.p. [London], 1897. 5 vol.

Farmer, John S., and (for vol. iii–vii) Henley, W. E. (comp. and ed.). *Slang and its Analogues Past and Present*. n.p. [London], 1890–1904. 7 vol. Revised edn, n.p. [London], vol. i, 1903–09 [no more published].

FERRIER, SUSAN. *Memoir and Correspondence . . . 1782–1854*. Ed. John A. Doyle. London, 1898.

FINLEY, RUTH E. *The Lady of Godey's. Sarah Josepha Hale*. Philadelphia and London, 1931.

FISHBEIN, MORRIS. 'The Misuse of Medical Terms.' *American Speech*, vol. i, no. 1, pp. 23–5. Oct. 1925.

FLINT, JAMES. *Letters from America*. Edinburgh, 1822.

FLORIO, IOHN. *A Worlde of Wordes, or Most copious and exact dictionarie in Italian and English*. London, 1598.

FOWLER, H. W. *A Dictionary of Modern English Usage*. Oxford, 1954.

FRANKLYN, JULIAN. *A Dictionary of Rhyming Slang*. London, 1960.

The Fruit-shop, a Tale. London, 1765. 2 vol.

G., Hon. F. L. [*sc.* F. Levison Gower?]. *The Swell's Night Guide through the Metropolis*. London, n.d. [1841].

GELLING, MARGARET. *The Place-Names of Oxfordshire*. Cambridge, 1953–54. 2 pt. English Place-Name Soc., vol. xxiii, xxiv.

Gove, Philip Babcock, and others (ed.). *Webster's Third New International Dictionary of the English Language Unabridged*. London and Springfield, Mass., 1961.

GOVER, J. E. B., and others. *The Place-Names of Northamptonshire*. Cambridge, 1933. English Place-Name Soc., vol. x.

GRATTAN, THOMAS COLLEY. *Civilized America*. London, 1859. 2 vol.

GRAVES, ROBERT. *Lars Porsena or The Future of Swearing and Improper Language*. London and New York, n.d. [1927].

GRAVES, ROBERT. *The Future of Swearing and Improper Language*. London, 1936.

GRAVES, ROBERT. *Occupation: Writer.* London, 1951.

GREENOUGH, JAMES BRADSTREET, and KITTREDGE, GEORGE LYMAN. *Words and Their Ways in English Speech.* New York and London, 1901.

[GROSE, FRANCIS.] *A Classical Dictionary of the Vulgar Tongue.* London, 1785. 2nd edn, 1788. 3rd edn, 1796. 3rd edn, with a biographical and critical sketch and an extensive commentary by Eric Partridge, London, 1931.

[HALIBURTON, THOMAS CHANDLER.] *The Clockmaker; or The Sayings and Doings of Samuel Slick, of Slickville.* 2nd ser. London, 1838.

HALPERT, HERBERT, and others. 'Symposium on Obscenity in Folklore.' *Journal of American Folklore,* vol. lxxv, no. 297, pp. 189–265. Jul.–Sept. 1962.

Harris's List of Covent-Garden Ladies: or, Man of Pleasure's Kalender For the Year, 1788. London, n.d. [1788].

HAWTHORNE, NATHANIEL. *The American Notebooks.* Ed. Randall Stewart. 2nd printing, New Haven and London, 1933.

Rolph, C. H. [pseud., *sc.* CECIL ROLPH HEWITT] (ed.). *The Trial of Lady Chatterley.* Harmondsworth, 1961.

H[OWELL], J[AMES]. Παροιμιογραφια. *Proverbs, or Old Sayed Savves & Adages.* London, 1659.

The Autobiography of Leigh Hunt. London, 1850. 3 vol.

JESPERSEN, OTTO. 'Veiled Language.' *S.P.E. Tract No. XXXIII,* Oxford, 1929, pp. 420–30.

JOHNSON, FALK. 'The History of Some "Dirty" Words.' *American Mercury,* vol. lxxi, no. 323, pp. 538–45. Nov. 1950.

JOHNSON, SAMUEL. *A Dictionary of the English Language.* London, 1755. 2 vol.

JOFFE, NATALIE F. 'The Vernacular of Menstruation.' *Word* (Linguistic Circle of New York), vol. iv, no. 3, pp. 181–6. Dec. 1948.

[JONES, JOHN.] *Adrasta: or, The Womans Spleene, And Loves Conquest.* London, 1635.

Justinian [pseud.]. *Americana Sexualis.* Chicago, 1939.

KANNER, LEO. 'A Philological Note on Sex Organ Nomenclature.' *Psychoanalytic Quarterly,* vol. xiv, no. 2, pp. 228–33. 1945.

Forman, Maurice Buxton (ed.). *The Letters of John Keats.* Oxford, 1931. 2 vol.

KELLER, H. VON. 'Englisches erotisches und skatologisches Idiotikon.' *Anthropophyteia,* VII Bd., S. 36–9. 1910.

KEUN, ODETTE. *I Discover the English.* London, 1934.

[Kopernicky, Ignaz; Krauss, Friedrich S.; Paris, Gaston; and others (ed.).] Κρυπτάδια. *Recueil de documents pour servir à l'étude des traditions populaires.* Heilbronn, 1883–88 (vol. i–iv); Paris, 1898–1911 (vol. v–xi). 11 vol.

Koštiál, Dr. Hermann. 'Englisches erotisches und skatologisches Idiotikon.' *Anthropophyteia*, VI Bd., S. 19–23. 1909.

Kronhausen, Eberhard and Phyllis. *Pornography and the Law. The Psychology of Erotic Realism and Pornography.* 2nd printing, New York, 1960.

Krumpelmann, John T. 'Charles Sealsfield's Americanisms.' *American Speech*, vol. xvi, no. 2, pp. 104–11. Apr. 1941.

The Collected Poems of D. H. Lawrence. London, 1932.

Lawrence, D. H. *Lady Chatterley's Lover.* Harmondsworth, 1960.

Lawrence, D. H. *Pansies.* Limited edn, London, 1929.

Lessing, Doris. *The Golden Notebook.* London, 1962.

Lewis, C. S. 'Four-Letter Words.' *Critical Quarterly*, vol. iii, no. 2, pp. 118–22. Summer 1961.

Hamer, Douglas (ed.). *The Works of Sir David Lindsay of the Mount 1490–1555.* Edinburgh, 1931–36. 4 vol.

Little Merlin's Cave. As it was lately discover'd, by a Gentleman's Gardener, in Maidenhead-Thicket. 4th edn, London, 1737.

Longfellow, Henry Wadsworth. *Kavanagh, A Tale.* London, 1849.

Yelverton, Thérèse (Viscountess Avonmore) [*sc.* Maria Theresa Longworth]. *Teresina in America.* London, 1875.

Loth, David. *The Erotic in Literature.* London, 1962.

Lyall, Archibald. *The Future of Taboo in These Islands.* London, 1936.

McCullers, Carson. *Clock without Hands.* London, 1961.

MacDougald, Duncan, Jr. 'Language and Sex.' Albert Ellis and Albert Abarbanel (ed.), *The Encyclopædia of Sexual Behaviour*, London, 1961, vol. ii, pp. 585–98.

McKnight, George H. *English Words and their Background.* New York and London, 1923.

McMillan, James B. 'Lexical Evidence from Charles Sealsfield.' *American Speech*, vol. xviii, no. 2, pp. 117–27. Apr. 1943.

Manchon, J. *Le Slang. Lexique de l'anglais familier et vulgaire.* Paris, 1923.

[Manning, Frederic.] *Her Privates We* by Private 19022. London, 1930.

[Manning, Frederic.] *The Middle Parts of Fortune. Somme and Ancre, 1916.* n.p. [London], 1929. 2 vol.

[Marchant, John and Gordon, ——.] *A New Complete English Dictionary.* London, 1760.

Marcy, Randolph B. *The Prairie Traveler.* Ed. Richard F. Burton. London, 1863.

Marryat, Capt. [Frederick]. *A Diary in America.* [pt i.] London, 1839. 3 vol.

[Marryat, Frederick.] *Jacob Faithful.* London, 1834. 3 vol.

[Marryat, Frederick.] *Peter Simple.* London, 1834.

MASEFIELD, JOHN. *The Everlasting Mercy*. London, 1911.

MATTHEWS, [JAMES] BRANDER. *Parts of Speech*. New York, 1916.

A Member of the Whip Club. Assisted by Hell-Fire Dick, etc. *Lexicon Balatronicum. A Dictionary of Buckish Slang, University Wit, and Pickpocket Eloquence*. London, 1811.

MENCKEN, H. L. *The American Language*. 2nd edn, London, 1922. 4th edn, 1936. Supp. I, New York, 1945.

MENCKEN, H. L. *A Book of Burlesques*. London, 1923.

MEREDITH, GEORGE. *The Ordeal of Richard Feverel*. London, 1859. 3 vol.

MEREDITH, MAMIE. 'Inexpressibles, Unmentionables, Unwhisperables, and Other Verbal Delicacies of Mid-Nineteenth Century Americans.' *American Speech*, vol. v, no. 4, pp. 285–7. Apr. 1930.

[Perry, James?] *Mimosa: or, The Sensitive Plant; A Poem*. London, 1779.

MINSHEU, IOHN. Ἡγεμὼν εἰς τὰς Γλωσσας. *id est, Ductor in Linguas, The Guide Into Tongues*. London, 1617.

Travels of Carl Philipp Moritz in England in 1782. London, 1924.

MURDOCH, IRIS. *An Unofficial Rose*. London, 1962.

Murray, James A. H., and others (ed.). *The Oxford English Dictionary*. Oxford, 1933. 13 vol.

PALSGRAVE, JEAN. *L'Éclaircissement de la langue française*. Ed. F. Genin. Paris, 1852.

PARTRIDGE, ERIC. *A Dictionary of Slang and Unconventional English*. 5th edn, London, 1961. 2 vol.

PARTRIDGE, ERIC. *Origins. A Short Etymological Dictionary of Modern English*. 3rd edn, London, 1961.

PARTRIDGE, ERIC. *Shakespeare's Bawdy*. London, 1947.

PARTRIDGE, ERIC. *Slang To-day and Yesterday*. 3rd edn, London, 1950.

PARTRIDGE, ERIC. *Words, Words, Words!* London, 1933.

Strong, Adam [pseud., sc. JAMES PERRY]. *The Electrical Eel; or, Gymnotus Electricus: and, The Torpedo; A Poem*. n.p., n.d. [1774?].

[PINKERTON, JOHN.] *Ancient Scotish Poems, never before in print*. London and Edinburgh, 1786. 2 vol.

[POTTER, WILLIAM S., and others.] *The Romance of Lust; or, Early Experiences*. London, 1873–76. 4 vol.

PUDNEY, JOHN. *The Smallest Room*. London, 1954.

PYLES, THOMAS. 'Innocuous Linguistic Indecorum: a Semantic Byway.' *Modern Language Notes*, vol. lxiv, no. 1, pp. 1–8. Jan. 1949.

RANDOLPH, VANCE. 'Verbal Modesty in the Ozarks.' *Dialect Notes*, vol. vi, pt i, pp. 57–64. 1928.

RATTRAY, R. F. 'On Lips of Living Men.' *Quarterly Review*, vol. ccxcix, no. 627, pp. 13–22. Jan. 1961.

READ, ALLEN WALKER. 'Noah Webster as a Euphemist.' *Dialect Notes*, vol. vi, pt viii, pp. 385–91. 1934.

READ, ALLEN WALKER. 'An Obscenity Symbol.' *American Speech*, vol. ix, no. 4, pp. 264–78. Dec. 1934.

REANEY, P. H. *The Place-Names of Essex*. Cambridge, 1935. English Place-Name Soc., vol. xii.

Registration and Licensing Authorities in Great Britain, Northern Ireland and the Republic of Ireland. Index Marks and Addresses. London, 1961.

Bernard, Oliver (ed.). *Rimbaud*. Harmondsworth, 1962.

Thorpe, James (ed.). *Rochester's Poems on Several Occasions*. Princeton, 1950. Princeton Studies in English, no. 30.

Ross, ALAN S. C. 'Linguistic Class-Indicators in Present-Day English.' *Neuphilologische Mitteilungen*, LV. Jahrgang, nr. 1–2, 20–56. 1954.

ROWE, H. D. 'New England Terms for "Bull": Some Aspects of Barnyard Bowdlerism.' *American Speech*, vol. xxxii, no. 2, pp. 110–16. May 1957.

Cook, E. T., and Wedderburn, Alexander (ed.). *The Works of John Ruskin*. London, 1903–12. 39 vol.

SADLEIR, MICHAEL. *Trollope. A Commentary*. London, 1927.

SAGARIN, EDWARD. *The Anatomy of Dirty Words*. New York, 1962.

Scott, Alexander (ed.). *The Poems of Alexander Scott*. n.p. [Edinburgh], 1952.

SEMPER, I. J. 'The King's English.' *English Journal* (college edn), vol. xviii, no. 4, pp. 307–12. Apr. 1929.

The Sempill Ballates. A Series of . . . Poems Ascribed to Robert Sempill. Edinburgh, 1872.

SHAKESPEARE, WILLIAM. *The Tragedy of Hamlet*. Ed. Edward Dowden. 8th edn, London, 1938.

SHAKESPEARE, WILLIAM. *The Second Part of King Henry the Fourth*. Ed. R. P. Cowl. London, 1923.

SHAKESPEARE, WILLIAM. *King Henry V*. Ed. J. H. Walter. London, 1960.

SHAKESPEARE, WILLIAM. *The Tragedy of King Lear*. Ed. Kenneth Muir. 8th edn, London, 1952.

SHAKESPEARE, WILLIAM. *The Merry Wives of Windsor*. Ed. H. C. Hart. 2nd edn, London, 1932.

SHAKESPEARE, WILLIAM. *The Tragedy of Romeo and Juliet*. Ed. Edward Dowden. 3rd edn, London, 1927.

SHAKESPEARE, WILLIAM. *Twelfth Night or What You Will*. Ed. Morton Luce. 4th edn, London, 1929.

SHOEMAKER, ERVIN C. *Noah Webster. Pioneer of Learning*. New York, 1936.

SKINNER, STEPHEN. *Etymologicon Linguæ Anglicanæ*. [Ed. Thomas Henshaw.] London, 1671.

[Cary, Henry N. ?] *The Slang of Venery and its Analogues*. Chicago, 1916. 3 vol. [vol. iii being entitled *Synonyms of the Slang of Venery*].

SMITH, A. H. *The Place-Names of the East Riding of Yorkshire and York.* Cambridge, 1937. English Place-Name Soc., vol. xiv.

SPIES, HEINRICH. *Kultur and Sprache im neuen England.* 2nd edn, Leipzig, Berlin, 1928.

STEADMAN, J. M., Jr. 'A Study of Verbal Taboos.' *American Speech,* vol. x, no. 2, pp. 93–103. Apr. 1935.

STEADMAN, J. M., Jr. 'Language Taboos of American College Students.' *English Studies* (Amsterdam), vol. xvii, no. 2, pp. 81–91. Apr. 1935.

STONE, LEO. 'On the Principal Obscene Word of the English Language (An Inquiry, with Hypothesis, Regarding its Origin and Persistence).' *International Journal of Psycho-Analysis,* vol. xxxv, pt 1, pp. 30–56. 1954.

[STRETSER, THOMAS.] *The Natural History of the Arbor Vitæ, or, Tree of Life.* London, 1732.

Pheuquewell, Roger [pseud., *sc.* THOMAS STRETSER.] *A New Description of Merryland.* 7th edn, Bath [or rather, London], 1741.

A Studious Enquirer into the Mysteries of Nature. *Wisdom Revealed; or, The Tree of Life Discover'd and Describ'd. . . . To which is added, The Crab-Tree: or, Sylvia Discover'd.* London, n.d. [1750?].

Partridge, Eric (ed.). *Swift's Polite Conversation.* London, 1963.

Scott, Temple (ed.). *The Prose Works of Jonathan Swift, D.D.* London, 1897–1908. 12 vol.

TACEY, WILLIAM S. 'Euphemisms for "Bull".' *American Speech,* vol. xxxiv, no. 2, pp. 146–7. May 1959.

THORNTON, RICHARD H. *An American Glossary.* London, 1912. 2 vol.

TILLEY, MORRIS PALMER. *A Dictionary of the Proverbs in England in the Sixteenth and Seventeenth Centuries.* Ann Arbor, Mich., 1950.

TILLEY, MORRIS P. 'Some Evidence in Shakespeare of Contemporary Efforts to Refine the Language of the Day.' *Publications of the Modern Language Association of America,* vol. xxxi (n.s., vol. xxiv), no. 1, pp. 65–78. 1916.

Touchit, Timothy [pseud.]. *La Souricière. The Mouse-trap.* London, 1794. 2 vol.

TROLLOPE, Mrs. [FRANCES]. *Domestic Manners of the Americans.* 2nd edn, London, 1832. 2 vol.

'Uncle Sam's Peculiarities. American Boarding-Houses.' *Bentley's Miscellany,* vol. iv, pp. 581–90. 1838.

Untermeyer, Louis (ed.). *The Albatross Book of Living Verse.* London, 1933.

VALDES, EDGAR. 'The Art of Swearing.' *Belgravia,* vol. lxxxviii, pp. 366–79. Dec. 1895.

Vanity of Vanities or Sir Harry Vane's Picture. London, n.d. [1659].

VENDRY's, J. *Le Langage. Introduction linguistique à l'histoire.* Paris, 1921. Trans. Paul Radin, *Language. A Linguistic Introduction to History.* London and New York, 1925.

Vié, Léonce. *L'Euphémisme.* Paris, 1905.

Wall, O. A. *Sex and Sex Worship (Phallic Worship).* London, 1919.

Ware, J. Redding. *Passing English of the Victorian Era.* London, n.d. [1909].

Webster, Noah. *The Holy Bible . . . with Amendments of the Language.* New Haven, 1833.

Webster, Noah. *Mistakes and Corrections.* New Haven, 1837.

Weekley, Ernest. *The Romance of Words.* 3rd edn, London, 1917.

Weekley, Ernest. *Words Ancient and Modern.* London, 1926.

Wentworth, Harold, and Flexner, Stuart Berg. *Dictionary of American Slang.* London, 1960.

White, Richard Grant. *Words and Their Uses, Past and Present.* New York, 1871.

Wilde, Oscar. *Salome . . . Pictured by Aubrey Beardsley.* London and Boston, Mass., 1894.

Wilson, Angus. *The Old Men at the Zoo.* London, 1961.

Wilson, Edmund. *Memoirs of Hecate County.* London, n.d. [1951].

Withington, Robert. 'Children of Linguistic Fashion.' *American Speech,* vol. ix, no. 4, pp. 255–9. Dec. 1934.

Withington, Robert. 'A Note on "Bloody".' *American Speech,* vol. vi, no. 1, pp. 29–35. Oct. 1930.

[Wolcot, John.] *The Works of Peter Pindar, Esq.* London, 1794–1801. 5 vol.

Wright, Thomas. *Anglo-Saxon and Old English Vocabularies.* Ed. and coll. Richard Paul Wülcker. London, 1884. 2 vol.

Wright, Thomas (ed.). *Political Ballads Published in England during the Commonwealth.* London, 1841. Early English Poetry, Ballads, and Popular Literature of the Middle Ages, vol. iii.

Wycherley, [William]. *The Country-Wife, A Comedy.* London, 1675.

Wycliffe, John, and his followers. *The Holy Bible.* Ed. the Rev. Josiah Forshall and Sir Frederic Madden. Oxford, 1850. 4 vol.

Wyld, Henry Cecil. *A History of Modern Colloquial English.* London, 1920.

PART II

THE GRUNDY SUNDAY (pp. 89–125)

Anglo-Phile Eutheo [pseud.]. *A second and third blast of retrait from plaies and Theaters.* London, 1580. [W. C. Hazlitt (ed.)], *The English Drama and*

Stage under the Tudor and Stuart Princes 1543–1664, n.p. [London], 1869, pp. 97–156.

ARCHENHOLTZ, W. DE. *A Picture of England.* London, 1797.

ARTHUR, WILLIAM. *'The People's Day'.* London, 1855.

Atkinson, J. C. (ed.). *Quarter Sessions Records.* London, 1888. North Riding Record Soc., vol. vi.

BAINES, EDWD. *On the Attempt to Change the Character of the Christian Sabbath.* London and Leeds, 1853.

BAINES, EDWARD. *Value of the Sabbath to the Working Classes.* Leeds, 1855.

BAKER, W. P. 'The Observance of Sunday.' Reginald Lennard (ed.), *Englishmen at Rest and Play,* Oxford, 1931, pp. 81–144.

Bates [afterwards Bates Harbin], E. H. (ed., vol. i-iii). *Quarter Sessions Records for the County of Somerset.* London, 1907–19. 4 vol.

BAXTER, —— [Richard ?]. *A Dreadful Warning to Lewd Livers.* London, n.d. [c. 1682].

Ayre, John (ed.). *The Catechism of Thomas Becon, S.T.P.* Cambridge, 1845.

[BOLTON, ROBERT.] *A Letter to a Lady, on Card-Playing on the Lord's Day.* London, 1748.

[BOLTON, ROBERT.] *A Letter to an Officer of the Army, on Travelling on Sundays.* London, 1757.

BOWNDE, NICOLAS. *The Doctrine of the Sabbath, Plainely layde forth.* London, 1595.

BOWND, NICOLAS. *Sabbathum Veteris et Novi Testamenti: Or The true doctrine of the Sabbath.* London, 1606.

Cowper, J. Meadows (ed.). *Henry Brinklow's Complaynt of Roderyck Mors.* London, 1874. Early English Text Soc. Extra ser., xxii.

Bruce, John (ed.). *Calendar of State Papers, Domestic Series, of the Reign of Charles I, 1634–1635.* London, 1864.

[BURTON, HENRY; attributed sometimes to William Prynne.] *A Divine Tragedie Lately Acted.* n.p. [London], 1636.

Diary of Thomas Burton, Esq. Member in the Parliaments of Oliver and Richard Cromwell. London, 1828. 4 vol.

Certain Sermons Appointed by the Queen's Majesty to be Declared and Read. Cambridge, 1850.

CHAMBERS, E. K. *The Elizabethan Stage.* Oxford, 1923. 4 vol.

CLIFFORD, ARTHUR BALDWIN. *The Sabbath Question Fully and Impartially Considered.* London, 1856.

COLLIER, J. PAYNE. *The History of English Dramatic Poetry to the Time of Shakespeare.* London, 1879. 3 vol.

COTTON, W., and WOOLLCOMBE, HENRY. *Gleanings from the Municipal and Cathedral Records relative to the History of the City of Exeter.* Exeter, 1877.

COULTON, G. G. *Medieval Panorama*. Cambridge, 1949.

COULTON, G. G. *The Medieval Village*. Cambridge, 1925.

COX, ROBERT. *The Literature of the Sabbath Question*. Edinburgh and London, 1865. 2 vol.

COX, ROBERT. *Sabbath Laws and Sabbath Duties*. Edinburgh and London, 1853.

Jenkyns, Henry (ed.). *The Remains of Thomas Cranmer, D.D.* Oxford, 1833. 4 vol.

Cowper, J. M. (ed.). *The Select Works of Robert Crowley*. London, 1872. Early English Text Soc. Extra ser., xv.

DE COETLOGON, C. *The Nature, Necessity, and Advantage of the Religious Observation of the Lord's Day*. London, 1776.

D'EWES, Sir SIMONDS. *The Journals of all the Parliaments During the Reign of Queen Elizabeth*. London, 1682.

DISNEY, JOHN. *An Essay upon the Execution of the Laws against Immorality and Prophaneness*. 2nd edn, London, 1710.

DISNEY, JOHN. *A Second Essay upon the Execution of the Laws against Immorality and Prophaneness*. London, 1710.

Divine Examples of God's Severe Judgment upon Sabbath-Breakers, in their unlavvful Sports. London, 1672.

DOMVILLE, WM. *The Sunday Band at Eastbourne*. London, 1856.

De Beer, E. S. (ed.). *The Diary of John Evelyn*. Oxford, 1955. 6 vol.

FABYAN, ROBERT. *The New Chronicles of England and France*. Ed. Henry Ellis. London, 1811.

FAIRBROTHER, E. H. 'Sunday Observance in the Eighteenth Century.' *Notes and Queries*, 12th ser., vol. iii, p. 145. Feb. 24, 1917.

FIELD, IOHN. *A godly exhortation, by occasion of the late iudgement of God, shewed at Parris-garden*. London, 1583.

Firth, C. H., and Rait, R. S. (ed.). *Acts and Ordinances of the Interregnum, 1642–1660*. London, 1911. 3 vol.

Frere, Walter Howard (and, for vol. ii, W. M. Kennedy) (ed.). *Visitation Articles and Injunctions of the Period of the Reformation*. London, etc., 1910. 3 vol. Alcuin Club Collections, xiv–xvi.

FULLER, THOMAS. *The Church-History of Britain*. London, 1655.

Fyfe, J. G. (ed.). *Scottish Diaries and Memoirs 1746–1843*. Stirling, 1942.

GIBSON, EDMUND. *Codex Juris Ecclesiastici Anglicani*. London, 1713. 2 vol.

GOLDING, ARTHUR. *A discourse vpon the Earthquake that hapned through this Realme of Englande*. London, n.d. [1580]. Louis Thorn Golding, *An Elizabethan Puritan*, New York, 1937, pp. 184–98.

GOVETT, L. A. *The King's Book of Sports*. London, 1890.

Strachey, Lytton, and Fulford, Roger (ed.). *The Greville Memoirs 1814–1860*. London, 1938. 8 vol.

Hall, Hubert (ed.). 'Some Elizabethan Penances in the Diocese of Ely.' *Transactions of the Royal Historical Soc.*, 3rd ser., vol. i, pp. 263–77. 1907.

HAMERSLEY, RICHARD. *Advice to Sunday Barbers.* London, 1706.

HAMILTON, ELIZABETH. *Letters on the Elementary Principles of Education.* 2nd edn, Bath, 1801–02. 2 vol.

HANSFORD, F. E. *Champions of Sunday Observance.* London, 1951.

Hardy, William John (ed.). *Calendar of State Papers, Domestic Series, of the Reign of William and Mary. May 1690-October 1691.* London, 1898.

HARRIS, M. DORMER. 'Unpublished Documents relating to Town Life in Coventry.' *Transactions of the Royal Historical Soc.*, 4th ser., vol. iii, pp. 103–14. 1920.

HARRISON, FREDERIC. *Sundays and Festivals.* London, 1867.

The Heaven-Drivers. A Poem. London, 1701.

HESSEY, JAMES AUGUSTUS. *Sunday: its Origin, History, and Present Obligation.* 5th edn, London, etc., 1889.

HEYLYN, PET. *The History of the Sabbath.* London, 1636. 2 pt.

Ninth Report of the Royal Commission on Historical Manuscripts, pt i. London, 1883.

Historical Manuscripts Commission. *Report on Manuscripts in Various Collections*, vol. i. London, 1901.

HODGKINS, WILLIAM. *Sunday: Christian and Social Significance.* London, 1960.

HODGSON, ROBERT. *The Life of the Right Reverend Beilby Porteus, D.D. Works of Porteus*, London, 1811, vol. i.

Hockliffe, E. (ed.). *The Diary of the Rev. Ralph Josselin 1616–1683.* London, 1908. Camden 3rd ser., vol. xv.

Joy and Light. See under Society for Promoting the Due Observance of the Lord's-day.

KENNICOTT, BENJAMIN. *The Sabbath. A Sermon.* Oxford and London, 1781.

KETHE, WILLIAM. *A Sermon made at Blandford Forũ.* London, 1571.

KIRTLAND, CHARLES. *The Voice of Truth in relation to the Sabbath Controversy.* Canterbury, 1857.

LA COMBE [FRANÇOIS]. *Tableau de Londres et de ses environs.* London and Brussels, 1784.

The Lamentable Complaints of Nick Froth the Tapster, and Rulerost the Cooke. n.p. [London ?], 1641.

Furnivall, Frederick J. (ed.). *Robert Laneham's Letter.* London, 1890. New Shakspere Soc., ser. vi, no. 14.

LEY, JOHN. *Sunday a Sabbath.* London, 1641.

Lloyd, Charles (ed.). *Formularies of Faith Put Forth by Authority during the reign of Henry VIII.* Oxford, 1825.

London and the Londoners. A Letter Addressed to the Inhabitants of Llanfairmathafarneithaf. . . . London, 1856.

The Lord's Day. See under Society for Promoting the Due Observance of the Lord's-day.

The Lord's Day Magazine. See under Society for Promoting the Due Observance of the Lord's-day.

Lord's Day Observance Society. See Society for Promoting the Due Observance of the Lord's-day.

LOWTH, SIMON. *A Letter to Edw. Stillingfleet, D.D.* London, 1687.

M'CRIE, THOMAS. *Memoirs of Sir Andrew Agnew of Lochnaw, Bart.* London and Edinburgh, 1850.

Nichols, John Gough (ed.). *The Diary of Henry Machyn.* London, 1848.

MANNING, BERNARD LORD. *The People's Faith in the Time of Wyclif.* Cambridge, 1918.

MARKUN, LEO. *Mrs Grundy. A History of Four Centuries of Morals.* New York and London, 1930.

MARTIN, H[ERBERT] H[ENRY]. *The Happy Man.* London, n.d. [1921].

MARTIN, H[ERBERT] H[ENRY]. *Shall We Copy the Continental Sunday?* London, n.d. [1923].

Memorial to Her Majesty the Queen, against the Playing of Military Bands for Public Amusement. . . . London, 1856.

The vvorkes of Sir Thomas More Knyght. . . . London, 1557.

MORRISH, REGINALD. *To Whom Ye Yield.* London, 1959.

The National Sunday League. . . . London, n.d. [c. 1856].

NEALE, EDW.^D VANSITTART. *Feasts and Fasts.* London, 1845.

[NEWTE, THOMAS.] *A Tour in England and Scotland in 1785.* London, 1785.

NEWTON, JOHN. *Memoirs of the Life of the Late Rev. William Grimshaw, A.B.* London, 1799.

Occasional Paper. See under Society for Promoting the Due Observance of the Lord's-day.

OSBORN, WILLIAM. *Moral and Physical Evils of Sabbath Desecration Considered.* Brighton, 1875.

Our Year Book. See under Society for Promoting the Due Observance of the Lord's-day.

PARKINSON, HENRY W. *Two Addresses Delivered in the Public Hall, Baillie-Street, Rochdale.* Rochdale, 1857.

Peel, Albert (ed.). *The Seconde Parte of a Register. Being a Calendar of Manuscripts.* . . . Cambridge, 1915. 2 vol.

Wheatley, Henry B. (ed.). *The Diary of Samuel Pepys.* London and Cambridge, 1903–04. 10 vol.

The Petition and Articles, or Severall Charges exhibited in Parliament against John Pocklington. London, 1641.

Peyton, Sidney A. (ed.). *The Churchwardens' Presentments in the Oxfordshire*

Peculiars of Dorchester, Thame and Banbury. n.p. [Oxford], 1928. Oxfordshire Record Soc. ser., vol. x.

PICKARD, JAMES. *The Sabbath, its Origin, History, and Obligations.* 2nd edn, Leeds and London, n.d. [c. 1857].

POCKLINGTON, JOHN. *Sunday no Sabbath. A Sermon.* London, 1636.

The Works of the Right Reverend Beilby Porteus, D.D. London, 1811. 6 vol.

PORTUS, GARNET V. *Caritas Anglicana or, An Historical Inquiry into those Religious and Philanthropical Societies that Flourished in England between the Years 1678 and 1740.* London and Oxford, 1912.

The Post Office and the Sabbath Question. London, 1850.

PRENTICE, ARCHIBALD. *One Day's Rest in Seven the Right of the Working Classes.* n.p. [Manchester ?], 1855.

PRIEBSCH, ROBERT. *Letter from Heaven on the Observance of the Lord's Day.* Oxford, 1936.

Quarterly Publication. See under Society for Promoting the Due Observance of the Lord's-day.

Report from Select Committee on the Observance of the Sabbath Day: with the Minutes of Evidence, and Appendix. n.p. [London], 1832.

ROBERTS, H[UMFREY]. *An earnest Complaint of diuers vain, wicked and abused Exercises, practised on the Saboth day.* London, 1572. [Photostat edn, 1935.]

[ROGERS, THOMAS.] *The Faith, Doctrine, and religion, professed, & protected in the Realme of England. . . .* n.p. [Cambridge?], 1607.

Sabbath-keeping the Support of our Religion and Nation; or, The . . . Address of a Clergyman. . . . London, 1767.

A Scotchman. *Letter to Joseph Locke, Esq. M.P. for Honiton.* Glasgow, 1849.

Sermons in Glass: or, a Sunday Visit to the Crystal Palace Defended. London, 1854.

A Short Account of the Origin of the National Sunday League. London, 1856.

Societies for the Reformation of Manners

Proposals for a National Reformation of Manners, Humbly offered to the Consideration of our Magistrates and Clergy. London, 169¾.

An Account of the Societies for Reformation of Manners. London, 1699.

A Short Account of the Several Kinds of Societies, set up of late Years, for the Promoting of God's Worship, for the Reformation of Manners, and for the Propagation of Christian Knowledge. n.p. [London], n.d. [c. 1700].

An Account of the Progress of the Reformation of Manners. . . . 13th edn, London, 1705.

The Fourteenth Account of the Progress made in Suppressing Profaneness and Debauchery, by the Societies for Reformation of Manners. . . . London, 1709.

The Fifteenth Account of the Progress made . . . by the Societies for Reformation of Manners. London, 1710.

A Representation of the State of the Societies for Reformation of Manners. London, 1715.

The Two and Twentieth Account of the Progress made . . . by the Societies . . . George [Ash] Lord Bishop of Clogher, *A Sermon Preached to the Societies for Reformation of Manners,* London, 1717.

The Four and Twentieth Account. . . . John Leng, *A Sermon. . . .* London, 1719.

The Six and Twentieth Account. . . . n.p. [London], n.d. [1721].

The Seven and Twentieth Account. . . . William Butler, *A Sermon. . . . ,* London, 1722.

The Thirtieth Account. . . . Edward [Chandler] Lord Bishop of Coventry, *A Sermon. . . . , London,* 1724.

The One and Thirtieth Account. . . . John [Wynne] Lord Bishop of St. Asaph, *A Sermon. . . . ,* London, 1726.

The Six and Thirtieth Account. . . . Francis [Hare] Lord Bishop of St. Asaph, *A Sermon. . . . ,* London, 1731, pp. 55–62.

The Eight and Thirtieth Account. . . . James Knight, *A Sermon. . . . ,* London, 1733, pp. 35–40.

The Fortieth Account. . . . Robert Drew, *A Sermon. . . . ,* London, 1735, pp. 21–8.

The Forty-first Account. . . . Edward Cobden, *A Sermon. . . . ,* London, 1736, pp. 25–32.

The Forty-third Account. . . . William Simpson, *A Sermon. . . . ,* London, 1738, pp. 25–31.

The Forty-fourth Account. . . . Samuel Smith, *A Sermon. . . . ,* London, 1738, pp. 23–8.

A Sermon Preached before the Former Societies for Reformation of Manners . . . Whereunto is subjoined, A Declaration from the Present Society. London, 1760.

Report of the Committee of the Society for Carrying into Effect His Majesty's Proclamation against Vice and Immorality, for the Year 1799. London, n.d. [1800].

Society for Promoting the Due Observance of the
Lord's-day (afterwards Lord's Day Observance Society)

Abraham Duquesne. A Paper for Young People. n.p. [London], n.d. [1905].

The Third (–Ninety Fourth) Annual Report of the Society for Promoting the Due Observance of the Lord's-day. London, 1834(–1925). [Continued as:]

Our Year Book. Being the 95th (–120th) Annual Report of the Lord's Day

Observance Society. [1926](–1951). [Later issues included in *Joy and Light.*]

Society for Promoting the Due Observance of the Lord's-day. Quarterly Publication. no. 1–55, Oct. 1843–Jan. 1856 [i.e., 1857]. [Continued as:]

Occasional Paper of the Society for Promoting the Due Observance of the Lord's-day. no. 56–129, Jun. 1857–Dec. 1900. [Continued as:]

The Lord's Day. no. 1–100, Jan. 1902–Oct.-Dec. 1926. [Continued as:]

The Lord's Day Magazine. no. 101–202, Jan.-Mar. 1930–Jan.-Mar. 1952. [Continued as:]

Joy and Light. no. 203–   , Apr.-Jun. 1952–   . [In progress.]

To Cyclists. This Hill Is Dangerous. London, n.d. [1901].

Address of the Society for Promoting the Observance of the Christian Sabbath, conformably to the Divine Command and to the Laws of the Land. London, n.d. [1809].

[Bowles, John?] *An Address to the Public, from the Society for the Suppression of Vice, Instituted in London, 1802, Part the Second.* London, 1803.

Some Account of the Lord's Day Conference Meeting Held at the Athenæum Room, Derby, on the 27th and 28th of November, 1860. Derby, 1861.

STONHOUSE, JAMES. *Admonitions against Swearing, Sabbath-Breaking, and Drunkenness.* London, 1800.

STRICKLAND, AGNES. *Lives of the Queens of England,* vol. xi. London, 1847.

Strong, S. A. (comp.). *A Catalogue of Letters and Other Historical Documents Exhibited in the Library at Welbeck.* London, 1903.

STRUTT, JOSEPH. *Glig-Gamena Angel-Ðeod. Or, The Sports and Pastimes of the People of England.* London, 1801.

STRYPE, JOHN. *Annals of the Reformation and Establishment of Religion.* Oxford, 1824. 4 vol.

Furnivall, Frederick J. (ed.). *Phillip Stubbes's Anatomy of the Abuses in England in Shakspere's Youth, A.D. 1583.* London, 1877–82. 2 pt. New Shakspere Soc., ser. vi, no. 4, 6, 12.

TAINE, H[IPPOLYTE]. *Notes sur l'Angleterre.* Paris, 1872.

TAIT, JAMES. 'The Declaration of Sports for Lancashire (1617).' *English Historical Review,* vol. xxxii, no. 128, pp. 561–8. Oct. 1917.

[TAYLOR, JEREMY.] *The Rule and Exercises of Holy Living.* London, 1650.

TAYLOR, JOHN. *A Short Relation of a Long Iourney Made Round or Ovall.* n.p. [London], n.d. [1653].

THURSTON, HERBERT. 'The Medieval Sunday.' *Nineteenth Century,* vol. xlvi, no. 269, pp. 36–50. Jul. 1899.

[TODD, JOHN.] *Todd's Lectures to Children,* 1st and 2nd ser. London, n.d. [1860].

Russell, Thomas (ed.). *The Works of the English Reformers: William Tyndale and John Frith.* London, 1831. 3 vol.

Voltaire [*sc.* FRANÇOIS MARIE AROUET]. *Lettres philosophiques* [1734]. *Œuvres complètes de Voltaire*, [vol. xxii,] Mélanges, ii, Paris, 1879, pp. 75–187.

WEBB, SIDNEY and BEATRICE. *The History of Liquor Licensing in England Principally from 1700 to 1830.* London, etc, 1903.

WEBSTER, W. *Two Sermons upon the Sabbath.* London, 1751.

WELLS, JOHN. *The Practical Sabbatarian.* London, 1668.

WENDEBORN, FRED. AUG. *A View of England towards the Close of the Eighteenth Century.* Trans. by the author. London, 1791. 2 vol.

WHITAKER, W. B. *The Eighteenth-Century English Sunday.* London, 1940.

WHITAKER, W. B. *Sunday in Tudor and Stuart Times.* London, 1933.

W[HITE], T[HOMAS]. *A Sermon Preached at Pawles Crosse.* London, 1578.

WILBERFORCE, ROBERT ISAAC and SAMUEL. *The Life of William Wilberforce.* London, 1838. 5 vol.

WILBERFORCE, WILLIAM. *A Practical View of the Prevailing Religious System of Professed Christians.* London, 1797.

WILKINS, DAVID. *Concilia Magnae Britanniae et Hiberniae.* . . . London, 1737. 4 vol.

W[ILLISON], J[OHN]. *A Treatise concerning the Sanctification of the Lord's Day.* 3rd edn, Edinburgh, 1745.

Beresford, John (ed.). *The Diary of a Country Parson: the Rev. James Woodforde, 1785–1802.* London, 1924–31. 5 vol.

WOODWARD, JOSIAH. *An Account of the Rise and Progress of the Religious Societies in the City of London, &c.* 2nd edn, London, 1698.

A short View of the Religious Societies in and about London. Being an Abridgement of the larger Account of them, given by Josiah Woodward, D.D. London, 1703.

YOUNG, SIDNEY. *The Annals of the Barber-Surgeons of London.* London, 1890.

PART III

THE TEETOTALITARIANS (pp. 129–63)

ACKROYD, WILLIAM. *The History and the Science of Drunkenness.* London and Manchester, 1883.

AGG-GARDNER, Sir JAMES. *Some Parliamentary Recollections.* London, n.d. [1927].

Alcohol versus *Teetotalism.* London, 1863.

Ancient Order of Froth Blowers. *A.O.F.B.* n.p. [London], n.d. [1925]. Revised edn, n.p. [London], n.d. [1928].

ASTOR, [NANCY,] Viscountess. *A Problem for Women.* London, n.d. [1920].

ATKIN, FREDERIC. *The Philosophy of the Temperance Reformation.* London and Bolton, n.d. [1874].

ATKIN, FRED. *Reminiscences of a Temperance Advocate.* London, 1899.

ATKIN, F. *Temperance Shots at Random: or, Incidents in the Life of Mr. Christopher Hodgson.* Manchester, 1887.

BAKER, J. JOHNSON. *The Historical Syllabus: being Elementary Lessons on the Temperance Movement in Church and Nation.* London, n.d. [1900].

BALFOUR, Mrs. C[LARA] L[UCAS]. *The Victim; or, An Evening's Amusement at the 'Vulture Tavern'.* London, 1860.

Band of Hope and Children's Circle Message. See under Lancashire and Cheshire Band of Hope [and Temperance] Union.

BATEMAN, CHAS W. *Tippling and Temperance.* London, 1890.

BATES, FRANK. *Lights and Landmarks of the Temperance Movement in Northamptonshire.* Northampton, 1898.

Beardsall, Rev. F. (comp.). *New Selection of Hymns and Songs Suitable for Public and Social Temperance Meetings.* Manchester, n.d. [1836?].

BLACKWELL, ERNEST. *Booth of the Blue Ribbon Movement.* London, 1883.

Blasius Multibibus, aliàs Drinkmuch [pseud., *sc.* RICHARD BRATHWAIT]. *A Solemne Ioviall Disputation, Theoreticke and Practicke; briefely Shadowing The Law of Drinking.* OENOZ*Y*THOPOLIS [*sc.* London], At the Signe of Red-eyes, 1617.

BROMLEY, JAMES. *Observations on Totalism.* 2nd edn, Sheffield, 1841.

BROTHERTON, JOSEPH. *The First Teetotal Tract. On Abstinence from Intoxicating Liquor. First published in 1821.* Manchester and London, 1890.

[BROWNE,] PETER. *A Discourse of Drinking Healths.* Dublin, 1716.

[BROWNE, PETER.] *On Drinking to the Memory of the Dead.* Dublin, 1713.

BROWNE, PET. *A Second Part of Drinking in Remembrance of the Dead.* Dublin, 1714.

BURNS, [JAMES] DAWSON. *The Juvenile Temperance Catechism.* London, n.d. [1873].

BURNS, [JAMES] DAWSON. *Temperance Ballads, with Other Metrical Compositions, for Recitation by Young Teetotalers.* London, etc., n.d. [1884].

BURNS, [JAMES] DAWSON. *Temperance History. A Consecutive Narrative of the Rise, Development, and Extension of the Temperance Reform.* London, n.d. [1889–91]. 2 vol.

BURNS, [JAMES] DAWSON. *Temperance in the Victorian Age: Sixty Years of Temperance Toil and Triumph.* London, 1897.

BURROUGHS, JOSEPH B. *A Medical Substitute for Alcohol in Cases of Emergency.* London, n.d. [1890].

BURTON, C. *Drunkards, Moderate Drinkers, Teetotalers.* London and Birmingham, 1902.

BURY, EDWARD. *England's Bane, or The Deadly Danger of Drunkenness.* London, 1677.

CARTER, HENRY. *The English Temperance Movement: A Study in Objectives.* vol. i: The Formative Period 1830–1899. London, 1933 [no more published].

The Case against the United Kingdom Alliance and the Permissive Bill. Manchester and London, 1872.

CATLIN, GEORGE E. G. *Liquor Control.* London, 1931.

Church of England Temperance Society. *Enforcement Committees.* London, n.d. [1900].

Church of England Temperance Society. *Enforcement of the Licensing Laws. Instructions to Agents.* London, n.d. [1900].

A Complete Catalogue of Temperance Literature. London, n.d. [1887].

A Correct Outline of the Public Discussion between Mr. Thomas Furneaux Jordan . . . and Frederic Richard Lees. 2nd edn, Leeds, 1839.

COULING, SAMUEL. *History of the Temperance Movement in Great Britain and Ireland.* London, 1862.

CRICHTON-BROWNE, Sir JAMES, and others. *Liberty.* London, 1917.

CROSLAND, T. W. H. *The Beautiful Teetotaller.* London, 1907.

DANIELL, MORTLOCK. *Via Media between Teetotalism and Drunkenness.* London, n.d. [1840?].

[DARBY, CHARLES.] *Bacchanalia: or A Description of a Drunken Club.* London, 1680.

DARK, SIDNEY. *The Passing of the Puritan.* London, etc., n.d. [1946].

DEARDEN, JOSEPH. *A Brief History of Ancient and Modern Tee-totalism.* Preston, n.d. [1840].

Democritus [pseud., *sc.* Henry Glasford Potter?]. *Democritus' Reply to the Teetotal Pamphleteers.* Newcastle-upon-Tyne, 1840.

Democritus [pseud., *sc.* Henry Glasford Potter?]. *A Medical, Moral, and Christian Dissection of Teetotalism.* 11th edn, London, etc., 1846.

DOVVNAME, IOHN. *Foure Treatises, Tending to Disswade All Christians from foure no lesse hainous then common sinnes.* London, 1613.

DRAPER, J. P. *Jubilee Sketch of the Fitzroy Teetotal Association, London, W.* London, 1889.

DUNLOP, JOHN. *The Philosophy of Artificial and Compulsory Drinking Usages in Great Britain and Ireland.* London, 1839.

Edmunds, Mrs. E. L. (ed.). *The Life and Memorials of the Late Rev. W. R. Baker.* London, 1865.

ENGELS, FREDERICK. *The Condition of the Working-Class in England in 1844.* Trans. Florence Kelley Wischnewetzky. London, 1936.

EVANS, T. H. *The Picture Gallery of Bacchus; or, Temperance Readings on Public House Signs.* London, n.d. [1883].

FARQUHARSON, ROBERT. *The Case for Moderate Drinking.* Edinburgh and London, 1892.

Final Words in Gough versus Lees. Leeds, 1860.

FIRTH, R. *An Essay on Sacramental Wine.* London, etc., 1841.

Freedom Association. *Handbook for Speakers and Writers on the [(]so-called[)] Temperance Question.* 5th edn, London, 1920. 8th edn, London, 1929.

FREMAN, GEORGE. *A Dehortation from all Sinne, but Particularly the Sinne of Drinking.* London, 1663.

FRENCH, RICHARD VALPY. *The History of Toasting, or Drinking of Healths in England.* London, n.d. [1882].

GOURLAY, WILLIAM. *'National Temperance'. A Jubilee Biograph of the National Temperance League.* London, 1906.

GOURLAY, WILLIAM. *Oinosville: An Unconventional Novel.* London, 1902.

GRINDROD, RALPH BARNES. *Bacchus: An Essay on the Nature, Causes, Effects, and Cure of Intemperance.* 2nd edn, London, 1848.

GUSTAFSON, AXEL. *The Foundation of Death. A Study of the Drink-Question.* London, 1884.

H., C. P. *Teetotalism Examined and Exposed.* London, 1872.

H., G. B. *Teetotalism Unmasked: Being a Tract for the Times.* London, 1845.

HALL, THO. *Funebria Floræ, the Downfall of May-Games.* London, 1660.

H[AMILTON], T[HOMAS] W[ELSH]. *The Temperance Reformation in Scotland.* Greenock, 1929.

HAYLER, GUY. *Towards World Sobriety.* London, 1937.

HAYLER, MARK H. C. *The Vision of a Century 1853–1953. The United Kingdom Alliance in Historical Retrospect.* London, 1953.

HAYNES, MATTHEW P. *An Interesting Account of the Extraordinary Grand Tee-total Gala.* London, n.d. [1840].

H[EYWOOD], T[HOMAS]. *Philocothonista, or, The Drunkard, Opened, Dissected, and Anatomized.* London, 1635.

HICKMAN, C. D., and DARBYSHIRE, W. *The Trial of John & Jane Temperance.* Manchester, n.d. [1882].

HICKS, GEORGE W. *The Temperance Pioneers.* Lydney, Glos., n.d. [1957].

HILTON, J. DEANE. *A Brief Memoir of James Hayes Raper Temperance Reformer, 1820–1897.* London, 1898.

History and Work of the Church of England Temperance Society. London, n.d. [1895].

HOPKINS, J. W. *The Rise and Progress of the Temperance Movement.* Birmingham, n.d. [1905].

HUDSON, THOMAS. *Temperance Pioneers of the West. Personal and Incidental Experiences.* London, 1887.

HYSLOP, Sir R. MURRAY. *The Centenary of the Temperance Movement 1832–1932.* London, 1931.

The Illustrated Temperance Reciter, vol. i. London, n.d. [1894].

INWARD, JABEZ. *Pictures of the Traffic; Consisting of Remarks on Public House Signs*. London, n.d. [1881].

The Ipswich Series of Temperance Tracts, vol. i. London and Ipswich, n.d. [c. 1853].

JAKEMAN, JOHN J. *Some Fallacies about Alcohol. A Little Book for Boys and Girls*. n.p. [Birkenhead], n.d. [1908].

Joint Committee on the Employment of Barmaids. *The Barmaid Problem*. London, n.d. [1904].

Joint Committee on the Employment of Barmaids. *Women as Barmaids*. London, 1905.

J[ORDAN], T. F. *Tee-totalism Weighed in the Balances and Found Wanting*. Leeds, 1837.

Junius, R. [pseud., *sc.* Richard Younge?]. *The Drunkard's Character*. London, 1638.

KEMPSTER, JOHN. *The Dean and the Drink*. London, n.d. [1892].

KERR, NORMAN. *Stimulants in Workhouses*. London, n.d. [1882].

KILLEN, W. D. *Memoir of John Edgar, D.D., Ll. D*. Belfast, etc., 1867.

KIMBALL, ARTHUR REED. *The Blue Ribbon*. London, 1894.

Lancashire and Cheshire Band of Hope [and Temperance] Union. *Uncle David's Message*, Mar. 1, 1946. [Continued as:]

Band of Hope and Children's Circle Message. no. 2–   , May 1, 1946–   . [In progress.]

LEES, F. R. *The Text-Book of Temperance in relation to Morals, Science, Criticism, and History*. London and York, 1871.

LEVY, HERMANN. *Drink. An Economic and Social Study*. London, 1951.

[LEWES, G. H.] 'The Physiological Errors of Teetotalism.' *Westminster Review*, n.s., vol. viii, no. 15, pp. 94–124. Jul. 1855.

The Life and Teachings of Joseph Livesey Comprising his Autobiography with an Introductory Review of his Labours as Reformer and Teacher. London, etc., n.d. [1886].

LIVESEY, J. *Reminiscences of Early Teetotalism*. Preston and London, n.d. [1868].

LIVESEY, JOSEPH. *The Staunch Teetotaler*. London, etc., no. 1–24. 1867–68.

London Alliance Review. no. 1–14. Apr. 1899–Apr.-Jun. 1902.

LUCAS, D. V. *Wine Bad and Good*. London, 1894.

LUKE, W. B. *Sir Wilfrid Lawson*. London, 1900.

McCANN, J. E. *The Birth and Progress of the Temperance Movement*. Newcastle-on-Tyne, n.d. [1932].

M'CREE, GEORGE WILSON. *Old Friends and New Faces*. London, 1883.

M'CREE, GEORGE WILSON. *Poets, Painters, and Players*. London, n.d. [1882].

The Life of James McCurrey (From 1801 to 1876). London, n.d. [1876].

McKENZIE, F. A. *'Pussyfoot' Johnson*. London, n.d. [1920].

MacNALTY, Sir ARTHUR S. *The Mirage of Alcohol*. n.p. [printed, Bedford], n.d. [1946].

MALINS, JOSEPH. *Wilson Stuart. A Memoir*. London, 1935.

MARTYN, CARLOS. *John B. Gough The Apostle of Cold Water*. New York, etc., 1893.

MEE, ARTHUR. *The Fiddlers. Drink in the Witness Box*. London, 1917.

MEE, ARTHUR. *The Parasite*. London, 1917.

MEE, ARTHUR, and HOLDEN, J. STUART. *Defeat or Victory? The Strength of Britain Book*. 2nd edn, London, 1917.

Moffat, Robert Scott (ed.). *'The Times' Drinking Bout*. London, n.d. [1892].

MOUNFIELD, ARTHUR. *The Beginnings of Total Abstinence. The Warrington Societies of 1830*. Warrington and London, n.d. [1903].

MUDGE, HENRY. *A Guide to the Treatment of Disease without Alcoholic Liquors*. London, 1863.

National Prohibition Party Bulletin. no. 30–38. Feb. 1929–Oct. 1929. [Continued as:]

The Prohibition Bulletin. no. 39–76. Nov. 1929–Dec. 1932. [Continued as:]

The Prohibitionist. no. 77–173. Jan. 1933–Jan.-Feb. 1949.

No Case against the United Kingdom Alliance and the Permissive Bill. Manchester and London, n.d. [1872].

Onward Reciter. 'For the Child.' Campaign No. XC, 1920. Manchester, 1920.

OVERTON, ROBERT. *Water-Works! Temperance Readings and Recitations*. London, 1896.

A Physician. *An Account of the Drunken Sea*. London, n.d. [1877].

The Politics of Temperance. The United Kingdom Alliance Monthly Papers. London and Manchester. no. 1–6. Jan.–Jun. 1859.

The Preston Temperance Advocate. no. 1–11. Jan.–Nov. 1837.

The Prohibition Bulletin. See *National Prohibition Party Bulletin*.

The Prohibitionist. See *National Prohibition Party Bulletin*.

PRYNNE, WILLIAM. *Healthes: Sicknesse*. London, 1628.

Rae, Robert (ed.). *The National Temperance League's Annual for 1882*. London, n.d. [1881].

REEVE, THOMAS. *God's Plea for Nineveh: or, London's Precedent for Mercy*. London, 1657.

REID, Rev. WILLIAM. *Temperance Memorials of the Late Robert Kettle, Esq.* Glasgow, etc., 1853.

Report from the Select Committee on Inquiry into Drunkenness, with Minutes of Evidence, and Appendix. London, 1834.

RIDGE, J. JAMES. *The Band of Hope Catechism*. London, n.d. [1894].

ROAF, WILLIAM. *The Pastor's Pledge of Total Abstinence*. 2nd edn, London, 1861.

ROWLEY, Rev. SAM. *Who Are the Frothblowers?* Bradford, n.d. [1927].

Russell, George W. E. (ed.). *Sir Wilfrid Lawson. A Memoir.* London, 1909.

Sabbaforry [pseud.]. *A Social Viper. Drunkenness.* London and Liverpool, 1869.

SAVILLE, JOHN. *Ernest Jones: Chartist.* London, 1952.

SHADWELL, ARTHUR. *Drink, Temperance and Legislation.* London, etc., 1902.

SHAW, J. G. *Life of William Gregson Temperance Advocate.* Blackburn, 1891.

SHERLOCK, FREDERICK. *Illustrious Abstainers.* London, 1879.

SMEETON, THOMAS. *Confessions of a Convert from Teetotalism to Temperance.* London, 1849.

SMITH, J. MILTON. *Nuts to Crack for Moderate Drinkers.* London, n.d. [1890].

STEPHENSON, JAMES; DEARDEN, JOSEPH; and TOULMIN, GEORGE. '*The Origin and Success of Teetotalism*', *being a Refutation of the Statements Made by Mr. James Teare.* Preston, 1864.

TAYLER, ROBERT. *Shawn in Peril.* London, n.d. [*c.* 1948]. Shawn of the Frozen North, no. 2.

Temperance Drinks for the Harvest and Home. Denbigh, n.d. [*c.* 1913].

TROTTER, THOMAS. *An Essay, Medical, Philosophical and Chemical, on Drunkenness, and its Effects on the Human Body.* 2nd edn, London, 1804.

Two Lady Nurses. *Hospital Nursing without Alcoholic Drinks.* London, n.d. [1882].

[*29th*](*-42nd*) *Annual Report (for 1890(-1930)) of the* [*Executive*] *Committee of the London Auxiliary of the United Kingdom Alliance.* London, 1891(-1904).

Twelfth (*-106th*) [*Annual*] *Report of the Executive Committee of the United Kingdom Alliance.* . . . Manchester [afterwards, London]. [1864](-1959).

United Kingdom Alliance, (Formed June 1st, 1853,) to Procure the Total and Immediate Legislative Suppression of the Traffic in All Intoxicating Liquors. Manchester, 1853.

The United Kingdom Alliance. A Full Report of the Speeches Delivered at the Annual Public Meeting . . . 1870. London, n.d. [1870].

URWIN, E. C. *Henry Carter, C.B.E. A Memoir.* London, 1955.

URWIN, E. C. *The Teaching of Temperance and Self-Control.* London, n.d. [1934].

WARD, GEORGE MATTHEW. *The Poisoning Conqueror, Alcohol.* London, n.d. [1883].

A Warning-piece to all Drunkards and Health-Drinkers. London, 1682.

Curnock, Nehemiah (ed.). *The Journal of the Rev. John Wesley, A.M.* London, n.d. [1909-16]. 8 vol.

What the United Kingdom Alliance Wants. Manchester, n.d. [*c.* 1900].

WHYTE, JAMES. *The United Kingdom Alliance Vindicated.* Manchester and London, n.d. [1902].

WINSKILL, P. T. *The Comprehensive History of the Rise and Progress of the Temperance Reformation from the Earliest Period to September, 1881.* Warrington, 1881.

WINSKILL, P. T. *The Temperance Movement and its Workers. A Record of Social, Moral, Religious, and Political Progress.* London, etc., 1892. 4 vol.

WINSLOW, FORBES E. *Come out from among them. An Expostulation with Christian Lovers of Alcoholic Drinks.* London, n.d. [1882].

WOOD, Mrs Henry [*sc.* ELLEN]. *Danesbury House.* Glasgow and London, 1860.

[YOUNG, A. S. W.] *The Blue Ribbon v. The Cross.* London, 1883.

YOVNG, THOMAS. *Englands Bane: or, The Description of Drunkennesse.* London, 1617.

PART IV

UNKINDLING A WANTONNESS (pp. 167–208)

ADBURGHAM, ALISON. *A* Punch *History of Manners and Modes 1841–1940.* London, 1961.

Amateur Swimming Association. *Handbook for 1899.* London, n.d. [1899].

A[VERELL], W[ILLIAM]. *A meruailous combat of contrarieties.* London, 1588.

BANSLEY, CHARLES. *A Treatyse Shewing and Declaring the Pryde and Abuse of Women now a dayes.* [*c.* 1550]. [Ed. J. P. Collier]. n.p. [London], n.d. [1841].

Barry, Gerald (ed.). *This England. The Englishman in Print.* London, 1933.

BARWICK, G. F. *The Reading Room of the British Museum.* London, 1929.

[BECON, THOMAS.] *The Jewel of Joye.* n.p. [London], n.d. [1553].

BINDER, PEARL. *Muffs and Morals.* London, etc., 1953.

Dickberry, F. [pseud., *sc.* F. BLAZE DE BURY]. *The Storm of London. A Social Rhapsody.* London, 1904.

O'Rell, Max [pseud., *sc.* LÉON PAUL BLOUET]. *John Bull's Womankind.* London, n.d. [1884].

[BOILEAU, JACQUES.] *A Just and Seasonable Reprehension of Naked Breasts and Shoulders. Written by a Grave and Learned Papist.* Trans. Edward Cooke. London, 1678.

BURNET, GILBERT. *Some Passages of the Life and Death of the Right Honourable John Earl of Rochester.* London, 1680.

BURNS, JOHN. *The Principles of Midwifery.* 3rd edn, London, 1814.

BURTON, JOHN. *An Essay towards a Complete New System of Midwifery, Theoretical and Practical.* London, 1751. 4 pt.

CHESTERTON, G. K. *All Is Grist. A Book of Essays*. London, 1931.

CLIMENSON, EMILY J. *Elizabeth Montagu, The Queen of the Blue-Stockings. Her Correspondence from 1720 to 1760*. London, 1906. 2 vol.

Mr. Clothes [pseud.]. 'Mahatma Gandhi on Nudism.' *Modern Review* (Calcutta), vol. lix, no. 1 (349), pp. 16–17. Jan. 1936.

COHEN, LUCY. *Lady de Rothschild and her Daughters 1821–1931*. London, 1935.

COLLEY MARCH, HY. 'The Giant and the Maypole of Cerne.' *Proceedings of the Dorset Natural History and Antiquarian Field Club*, vol. xxii, pp. 101–18. 1901.

COLLIER, JOHN, and LANG, IAIN. *Just the Other Day. An Informal History of Great Britain since the War*. London, 1932.

A Compassionate Conformist. *Englands Vanity: or the Voice of God Against the Monstrous Sin of Pride, in Dress and Apparel: Wherein Naked Breasts and Shoulders . . . are condemned as Notoriously Unlawful*. London, 1683.

[CRAIG, ALEC.] *The Bibliography of Nudism*. London, n.d. [1954]. Off-printed from *Sun and Health*, no. 14 (no. 2, 1954).

CRAIG, ALEC. 'Sun Bathing in War Time.' *Plan*, vol. x, no. 6, pp. 3–4. Jun. 1943.

CUNNINGTON, C. WILLETT. *The Art of English Costume*. London, 1948.

CUNNINGTON, C. WILLETT. *English Women's Clothing in the Nineteenth Century*. London, 1937.

CUNNINGTON, C. WILLETT. *English Women's Clothing in the Present Century*. London, 1952.

CUNNINGTON, C. WILLETT. *Handbook of English Mediaeval Costume*. London, 1952.

CUNNINGTON, C. WILLETT. *Why Women Wear Clothes*. London, 1941.

CUNNINGTON, C. WILLETT and PHILLIS. *Handbook of English Costume in the Nineteenth Century*. London, 1959.

CUNNINGTON, C. WILLETT and PHILLIS, and BEARD, CHARLES. *A Dictionary of English Costume*. London, 1960.

DINGWALL, E. J. *The Girdle of Chastity. A Medico-Historical Study*. London, 1931.

DUNLAP, KNIGHT. 'The Development and Function of Clothing.' *Journal of General Psychology*, vol. i, pp. 64–78. 1928.

Eden, Adam [pseud.]. *A Vindication of the Reformation, On Foot, among the Ladies, to Abolish Modesty and Chastity, and Restore the Native Simplicity of going Naked*. 2nd edn, London, 1755.

ELLIS, [HENRY] HAVELOCK. *Studies in the Psychology of Sex*. New York, 1936. 4 vol.

EVANS, I. O. *Sensible Sun-Bathing*. London, 1935.

In a Nudist Camp! (Somewhere in England.) or The Naked Truth. By an Eye-Witness. An Exposure of Nudism, The New Menace to Christianity. Glasgow, 1933.

FAIRHOLT, F. W. *Costume in England.* 2nd edn, London, 1860.

[Steele, Sir R. ?]. *Female Folly: or, The Plague of a Woman's Riding-Hood and Cloak.* By the Author of *The Satyr upon Hoop'd Petticoats.* London, 1713.

FLÜGEL, J. C. 'On the Mental Attitude to Present-day Clothes. Report on a Questionnaire.' *British Journal of Medical Psychology,* vol. ix, pt ii, pp. 97–149. 1929.

FLÜGEL, J. C. *The Psychology of Clothes.* London, 1930. International Psycho-analytical Library, no. 18.

Blunt, John [pseud., sc. S. W. FORES]. *Man-midwifery Dissected; or, the Obstetric Family-Instructor.* London, 1793.

FOWLER, O. S. *Intemperance and Tight Lacing Considered in Relation to the Laws of Life.* London and Wortley, 1849.

Nakedness Consider'd: or, Reasons For Not Wearing of Clothes. By a Gentleman of Great Parts. London, 1729.

GIBBONS, A. O. *Cerne Abbas. Notes and Speculations on a Dorset Village.* Dorchester, n.d. [1963].

GILCHRIST, ALEXANDER. *Life of William Blake, 'Pictor Ignotus'.* London and Cambridge, 1863. 2 vol.

GLADSTONE, Right Hon. W. E. *Studies on Homer and the Homeric Age.* Oxford, 1858. 3 vol.

GLYN, ELINOR. *The Vicissitudes of Evangeline.* London, 1905.

GORDON, JAN & CORA. *The London Roundabout.* London, etc., 1933.

GRAVES, ROBERT, and HODGE, ALAN. *The Long Week-end. A Social History of Great Britain 1918–1939.* London, 1940.

Gymnos. The Official Organ of the Gymnic Association of Great Britain. vol. i, no. 1–vol. ii, no. 4. Feb. 1933–May 1934. [Continued as:]

Illustrated Sun Bathing News. vol. i, no. 2–vol. i, no. 3. Summer 1935–Autumn 1935.

HALL, CARRIE A. *From Hoopskirts to Nudity.* Caldwell, I., 1938.

HALL, JOHN. *The Court of Virtue (1565).* Ed. Russell A. Fraser. London, 1961.

HALL, THOMAS. *Comarum ἀκοσμία. The Loathsomnesse of Long Haire.* London, 1653.

Ellis, S. M. (ed.). *A Mid-Victorian Pepys. The Letters and Memoirs of Sir William Hardman, M.A., F.R.G.S.* London, 1923.

[HARRIS, JAMES H.,] Earl of Malmesbury. *Memoirs of an Ex-Minister. An Autobiography.* London, 1884. 2 vol.

Furnivall, Frederick J. (ed.) [William] *Harrison's Description of England in Shakspere's Youth.* pt i. London, 1877. New Shakspere Soc., ser. vi, no. 1.

[HAYWOOD, ELIZA.] *The Female Spectator.* London, 1745. 4 vol.

Health & Efficiency. vol. xviii, no. 209 (80)–vol. xxxi, no. 388. Aug. 1918–Jun. 20, 1931. n.s., vol. i, no. 1– . Aug. 1931– . [In progress.]

HILL, GEORGIANA. *Women in English Life From Mediæval to Modern Times.* London, 1896. 2 vol.

HOGGART, RICHARD. *The Uses of Literacy.* London, 1957.

HOLDEN, ANGUS. *Elegant Modes in the Nineteenth Century from High Waist to Bustle.* London, 1935.

Illustrated Sun Bathing News. See *Gymnos.*

JOHNSON, SAMUEL. *Lives of the English Poets.* Ed. George Birkbeck Hill. Oxford, 1905. 3 vol.

JOHNSTONE, R. W. *William Smellie the Master of British Midwifery.* Edinburgh and London, 1952.

JONES, MARY D. *Cerne Abbas. The Story of a Dorset Village.* London, 1952.

JOYCE, JAMES. *Ulysses.* London, 1954.

KENNEDY, HUGH A. STUDDERT. 'Short Skirts.' *Forum,* vol. lxxv, no. 6, pp. 829–36. Jun. 1926.

Plomer, William (ed.). *Kilvert's Diary.* vol. ii. Selections from the Diary of the Rev. Francis Kilvert 23 August 1871–13 May 1874. London, 1939. vol. iii. . . . 14 May 1874–13 March 1879. London, 1940.

LAMBERT, RICHARD S. *The Universal Provider. A Study of William Whiteley and the Rise of the London Department Store.* London, 1938.

[LANCASTRE SALDANHA, ADELINE LOUISE MARIA,] Countess of Cardigan and Lancastre. *My Recollections.* 2nd impression, London, 1909.

LANG, G. H. *The Churches of God. A Treatise for the Times.* London, 1928. Bible Studies, no. 2.

LANGDON-DAVIES, JOHN. *The Future of Nakedness.* London, 1929.

LANGNER, LAWRENCE. *The Importance of Wearing Clothes.* London, n.d. [1960].

LAVER, JAMES. *Clothes.* London, 1952. Pleasures of Life ser.

LAVER, JAMES. *Edwardian Promenade.* London, 1958.

LAVER, JAMES. *The Literature of Fashion. An Exhibition arranged . . . for the National Book League.* London, 1947.

LAVER, JAMES. *Taste and Fashion from the French Revolution to the Present Day.* 2nd edn, London, etc., 1945.

LIVESEY, J. *The Moral Reformer, and Protestor against the Vices, Abuses, and Corruptions of the Age.* London and Preston, 1831–33. 3 vol.

L[ODGE], T[HOMAS]. *VVits Miserie, and the VVorlds Madnesse: Discouering the Deuils Incarnat of this Age.* London, 1596.

London Council for the Promotion of Public Morality (afterwards Public Morality Council). [1st] (–62nd) *Annual Report.* 1901(–62). [From 1954 onwards, issues are entitled *Public Morals.*]

MACQUOID, PERCY. 'Costume.' *Shakespeare's England, An Account of the Life & Manners of his Age*, vol. ii. Oxford, 1926. pp. 91–118.

MALINS, EDWARD. 'An Address on Midwifery and Midwives.' *British Medical Journal*, Jun. 22, 1901, pp. 1529–32.

MANNIN, ETHEL. *Rolling in the Dew*. London, n.d. [1940].

MARPLES, MORRIS. *White Horses & Other Hill Figures*. London and New York, 1949.

Mee, Arthur (ed.). *Dorset. Thomas Hardy's Country*. London, 1939. The King's England.

MERRIFIELD, Mrs. [MARY PHILADELPHIA]. *Dress as a Fine Art*. London, 1854.

Lupton, J. H. (ed.). *The Utopia of Sir Thomas More*. Trans. Ralph Robynson. Oxford, 1895.

An Itinerary VVritten By Fynes Moryson Gent. First in the Latine Tongue, and then Translated By him into English. London, 1617.

MURPHY, ARTHUR. *The Gray's Inn Journal*. Numb. 1–104. Oct. 21, 1752–Oct. 12, 1754. London, 1756. 2 vol.

NASHE, THO. *Christs Teares over Ierusalem*. London, 1593.

The Naturist. vol. i, no. 1– . Dec. 1937– . [In progress.]

NORWOOD, Rev. C. E. *Nudism in England*. London, 1933.

Nudelife. vol. i, no. 1–vol. v, no. 23. Mar. 1932–Apr.-Sept. 1936.

Observations on the Impropriety of Men Being Employed in the Business of Midwifery. London, 1827.

PARTRIDGE, BURGO. *A History of Orgies*. London, 1958.

PEARL, CYRIL. *The Girl with the Swansdown Seat*. London, 1955.

PEEL, Mrs. C. S. *A Hundred Wonderful Years: Social and Domestic Life of a Century, 1820–1920*. London, 1926.

PETRIE, Sir FLINDERS. *The Hill Figures of England*. London, 1926. Royal Anthropological Inst. Occ. Papers, no. 7.

PICKMERE, J. R. *An Address to the Public on the Propriety of Midwives, instead of Surgeons, Practising Midwifery*. 4th edn, The Pamphleteer, vol. xxviii, no. lv, pp. 63–117. 1827.

PINTO, V. DE SOLA. *Sir Charles Sedley 1639–1701. A Study in the Life and Literature of the Restoration*. London, 1927.

Public Morality Council. See London Council for the Promotion of Public Morality.

Quippes for Vpstart Newfangled Gentlewomen, Or, A Glasse, to view the Pride of vainglorious women. London, 1595.

RASCH, GUSTAV. *London bei Nacht. Culturbilder*. Berlin, 1873.

RUSSELL, BERTRAND. *Unpopular Essays*. London, 1950.

RUTHERFORD, MICHAEL. *British Naturism*. London, 1946.

ST. CLAIR, MIRIAM T. *The Vice of To-day*. 2nd edn, Limerick, n.d. [1943].

SANBORN, HERBERT C. 'The Function of Clothing and of Bodily Adornment.'

American Journal of Psychology, vol. xxxviii, no. 1, pp. 1–20. Jan. 1926.

SCOTT, GEORGE RYLEY. *The Common Sense of Nudism.* London, 1934.

SHAYLER, HUGH. 'Looking Backward.' *Dawn: 1954. The Official Year Book of the British Sun Bathing Association.* London, 1954, pp. 9–10, 15, 38.

SMELLIE, W[ILLIAM]. *A Treatise on the Theory and Practice of Midwifery.* London, 1752.

SPENCER, HERBERT R. *The History of British Midwifery from 1650 to 1800.* London, 1927. The Fitz-Patrick Lectures for 1927.

STOKES, H. G. *The very first history of the English Seaside.* London, 1947.

STRACHEY, RAY. 'Prudery and Nakedness.' *Nation and Athenæum*, vol. xlv, no. 24, p. 763. Sept. 14, 1929.

STRUTT, JOSEPH. *A Complete View of the Dress and Habits of the People of England.* London, 1796–99. 2 vol.

SUMNER, WILLIAM GRAHAM. *Folkways. A Study of the Sociological Importance of Usages, Manners, Customs, Mores, and Morals.* Boston, Mass., 1907.

Sun Bathing Review. vol. i, no. 1–vol. xxvii, no. 107. Spring 1933–Autumn 1959. [Thereafter incorporated in *Health & Efficiency.*]

[SWIFT, JONATHAN.] *Travels into Several Remote Nations of the World. In Four Parts. By Lemuel Gulliver.* London, 1726. 2 vol.

TEXIER, EDMOND. *Lettres sur l'Angleterre (Souvenirs de l'Exposition universelle).* Paris, 1851.

These Tremendous Years 1919–1938. London, 1938.

[THICKNESSE, PHILIP.] *Man-Midwifery Analysed: and the Tendency of that Practice Detected and Exposed.* London, 1764.

TILT, E. J. *Elements of Health, and Principles of Female Hygiene.* London, 1852.

A Christian Business Man [*sc.* T.I.W.]. '*Modest Apparel*'. *An Earnest Word to Christian Women.* 2nd edn, London, n.d. [1931].

WALLIS, REGINALD. *The New Adorning. The Spiritual Significance of Dress and Clothing in the Word of God.* London, n.d. [1938].

WARD, LESTER F. *Dynamic Sociology or Applied Social Science.* 2nd edn, New York, 1907. 2 vol.

WEBSTER, NESTA H. *The Socialist Network.* London, 1926.

Wellesley, Col. the Hon. F. A. (ed.). *The Paris Embassy during the Second Empire. Selections from the Papers of Henry Richard Charles Wellesley, 1st Earl Cowley.* London, 1928.

WESTCOTT, WM. WYNN. 'An Address on Sudden and Unexpected Deaths.' *British Medical Journal*, Feb. 29, 1908, pp. 490–3.

WEY, FRANCIS. *Les Anglais chez eux.* Paris, 1856.

WILLUGHBY, PERCIVALL. *Observations in Midwifery. As also The Countrey Midwifes Opusculum.* Ed. Henry Blenkinsop. Warwick, 1863.

[Sir J. Mennis and Capt. J. Smith?]. *Wit Restor'd In severall Select Poems Not formerly publish't.* London, 1658.

WITKOWSKI, G.-J. *Histoire des accouchements chez tous les peuples.* Paris, n.d. [1887].

WOLLSTONECRAFT, MARY. *A Vindication of the Rights of Woman: with Strictures on Political and Moral Subjects.* London, 1792.

WOOD, ANTHONY À. *Athenæ Oxonienses.* Ed. Philip Bliss. London, 1813–20. 4 vol.

PART V

DON'T DANCE, LITTLE LADY (pp. 211–53)

ALLSOP, KENNETH. 'Brave New Underworld.' *Spectator,* no. 6894, pp. 240–1. Aug. 12, 1960.

Andrée, Rosemary [pseud.]. *My Life Story.* London, 1945.

AVERY, EMMETT L. 'Dancing and Pantomime on the English Stage, 1700–1737.' *Studies in Philology* (Chapel Hill), vol. xxxi, no. 3, pp. 417–52. Jul. 1934.

BAILEY, LESLIE. *Scrapbook 1900 to 1914.* London, 1957.

BARRÈRE, ALBERT, and LELAND, CHARLES G. *A Dictionary of Slang, Jargon & Cant.* n.p. [Edinburgh], 1889–90. 2 vol.

[BEHN, APHRA.] *The Rover. Or, The Banish't Cavaliers.* London, 1677.

BENTHAM, JOSEPH. Χοροθεολογον *or Two Briefe but Usefull Treatises, The One Touching the Office and Quality of the Ministry of the Gospel. The Other Of the Nature and Accidents of Mixt Dancing.* London, 1657.

BERGLER, EDMUND. *Fashion and the Unconscious.* New York, 1953.

BINDER, PEARL. *The English Inside Out. An up-to-date report on morals and manners in England.* London, 1961.

BOWEN, MARJORIE. *Patriotic Lady. A Study of Emma, Lady Hamilton, and the Neapolitan Revolution of 1799.* London, 1935.

BURDER, GEORGE. *Lawful Amusements; A Sermon.* London, 1805.

Democritus Iunior [pseud., *sc.* RICHARD BURTON]. *The Anatomy of Melancholy.* Oxford, 1621.

Hornem, Horace, Esq. [pseud., *sc.* GEORGE BYRON]. *Waltz: an Apostrophic Hymn.* London, 1813.

'The "Can-Can".' *The Era,* vol. xxxvii, no. 1,890, p. 11. Dec. 13, 1874.

CHAMBERS, E. K. *The Mediaeval Stage.* London, 1903. 2 vol.

Chujoy, Anatole (comp. and ed.). *The Dance Encyclopedia.* New York, 1949.

Twain, Mark [pseud., *sc.* SAMUEL L. CLEMENS]. *The Innocents Abroad, or The New Pilgrims' Progress.* Hartford, Conn., 1869.

COCHRAN, CHARLES B. *Cock-A-Doodle-Do.* London, 1941.

COCHRAN, CHARLES B. *I had almost Forgotten . . .* London, 1932.

COCHRAN, CHARLES B. *The Secrets of a Showman.* London, 1925.

COLLIER, J. PAYNE. *A Bibliographical and Critical Account of the Rarest Books in the English Language.* London, 1865. 2 vol.

COOPER, DIANA. *The Rainbow Comes and Goes.* London, 1958.

CROUCH, JOSEPH. *Puritanism and Art. An Inquiry into a Popular Fallacy.* London, etc., 1910.

Dancing, in a Right Spirit, a Delightful and Scriptural Pleasure. London, n.d. [1865].

DAVIES, Rev. JAMES. *Our Morals.* London, 1873.

DAVIS, M. *Thoughts on Dancing: Occasioned by Some Late Transactions among the People called Methodists.* London, 1791.

E., B. *Folly's Advocate; or, The Dancing-Master in Search of Pupils.* London, 1827.

F., A. *The Ladies' Pocket-Book of Etiquette.* 7th edn, London, 1840.

FITZ GEORGE, MARY. *Ball Room Refinement . . . with a Descriptive Outline of the Deux Temps Valse, and Some Strictures on its Present Style.* London, n.d. [1851].

FLITCH, J. E. CRAWFORD. *Modern Dancing and Dancers.* London, 1912.

Ford, Boris (ed.). *The Age of Chaucer.* Harmondsworth, 1954. A Guide to English Literature, vol. i.

GORER, GEOFFREY. *Hot Strip Tease and Other Notes on American Culture.* London, 1937.

GRAHAM, LAWRENCE. 'Reflections on Dancing.' *The Millgate,* vol. xxxv, pt i, no. 412, pp. 235–8. Jan. 1940.

GRAVES, CHARLES. *The Cochran Story. A Biography of Sir Charles Blake Cochran, Kt.* London, n.d. [1951].

GREENWOOD, JAMES. *In Strange Company: Being the Experiences of a Roving Correspondent.* London, 1873.

GRIBBLE, FRANCIS. 'The Origin of the Can-Can.' *Dancing Times,* n.s., no. 271, pp. 19–22. Apr. 1933.

GROVE, Mrs. LILLY, and others. *Dancing.* London, 1895.

GUEST, IVOR. *The Alhambra Ballet.* New York, 1959. *Dance Perspectives,* no. 4.

HIBBERT, H. G. *Fifty Years of a Londoner's Life.* London, 1916.

HILL, ROWLAND. *A Warning to Professors; Containing Aphoristic Observations on the Nature and Tendency of Public Amusements.* London, 1833.

HINGESTON, HENRY. מְחִין קְדָל *or, A Dreadful Alarm upon the Clouds of Heaven, Mix'd with Love.* London, 1703.

The History of the Human Heart; or The Adventures of a Young Gentleman. London, 1749. [Reprinted 1885 in] Rochester ser. of reprints, no. iv.

HOLLINGSHEAD, JOHN. *Gaiety Chronicles.* London, 1898.

HOLLINGSHEAD, JOHN. *My Lifetime.* London, 1895. 2 vol.

Hop [pseud.]. 'Waltzing.' *The Sporting Magazine,* vol. xl, no. 239, pp. 213–14. Aug. 1812.

JEAFFRESON, JOHN CORDY. *Lady Hamilton and Lord Nelson.* London, 1888. 2 vol.

KELLOGG, J. H. *Ladies' Guide in Health and Disease.* London, etc., 1890.

Stoddard, Richard Henry (ed.). *Personal Reminiscences by Cornelia Knight and Thomas Raikes.* New York, 1875. Bric-a-Brac ser.

KNIGHT, RICHARD PAYNE. *A Discourse on the Worship of Priapus . . . to which is added An Essay* [by Thomas Wright, Sir James Emerson Tennent, and George Witt] *on the Worship of the Generative Powers during the Middle Ages of Western Europe.* London, 1865.

[LEMERCHER DE LONGPRÉ, CHARLES,] Baron D'HAUSSEZ. *La Grande-Bretagne en mil huit cent trente-trois.* Brussels, 1833. 2 vol.

LOCKYER, Rev. HERBERT. *Dancing Ancient and Modern.* London, etc., n.d. [1927]. 2nd edn, London, 1930.

MAETERLINCK, MAURICE. *Monna Vanna.* Paris, 1902.

MALCOLM, JAMES PELLER. *Anecdotes of the Manners and Customs of London during the Eighteenth Century.* London, 1808.

Memoirs of Lady Hamilton. London, 1815.

The Midnight Spy. London, 1766.

Morton, W. H., and Newton, H. Chance (comp.). *Sixty Years' Stage Service, Being a Record of the Life of Charles Morton, 'The Father of the Halls'.* London, 1905.

National Vigilance Association. [1st](*–64th Annual*) *Report of the Executive Committee.* 1887(–1951).

National Vigilance Association. *Work Accomplished by the Association.* April 1906.

'New Twist to an Old Story.' *Weekend,* no. 2972, pp. 3–5. Feb. 7–11, 1962.

NICHOLSON, The Lord Chief Baron [RENTON]. *An Autobiography.* London, n.d. [1860].

The Lord Chief Baron [*sc.* RENTON NICHOLSON]. *The Swell's Night Guide; or, A Peep through the Great Metropolis under the Dominion of Nox.* 20th edn, London, 1846.

NICOLL, ALLARDYCE. *Masks Mimes and Miracles. Studies in the Popular Theatre.* London, etc., 1931.

NORTHBROOKE, JOHN. *A Treatise against Dicing, Dancing, Plays, and Interludes.* [c. 1577.] London, 1843.

OWST, G. R. 'The People's Sunday Amusements in the Preaching of Mediæval England.' *Holborn Review*, vol. xvii (n.s.), pp. 32–45. Jan. 1926.

PERKINS, W[ILLIAM]. *The VVhole Treatise of the Cases of Conscience*. London, 1608.

Phallic Worship. A Description of the Mysteries of the Sex Worship of the Ancients. n.p., 1886.

Phallism: A Description of the Worship of Lingam-Yoni in Various Parts of the World. London, 1889.

RAE, W. FRASER. *Sheridan. A Biography*. London, 1896. 2 vol.

RENDLE, T. MCDONALD. *Swings and Roundabouts. A Yokel in London*. London, 1919.

Report from the Joint Select Committee of the House of Lords and the House of Commons on the Stage Plays (Censorship); together with the Proceedings of the Committee, Minutes of Evidence, and Appendices. London, 1909.

Report from the Select Committee on Public Houses; together with the Proceedings of the Committee, Minutes of Evidence, Appendix and Index. 1854.

Report of the Royal Commission on Alien Immigration with Minutes of Evidence and Appendix. London, 1903–04. 4 vol. Cd 1741–3.

RICHARDSON, PHILIP J. S. *A History of English Ballroom Dancing (1910–45)*. London, n.d. [1946].

SACHS, CURT. *World History of the Dance*. Trans. Bessie Schönberg. London, 1938.

'Scandalous Dances Brought from French Casinos to American Parlors.' *International Monthly Magazine of Literature, Science, and Art*, vol. ii, no. 3, p. 333. Feb. 1, 1851.

SCHOLES, PERCY A. *The Puritans and Music in England and New England*. London, 1934.

SCOTT, EDWARD. 'Manner in Social Dancing.' *Dancing Times*, n.s., no. 87, pp. 65–7. Dec. 1917.

SCOTT, HAROLD. *The Early Doors. Origins of the Music Hall*. London, 1946.

SHERSON, ERROLL. *London's Lost Theatres of the Nineteenth Century With Notes on Plays and Players Seen There*. London, 1925.

Darton, F. J. Harvey (ed.). *The Life and Times of Mrs. Sherwood (1775–1851)*. London, 1910.

SHORT, ERNEST. *Fifty Years of Vaudeville*. London, 1946.

SHORT, ERNEST, and COMPTON-RICKETT, ARTHUR. *Ring up the Curtain*. London, 1938.

SICHEL, WALTER. *Emma Lady Hamilton*. London, 1905.

SIMS, GEO. R. *Glances Back*. London, 1917.

SLONIMSKY, NICOLAS. *Music of Latin America*. London, etc., 1946.

SOLDENE, EMILY. *My Theatrical and Musical Recollections*. London, 1897.

Stirling, A. M. W. (comp.). *The Letter-Bag of Lady Elizabeth Spencer-Stanhope*. London, 1913. 2 vol.

STOW, JOHN. *A Survey of London.* 2nd edn, 1603. Ed. Charles Lethbridge Kingsford. Oxford, 1908. 2 vol.

THOMSON, GEORGE. *Studies in Ancient Greek Society.* [vol. i:] *The Prehistoric Ægean.* London, 1949.

[WARD, EDWARD.] *The London-Spy Compleat.* 2nd edn, London, 1704.

The Works of the Rev. John Wesley, A.M. vol. vii. London, 1878.

WITKOWSKI, G.-J., and NASS, L. *Le Nu au théâtre depuis l'antiquité jusqu'à nos jours.* Paris, 1909.

WRIGHT, THOMAS. *A History of Domestic Manners and Sentiments in England During the Middle Ages.* London, 1862.

YATES, G. *The Ball; or, A Glance at Almack's in 1829.* London, 1829.

INDEX

Figures in bold type refer to the plates.